DATE DUE

ANTISEMITISM

GARLAND REFERENCE LIBRARY
OF SOCIAL SCIENCE
(Vol. 366)

Academic Committee Chairman
of the Bibliographic Project: Otto Dov Kulka

Executive Editor: Sue Fox
Assistant Editor: Louise Fischer
Technical Editors: Rosalind N. Arzt, Rachel Schwartz
Abstractors: Alexander Avram, Naomi Bar-Yosef, Elliott Green, Boris Korsch, Ephraim Meier, Doron Niederland, Beatrice Senkman, Hanna Volovici

The Vidal Sassoon International Center
for the Study of Antisemitism
The Hebrew University of Jerusalem

ANTISEMITISM
An Annotated Bibliography

Volume 1
1984–1985

Edited by Susan Sarah Cohen

GARLAND PUBLISHING, INC. • NEW YORK & LONDON
1987

Library of Congress Cataloging-in-Publication Data

Antisemitism : an annotated bibliography.

(Garland reference library of social science ;
vol. 366-)
Includes indexes.
1. Antisemitism—Bibliography. I. Cohen, Susan Sarah.
II. Vidal Sassoon International Center for the Study of
Antisemitism (Universiṭah ha-'Ivrit bi-Yerushalayim)
III. Series: Garland reference library of social
science ; v. 366, etc.
Z6374.A56A57 1987 016.3058′924 87-11842
[DS145]
ISBN 0-8240-8532-9 (v. 1 : alk. paper)

Printed on acid-free, 250-year-life paper
Manufactured in the United States of America

CONTENTS

PREFACE

The Vidal Sassoon International Center for the Study of Antisemitism of the Hebrew University of Jerusalem was established by an international group of scholars in 1983 as an academic research center to sponsor and to support basic research in the study of antisemitism. It has grown into a broad-based educational and information resource center, sponsoring study seminars, international conferences, and publishing research studies and papers.

This publication is an outgrowth of the Center's Bibliographic Project, which is comprised of an on-line data base and a bienniel printed bibliography. This volume, the first of the series, includes works *about* antisemitism—books, dissertations, masters' theses, and articles from periodicals and collections—published in 1984–1985. It does not include newspaper articles, reviews, and works of fiction. No other bibliography published today presents as comprehensive a list of current written works on the subject of antisemitism.

For the purpose of this bibliography, antisemitism was defined as antagonism towards Jews and Judaism as expressed in writings (e.g., the New Testament, polemical literature, works of fiction, etc.), in the visual arts (e.g., art, caricatures, films), and in actions (e.g., massacres and pogroms, discriminatory legislation, the Holocaust, etc.). Works were also included which deal with Gentile philosemitism, with Jewish responses to antisemitism, and with Jewish self-hatred, since these are all influenced by antisemitism. In borderline cases (e.g., Christian-Jewish relations, anti-Israel and anti-Zionism, works of fiction and films), books and articles were listed when the author of the work related the subject to antisemitism.

The coverage of four specific subjects has been limited in the following manner:

1) *The Holocaust Period (1933–1945).* Due to the huge amount of

published material on this subject, it was decided to include those works which deal with the ideology and policy of the Nazis towards Jews; the ideologies and policies of Nazi-occupied or allied countries; the policies of governments of the free world towards Jews; and the attitudes of non-Jews towards Jews—individuals, political groups, religious bodies, the press, etc. Not included are works describing Jewish life as experienced during the Holocaust unless they contain, to some extent, a discussion of the above-mentioned subjects. For example, the Jewish experience in the ghettos and in the concentration and extermination camps is not dealt with, but material dealing with the Nazis' establishment of the camps and their policy of extermination is included. As a general rule, memorial books published by Jewish groups which commemorate their city, town, or village and those who perished, are not listed, but the many memorial books to the Jews published in Germany by non-Jews are included.

2) *Soviet Jewry*. Works are included which deal with Soviet ideology and policy towards the Jews, but not with the Jewish experience as such.

3) *Anti-Zionism*. Works are included which describe anti-Zionism as antisemitism, particularly those which discuss antisemitic accusations vaunted against Zionism and Israel, such as the Jewish "world conspiracy," Zionist collaboration with Nazis, the "Zionism equals racism" formula, and the comparison of Israelis with Nazis.

4) *The Arab-Israeli Conflict*. Works are included which deal with antisemitism in the Arab world, but not with the political conflict between the State of Israel and its Arab neighbors.

This bibliography does not cover antisemitic publications. The list of antisemitic periodicals in Appendix I (provided by the Institute of Jewish Affairs in London, and specifically by Michael May, Assistant Director) fills this gap to some extent.

The listings were compiled mainly from the holdings of the Jewish National and University Library in Jerusalem, which receives the majority of works on Jewish subjects published throughout the world. The works listed come from a diverse range of disciplines—history, psychology, sociology, anthropology, literature, and art. Books and articles which deal only in part with antisemitism, or articles of one-page length, are included when they provide information worthy of attention.

The bibliography is multi-lingual—this volume contains works in English, European languages, Hebrew, and Yiddish. An English translation of the title is given in brackets for languages other than French, German, Italian, and Spanish.

Each item has been listed only once—a work dealing with two or more of the chronological or geographical sub-divisions is listed in the appropriate "General" section. (The detailed subject index at the end of the volume compensates for the "general" classifications.) The format of each entry follows the rules of the "Chicago Manual of Style," with slight modification. Articles from collections were listed separately unless the entire collection, or a major part of it, deals with antisemitism, in which case the collection was listed as one entry with a detailed list of contents but without annotations. The articles of a collection which have been dispersed may be located by referring to the editor's name in the author index.

The annotation expresses the views of the author(s) of the work described, and not those of the annotator. The length of the annotation does not indicate the importance of a particular work. Material published in 1984–1985 and not listed in Volume I will appear in Volume II. Suggestions for additions and corrections are welcomed.

Acknowledgments

The Vidal Sassoon Center for the Study of Antisemitism wishes to thank the staff of the Jewish National and University Library for their support and cooperation, without which this volume could not have been produced, and especially Malachi Beit-Arie, Director of the JNUL, Jonathan Yoel, Assistant Director of the JNUL, Rachel Mayer, head of the

Periodicals Department, and Theodor Armon of the Acquisitions Department; Judy Levy of the Hebrew University's Department of Information Systems and Myra Levine of the Bibliographic Center of the Institute for Contemporary Jewry for helping to design the computer program for the storage and retrieval of data; Richard Cohen of the Hebrew University for reading the text and making valuable suggestions.

Jerusalem
February 1987—Shevat 5747

S.S.C.

LIST OF PERIODICALS AND COLLECTIONS

Acta Poloniae Historica. Wroclaw: Polska Akademia Nauk
Acta Psychiatrica Belgica. Bruxelles: Association des Sociétés Scientifiques Medicales Belges
Actes de la Recherche en Sciences Sociales. Paris: Centre de Sociologie Européenne
ADL Bulletin. New York: Anti-Defamation League of B'nai B'rith
ADL European Report. New York: ADL
ADL Fact Finding Report. New York: ADL
ADL Facts. New York: ADL
ADL Special Report. New York: ADL
America: National Catholic Weekly Review. New York: America Press
American Film. New York: American Film Institute
American Jewish Archives. Cincinnati, OH: American Jewish Archives
American Jewish History. Waltham, MA: American Jewish Historical Society
American Quarterly. Philadelphia: University of Pennsylvania, for the American Studies Association
American Sociological Review. Washington, DC: American Sociological Association
Analytische Psychologie. Basel: S. Karger
Anti-Semitism and Human Rights, ed. S. Liberman. Melbourne: Australian Institute of Jewish Affairs, 1985
Anti-Semitism in the Soviet Union: Its Roots and Consequences, ed. T. Freedman. New York: Freedom Library Press of the ADL, 1984
The Antisemitism in Our Time: A Threat Against Us All, ed. L. Eitinger. Oslo: The Nansen Committee, 1984
Antisemitismus: Von der Judenfeindschaft zum Holocaust, eds. A. Strauss, N. Kampe. Bonn: Bundeszentrale fuer Politische Bildung, 1984
Anzeiger, see Oesterreichische Akademie der Wissenschaften . . .

Approaches to Judaism in Medieval Times, ed. D. R. Blumenthal. Chico, CA: Scholars Press, 1984

Arcadia: Zeitschrift fuer vergleichende Literaturwissenschaft. Berlin: Walter de Gruyter

L'Arche. Paris: Fonds Social Juif Unifié

Archiv fuer Kulturgeschichte. Koeln: Boehlau Verlag

Argumenty. Warszawa: Stowarzyszenie Ateistów i Wolnoymślicieli

Arthur Schnitzler und seine Zeit: Akten des Internationalen Symposiums, Bari 1981, ed. G. Farese. Bern: P. Lang, 1985 (Jahrbuch fuer Internationale Germanistik, Reihe A, Bd. 13)

Artists against Hitler: Persecution, Exile, Resistance, ed. G. Schoenberner. Bonn: Inter Nationes, 1984

Australian Journal of Politics and History. St. Lucia, Queensland: University of Queensland Press

Backgrounder. New York: American Jewish Committee

B'Eretz Israel. Tel-Aviv: Chevrat "Hayom" (Hebrew)

La Bibliofilia: Rivista di storia del libro e di bibliografia. Firenze: Leo S. Olschki

Bibliothèque d'Humanisme et Renaissance: Travaux et documents. Genève: Librairie Droz

Das Bild des Juden in der Volks- und Jugendliteratur vom 18. Jahrhundert bis 1945, ed. H. Pleticha. Wuerzburg: Koenigshausen und Neumann, 1985

Bitzaron. New York: Hebrew Literary Foundation (Hebrew)

Biuletyn Żydowskiego Instytutu Historycznego w Polsce. Warszawa: Żydowski Instytut Historyczny w Polsce

Bleter far Geszichte. Warszawa: Żydowski Instytut Historyczny w Polsce (Yiddish)

B'nai B'rith International Jewish Monthly. Washington, DC

B'nai B'rith Journal. Basel: B'nai B'rith Distrikt 19

Bulletin de la Société Archéologique de Tarn et Garonne. Montauban, France

Bulletin of Hispanic Studies. Liverpool: Liverpool University Press

Bulletin of the Atomic Scientists. Chicago: Educational Foundation for Nuclear Science

Cahiers Bernard Lazare: La revue de la gauche juive en France. Paris: Cercle Bernard Lazare

Cahiers du Monde Russe et Soviétique. Paris: L'Ecole des Hautes Etudes en Sciences Sociales

Canadian Forum. Toronto: Survival Foundation
Canadian Jewish Archives. Montreal: Canadian Jewish Congress
Canadian Jewish Historical Society Journal. Montreal
Canadian Jewish Outlook. Vancouver, B.C.: Canadian Jewish Outlook Society
Canadian Journal of Philosophy. Calgary, Alta.: University of Calgary Press
Canadian Review of Sociology and Anthropology. Toronto: University of Toronto Press
Catholica: Vierteljahresschrift fuer oekumenische Theologie. Muenster: Aschendorffsche Verlagsbuchhandlung, for the Johann Adam Moehler-Institut, Paderborn
Central European History. Atlanta, GA: Emory University, for the American Historical Association
De Centrale. Antwerpen: Centraal Beheer van Joodse Weldadigheid en Maatschappelijk Hulpbetoon
Centrale. Bruxelles: Centrale d'Oeuvres Sociales Juives
The Century of Moses Montefiore, eds. S. and V. D. Lipman. Oxford: Oxford University Press, 1985
The Chaucer Review. University Park, PA: Pennsylvania State University Press
Cheschbon. Muenchen: Cheschbon—Bundesverband Jued. Studenten in Deutschland
Christian Jewish Relations. London: Institute of Jewish Affairs
CinémAction. Paris: Ed. du Cerf
Civiltà Cattolica. Roma: Compagnia di Gesù
Coloquio. Buenos Aires: Congreso Judío Latinoamericano
Commentary. New York: American Jewish Committee
Conflict: All Warfare Short of War. New York: Crane, Russak
Congress Monthly. New York: American Jewish Congress
Contemporary Crises: Crime, Law, Social Policy. Amsterdam: Elsevier
Contemporary Jewry: Studies in Honor of Moshe Davis, ed. G. Wigoder. Jerusalem: Hebrew University, Institute of Contemporary Jewry, 1984
Corrente. São Paulo: WIZO
Criterio. Buenos Aires: Editorial Criterio
Critical Social Policy. Oxford: Basil Blackwell
Criticism: A Quarterly for Literature and the Arts. Detroit, MI: Wayne State University Press

Cross Currents: A Yearbook of Central European Culture. Ann Arbor, MI: University of Michigan
Crusade and Settlement, ed. P. H. Ebury. Cardiff: University College Cardiff Press, 1985
Daat: A Journal of Jewish Philosophy and Kabbalah. Ramat-Gan: Bar Ilan University (Hebrew)
Danzig, between East and West: Aspects of Modern Jewish History, ed. I. Twersky. Cambridge, MA: Harvard University Press, 1985
"Das war ein Vorspiel nur": Berliner Colloquium zur Literaturpolitik im "Dritten Reich," eds. H. Denkler, E. Laemmert. Berlin (West): Akademie der Kuenste, 1985
Department of State Bulletin, see U.S. Department of State . . .
Deutschland 1933: Machtzerfall der Demokratie und nationalsozialistische "Machtergreifung," eds. W. Treue, J. Schmaedeke. Berlin (West): Colloquium Verlag, 1984
Der Deutschunterricht. Seelze: Erhard Friedrich Verlag
Dialectical Anthropology. Amsterdam: Elsevier
Dissent. New York: Foundation for the Study of Independent Social Ideas
Dorem Afrike. Johannesburg: Yiddish Cultural Federation (Yiddish)
Le Droit de Vivre. Paris: Ligue Internationale Contre le Racisme et l'Antisémitisme (LICRA)
Dutch Jewish History: Proceedings of the Symposium . . . Nov. 28-Dec. 3, 1982, Tel-Aviv-Jerusalem, ed. J. Michman. Jerusalem: Hebrew University, Institute for Research on Dutch Jewry, 1984
Dynamische Psychiatrie. Berlin (West): Pinel-Publikationen, for the Deutsche Akademie fuer Psychoanalyse
Dzieje Najnowsze. Wroclaw: Polska Akademia Nauk
East European Quarterly. Boulder, CO: University of Colorado
Ecumenical Institute for Theological Research Yearbook. Tantur/Jerusalem
Ecumenical Review. Geneva: World Council of Churches
Eit-Mol. Tel-Aviv: Tel-Aviv University (Hebrew)
Encounter. London: Encounter, Ltd.
Encounter: Creative Theological Scholarship. Indianapolis, IN: Christian Theological Seminary
English Studies. Lisse, Netherlands; Swets Publishing Service
Estudios Bíblicos. Madrid: Consejo Superior de Investigaciones Científicas, Instituto de Teología "Francisco Suarez"

European Judaism. London: Foundation for European Judaism
Evangelische Theologie. Muenchen: Chr. Kaiser Verlag
Exil—Forschung, Erkenntnisse, Ergebnisse 1933–1945. Maintal, West Germany
Exile in Great Britain: Refugees from Hitler's Germany, ed. G. Hirschfeld. Tr. from the German. Leamington Spa: Berg, 1984
Exilforschung. Muenchen: Text und Kritik
Az 1944 év hístoriája, ed. F. Glatz. Budapest: Lapkiado Vallalat, 1984
Fabula: Zeitschrift fuer Erzaehlforschung. Berlin (West): Walter de Gruyter
Face to Face. New York: Anti-Defamation League of B'nai B'rith
Film Comment. New York: Film Society of Lincoln Center
Foi et Vie. Paris: Association des Amis de Foi et Vie
Folk un Zion. Jerusalem: World Zionist Organization (Yiddish)
For a Palestinian: A Memorial to Wael Zuaiter, ed. J. Venn-Brown. London: Kegan Paul, 1984
Foreign Policy. Farmingdale, NY: Carnegie Endowment for International Peace
Forrás. Kecskemet: Bacs Kiskun Megyei Lapkiado Vallalat
Forschungen zur Osteuropaeischen Geschichte. Berlin (West): Freie Universitaet, Osteuropa-Institut
Forum on the Jewish People, Zionism and Israel. Jerusalem: World Zionist Organization
France-Israël Information. Paris: France-Israël Information
Frankfurter Hefte: Zeitschrift fuer Kultur und Politik. Frankfurt a.M.: Der Neuen Verlagsgesellschaft der Frankfurter Hefte
Frankfurter Juedisches Gemeindeblatt. Frankfurt a.M.: Juedische Gemeinde
Der Freund Israels. Basel: Stiftung fuer Kirche und Judentum
Gal-Ed: On the History of the Jews in Poland. Tel-Aviv: Tel-Aviv University, for the Society for Historical Research of Polish Jewry
Die Gemeinde. Wien: Israelitische Kultusgemeinde
Genesis 2. Cambridge, MA: D. J. Perlstein
Le Genre Humain. Paris: Editions Complexe
German Nationalism and the European Response, 1890–1945, eds. C. Fink et al. Norman, OK: University of Oklahoma Press, 1985
Geschichte in Wissenschaft und Unterricht: Zeitschrift des Verbandes der Geschichtslehrer Deutschlands. Seelze: E. Friedrich Verlag; Stuttgart: E. Klett Verlag

Geschichte und Gesellschaft: Zeitschrift fuer historische Sozialwissenschaft. Goettingen: Vandenhoeck und Ruprecht
Gesher: Quarterly Review of Jewish Affairs. Jerusalem: Israel Executive of the World Jewish Congress (Hebrew)
Grenzfeste deutscher Wissenschaft: Ueber Faschismus und Vergangenheitsbewaeltigung an der Universitaet Graz, von C. Fleck et al. Graz: Verlag fuer Gesellschaftskritik, 1985
Ha-Umma. Tel-Aviv: Misdar Jabotinsky (Hebrew)
Hadassah Magazine. New York: Hadassah
Hadoar. New York: Histadruth Ivrith of America (Hebrew)
The Hammer: Anti-Racist, Anti-Fascist News and Analysis. Kansas City, MO: Institute for Research and Education on Human Rights
Harper's Magazine. New York: Harper's Magazine Co.
Harvard Ukrainian Studies. Cambridge, MA: Harvard University, Ukrainian Research Institute
O Hebreu. São Paulo: Empresa Jornalística O Hebreu Ltda.
Hebrew University. Soviet and East European Research Centre: Research Papers. Jerusalem
Heidelberg unter dem Nationalsozialismus, eds. J. Schadt, M. Caroli. Heidelberg: C. F. Mueller Juristischer Verlag, 1985
Heidelberger Jahrbuecher. Berlin (West): Springer-Verlag
Heine Jahrbuch. Hamburg: Hoffmann und Campe Verlag
Helmantica: Revista de filología clásica y hebrea. Salamanca: Universidad Pontificia
Herança Judaica. São Paulo: B'nai B'rith
Herencia Judía. Bogotá: B'nai B'rith Distrito 23 (Caribe)
Ter Herkenning: Tijdschrift voor Christenen en Joden. 's-Gravenhage: Boekencentrum
Hispanic American Historical Review. Durham, NC: Duke University Press
Hispanófila. Chapel Hill, NC: University of Carolina
L'Histoire. Paris: Société d'Editions Scientifiques
Historische Zeitschrift. Muenchen: R. Oldenbourg Verlag
History Today. London: History Today, Ltd.
Hochschule und Wissenschaft im Dritten Reich, ed J. Troeger. Frankfurt a.M.: Campus-Verlag, 1984
The Holocaust as Interruption, eds. E. Schuessler Fiorenza, D. Tracy. Edinburgh: T. & T. Clark, 1984 (Concilium, 175). In French, see Le Judaïsme après Auschwitz

Holocaust Studies Annual. Greenwood, FL: Penkevill Pub. Co.
Humanistic Judaism. Farmington Hills, MI: Society for Humanistic Judaism
Ideas into Politics: Aspects of European History 1880–1950, eds. R. J. Pullen et al. London: Croom Helm; Totowa, NJ: Barnes and Noble, 1984
Illustrierte Neue Welt. Wien: "INW-Pressedienst"
Immanuel: A Journal of Religious Thought and Research in Israel. Jerusalem; Ecumenical Theological Research Fraternity in Israel; New York: ADL
Immigration History Newsletter. St. Paul, MN: Immigration History Society
Indiana Social Studies Quarterly. Muncie, IN: Ball State University, for the Indiana Council for the Social Studies
L'Infini. Paris: Denoël
Institute of British Geographers: Transactions. London
Institute of Jewish Affairs: Research Reports. London.
L'Interdit de la représentation: Colloque de Montpellier, eds. A. et J.-J. Rassial. Paris: Ed. du Seuil, 1984
International Journal of Group Tensions. New York: International Organization for the Study of Group Tensions
International Journal of Political Education. Amsterdam: Elsevier
Interpretation: A Journal of Bible and Theology. Richmond, VA: Union Theological Seminary
Irish-Jewish Year Book. Dublin: Chief Rabbinate of Ireland
Israel. Den Haag: Genootschap Nederland-Israel
Israel Horizons. New York: Americans for Progressive Israel—Hashomer Hatzair
Israel Journal of Psychiatry and Related Sciences. Jerusalem: Israel Science Pub.
Israel Yearbook on Human Rights. Tel-Aviv: Tel-Aviv University, Faculty of Law
Izvoare. Tel-Aviv: Asociaţia Scriitorilor Israelieni de Limbă Română
Jahrbuch des Instituts fuer Deutsche Geschichte. Tel-Aviv: Tel-Aviv University
Jahrbuch fuer Internationale Germanistik, see Arthur Schnitzler und seine Zeit
Jahrbuecher fuer Geschichte Osteuropas. Wiesbaden: Franz Steiner Verlag, for the Osteuropa-Institut, Muenchen

Jerusalem Quarterly. Jerusalem: Middle East Institute
Jerusalem Studies in Jewish Folklore. Jerusalem: Magnes Press, Hebrew University (Hebrew)
Jerushalaimer Almanach. Jerusalem: Yiddish Writers Group
Jewish Affairs. Johannesburg: South African Jewish Board of Deputies
Jewish Currents. New York: Association for Promotion of Jewish Secularism
Jewish Defender. Downsview, Ont.: Jewish Defense League
Jewish Frontier. New York: Labor Zionist Letters Inc.
Jewish Journal of Sociology. London: World Jewish Congress
Jewish Monthly, see B'nai B'rith International Jewish Monthly
The Jewish People in Christian Preaching, ed. D. J. Fasching. New York: Edwin Mellen Press, 1984
Jewish Quarterly. London: Jewish Literary Trust
Jewish Quarterly Review. Winona Lake, IN: Eisenbrauns, for Dropsie College, Merion Station, PA
Jewish Social Studies. New York: Conference on Jewish Social Studies
Jewish Spectator. Santa Monica, CA: The Jewish Spectator
Jews and Conversos: Studies in Society and the Inquisition, ed. Y. Kaplan. Jerusalem: World Union of Jewish Studies; Magnes Press, Hebrew University, 1985
Jews and Jewish Topics in Soviet and East European Publications. Jerusalem: Hebrew University
Jews in Black Perspectives: A Dialogue, ed. J. R. Washington. Rutherford, NJ: Fairleigh Dickinson University Press, 1984
Jews in Economic Life, ed. N. Gross. Jerusalem: Zalman Shazar Center, 1985 (Hebrew)
The Jews in Modern France, eds. F. Malino, B. Wasserstein. Hanover, NH: University Press of New England, 1985
Jews in Soviet Culture, ed. J. Miller, New Brunswick, NJ: Transaction Books, 1984
The Jews of Czechoslovakia, ed. A. Dagan. Vol. 3. Philadelphia: Jewish Publication Society of America; New York: Society for the History of Czechoslovak Jews, 1984
The Jews of the Soviet Union. Jerusalem: Publications on Soviet Jewry, Hebrew University (Hebrew)
Journal of American Ethnic History. New Brunswick, NJ: Transaction Periodicals Consortium, Rutgers University, for the Immigration History Society

Journal of American History. Bloomington, IN: Organization of American Historians
Journal of Contemporary History. London: Sage
Journal of Ecumenical Studies. Philadelphia: Temple University
Journal of Ethnic Studies. Bellingham, WA: Western Washington University
Journal of European Studies. Chalfont St. Giles, Bucks.: Alpha Academic
Journal of Jewish Communal Service. New York: Conference of Jewish Communal Services
Journal of Jewish Studies. Oxford: Oxford Centre for Postgraduate Hebrew Studies
Journal of Library History. Austin: University of Texas Press
Journal of Modern History. Chicago: University of Chicago Press
Journal of Modern Literature. Philadelphia: Temple University
Journal of Reform Judaism. New York: CCAR (Central Conference of American Rabbis) Press
Journal of Social Psychology. Washington, DC: Heldref Publications, for the Helen Dwight Reid Educational Foundation
Journal of Sport History. University Park, PA: North American Society for Sport History
Journal of the Economic and Social History of the Orient. Leiden: E. J. Brill
Journal of the History of Ideas. Philadelphia: Temple University
Journal of the History of the Behavioral Sciences. Brandon, VT: Clinical Psychology Pub. Co.
Journal of the Royal Asiatic Society. London
Journal of Theological Studies. Oxford: Oxford University Press
Journal of Theology for Southern Africa. Cape Town: University of Cape Town, Department of Religious Studies
Journalism Quarterly. Columbia, SC: Association for Education in Journalism and Mass Communications, University of South Carolina
Judaica: Beitraege zum Verstaendnis des juedischen Schicksals in Vergangenheit und Gegenwart. Basel: Stiftung fuer Kirche und Judentum
Judaism. New York: American Jewish Congress
Le Judaïsme après Auschwitz, eds. E. Schuessler Fiorenza, D. Tracy. Paris: Beauchesne, 1984 (Concilium, 195). In English, see The

Holocaust as Interruption
Judaïsme et droits de l'homme, ed. E. Hirsch. Paris: Librairie des Libertés, 1984
Juden als Darmstaedter Buerger, ed. E. G. Franz. Darmstadt: E. Roether Verlag, 1984
Die Juden und Martin Luther—Martin Luther und die Juden, ed. H. Kremers. Neukirchen-Vluyn: Nerkirchener Verlag, 1985
Judentum und Antisemitismus von der Antike bis zur Gegenwart, eds. T. Klein et al. Duesseldorf: Droste Verlag, 1984
Judisk Kroenika. Stockholm: Judiska Foersamlingarnas i Sverige
Die Juedische Emigration aus Deutschland, 1933–1941: Die Geschichte einer Austreibung, ed. G. Pflug. Frankfurt a.M.: Buchhaendler-Vereinigung, 1985
Juedischer Pressedienst. Bonn: Zentralrat der Juden in Deutschland
Les Juifs au regard de l'histoire: Mélanges en l'honneur de Bernhard Blumenkranz, ed. G. Dahan. Paris: Picard, 1985
Juifs et Judaïsme en Afrique du Nord dans l'Antiquité et le Haut Moyen-Age, eds. C. Iancu, J.-M. Lassere. Montpellier: Université Paul Valéry, 1985
Kairos: Zeitschrift fuer Religionswissenschaft und Theologie. Salzburg: Otto Mueller Verlag
Kiryat Sefer. Jerusalem: Jewish National and University Library Press (Hebrew)
Kivunim. Jerusalem: World Zionist Organization (Hebrew)
Koeln und das rheinische Judentum, ed. J. Bohnke-Kollwitz et al. Koeln: J. P. Bachem, 1984
Kultur un Lebn. New York: Workmen's Circle (Yiddish)
Kultura: Szkice, opowiadania, sprawozdania. Paris: Instytut Literacki
Der Landesverband der Israelitischen Kultusgemeinden in Bayern. [Bulletin]. Muenchen: Der Verband
Le-Ezrat ha-Am—Het volk ter hulpe: Het eerste joodse blad in 1945, eds. T. Benima, F. J. Hoogewoud. Assen: Van Gorcum, 1985
Leo Baeck Institute Year Book. London
Liberty: A Magazine of Religious Freedom. Hagerstown, MD: Review and Herald Pub.
Library Quarterly. Chicago: University of Chicago Press
The Listener. London: BBC Enterprises
Lithuanian Jewry, ed. L. Garfunkel. Vol. 4: The Holocaust. Tel-Aviv: Igud Yots'ei Lita b'Israel, 1984 (Hebrew)

Littérature. Paris: Larousse
Luther, Lutheranism and the Jews, eds. J. Halpérin, A. Sovik. Geneva: Lutheran World Federation, 1984
Mankind. Sydney: Anthropological Society of New South Wales
Massuah: A Yearbook on the Holocaust and Heroism. Tel-Aviv: Massuah (Hebrew)
Me'asef: Studies in the History and Problems of the Jewish Labor Movement. Givat Haviva: Beit Baruch Lin (Hebrew)
Mechkerei Yerushalayim be-Folklor, see Jerusalem Studies in Jewish Folklore
Medieval Studies. Toronto: Pontifical Institute of Medieval Studies
Melbourne Chronicle. Melbourne: Jewish National Library and Cultural Centre "Kadimah"
A Memorial to the Brzozów Community, ed. A. Levite. Tel-Aviv: Survivors of Brzozów, 1984 (Hebrew)
Menorah Review. Richmond, VA: Virginia Commonwealth University, Judaic Studies Program
Merkur: Deutsche Zeitschrift fuer europaeisches Denken. Stuttgart: Klett-Cotta
Mibifnim. Ein Harod: United Kibbutz Movement (Hebrew)
Michael: On the History of the Jews in the Diaspora. Tel-Aviv: Tel-Aviv University (Hebrew)
Michigan Germanic Studies, Ann Arbor: University of Michigan, Department of German
Michigan Jewish History. Oak Park, MI: Jewish Historical Society of Michigan
Midland History. Birmingham: University of Birmingham
Midstream. New York: Theodor Herzl Foundation
Miscellanea Historiae Ecclesiasticae. Bruxelles: Editions Nauwelaerts
Modern Jewish Studies Annual/Yiddish. Flushing, NY: Queens College Press
Modern Judaism. Baltimore, MD: Johns Hopkins University Press
Modern Language Quarterly. Seattle: University of Washington
Moment. Farmingdale, NY: Moment Magazine, a division of Jewish Educational Ventures, Boston
Monatsschrift fuer Kriminologie und Strafrechtsreform. Koeln: Carl Heymanns Verlag, for the Gesellschaft fuer die Gesamte Kriminologie
Le Monothéisme contre le racisme: Les actes du Colloque organisé le

29 mars 1981 par la Loge Saädia Gaon du B'nai B'rith. Paris: Union Française des Associations B'nai B'rith, 1984
Moral Education Forum. New York: Hunter College
Der Mord an den Juden im Zweiten Weltkrieg: Entschlussbildung und Verwirklichung, eds. E. Jaeckel, J. Rohwer. Stuttgart: Deutsche Verlags-Anstalt, 1985
Mouvements de jeunesse chrétiens et juifs, eds. G. Cholvy et al. Paris: Ed. du Cerf, 1985
The Nation. New York: Nation Enterprises
Nation and History: Studies in the History of the Jewish People, ed. S. Ettinger. Vol. 2. Jerusalem: Zalman Shazar Center, 1984 (Hebrew)
National Review. New York: National Review, Inc.
Nationalities Papers. Omaha, NE: Association for the Study of Nationalities
Nazism 1919–1945. Vol. 2: State, Economy and Society 1933–1939: A Documentary Reader, eds. J. Noakes, G. Pridham. Exeter: University of Exeter, 1984
Neohelicon. Budapest: Akademiai Kiado, for the International Comparative Literature Association
Nes Ammim Lezingen: Gesprekken in Israel. Nes Ammim
Das Neue Israel: Zeitschrift fuer Politik, Kultur und Wirtschaft. Zuerich: AG Juedischer Verlag
New Community. London: Community Relations Commission
New German Critique. Milwaukee, WI: University of Wisconsin
New Left Review. Oxford: Alden Press
New Outlook. Tel-Aviv: Tazpiot, for the Jewish-Arab Institute
New Republic. Washington, DC: The New Republic, Inc.
New Statesman. London: Statesman and Nation Pub. Co.
New Testament Studies. Cambridge: Cambridge University Press
New Times: A Soviet Weekly of World Affairs. Moscow: Trud
New York Review of Books. New York: New York Review
Newsweek. New York: Newsweek, Inc.
Nordisk Judaistik: Scandinavian Jewish Studies. Stockholm: Saellskapet foer Judaistisk Forskning
Les Nouveaux Cahiers. Paris: Alliance Israélite Universelle
Observations on the "Spiritual Situation of the Age": Contemporary German Perspectives, ed. J. Habermas. Trans. from the German. Cambridge, MA: MIT Press, 1984

Oesterreichische Akademie der Wissenschaften. Phil.-Hist. Klasse. Anzeiger. Wien
El Olivo: Documentación y estudios para el diálogo entre Judíos y Cristianos. Madrid: Centro de Estudios Judeo-Cristianos
Ori: Mensuel israélien de pensée et d'actualité juives. Jerusalem: Ori
Pardès: Anthropologie, histoire, philosophie, littérature. Paris: J. C. Lattès
Patterns of Prejudice. London: Institute of Jewish Affairs
Pe'amim: Studies in the Cultural Heritage of Oriental Jewry. Jerusalem: Ben-Zvi Institute (Hebrew)
Persecution and Toleration, ed. W. J. Sheils. Oxford: Blackwell, 1984 (Studies in Church History, 21)
Pfaelzisches Pfarrerblatt. Homburg: Pfaelzischer Pfarrerverein
Philosophical Forum. New York: Philosophical Forum, Inc.
Philosophy of the Social Sciences. Waterloo, Ont.: Wilfrid Laurier University Press
Pierre Mendès France et le mendésisme, eds. F. Bédarida, J.-P. Rioux. Paris: Fayard, 1985
Pioneer Woman. New York: Pioneer Women/Na'amat
Political Affairs. New York: Communist Party, USA
Political Communication and Persuasion. New York: Crane Russak
Political Psychology. New York: International Society of Political Psychology
Political Science Quarterly. New York: Academy of Political Science
Political Theory. Beverly Hills, CA: Sage
Los políticos argentinos y el antisemitismo, comp. A. Kleiner. Buenos Aires: Libreros y Editores del Polígono, 1984
Polityka. Warszawa: "Prasa-Książka-Ruch" RSW
Popular Music. Cambridge: Cambridge University Press
Praxis International: A Philosophical Journal. Oxford: Blackwell
Il pregiudizio antisemitico in Italia: La coscienza democratica di fronte al razzismo strisciante. Roma: Newton Compton, 1984
Present Tense. New York: American Jewish Committee
Proceedings of the Eighth World Congress of Jewish Studies, August 1981. Panel Sessions: Jewish History, ed. D. Assaf. Jerusalem: World Union of Jewish Studies, 1984 (Hebrew)
Prologue. Washington, DC: National Archives
Przegląd Historyczny. Warszawa: Towarzystwo Miłośników Historii
Przegląd Zachodni. Poznań: Instytut Zachodni

Psyche: Zeitschrift fuer Psychoanalyse und ihre Anwendungen. Stuttgart: Klett-Cotta
Psychoanalytic Reflections on the Holocaust, eds. S. A. Luel, P. Marcus. Denver: University of Denver; New York: Ktav, 1984
Psychohistory Review. Springfield, IL: Sangamon State University
Quaderni Storici. Bologna: Il Mulino
Quadrant. Sydney: Quadrant Magazine Co., for the Australian Association for Cultural Freedom
Radio Free Europe Research Reports. Situation Report: Romania. Munich: RFERL Inc.
La Rassegna Mensile di Israel. Roma: Unione delle Comunità Israelitiche Italiane
Recht, Verwaltung und Justiz im Nationalsozialismus: Ausgewaehlte Schriften, Gesetze und Gerichtsentscheidungen von 1933 bis 1945, eds. M. Hirsch et al. Koeln: Bund Verlag, 1984
Rechtsextremismus in der Bundesrepublik: Voraussetzungen, Zusammenhaenge, Wirkungen. Frankfurt a.M.: Fischer Verlag, 1984
Reference Services Review. Ann Arbor, MI: Pierian Press
Reform Judaism. New York: Union of American Hebrew Congregations
Regards: Revue juive de Belgique. Bruxelles: Les Amis de Regards
Les Relations intercommunautaires juives en Méditerranée occidentale, XIIe-XXe siècles: Actes du Colloque international . . . Sénanque, mai 1982, ed. J. L. Miège. Paris: Centre National de la Recherche Scientifique, 1984
Rencontre—Chrétiens et Juifs. Paris: Les Rencontres entre Chrétiens et Juifs
Review of Politics. Notre Dame, IN: University of Notre Dame
Revue d'Histoire de la Médecine Hébraïque. Paris: Société d'Histoire de la Médecine Hébraïque
Revue d'Histoire et de Philosophie Religieuses. Paris: Presses Universitaires de France
Revue des Deux Mondes. Paris: Revue des Deux Mondes
Revue des Etudes Juives. Paris: Société des Etudes Juives
Revue des Sciences Religieuses. Strasbourg: Université des Sciences Humaines
Revue Française de Science Politique. Paris: Presses de la Fondation Nationale des Sciences Politiques
Rivista di Storia Contemporanea. Torino: Loescher Editore
Romanic Review. New York: Columbia University

Rumbos en el Judaísmo, el Sionismo e Israel. Jerusalem: World Zionist Organization
Russia. Silver Spring, MD: Foundation for Soviet Studies
Schatten der Vergangenheit: Deutsche und Juden Heute, ed. A. Wojak. Guetersloh: Guetersloher Verlagshaus Mohn, 1985
Sefárdica. Buenos Aires: Centro de Investigación y Difusión de la Cultura Sefaradi
Sefer Bar-Ilan. Netanya: Bar Ilan High-School (Hebrew)
Semana. Jerusalem: Semana
Sens: Juifs et Chrétiens dans le monde aujourd'hui. Paris: L'Amitié Judéo-Chrétienne de France
Shdemot: Cultural Forum of the Kibbutz Movement. Tel-Aviv: Federation of Kibbutz Movements
The Shekel. Tamarac, FL: American Israel Numismatic Association
Shevet Ve'am: Literary and Research Forum for History and Social Problems of Sephardi and Oriental Jewry in Israel and Abroad. Jerusalem: Council of the Sephardi Community (Hebrew)
Sh'ma: A Journal of Jewish Responsibility. Port Washington, NY: Sh'ma, Inc.
Shvut: Jewish Problems in the USSR and Eastern Europe. Tel-Aviv: Tel-Aviv University (Hebrew)
Simon Wiesenthal Center Annual. Los Angeles
Sixteenth Century Journal. Kirksville, MO: Sixteenth Century Studies Conference, Northeast Missouri State University
Skira Chodshit. Tel-Aviv: Ministry of Defense (Hebrew)
Śląski Kwartalnik Historyczny "Sobótka". Wroclaw: Ossolineum, for the Wroclawskie Towarzystwo Milośników Historii
Slavica Hierosolymitana. Jerusalem: Magnes Press, Hebrew University
Social, Cultural and Educational Association of the Jews in the People's Republic of Bulgaria: Annual. Sofia
Social Education. Washington, DC: National Council for the Social Studies
Sociological Review. Henley-on-Thames, Oxon: Routledge and Kegan Paul
South Atlantic Quarterly. Durham, NC: Duke University Press
Soviet Jewish Affairs: A Journal of Jewish Problems in the USSR and Eastern Europe. London: Institute of Jewish Affairs
Soviet Jewry in the Decisive Decade 1971–1980, ed. R. O. Freedman. Durham, NC: Duke University Press, 1984

The Spectator. London: The Spectator, Ltd.
Speculum: A Journal of Medieval Studies. Cambridge, MA: Medieval Academy of America
Der Spiegel. Hamburg: Spiegel-Verlag Rudolf Augstein
Staatsrecht und Staatsrechtlehre im Dritten Reich, ed. E. W. Boeckenfoerde. Heidelberg: C. F. Mueller Juristischer Verlag, 1985
State, Culture and Society. New York: Associated Faculty Press
Storia Contemporanea. Bologna: Il Mulino
Storia delle idee politiche, economiche e sociali, ed. L. Firpo. Vol. 2, pt. 1: Ebraismo e cristianesimo, eds. G. Barbero et al. Torino: Unione Tipografico-Editrice Torinese, 1985
Studi Veneziani. Pisa: Giardini editori
Studia Monastica. Barcelona: Publicacions de l'Abadia de Montserrat
Studia nad Faszyzmem i Zbrodniami Hitlerowskimi. Wroclaw: Wydawnictwo Universytetu Wroclawskiego
Studia Rosenthaliana: Tijdschrift voor Joodse wetenschap en geschiedenis in Nederland. Assen: Van Gorcum, for the University Library of Amsterdam, Bibliotheca Rosenthaliana
Studies in Contemporary Jewry. Bloomington, IN: Indiana University Press, for the Hebrew University, Institute of Contemporary Jewry
Studies in Memory of R. Yitzhak Nissim. Vol. 4: Documents on Communities and Persons, ed. M. Benayahu. Jerusalem: Yad Ha-Rav Nissim, 1985 (Hebrew)
Studies in Zionism. Baltimore, MD: Johns Hopkins University Press, for Tel-Aviv University, Institute for Zionist Research
Survey of Jewish Affairs. Cranbury, NJ: Associated University Presses
Tefutsot Israel. Jerusalem: American Jewish Committee, Israel Office (Hebrew)
Temenos: Studies in Comparative Religion. Helsinki: Suomen Uskontotieteellinen Seura
Les Temps Modernes. Paris: Les Temps Modernes
La Terre Retrouvée: Tribune sioniste. Paris: Terre Retrouvée
Then and Now: Annual Lectures on the Jews of Greece (1977–1983), ed. Z. Ankori. Tel-Aviv: Chair for the History and Culture of the Jewry of Salonica and Greece, Tel-Aviv University, 1984 (Hebrew)
Theologische Literaturzeitung. Berlin (East): Evangelische Verlagsanstalt
Theology Today. Princeton, NJ [Publisher unknown]
Threepenny Review. San Francisco: Garnett Press

Tidsskrift for Teologi og Kirke. Oslo: Universitetsforlaget
Time. New York: Time, Inc.
Toward the Understanding and Prevention of Genocide: Proceedings of the International Conference on the Holocaust and Genocide. Boulder, CO: Westview Press, 1984
Traces. Paris: Traces
Tribuene: Zeitschrift zum Verstaendnis des Judentums. Frankfurt a.M.: Tribuene Verlag
Tribune Juive. Paris: Publications Juives Réunies
Twentieth Century Literature. Hempstead, NY: Hofstra University Press
Tygodnik Powszechny: Katolickie pismo spoleczno-kulturalne. Kraków: Spoleczny Instytut Wydawniczy "Znak"
Understanding Popular Culture: Europe from the Middle Ages to the Nineteenth Century, ed. S. L. Kaplan. Berlin (West): Mouton, 1984
La Unión. Lima: Asociación Judía del Perú
U.S. Department of State Bulletin. Washington, DC
Unser Tsait. New York: Unser Tsait (Yiddish)
"Unternehmen Barbarossa": Der deutsche Ueberfall auf die Sowjet Union 1941, eds. G. R. Ueberschaer, W. Wette. Paderborn: Schoening, 1984
Valóság. Budapest: Tudományás Ismeretterjesztoe Társulat
Verfolgung, Vertreibung, Vernichtung: Dokumente des faschistischen Antisemitismus 1933–1942, ed. K. Paetzold. Frankfurt a.M.: Roederberg-Verlag, 1984
Versunkene Welt, eds. J. Riedl, H. P. Hofmann. Wien: Jewish Welcome Service, 1984
Vichy France and the Resistance; Culture and Ideology, eds. R. Kedward, R. Austin. London: Croom Helm, 1985
Vierteljahrshefte fuer Zeitgeschichte. Muenchen: Institut fuer Zeitgeschichte; Stuttgart: Deutsche Verlags-Anstalt
Viewpoints. Montreal: Labor Zionist Movement of Canada
Vision and Conflict in the Holy Land, ed. R. I. Cohen. Jerusalem: Yad Izhak Ben-Zvi; New York: St. Martin's Press, 1985
The Voice of Auschwitz Survivors in Israel. Jerusalem: Public Committee in Israel of Survivors of Auschwitz
The Voice of Auschwitz Survivors in Israel: Forty Years after, ed. S. Nahari. Jerusalem: Public Committee in Israel of Survivors of

Auschwitz, 1985
Vous avez dit fascismes?, eds. A. Spire, R. Badinter. Paris: Editions Montalba, 1984
Wagnerism in European Culture and Politics, eds. D. C. Large, W. Weber. Ithaca, NY: Cornell University Press, 1984
Wenn der Messias kommt: Das juedisch-christliche Verhaeltnis im Spiegel mittelalterlicher Kunst, eds. L. Koetzsche, P. von der Osten-Sacken. Berlin (West): Institut Kirche und Judentum, 1984
Western European Education. White Plains, NY: International Arts and Sciences Press
Western Political Quarterly. Salt Lake City: University of Utah
Western States Jewish History. Santa Monica, CA: Western States Jewish History Association
Wetterauer Geschichtsblaetter. Beiheft. Friedberg, Hessen: Bindernagelschen Verlag
When Biology Became Destiny: Women in Weimar and Nazi Germany, eds. R. Bridenthal et al. New York: Monthly Review Press, 1984
Who's Afraid of Richard Wagner:: Aspects of a Controversial Personality, eds. R. Litvin, H. Shelach. Jerusalem: Keter, 1984 (Hebrew)
Widerstand, Flucht, Kollaboration: Literarische Intelligenz und Politik in Frankreich, ed. J. Siess. Frankfurt a.M.: Campus Verlag, 1984
Widerstand und Verfolgung in Wien 1934–1945: Eine Dokumentation. Vol. 3: 1938–1945. 2nd ed. Wien: Oesterreichischer Bundesverlag, 1984
Wien 1870–1930: Traum und Wirklichkeit, ed. R. Waissenberger. Salzburg: Residenz Verlag, 1984
The World of Anne Frank/Die wereld van Anne Frank, by S. A. Cohen et al. Amsterdam: Anne Frank Stichting, 1985
World Today. London: Royal Institute of International Affairs
Wuppertal in der Zeit des Nationalsozialismus, ed. K. Goebel. Wuppertal: Peter Hammer Verlag, 1984
Yad Vashem Studies. Jerusalem: Yad Vashem
Yahadut Zemanenu. Jerusalem: Magnes Press, Hebrew University (Hebrew)
Yehudei Berit ha-Moetzot, see The Jews of the Soviet Union
Yiddish, see Modern Jewish Studies Annual
Yiddishe Vort. New York: Agudath Israel of America (Yiddish)

Yod: Revue des études hébraïques et juives. Paris: Publications Langues'O
Zeitgeschichte. Wien: Geyer-Edition
Zeitschrift fuer Evangelische Ethik. Guetersloh: Guetersloher Verlagshaus Gerd Mohn
Zeitschrift fuer Historische Forschung. Berlin (West): Duncker und Humblot
Zeitschrift fuer Religions- und Geistesgeschichte. Koeln: E. J. Brill
Zeszyty Historyczne. Paris: Instytut Literacki
Zion: A Quarterly for Research in Jewish History. Jerusalem: Historical Society of Israel (Hebrew)
Zionist Ideas. Jerusalem: World Zionist Organization
Zmanim: A Historical Quarterly. Tel-Aviv: Tel-Aviv University (Hebrew)
Zukunft. New York: Congress of Jewish Culture (Yiddish)

ANTISEMITISM

B I B L I O G R A P H I E S
A N D   R E F E R E N C E   W O R K S

0001. הטל, אברהם. יהדות יוון, מגירוש ספרד ועד ימינו: ביבליו- גראפיה. ירושלים: מכון בן-צבי, 1984. 215, xxiv עמ'.

[Attal, Robert. THE JEWS OF GREECE, FROM THE EXPULSION FROM SPAIN UNTIL THE PRESENT: A BIBLIOGRAPHY. Jerusalem: Ben-Zvi Institute, 1984. 215, xxiv pp.]

2297 entries, including books and articles from journals and newspapers, in the European languages, Hebrew, and Greek. See the subject index for antisemitism.

0002. Braham, Randolph L. THE HUNGARIAN JEWISH CATASTROPHE: A SELECTED AND ANNOTATED BIBLIOGRAPHY. 2nd ed., rev. and enlarged. New York: Social Science Monographs and Institute for Holocaust Studies, CUNY, distributed by Columbia University Press, 1984. xvi, 501 pp. (East European Monographs, 162) (Holocaust Studies Series).

2479 entries, many annotated, in the European languages, Hebrew, and Yiddish. Deals with the Holocaust and the period before and after World War II, including sections on antisemitism and racism, antisemitic literature, anti-Jewish legislation, antisemitic professional associations, the Holocaust, war criminals and war crimes trials, neo-Nazism, neo-antisemitism.

0003. Davis, Lenwood G. BLACK-JEWISH RELATIONS IN THE UNITED STATES, 1752-1984: A SELECTED BIBLIOGRAPHY. Westport, CT: Greenwood Press, 1984. xv, 130 pp. (Bibliographies and Indexes in Afro-American and African Studies, 1).

An annotated bibliography of articles, books, pamphlets and dissertations in English. 1241 entries. On Black antisemitism, see pp. 10-17, 56-62.

0004. Fisher, Eugene J. A New Maturity in Christian-Jewish Dialogue: An Annotated Bibliography, 1973-1983. FACE TO FACE 11 (Spr 1984) 29-43.

Describes and analyzes various works in English on Christian-Jewish dialogue and on attempts to eradicate antisemitism. Includes works on the New Testament and Judaism, the trial of Jesus, medieval and modern Jewish-Christian relations, the Churches and the Holocaust.

0005. Flem, Lydia. LE RACISME. Paris: MA Editions, 1985. 205 pp.

A lexicon of subjects and persons associated with racism, including antisemitism.

0006. Fritsch, Christopher. America and the Holocaust: A Selected Bibliography. HOLOCAUST STUDIES ANNUAL 1 <1983> (1984) 167-178.

109 entries in English and Hebrew, including bibliographies, articles, books, and dissertations.

0007. Gilbert, Victor F.; Tatla, Darshan Singh. IMMIGRANTS, MINORITIES AND RACE RELATIONS: A BIBLIOGRAPHY OF THESES AND DISSERTATIONS PRESENTED AT BRITISH AND IRISH UNIVERSITIES, 1900-1981. With an introductory essay by Colin Holmes. London: Mansell, 1984. xxxiii, 153 pp.

1716 entries. See the index for antisemitism.

0008. Hundert, Gershon David; Bacon, Gershon C. THE JEWS IN POLAND AND RUSSIA: BIBLIOGRAPHICAL ESSAYS. Bloomington, IN: Indiana University Press, 1984. xii, 276 pp. (Modern Jewish Experience Series).

Includes works in the European languages, Hebrew and Yiddish. For antisemitism, see especially pp. 45-48 on Jewish-Christian relations and persecution in Poland in the 16th-17th centuries; pp. 170- 174 on antisemitism in Tsarist Russia; pp. 187-188 on antisemitism in inter-war Poland; pp. 224-225 on antisemitism in the Soviet Union today.

0009. Kaplan, Jonathan. INTERNATIONAL BIBLIOGRAPHY OF JEWISH HISTORY AND THOUGHT. Muenchen: K.G. Saur; Jerusalem: Magnes Press, 1984. xviii, 483 pp.

A selective bibliography of books published in the 20th century. 2190 entries in Hebrew and European languages. Pp. 185-193 include works on antisemitism in the Middle Ages. Pp. 261-271: "Modern Anti-Semitism."

0010. Klenicki, Leon; Wigoder, Geoffrey, eds. A DICTIONARY OF THE JEWISH CHRISTIAN DIALOGUE. New York: Paulist Press, 1984. vii, 213 pp. (Studies in Judaism and Christianity).

Pp. 9-15: "Antisemitism."

0011. Laska, Vera. NAZISM, RESISTANCE AND HOLOCAUST IN WORLD WAR II: A BIBLIOGRAPHY. Metuchen, NJ: Scarecrow Press, 1985. 183 pp.

A bibliography of books, mostly English, partially annotated. 1907 entries. See pp. 1-7: "Jews and Anti-Semitism"; pp. 127-139: "War Crimes."

0012. Rees, Philip. FASCISM AND PRE-FASCISM IN EUROPE 1890-1945: A BIBLIOGRAPHY OF THE EXTREME RIGHT. Brighton, Sussex: Harvester Press; Totowa, NJ: Barnes and Noble Books, 1984. xxii, 330 pp.

Includes books, articles, and dissertations in the European languages. Partially annotated. Consists mostly of works published after 1945.

0013. Schlesinger, Hugo; Porto, Humberto. GUIA BIBLIOGRAFICO DO DIALOGO CRISTAO-JUDAICO [A Bibliographical Guide to Christian-Jewish Dialogue]. São Paulo: Conselho de Fraternidade Cristão-Judaica, 1985. 144 pp.

Ca. 780 entries, in European languages. Includes books, documents, and a list of periodicals.

0014. Senkman, B.; Weinstein, A. Fuentes para el estudio de la cultura sefaradi en revistas judéo-argentinas. SEFARDICA 1, 2 (Nov 1984) 145-164.

A bibliography of articles published in thirteen different periodicals in Argentinia between 1911 and 1984. Many of the entries discuss antisemitism, the Inquisition, crypto-Jews, and antisemitism in Arab countries.

0015. Szonyi, David M. THE HOLOCAUST: AN ANNOTATED BIBLIOGRAPHY AND RESOURCE GUIDE. New York: Ktav, 1985. xiv, 396 pp.

Includes books, articles, memoirs, literature about the Holocaust, children's books, audio-visual material, music, lists of memorial sites and resources centers, lists of groups for survivors and children of survivors. English only.

0016. THE THIRD REICH, 1933-1939: A HISTORICAL BIBLIOGRAPHY. Santa Barbara, CA: ABC-Clio Information Services, 1984. 239 pp. (ABC-Clio Research Guides, 10).

1024 abstracts of articles in European languages, published between 1973 and 1982. See the index for antisemitism.

0017. THE THIRD REICH AT WAR: A HISTORICAL BIBLIOGRAPHY. Santa Barbara, CA: ABC-Clio Information Services, 1984. xii, 270 pp. (ABC-Clio Research Guides, 11).

1061 abstracts of articles in European languages, published between 1972 and 1982. See the index for antisemitism.

0018. Zentner, Christian; Beduerftig, Friedemann, eds. DAS GROSSE LEXIKON DES DRITTEN REICHES. Muenchen: Suedwest Verlag, 1985. 686 pp.

On antisemitism, see the following entries: "Antisemitismus," by Herbert Obenhaus (29-31); "Endloesung," by Alfred Streim (150-153); "Judenverfolgung," by A. Streim (289-291); "Konzentrationslager," by Willy Dressen (325-326); "Nationalsozialismus," by Reinhart Beck (403-406); "Die Weltanschauung Hitlers," by C. Zentner (632-635), and other shorter entries.

A N T I S E M I T I S M

T H R O U G H O U T T H E A G E S

GENERAL

0019. אנקורי, צבי. יהדות ויוונות נוצרית: מיפגש ועימות במרוצת הדורות. תל-אביב: אוניברסיטת תל-אביב, 1984. 198 עמ'. (יהודי-יוון לדורותם, 1).

[Ankori, Zvi. ENCOUNTER IN HISTORY: JEWS AND CHRISTIAN GREEKS IN THEIR RELATION THROUGH THE AGES. Tel-Aviv: Tel-Aviv University, 1984. 198 pp. (Greek Jewish Themes in Historical Perspective, 1).]

A history of the ambivalent relations between Greek Jewry and Greek Orthodox Christians, from the 4th to the 19th centuries. Stresses the fact that respect and admiration for Jews existed side by side with religious and political antisemitism expressed in anti-Jewish legislation, forced conversion, etc. Economic antisemitism was introduced only in the 19th century.

0020. לאסדאן, טוביה. צו דער געשיכטע פון עלילת דם. דאס אידישע ווארט 245 (ניסן תשמד) 13-16.

[Lasdan, Tuvia. On the History of the Blood Libel. DOS YIDDISHE VORT 245 (Nissan 5744 = Apr 1984) 13-16.]

A brief history of the blood libel from 1144 to the 20th century. Includes miraculous tales of how the Maharal (Judah Loew ben Bezalel, 16th century) saved the Jews of Prague from a blood libel accusation and an account of the efforts of Hermann Strack, a 19th century Christian scholar, to defend the Jews against blood libel charges by various antisemitic "experts."

0021. לואיס, ברנרד. המורשה היהודית-מוסלמית. פעמים 20 (1984)
.13-3

[Lewis, Bernard. The Judeo-Islamic Heritage. PE`AMIM 20 (1984) 3-13.]

Defends the use of the concept "Judeo-Islamic heritage." Muslim practice in relation to the Jews varied widely in different periods and regions. Muslim society saw discrimination against non-believers as a positive value, but persecution was rare. Examines similarities between Judaism and Islam as well as points of difference which could lead to conflict.

0022. משי זהב, יהודה, עורך. פרשיות עלילות הדם שהעלילו על עם
ישראל במשך הדורות שעברו ועד ימינו. ירושלים: י. משי זהב,
תשמד. שכ עמ׳.

[Meshi Zahav, Yehuda, ed. BLOOD LIBELS: BLOOD LIBEL ACCUSATIONS AGAINST THE JEWS THROUGHOUT THE PAST GENERATIONS UNTIL THE PRESENT. Jerusalem: Y. Meshi Zahav, 1984. 320 pp.]

The three sections of the book include descriptions of the blood libels in chronological order, tales of sages and pious men who prevented actions planned against the Jews, and miscellaneous cases.

0023. סטאו, קנת. ישראל בין האומות. האומה 74/75 (אביב/קיץ
1984) 10-19.

[Stow, Kenneth. Israel among the Nations. HA-UMMA 74/75 (Spr/Sum 1984) 10-19.] Trans. from "Midstream," Oct. 1983.

Western hostility to Israel embodies fundamentally medieval patterns and attitudes. Medieval Christianity saw the Jew as "emblematic of all that was evil or imperfect," and defined the proper social place of Jews as "perpetual servitude." From the 19th century, left-wing thinkers espoused this attitude in secular form and today Israel must play the role of the acquiescent inferior in external affairs. This attitude was expressed clearly during the 1982 Lebanon War.

0024. Amson, Fabienne; Gruber-Ejnes, Pascale. De la crucifixion au génocide. REGARDS 145 (12-25 Sept 1985) 70-73.

Describes the refusal of the Jews to recognize Jesus as the Messiah and the accusation of deicide, the growth of Christian antisemitism, persecution of the Jews in the Middle Ages, and modern antisemitism.

0025. Aufgebauer, Peter. DIE GESCHICHTE DER JUDEN IN DER STADT HILDESHEIM UND IN DER FRUEHEN NEUZEIT. Hildesheim: Bernward, 1984. 178 pp. (Schriftenreihe des Stadtarchivs und der Stadtbibliothek Hildesheim, 12).

Discusses the restrictive policies of the municipality and the Church towards the Jews up to the 19th century.

0026. Bach, H.I. THE GERMAN JEW: A SYNTHESIS OF JUDAISM AND WESTERN CIVILIZATION, 1730-1930. Oxford: Oxford University Press, 1984. 255 pp. (The Littman Library of Jewish Civilization).

Includes a short introduction, "German Jews in the Middle Ages" (pp. 17-43), describing the persecution of Jews in Germany, the attitude of the Catholic Church, and later of Protestantism, and the life of the Jews in the ghettos. The struggle for emancipation from social and political discrimination after the French Revolution is described as part of a gradual process of synthesis between German and Jewish culture. The chapter entitled "Nationalism and Anti-Semitism in the New German Empire" (pp. 122-135) shows the rise of reaction and of political antisemitism.

0027. Bat Yeor [=Littman, Gisèle]. THE DHIMMI: JEWS AND CHRISTIANS UNDER ISLAM. Rev. and enlarged English ed. Rutherford, NJ: Fairleigh Dickinson University Press, 1985. 444 pp. Originally published as "Le Dhimmi" (Paris: Ed. Anthropos, 1980).

The oppression of Jews under Islamic rule is based on an archetypal relationship established at the time of the Muslim conquest - "the victor-vanquished relationship," expressed in the status of the dhimmi, the inferior non-Muslim. Parts 1 and 2 (pp. 43-157) consist of a historical outline of the Jews' status under Islam and a description of modern formulations of this dhimmi status, its place in Arab nationalism, and its psychological effects on Oriental Jews. The rest of the book consists of documents reflecting persecution and oppression of the Jews in various Islamic countries from the time of Mohammed up to the present day.

0028. Baumann, Arnulf; Mahn, Kaete; Saeboe, Magne. LUTHERS ERBEN UND DIE JUDEN: DAS VERHAELTNIS LUTHERISCHER KIRCHEN EUROPAS ZU DEN JUDEN. Hannover: Lutherisches Verlagshaus, 1984. 144 pp.

An analysis of the attitudes of the Lutheran churches in Europe towards the Jews from the 16th century to the present. Focuses on the period from 1933 onwards, i.e. on the problem of the Protestant churches' response to Nazism and the Holocaust.

0029. Birnbaum, Henrik. Some Problems with the Etymology and the Semantics of Slavic Žid "Jew". SLAVICA HIEROSOLYMITANA 7 (1985) 1-11.

Discusses some etymological and semantic problems of the word "Žid" in the Slavic languages, its neutral meaning in Polish and its pejorative sense in Russian. To express a negative attitude in Polish one adds a suffix.

0030. Bochnik, Peter. DIE MAECHTIGEN DIENER: DIE MEDIZIN UND DIE ENTWICKLUNG VON FRAUENFEINDLICHKEIT UND ANTISEMITISMUS IN DER EUROPAEISCHEN GESCHICHTE. Reinbeck: Rowohlt, 1985. 123 pp.

From the Middle Ages, the medical profession gained political influence through an alliance with the Catholic Church, based on common interests. This alliance between the "healers of the body" and the "healers of the soul" made possible the attempt to exclude Jews and women from the profession. Ch. 4 (pp. 41-63) deals with 800 years of antisemitism in the medical profession.

0031. Bonfil, Robert. The Historian's Perception of the Jews in the Italian Renaissance: Towards a Reappraisal. REVUE DES ETUDES JUIVES 143, 1/2 (Jan-June 1984) 59-82.

Proposes moving away from the view of Renaissance Jewry offered by Cecil Roth and other historians. The men of the Renaissance (14th-16th centuries) were not as open to or accepting of Jews as Roth suggested. "Persecutions, blood-libels, expulsions" mar the idyllic image of a Jewish Italian renaissance of deep intellectual and social intermingling.

0032. Butraru, I.C. HOLOCAUSTUL UITAT...: CONSIDERATIUNI ISTORICE, POLITICE SI SOCIALE CU PRIVIRE LA ANTISEMITISMUL ROMANESC [The Holocaust Forgotten...: Historical, Political and Social Considerations in Regard to Romanian Antisemitism]. Tel Aviv: Asociaţia Culturală Mondială a Evreilor Originari din Romania, 1985. 528 pp.

A history of antisemitism in Romania, especially during the 20th century. Includes a short survey of events during the 14th to 19th centuries. Discusses anti-Jewish legislation and regulations, the situation between the two World Wars, and the activities of the Iron Guard and of other antisemitic parties, events during the Holocaust period, the pogroms, and the deportations of Jews to Transnistria. The last chapter deals with antisemitism in Romania since the Second World War.

0033. Calmann, Marianne. THE CARRIERE OF CARPENTRAS. Oxford: Oxford University Press, 1984. 286 pp.

A history of the Jews of the Comtat Venaissin (France), especially Carpentras under papal rule from 1273 to 1791, including the establishment of the ghettos (ca. 1460) and oppression and persecution of the Jews.

0034. Chary, Théophane. Glanes sur les sentiers de la méconnaissance. FOI ET VIE 84 (Jan 1985) 143-148.

Discusses antisemitism in Catholic literature and in the liturgy.

0035. Chevalier, Yves. Freud et l'antisémitisme - jalousie. SENS 37, 2 (Feb 1985) 45-50.

Part of a larger work about antisemitism. Discusses the causes of antisemitism as viewed by Freud, based on his books "Moses and Monotheism" and "Civilization and Its Discontents." There are many causes of antisemitism, but the two most preponderant from ancient times until today are the view of the Jew as a stranger, and jealousy of the Jews who claim to be God's chosen people.

0036. Cohn, Warren I. Five Hundred Years "Auf der Treppen": A History of the Trepp Family of Fulda. LEO BAECK INSTITUTE YEAR BOOK 30 (1985) 479-498.

A history of the Trepp family of Fulda since the 15th century, including details of persecution and restrictions suffered by the Jews of Fulda in medieval times, the expulsion of 1671, and the Nazi period.

0037. Cohn-Sherbok, Dan. Jews, Christians and Liberation Theology. CHRISTIAN JEWISH RELATIONS 17, 1 (Mar 1984) 3-11.

Examines anti-Judaism and antisemitism in Christianity, and anti-Christianity in Judaism. Discusses the possibilities for Jewish-Christian dialogue. Liberation theology creates a bridge between the two religions because of the "return to scriptural sources."

0038. Cortes y Cortes, Gabriel. HISTORIA DE LOS JUDIOS MALLORQUINES Y DE SUS DESCENDIENTES CRISTIANOS. Palma de Mallorca: Miguel Font, 1985. 370 pp. in 2 vols. (Collecció La Rodella, 5-6).

The book was written in 1944 and is now being published posthumously. Vol. 1 is a survey of Majorca Jewry since Roman times and describes various periods of persecution, focusing on the Christian period when Majorca was under the rule of Aragon. The pogrom of 1391 was followed by mass forced conversions. Includes lists of conversos, their addresses, the change brought against them, and their treatment by the Inquisition. Vol. 2 relates the fate of descendants of the conversos from 1535 to 1675.

0039. Craig, Gordon A. UEBER DIE DEUTSCHEN. Muenchen: Deutscher Taschenbuch Verlag, 1985. 392 pp. Originally published as "The Germans" (New York: G.P. Putnam's Sons, 1982).

An analysis of contemporary Germany and the Germans in historical perspective. Ch. 6 (pp. 143-167), "Deutsche und Juden," deals with German-Jewish relations from the Middle Ages to the present, particularly with anti-Jewish attitudes and actions.

0040. Eckstein, Jerome. Luther's Legacy in the Jewish Community. VIEWPOINTS 12, 10 (Apr/May 1984) 5-6.

Discusses the roots of Christian antisemitism in the New Testament and in the Early Church, Luther's anti-Judaism, the influence of his writings on Nazism, and recent attempts by theologians (Lutherans, Catholics) to revise the age-old trend of Christian anti-Judaism.

0041. Ehrlich, Ernst Ludwig; Vogel, Rolf. ERNST LUDWIG EHRLICH UND DER CHRISTLICH-JUEDISCHE DIALOG. Hrsg. von Rolf Vogel. Frankfurt a.M.: Verlag Josef Knecht, 1984. 206 pp.

Presents Erhlich's views on the Christian-Jewish dialogue, of which he was one of the initiators. Consists of an interview given to Vogel, a journalist, in 1983 and speeches and articles by Ehrlich over the last twenty years on subjects such as the origins of Christian anti-Judaism, connections between anti-Judaism and antisemitic persecutions, the attitude of Luther and the Protestant churches towards the Jews.

0042. Fasching, Darrell J., ed. THE JEWISH PEOPLE IN CHRISTIAN PREACHING. New York: Edwin Mellen Press, 1984. vi, 113 pp. (Symposium Series, 10).

Based on a symposium held in Syracuse, NY, Oct. 1979. A collection of papers and sermons based on the premise that words have the power to kill, and that Christian stereotypes of Jews and the doctrine of "supercession" of the Jews as the chosen people by the Christians were partly responsible for the Holocaust. Designed for Christian preachers, religious educators, and laymen to help them to form a new, non-antisemitic presentation of Christianity. Contents: Michael J. Cook: The Jewish People in Christian Theology: Past and Present (3-17); Paul M. Van Buren: The Jewish People in Christian Theology: Present and Future (19-33); Eugene Fisher: The Jewish People in Christian Preaching: A Catholic Perspective (37-60); Krister Stendahl: The Jewish People in Christian Preaching: A Protestant Perspective (61-76); Darrell J. Fasching: The Church, the Synagogue and the Gospel (79-86); Samuel Sandmel: Jews, Christians and the Future: What May We Hope for (89-104).

0043. Fisher, Eugene; Klenicki, Leon. Ajer y hoy - antisemitismo: Un esquema. HERENCIA JUDIA 32 (1985) 27-32.

A short analysis of the concept of antisemitism, Christian anti-Judaism, and modern secular antisemitism.

0044. Flannery, Edward H. THE ANGUISH OF THE JEWS: TWENTY-THREE CENTURIES OF ANTISEMITISM. Rev. and updated. New York: Paulist Press, 1985. vi, 369 pp.

A revised version of the 1964 edition, designed "to acquaint Christians generally with the sufferings of the Jews during the Christian era" and to give the Christian reader a chance of self-understanding and awareness of the "dark side of the Christian heritage." Reflects changing perspectives since publication of the first edition - a greater emphasis on the role of the Churches and rationalist antisemitism.

0045. Fontette, François de. Des calomnies d'Apion à la "solution finale": La haine du juif née après 1880. LE DROIT DE VIVRE 509 (Mar 1985) 16.

Reviews antisemitism since ancient times, including that found in Christianity. From 1880, this antisemitism evolved into racism, culminating in the Holocaust.

0046. Franz, Eckhart G., ed. JUDEN ALS DARMSTAEDTER BUERGER. Darmstadt: E. Roeter Verlag, 1984. 442 pp.

A collection of articles on the Jews of Darmstadt from the Middle Ages until the present. Antisemitism is mentioned throughout the volume; articles dealing specifically with antisemitism are listed separately.

0047. Franzheim, Liesel. JUDEN IN KOELN VON DER ROEMERZEIT BIS INS 20. JAHRHUNDERT: FOTO-DOKUMENTATION. [Bildauswahl und Texte: Liesel Franzheim. Redaktion: Jutta Bohnke-Kollwitz]. Koeln: Koelnisches Stadtmuseum, 1984. 352 pp.

Ch. 8 (pp. 257-293) deals with the development of antisemitism in Cologne before and after 1933. Earlier chapters include descriptions and documentation of massacres in the Middle Ages.

0048. Friedman, Daniel. Seven Lessons of Anti-Semitism. HUMANISTIC JUDAISM 13, 1 (Spr 1985) 12-13.

"Understanding anti-Semitism is a key to Jewish self-understanding." Describes antisemitism as a permanent and ubiquitous force which binds together Jews despite their different ideologies and which is aroused by their uniqueness as a people.

0049. Gilbert, Martin. JEWISH HISTORY ATLAS. 3rd rev. ed. Jerusalem: Steimatsky, 1985. 128 pp.

"If...persecution, expulsion, torture, humiliation and mass murder haunt these pages, it is because they also haunt the Jewish story." The 3rd edition emphasizes the story of Soviet Jewry in recent years.

0050. Giniewski, Paul. Qu'est-ce que la Dhimma? RENCONTRE - CHRETIENS ET JUIFS 18, 1 <77> (1984) 5-34.

A survey of the attitudes of Islam and Muslims towards the Jews, from Mohammed to the present, but particularly in the 20th century.

0051. Ginzel, Guenther B. Zur Geschichte des Antisemitismus von der Antike bis in die Gegenwart. SCHATTEN DER VERGANGENHEIT: DEUTSCHE UND JUDEN HEUTE, ed. Andreas Wojak. Guetersloh: Guetersloher Verlagshaus Mohn, 1985. Pp. 15-43.

A general survey of the history of antisemitism, stressing antisemitic literary and visual propaganda (poems, caricatures).

0052. Grossman, Vassilij. Antisemitismen. JUDISK KROENIKA 53, 3 (June 1985) 12-13. In Swedish.

0053. Herszlikowicz, Michel. PHILOSOPHIE DE L'ANTISEMITISME. Paris: Presses Universitaires de France, 1985. 170 pp.

Part I, "Myths," reconstructs the anti-Jewish mythology regarding money, sex, the sacred, and politics which lies at the basis of all persecution. Part II, "Traditions," describes how these myths are translated into reality. "Antisemitism is not only the verification of a legend or the confirmation of a prejudice, but also an every-day attitude."

0054. Huegen, Ludwig. JUEDISCHE GEMEINDEN AM NIEDERRHEIN: IHRE GESCHICHTE, IHR SCHICKSAL. Willich/Niederrhein: Enger, 1985. 208 pp.

After a short survey of the Middle Ages (including the Crusades and other anti-Jewish actions), the book concentrates on the 19th and 20th centuries, describing also discrimination against Jews. Ch. 5 (pp. 126-167) deals with antisemitism during the Weimar period and the destruction of the Jews in the Nazi period.

0055. Kastning-Olmesdahl, Ruth. Theological and Psychological Barriers to Changing the Image of Jews and Judaism in Education. JOURNAL OF ECUMENICAL STUDIES 21, 3 (Sum 1984) 452-469.

Surveys the image of the Jews as it developed in early Christianity, and as depicted in religious teachings to this day: enemies and killers of Jesus, fanatics, intolerant, particularistic, dishonest, hypocritical. Presents explanations for the reluctance of Christians to change these views: fear of that which is different; confirmation of one's identity by rejection of the other; fundamentalism; guilt and prejudice.

0056. Klein, Thomas; Losemann, Volker; Mai, Gunther, eds. JUDENTUM UND ANTISEMITISMUS VON DER ANTIKE BIS ZUR GEGENWART. Duesseldorf: Droste Verlag, 1984. 189 pp.

Contents: Robert M. Errington: Die Juden im Zeitalter des Hellenismus (1-15); Helmut Castritius: Die Haltung Roms gegenueber den Juden in der ausgehenden Republik und der Prinzipatszeit (15-41); Friedrich Lotter: Die Entwicklung des Judenrechts im christlichen Abendland bis zu den Kreuzzuegen (41-65); Michael Toch: Judenfeindschaft im deutschen Spaetmittelalter (65-77); Marianne Awerbuch: Judentum im 16. und 17. Jahrhundert zwischen Inquisition und Reformation (77-103); Hartwig Brandt: Stufen der Judenemanzipation im 18. und 19. Jahrhundert (103-113); G. Mai: Sozialgeschichtliche Bedingungen von Judentum und Antisemitismus im Kaiserreich (113-137); V. Losemann: Rassenideologien und antisemitische Publizistik in Deutschland im 19. und 20. Jhdt. (137-161); Uwe D. Adam: Der Aspekt der "Planung" in der NS-Judenpolitik (161-179); Stephan Dolezel: Das Judentum Osteuropas (179-188).

0057. Kobler, Franz, ed. JUDEN UND JUDENTUM IN DEUTSCHEN BRIEFEN AUS DREI JAHRHUNDERTEN. Koenigstein/Ts: Juedischer Verlag Athenaeum, 1984. 415 pp. Reprint of the 1935 ed. (Wien: Saturn Verlag).

A collection of letters dealing with Jews and Judaism written between 1648-1922 by German Jews and Gentiles. Some of them reflect and discuss antisemitism in thought and in deed in Germany. Included are letters by Marx, Wagner, Heine, Riesser, Nietzsche, and Hess.

0058. Kohn, Moshe. Crença oculta [Secret Faith]. HERANCA JUDAICA 56 (Mar 1984) 67-71.

Sketches the last years of the Inquisition in Portugal (1751-1821), its victims from the beginning, the lingering fear of the Inquisition among descendants of crypto-Jews, and an incident of modern antisemitism directed against these descendants.

0059. Kremers, Heinz, ed. DIE JUDEN UND MARTIN LUTHER - MARTIN LUTHER UND DIE JUDEN. Neukirchen-Vluyn: Neukirchener Verlag, 1985. 440 pp.

A collection of articles dealing with Luther's attitudes towards Jews and Judaism and his influence on the attitudes of the Protestant Church up to the present. Includes articles by Ben-Zion Degani, Johannes P. Boendermaker, Stefan Schreiner, Ernst L. Ehrlich, Martin Stoehr, Johannes Brosseder, Heiko A. Oberman, Adam Weyer, Pinchas E. Lapide, Guenther B. Ginzel, Eberhard Bethge, Juergen Seim, Albert H. Friedlander, Guenther van Norden, Johann M. Schmidt, Leonore Siegele-Wenschkewitz, Bertold Klappert, Heinz Kremers.

0060. Kriegel, Arthur. Racisme et science. SENS 36, 5/6 (May/June 1984) 189-195.

Modern antisemitism is seen as the racist, pseudo-scientific successor to religious anti-Judaism.

0061. Krigier, Rivon. Antisémitisme, christianisme ou le complex d'Oedipe. ORI 1 (Feb 1985) 19-20.

Explains Christian antisemitism as a phenomenon of the deep mysteries of the unconscious, in accordance with Freudian theory. Christianity is the negation of Judaism rather than its daughter religion. Antisemitism is characterized by an attraction-repulsion relationship with the Jews, similar to the Oedipal relationship.

0062. Landau, Lazare. Sources de l'antisémitisme et remèdes contre cette maladie. FOI ET VIE 84 (Jan 1985) 135-142. Unseen.

0063. Landmann, Salcia. War Nazismus Rassismus? ZEITSCHRIFT FUER RELIGIONS- UND GEISTESGESCHICHTE 36, 4 (1984) 364-370.

Compares components of Nazi antisemitism (biological, religious, economic) with Spanish antisemitism in the Middle Ages (blood purity, forced conversion), concluding that both were racist.

0064. Laubenthal, Wilhelm. DIE SYNAGOGENGEMEINDEN DES KREISES MERZIG. Saarbruecken: Saarbruecker Verlag, 1984. 207 pp.

A history of three communities - Merzig, Brotdorf, Hilbringen - between 1648-1942. Ch. 5 discusses the destruction of the communities by the Nazis.

0065. Lewis, Bernard. THE JEWS OF ISLAM. Princeton, NJ: Princeton University Press, 1984. xii, 245 pp. An extract appeared in COMMENTARY 77, 6 (June 1984) 44-54.

Examines the status of the Jews in the Islamic world from the early days of Islam to the present. Challenges accepted stereotypes of the Muslim attitude to non-believers as one of either utopian tolerance and harmony or fanaticism and persecution. Theologically, Islam has never accorded equality to non-believers, but the status of dhimmi, second-class citizens, assures rights established in law. Focuses on the attitude of those in power towards Jews, which varied at different times and places from persecution (which was rare) through humiliation to tolerance.

0066. Liberman, Serge, ed. ANTI-SEMITISM AND HUMAN RIGHTS. Melbourne: Australian Institute of Jewish Affairs, 1985. vi, 176 pp.

Proceedings of a seminar held in Melbourne, June 1984. Contents: Immanuel Jakobovits: Anti-Semitism: After the Holocaust, after the State of Israel (1-6); Stephen Roth: The Roots of Modern Anti-Semitism and the New Anti-Semitism (9-14); Shimon Samuels: Anti-Semitism, the Abiding Prejudice (15-18); Abraham H. Foxman: Anti-Semitism in the United States (19-26); John Foster: Fabricating History (27-30); Konrad Kwiet: The New Revisionism (31-32); Itamar Rabinovich: Anti-Semitism and the Muslim and Arab World (43-52); Allan Gerson: The United Nations and Anti-Semitism (53-56); William Korey: The Triumph of Evil: UN Anti-Semitism (57-60); Emanuel Litvinoff: Russian Anti-Semitism: From Czar to Chernenko (61-73); Zwi Werblowsky: Christian-Jewish Relations (91-96); Robert Anderson: The Church and Anti-Semitism: Beginning of a Tragedy (97-101); William G. Smith: The Religious Factor in Anti-Semitism (103-106); John Williams: The Churches, the Noahide Covenant and Anti-Semitism (107-113); William D. Rubinstein: The Politics of Anti-Semitism: The Australian Experience (131-138); Louis Waller: Legal Curbs on

Discrimination and Race Hatred (141-146); Peter H. Bailey: Institutional Protections against Anti-Semitism and Racism (147-155); S. Roth: The Legal Fight against Anti-Semitism: The National Aspect (157-164); Sam Lipski: Australia and the Jews (165-170).

0067. Link, Paul S. OUR FORGOTTEN BRETHREN: THE MARRANOS. Rehovot, Israel: The Author, 1985. 260 pp.

A description of the lives of 32 "outstanding" marranos (including Christopher Columbus), from the 15th to the 20th centuries, who flourished in the Iberian Peninsula, other European countries, Africa, and Latin America. The introduction (pp. 2-14) surveys the persecution of the Jews in medieval Spain and Portugal, the Inquisition, and the evolvement of the status of marranos, conversos, New Christians and crypto-Jews.

0068. Litman, Jacob. THE ECONOMIC ROLE OF JEWS IN MEDIEVAL POLAND: THE CONTRIBUTION OF YITZHAK SCHIPPER. Lanham, MD: University Press of America, 1984. xiv, 306 pp.

An evaluation of the work of Yitzhak (Ignacy) Schipper (1884-1943), the Polish Jewish historian. Working at a time of acute Polish hostility toward the Jews, much of Schipper's work (written in Polish and in Yiddish) was directed toward disproving antisemitic claims and showing the Jewish contribution to medieval Polish life. Schipper challenged Sombart's thesis that capitalism reflects the Jews' racial psyche, and gave a historical explanation of the origin of Jewish capital and usury. State exploitation of Jewish usury in the Middle Ages resulted in popular antisemitism and pogroms.

0069. Marrus, Michael R. Théorie et pratique de l'antisémitisme. SENS 37, 1 (Jan 1985) 17-25. Translated from "Commentary," Aug 1982.

The view that antisemitism is eternal and unchanging may lead to a preoccupation with general theories and ideas, neglecting the specific historical factors behind antisemitic outbreaks, and to a fatalistic determinism in which all forms of racism and anti-Judaism lead to the Final Solution. In his book "Vichy France and the Jews," written with Robert Paxton, Marrus presents an alternative model in which antisemitism is seen as a series of concentric circles becoming more intense at the center and liable in certain major crises to coalesce.

0070. Michael, Robert. Christian Theology and the Holocaust. MIDSTREAM 30, 4 (Apr 1984) 6-9.

Christian theology's anti-Jewish myths are the basis for antisemitism throughout the ages, including Nazi antisemitism.

0071. Michael, Robert. Luther, Luther Scholars and the Jews. ENCOUNTER: CREATIVE THEOLOGICAL SCHOLARSHIP 46, 4 (Fall 1985) 339-356.

Luther scholars who defend, censor or try to tone down his views on the Jews, ignore the murderous implications of Luther's antisemitism. Like the Nazis, Luther mythologized the Jews as completely evil: they should not be treated as humans and should be cast out of Germany. They could be saved if they converted to Christianity, but their demonic hostility to Christian society made this inconceivable. "There was a strong parallel between Luther's ideas and feelings about Jews and Judaism and the essentially anti-Jewish Weltanschauung of most German Lutherans throughout the Holocaust."

0072. Montefiore, Hugh W. Radical Review of Christian Teaching. CHRISTIAN JEWISH RELATIONS 18, 1 (Mar 1985) 31-33.

Christian antisemitism cannot be tolerated. "As I write this I have just received from the General Synod of the Church of England the draft text of its new Holy Week Services; and there, on Good Friday, reappear those terrible Reproaches, as terrible an anti-Jewish liturgical text as you will find anywhere in mainstream Christendom. We still have a long way to go."

0073. Monti, Joseph E. WHO DO YOU SAY THAT I AM? THE CHRISTIAN UNDERSTANDING OF CHRIST AND ANTISEMITISM. New York: Paulist Press, 1984. vii, 98 pp. On cover: An Essay in Christian-Jewish Dialogue.

Proposes to lead the way to "an adequate theological and moral response to our own legacy of anti-Judaism and anti-Semitism." Sketches early Christian anti-Judaism from a theological point of view and drafts proposals for a "reconstructed Christology," more tolerant of Judaism and other religions.

0074. Mueller-Serten, Gernot. PALAESTINAS FEINDLICHE BRUEDER. Duesseldorf: Econ-Verlag, 1984. 320 pp.

The religious, political, historical and psychological origins of the Arab-Jewish conflict in Palestine are discussed. Antisemitism and persecutions of the Jews are mentioned throughout the historical narrative, from antiquity to the present.

0075. Mussner, Franz. TRACTATE ON THE JEWS. Trans. by Leonard Swidler. Philadelphia: Fortress Press; London: SPCK, 1984. xii, 339 pp. Originally published as "Traktat ueber die Juden" (Muenchen: Koesel Verlag, 1979).

The anti-Jewish spirit has had a profound impact throughout history. Calls on Christians to question that spirit and to re-evaluate the Church's relationship to Judaism. Describes Christian theology regarding Judaism and gives an explanation of Judaism in its own terms. See index for references to anti-Judaism and antisemitism.

0076. Nekisz, Józef. Antysemityzm katolicki [Catholic Antisemitism]. ARGUMENTY 4 (1985). Unseen.

0077. Ortona, Guido. Appunti per una teoria generale dell'antisemitismo e dei fenomeni analoghi. RASSEGNA MENSILE DI ISRAEL 50, 5-8 (May-Aug 1984) 235-248.

Antisemitism is analagous to other social phenomena defined by a spontaneous hostile attitude of one social or ethnic group towards another. Analyzes the social and psychological mechanisms of antisemitism.

0078. Pazi, Margarita. Talmudverbrennungen. EXIL 1 (1984) 41-44.

A short survey from the 13th century to the 20th.

0079. Pedatella, R. Anthony. Reflections on Italian Attitudes toward Jewry. JEWISH FRONTIER 51, 2 (Feb 1984) 12-16.

"Italian history has been remarkably free of antisemitism." Surveys Italian Jewry throughout the ages, with special attention to the fascist period.

0080. Peters, Joan. FROM TIME IMMEMORIAL: THE ORIGINS OF THE ARAB-JEWISH CONFLICT OVER PALESTINE. New York: Harper and Row, 1984. x, 601 pp.

Refutes popular misconceptions and Arab propaganda claims regarding the Palestinian refugee problem, the status of the Jews in Arab lands, and the history of Palestine. Includes descriptions of the mistreatment of Jews under Arab rule, accusations of deliberate antisemitism on the part of British officials in concealing data on Arab immigration while excluding Jewish refugees from Nazism, and data on Arab collaboration with the Nazis. Describes Arab nationalism as an extension of traditional antagonism towards the Jews, due to their refusal to accept their subordinate dhimmi role.

0081. Petuchowski, Jakob J. "Jewish Survival" and Anti-Semitism. JUDAISM 33, 4 (Fall 1984) 391-401.

Many Jews, in the past, chose to convert in order to ensure physical or economic survival. In an open society they can disappear or become "non-affiliated." Theories calling for the preservation of Judaism in reaction to antisemitism will not persuade Jews to suffer the dangers or inconveniences of identifying as Jews. They will do so only if Judaism has intrinsic value.

0082. Poliakov, Léon. LA CAUSALITE DIABOLIQUE. Vol. 2: DU JOUG MONGOL A LA VICTOIRE DE LENINE, 1250-1920. Paris: Calmann-Lévy, 1985. 366 pp. (Collection "Liberté de l'esprit").

Vol. 1 (1980) analyzed "diabolical" explanations for the great revolutions in history. Vol. 2 traces the origins of the Jewish conspiracy theory in Russian history and its role in the Russian revolution which was viewed by the Whites as a "Jewish plot."

0083. Poliakov, Léon. DE MAOME AOS MARRANOS [From Mohammed to the Marranos]. São Paulo: Perspectiva, 1984. 288 pp. Originally published as Vol. II of his "Histoire de l'Antisémitisme" (Paris: Calmann-Lévy, 1961).

Covers the antisemitism of Mohammed and Islam, and Spain and Portugal from the Middle Ages to the 19th century, with an appendix on the Jews of Rome and the Holy See.

0084. Poliakov, Léon. Les sémites et les sauvages. SENS 36, 5/6 (May/June 1984) 197-202.

Examines the use of the term antisemitism, which began as a racist term but was later projected into historical epochs for which the term Judeophobia (i.e. non-racial hatred) would be more appropriate. After racism developed in the 16th century, certain antisemites made an analogy between Blacks, savages and Jews.

0085. Poliakov, Léon; Delacampagne, Christian; Girard, Patrick. UEBER DEN RASSISMUS. Frankfurt/M: Ullstein Taschenbuch Verlag, 1984. 207 pp.

Describes racism and traces its origins, based on theories from the fields of history, biology, sociology, and psychology. Examines whether racism is rooted in man's nature, or is dependent on special historical and sociological conditions. Antisemitism is a focal point in this discussion.

0086. Porter, Jack Nusan. Self-Hatred and Self-Esteem. JEWISH SPECTATOR 50, 3 (Fall 1985) 51-53.

Self-hatred is an extreme form of self-denial: denial of one's traits, including ancestry, religion or race, which are seen as negative or abhorrent. This is one type of response to minority status, defined as inferior and affected by discrimination and prejudice.

0087. Problemi e prospettive del dialogo tra cristiani ed ebrei. CIVILTA CATTOLICA 3235 (1985) 3-18.

Traces the history of Christian-Jewish relations throughout the ages, including the anti-Jewish polemics of the Church Fathers, the ritual murder charges, the accusations of deicide. The first positive document regarding the Jews, issued by the Catholic Church, is the "Nostra Aetate" declaration. Discusses its importance and expresses faith that the dialogue will continue.

0088. Rappaport, S. Martin Luther and the Jews. JEWISH AFFAIRS 39, 1 (Jan 1984) 19-23.

There is little the Nazis said and did that cannot be found in Luther's anti-Jewish writings. In "The Jews and Their Lies" Luther incorporated most of the calumnies against the Jews known in his day. The Nazis republished excerpts. On the other hand, Luther's Reformation paved the way for a new epoch in Christian-Jewish relations.

0089. Rassial, Jean-Jacques. Comme le nez au milieu de la figure. L'INTERDIT DE LA REPRESENTATION: COLLOQUE DE MONTPELLIER, eds. Adélie et Jean-Jacques Rassial. Paris: Editions du Seuil, 1984. Pp. 19-30.

An essay on problems of self-identity and identification by others in terms of psychoanalysis. In discussing the problems of identifying a Jew, touches on antisemitism.

0090. Rausch, David A. A LEGACY OF HATRED: WHY CHRISTIANS MUST NOT FORGET THE HOLOCAUST. Chicago: Moody Press, 1984. viii, 222 pp.

"Traces anti-Semitic attitudes since the beginning of the Christian era through the conflict in the Middle East today, concentrating on the horrifying events surrounding the Holocaust, its causes and effects." Emphasizes the dangers of antisemitism and racism in the US today and the special responsiblity of Christians to combat them.

0091. Reuter, Fritz. WARMAISA: 1000 JAHRE JUDEN IN WORMS. Worms: Stadtarchiv, 1984. 227 pp. (Der Wormsgau: Wissenschaftliche Zeitschrift der Stadt Worms und des Altertumsvereins Worms, Beiheft 29).

Pp. 30-34 deal with the persecution of the Jews during and after the First Crusade (1096); pp. 191-209 describe the fate of the Jews of Worms during the Holocaust.

0092. Rodinson, Maxime. Antisemitism as Myth, Judaeophobia as Reality. FOR A PALESTINIAN: A MEMORIAL TO WAEL ZUAITER, ed. Janet Venn-Brown. London: Kegan Paul International, 1984. Pp. 126-175. Originally published as "Per un Palestinese" (Roma: Mazotta Editore, 1979).

States that the term antisemitism was invented by 19th century German antisemites to give their Judaeophobia a scientific basis, and that Judaeophobia is a form of "ethnism," belief in one's ethnic superiority over one's enemies. Antisemitic attacks are explained as outbursts of Judaeophobia occurring under specific social, religious, and economic circumstances. However, some Jews spread the view that antisemitism is a universal hostility to an essential Jewishness which must therefore be innocent and superior. Criticism of Jewish jingoism or Zionism is then labelled antisemitic.

0093. Rothenberg, Joshua. Poles and Jews: Then and Now. MIDSTREAM 30, 9 (Nov 1984) 10-14.

In 1983 several well-known Jews issued a manifesto calling for a rapprochement between Jews and Poles. Gives the background to the Jews' position in Poland from the early Middle Ages to the present and shows differing Polish attitudes towards the Jews.

0094. Rylaarsdam, Coert. Judaism: The Christian Problem. FACE TO FACE 11 (Spr 1984) 4-8. Appeared in French in RENCONTRE CHRETIENS ET JUIFS 19 <79/80> (1985) 65-76.

The Christian cannot define himself without reference to the mother religion, Judaism. It cannot be simply ignored. In the past, Christians explained the refusal of the Jews to recognize the truth by their malevolence or by a curse blinding them, and responded with persecution and missionizing. Can a new definition of Judaism as a living religion with its own truth be found? Pp. 9-22 contain responses by James A. Carpenter, Alan Davies, Monika Hellwig, James Hitchcock, and Dorothea Soelle, and a reply by Dr. Rylaarsdam.

0095. Ryszka, Franciszek. Anti-Semitism: Ideas, Attitudes, Genocides. ACTA POLONIAE HISTORICA 50 (1984) 57-80.

Analyzes the historical origins of the crime of genocide. Refers to the "objective enemy" theory of Hannah Arendt and the "racism" theories of George Mosse, and views them as inadequate. In a short survey of the history of the Jews in Poland and Germany, traces the appearance of the Jewish stereotype or "syndrome." Denies charges that Polish antisemitism contributed to the Holocaust.

0096. Schafler, Samuel. Antisemitism in Historical Perspective. JOURNAL OF JEWISH COMMUNAL SERVICE 60, 3 (Spr 1984) 250-255.

The differences between various types of antisemitism - ancient, Christian, modern - should not be blurred. Nor should the normal hostility every people arouses be confused with antisemitism, which is based on irrational hatred of a demonic figure of the Jew. Christian antisemitism prepared the way for Hitler, but Nazism was post-Christian. Criticism of Israel's policies is valid, but denial of her right to exist is antisemitic.

0097. Schmidt, Johann M. Heine und Luther: Heines Lutherrezeption in der Spannung zwischen den Daten 1483 und 1933. HEINE JAHRBUCH 24 (1985) 9-79.

Compares Heine's attitude towards Luther to that of Lutheran Germans in 1933. Heine criticized Luther both on religious and political grounds. One of Heine's sharpest criticisms against Luther concerns his antisemitism and his appeal to the state authority for anti-Jewish action.

0098. Schmitz, Ernst; Hunder, Hans. DOCUMENTA JUDAICA. Dimona, Israel: Stadtverwaltung Dimona, 1985. 58, 50 pp. In German and Hebrew. Hebrew translation by Yosef Galon.

A descriptive and documented history of the Jews of the Rhineland, especially the community of Andernach, from ancient times until today. Antisemitic attitudes originating from economic, religious and racial prejudice, and sometimes resulting in pogroms, are frequently mentioned.

0099. See, Wolfgang. DER APOSTEL PAULUS UND DIE NUERNBERGER GESETZE: TRAKTAT UEBER DEN ABENDLANDLUNGEN ANTISEMITISMUS DER CHRISTEN ANLAESSLICH EINES FUENFZIGSTEN JAHRESTAGES (15.9.1935). Berlin (West): Wichern-Verlag, 1985. 124 pp.

A general history of Christian antisemitism. "Auschwitz was not an historical accident, but was the brutal result of the long and continuing antisemitism of the Christian majority society towards the Jewish minority."

0100. Segal, Alicia Freilich de. LEGITIMA DEFENSA: COMENTARIOS, POLEMICAS. Caracas: Publicaciones Seleven, 1984. 145 pp.

A collection of articles by a journalist, including articles on antisemitism, a new look at Shylock, the nature of anti-Jewish jokes, antisemitism in the USSR, in the media, etc.

0101. Skarsaune, O. Trekk fra dialogen mellom joedendom og kristendom i gammel og ny tid [The Character of the Dialogue between Judaism and Christianity in the Past and Today]. TIDSSKRIFT FOR TEOLOGI OG KIRKE 56, 1 (1985) 51-64. Unseen.

0102. Sperber, Manès. Jusqu'à la fin des temps? LE GENRE HUMAIN 11 (Fall/Win 1984/1985) 91-111.

Anti-Judaism arises from the psychological fear of the other. Explains the religious, historical and social/ psychological factors involved. Surveys Jewish history in ancient and medieval times, showing the development of Christian anti-Judaism. Racial antisemitism emerged in 15th century Spain in order to devalue the Jews and to separate them from society, and was later incorporated by the Nazis.

0103. Stein, Howard F. The Holocaust, the Uncanny and the Jewish Sense of History. POLITICAL PSYCHOLOGY 5, 1 (Mar 1984) 5-35.

A psychoanalytical interpretation of Jewish history, the persecution of Jews, and the Holocaust, based on the premise that the Jewish religion involves a complex of victimization and sacrifice. Persecution is experienced by Jews as sacred martyrdom - timeless, dreaded, and expected. They thus avoid facing their own active role as collaborators in a sado-masochistic social system.

0104. Strauss, Herbert A.; Kampe, Norbert, eds. ANTISEMITISMUS: VON DER JUDENFEINDSCHAFT ZUM HOLOCAUST. Bonn: Bundeszentrale fuer Politische Bildung, 1984. 288 pp.

A collection of articles dealing with the history of antisemitism, especially in Germany, from the Middle Ages until the post-World War II period. Contents: František Graus: Judenfeindschaft im Mittelalter (29-46); Ernst L. Ehrlich: Luther und die Juden (47-65); H.A. Strauss: Juden und Judenfeindschaft in der fruehen Neuzeit (66-87); Reinhard Ruerup: Emanzipation und Antisemitismus (88-98); Werner Jochmann: Struktur und Funktion des deutschen Antisemitismus, 1878-1914 (99-142); Arnold Paucker: Die Abwehr des Antisemitismus in den Jahren 1893-1933 (143-171); Walther Hofer: Stufen der Judenverfolgung im Dritten Reich 1933-1939 (172-185); Wolfgang Scheffler: Wege zur "Endloesung" (186-215); H.A. Strauss: Der Holocaust (215-234); Wolfgang Fritz Haug: Antisemitismus in marxistischer Sicht (234-255); Klaus-Henning Rosen: Vorurteile im Verborgenen: Zum Antisemitismus in der Bundesrepublik Deutschland (256-279).

0105. Terman, David. Anti-Semitism: A Study in Group Vulnerability and the Vicissitudes of Group Ideals. PSYCHOHISTORY REVIEW 12, 4 (Spr 1984) 18-24.

Reviews the history of antisemitism from the perspective of psychoanalytic theory. Both ancient and Christian antisemitism are explained as a psychological mechanism employed by a group which feels that its collective ideology is threatened.

0106. Willebrands, Johannes. Is Christianity Antisemitic? CHRISTIAN JEWISH RELATIONS 18, 2 (June 1985) 8-20.

A lecture delivered to the Oxford Union, 13 March 1985, by the President of the Vatican Secretariat for Promoting Christian Unity (Commission for Religious Relations with the Jews). Denies that Christianity as embodied in the New Testament and in the teaching of the Catholic Church is antisemitic. Even if the New Testament contains antisemitic texts or descriptions, they do not cancel or modify the "positive thrust" on Judaism. In the past, the Christian tradition was inspired by antisemitic images, and the Church as a body was antisemitic. Today there is an attempt to "link with that truer, normative past" of the New Testament.

0107. Wine, Sherwin T. Anti-Semitism: A Force for Jewish Survival. HUMANISTIC JUDAISM 13, 1 (Spr 1985) 7-11.

Antisemitism stimulated among Jews throughout the ages a series of survival responses which eventually defined the self-image of the Jew. Six positive skills were stimulated - ambition, community support, liberal democracy, alliance with vulnerable minority groups, skepticism, and humor. Negative skills developed were hostility to the outside world, claims of superiority, religious identity, and making survival the ultimate value.

0108. Wippermann, Wolfgang. JUEDISCHES LEBEN IM RAUM BREMERHAVEN: EINE FALLSTUDIE ZUR ALLTAGSGESCHICHTE DER JUDEN VOM 18. JAHRHUNDERT BIS ZUR NS-ZEIT. Bremerhaven: Stadtarchiv, 1985. 222 pp. (Veroeffentlichungen des Stadtarchivs Bremerhaven, 5).

A regional case study dealing with the everyday life of the Jews in Bremerhaven from the 18th century until the Nazi rise to power. Ch. 1 deals with the persecution and expulsion of the local Jews during the Middle Ages; ch. 3 analyzes the development of antisemitism in Germany during the Second Empire and the Weimar Republic; ch. 4 deals with the anti-Jewish policy of the Nazis in general and with the fate of Bremerhaven's Jews in particular.

0109. Wolfe, Robert. DARK STAR. New York: Memory Books, 1984. 266 pp.

A history of the Jewish people, written in a "strictly secular spirit," emphasizing the contribution of the Jews to history and how the Gentile's view of Jews and Judaism has been distorted by antisemitism.

0110. Wolff, Theodor. "DIE JUDEN": EIN DOKUMENT AUS DEM EXIL 1942/43. Hrsg. von Bernd Soesemann. Koenigstein/Ts.: Juedischer Verlag Athenaeum, 1984. 305 pp.

Six posthumously published essays by the liberal German-Jewish writer and long-time editor of the "Berliner Tageblatt" who was killed by the Nazis in 1943. Two of the essays deal with the origins of antisemitism and its manifestations throughout history.

0111. Yaseen, Leonard C. THE JESUS CONNECTION: TO TRIUMPH OVER ANTI-SEMITISM. New York: Crossroad, 1985. xvi, 154 pp.

Shows that Jesus's life and teachings were consistent with his Jewish heritage, and that true Christianity cannot be anti-Jewish. The author, an American Jewish businessman, describes his own encounters with social prejudice in the USA, and claims that a better understanding of Jesus's Jewishness will dispel antisemitism. Ch. 13 (pp. 85-143) consists of a collection of famous American Jewish figures, showing their contributions to American life.

THE ANCIENT PERIOD

0112. ראבילו, א. מרדכי. יהדות ויהודים בהחלטות של ועידות הכנסיה הקאתולית במאה הרביעית לסה"נ. ספר זכרון להרב יצחק נסים. סדר רביעי: תעודות על קהילות ואישים, בעריכת מאיר בניהו. ירושלים: יד הרב נסים, 1985. עמ' קנז-קעה.

[Rabello, Alfredo Mordechai. Judaism and Jews in the Canons of the Councils of the Catholic Church in the Fourth Century. STUDIES IN MEMORY OF R. YITZHAK NISSIM. VOL. 4: DOCUMENTS ON COMMUNITIES AND PERSONS, ed. Meir Benayahu. Jerusalem: Yad Ha-Rav Nissim, 1985. Pp. 157-175.]

Examines the canons of the Councils of Elvira (Spain), Nicaea, Antioch, Laodicea, Carthage, and the "Apostolic Canons." The decisions regarding Jews had a two-fold purpose - to reduce the influence of Jews on their Christian neighbors (which was apparently considerable), and to convert the Jews to Christianity.

0113. Aziza, Claude. Ponce Pilate. L'HISTOIRE 70 (Sept 1984) 46-54.

Sketches the rule of Pontius Pilate. Discusses his cruelties to the Jews as recorded in Josephus, Philo, Tacitus and the New Testament. Some commentators believe that Pilate came to Judea representing a conscious anti-Jewish policy of Sejanus, a minister of Tiberius.

0114. Aziza, Claude. Quelques aspects de la polémique judéo-chrétienne dans l'Afrique romaine (IIe-VIe siècles), I. JUIFS ET JUDAISME EN AFRIQUE DU NORD DANS L'ANTIQUITE ET LE HAUT MOYEN-AGE, eds. Carol Iancu, Jean-Marie Lassère. Montpellier: Université Paul Valéry, 1985. Pp. 49-56.

Describes the rivalry between Jews and Christians in Roman Africa in proselytizing among the pagans, which was a cause of conflict before 330 C.E. With Constantine's rise to power, the Judeo-Christian conflict became a political problem; to become a Christian meant entrance to the majority. In the Theodosian Code (408-409 C.E.) missionizing by Jews was considered a crime against the state.

0115. Benin, Stephen D. Commandments, Covenants, and the Jews in Aphrahat, Ephrem, and Jacob of Sarug. APPROACHES TO JUDAISM IN MEDIEVAL TIMES, ed. David R. Blumenthal. Chico, CA: Scholars Press, 1984. Pp. 135-156.

Discusses the anti-Jewish polemical writings of the three Syrian Church Fathers, Aphrahat (or Aphraates, 4th cent.), Ephrem the Syrian (c.306-373), and Jacob of Sarug (451-521). They criticized Jewish law and ritual practice and faulted the Jews for rejecting Christ.

0116. Blanchetière, F. "Privilegia Odiosa" ou non? L'évolution de l'attitude officielle à l'endroit des juifs et du judaïsme (312-395). REVUE DES SCIENCES RELIGIEUSES 59, 3/4 (July-Oct 1985) 222-251.

The main aim of imperial Roman restrictive legislation was to prevent any possibility of Jewish proselytizing. Judaism was considered a legal religion and Jews were treated less severely than pagans or heretics. The theological struggle between Jews and Christians had an influence on legislation which is difficult to define. Antisemitic expressions are found which may reflect intolerance and hostility to Judaism; however, the codes of laws were compiled by officials and Church historians and may not represent actual Gentile-Jewish relations.

0117. Brennan, Brian. The Conversion of the Jews of Clermont in A.D. 576. JOURNAL OF THEOLOGICAL STUDIES 36, 2 (Nov 1985) 321-337.

In the 6th century, Bishop Avitus adopted an active proselytization policy and accused his opponents of overly tolerant attitudes toward the Jews. The historian Gregory of Tours recounts that a Jewish attack on a converted Jew led to the destruction of a synagogue by a mob and to baptism of most of the Jews. Those refusing to convert were expelled. The poet Venantius Fortunatus wrote a poem emphasizing the Jews' responsibility for fracturing the Christian unity of the town, and its restoration by their conversion.

0118. Butin, J.D.; Schwartz, J. Post Philonis Legationem. REVUE D'HISTOIRE ET DE PHILOSOPHIE RELIGIEUSES 65, 2 (Apr-June 1985) 127-129.

An unedited papyrus found in the B.N.U., Strasbourg, sheds further light on events in Alexandria in 41 C.E., clarifying the circumstances under which the Emperor Claudius sent his "Letter to the Alexandrians," and fixing the date of the trial of Isidore and Lampon, the two antisemitic agitators mentioned by Philo.

0119. Cherlin, Leonard. The First Thousand Years of Christian Anti-Semitism. HUMANISTIC JUDAISM 13, 1 (Spr 1985) 21-23.

"Ecclesiastical rulings denigrate the Jews and become the basis for a Church-endorsed anti-Semitism." By the fourth century, hating the Jews had become a Christian duty.

0120. Chevalier, Yves. L'Antisémitisme antique. SENS 37, 1 (Jan 1985) 3-15.

A survey of works on antisemitism in the ancient world, discussing the question whether hostility to the Jews was a form of xenophobia or whether it was an early form of antisemitism. Analyzing attacks on Jewish communities, specifically in Egypt, and early polemics, concludes that hostility to Jewish "otherness" was irrational and based on fantasies.

0121. Cohen, Martin A. Severus' Epistle on the Jews: Outline of a New Perspective. HELMANTICA 35 <106> (Jan-Apr 1984) 71-79.

Describes the epistle on the conversion of 540 Jews of Menorca to Christianity, attributed to Severus, bishop in early 5th century Menorca. Discusses the authorship and historicity of the document, entitled "Epistola de Judaeis" by 16th century theologians.

0122. Donfried, Karl Paul. Paul and Judaism: I Thessalonians 2:13-16 as a Test Case. INTERPRETATION: A JOURNAL OF BIBLE AND THEOLOGY 38, 3 (July 1984) 242-253.

Examines various interpretations of anti-Jewish statements by Paul in I Thessalonians 2:13-16, and contends that the hostility of this passage is mitigated by statements made by Paul in Romans 9, 10 and 11 to the effect that God's wrath towards the Jews will turn to mercy on the last day.

0123. Drijvers, Hans J.W. Jews and Christians at Edessa. JOURNAL OF JEWISH STUDIES 36, 1 (Spr 1985) 88-102.

Examines ideological conflicts and struggles between Jewish and Christian minorities in Edessa, Syria during the 3rd to 5th century C.E. The 3rd century foundation legend of the Edessa Church, the Doctrina Addoi, claimed its origin from the time of Christ, and was used as propaganda to convert the Jews. Later, when religious tension increased, the legend was modified to express anti-Jewish feeling. Ephrem the Syrian condemned Edessa Christians who were attracted to Judaism.

0124. Firpo, Luigi, ed. STORIA DELLE IDEE POLITICHE, ECONOMICHE E SOCIALI. VOL. 2, PT. 1: EBRAISMO E CRISTIANESIMO, eds. Giorgio Barbero et al. Torino: Unione Tipografico-Editrice Torinese, 1985. 678 pp.

The chapter entitled "Il giudaismo alessandrino" (pp. 289-362) includes material on anti-Judaism in Alexandria as documented by the 2nd century historian Posidonius, in the "Letter of Aristeas," and in other documents of the 1st century C.E. Pp. 354-355 contain a bibliography on antisemitism in antiquity, and p. 458 - a bibliography on antisemitic elements in the trial of Jesus.

0125. Horst, P.W. van der. Het heidense antisemitisme in de oudheid [Pagan Antisemitism in Antiquity]. TER HERKENNING 13, 1 (Mar 1985) 45-52.

A survey of studies of ancient non-Christian works and attitudes toward Jews expressed in them. John Gager's "The Origins of Anti-Semitism: Attitudes toward Judaism in Pagan and Christian Antiquity" (New York: Oxford University Press, 1983) is a useful corrective to the current opinion that pagan authors had a generally negative attitude toward Jews.

0126. Kampling, Rainer. Die Darstellung der Juden und des Judentums in den Predigten des Zeno von Verona. KAIROS 26, 1/2 (1984) 16-28.

Analyzes the anti-Jewish sermons of the fourth-century bishop Zeno of Verona, who accused the Jews of cruel ritual practices.

0127. Kelly, Mary. The Good Friday Liturgy and the Jews. CHRISTIAN JEWISH RELATIONS 17, 1 (Mar 1984) 37-41.

Discusses the origin of the Good Friday liturgy and the elements of antisemitism in it.

0128. Levenson, Jon D. Is There a Counterpart in the Hebrew Bible to New Testament Antisemitism? JOURNAL OF ECUMENICAL STUDIES 22, 2 (Spr 1985) 242-260.

The stereotypical presentation of Judaism as an obsolete religion, still found in "objective" Christian writing, originates in the New Testament which demonizes the Jews and creates a sharp dualism between the old and limited Jewish world and the "new Israel," Christianity. Parallels can be found in the Hebrew Bible and tradition, justifying the appropriation of Canaan by condemning Canaanite religion, misrepresenting paganism as mere fetishism, and presenting the Amalekites as archetypes of evil. However, other traditions in Jewish thought soften this hostility.

0129. Linder, Amnon. Jerusalem as a Focus of Confrontation between Judaism and Christianity. VISION AND CONFLICT IN THE HOLY LAND, ed. Richard I. Cohen. Jerusalem: Yad Izhak Ben-Zvi; New York: St. Martin's Press, 1985. Pp. 1-22.

Examines early Christian anti-Jewish attitudes as they developed in the Jerusalem Church, particularly during the 4th-5th centuries and continuing through the Middle Ages. Jerusalem was the focus for concepts which found expression in ritual and in literature - because the Jews rejected Jesus they are to be persecuted, expelled, dispersed, subjugated, disintegrated as a people, and forcibly converted.

0130. Maccoby, Hyam. Anti-Judaism and Anti-Semitism. EUROPEAN JUDAISM 18, 2 (Spr 1985) 27-30. To be published in "A Handbook of Jewish Theology," eds. Arthur A. Cohen, Paul Mendes-Flohr.

Contends that the anti-Judaism of Gnosticism and of Pauline Christianity entail antisemitism, the Gnostics ascribing to the Jews the role of cosmic evil, instruments of a demonic Power, and Paul viewing them as agents of Satan, betrayers and murderers of Christ.

0131. Mamlak, Gershon. An Early Diaspora: The Point of Purim. MIDSTREAM 31, 5 (May 1985) 30-32.

In the multi-national, syncretic Persian Empire the alien nature of Judaism as a faith and Jews as a national entity gave rise to the first "Jewish problem." This phenomenon is inseparable from Jewish existence in the Diaspora; the solution is Zionism.

0132. Paul, André. Flavius Josephus' "Antiquities of the Jews": An Anti-Christian Manifesto. NEW TESTAMENT STUDIES 31, 3 (July 1985) 473-480.

The "Antiquities of the Jews" was produced in Rome as part of a process of Josephus' repentance and acceptance of Jewish thinking, and as an attempt to re-establish the truths of the Jewish tradition in the face of the Christian challenge. This is proved by textual analysis which shows a deliberate avoidance of Greek translations - i.e. use of Christian terminology.

0133. Rabello, Alfredo Mordechai. On the Relations between Diocletian and the Jews. JOURNAL OF JEWISH STUDIES 35, 2 (Fall 1984) 147-167.

Based on rabbinic sources (Talmud and Midrashim) and Roman legal texts, concludes that the Emperor Diocletian was not hostile to the Jews - in contrast to the opinion of the Jewish historian Yitzchak Fritz Baer - and that Diocletian, in fact, extended the Jews' privileges.

0134. Reim, Guenter. Joh. 8:44 - Gotteskinder/Teufelskinder: Wie antijudaistisch ist "die Wohl antijudaistischste Aeusserung des NT?" NEW TESTAMENT STUDIES 30, 4 (1984) 619-624.

Explains the view of Christians that "the father of the Jews is the devil" as a misinterpretation of John 8:44, which is considered to be the most anti-Jewish verse in the New Testament.

0135. Schottroff, Luise. Anti-Judaism in the New Testament. THE HOLOCAUST AS INTERRUPTION, eds. Elisabeth Schuessler Fiorenza, David Tracy. Edinburgh: T. and T. Clark, 1984. Pp. 53-59. Appeared in French in LE JUDAISME APRES AUSCHWITZ. Paris: Beauchèsne, 1984. Pp. 85-96.

States that the "heinous" influence of anti-Judaism in the New Testament was not recognized in the past as antisemitic. Examples of anti-Jewish distortions in the New Testament are described and shown to be a result of the history of the Early Church. Interpretations of the New Testament which claim absolute superiority for Christianity must be rejected.

0136. Stanton, G.N. Aspects of Early Christian-Jewish Polemic and Apologetic. NEW TESTAMENT STUDIES 31, 3 (July 1985) 377-392.

Early Christians were sensitive to Jewish allegations that Jesus was a sorcerer and a deceiver, and Christianity a lawless sect. In their polemics, the Christians responded that the exile and the destruction of the Temple were punishments for the Jews' non-recognition of Jesus.

THE MEDIEVAL PERIOD

0137. ביינארט, חיים. האם התערב מיסר אלפונסו די לה קבלריה למניעת גירוש היהודים מספרד? ציון 50 (1985) 265-275.

[Beinart, Haim. Did Micer Alfonso de la Caballería Intervene against the Expulsion of the Jews from Spain? ZION 50 (1985) 265-275.]

Alfonso de la Caballería, son of a converso, had close and diverse relations with Jews in Saragossa, as indicated in his trial by the Inquisition which was stopped through the intervention of King Fernando. The king also gave him a document (BM ms. described here) absolving him from the accusation of intervening on behalf of the Jews to revoke the order of expulsion.

0138. ביינארט, חיים. 500 שנה לייסוד האינקוויזיציה הלאומית בספרד. האומה 74/75 (אביב/קיץ 1984) 45-52.

[Beinart, Haim. 500 Years since the Founding of the National Inquisition in Spain. HA-UMMA 74/75 (Spr/Sum 1984) 45-52.]

Describes the origins and nature of the Spanish Inquisition. A large group of New Christians, converted forcibly in 1391 or voluntarily during the mass conversions, were prevented from entering Christian society. Attempts to bar them from public office led to a political struggle in which all New Christians were suspected of Judaizing. In the 1460s the Franciscan monk Alfonso de Espina proposed that the Inquisition prosecute judaizers, and that the Jews of Spain be expelled in order to destroy their influence on the converts.

0139. לימור, אורה. ויכוח מאיורקה 1286: מהדורה ביקורתית ומבוא. דיסרטציה - האוניברסיטה העברית בירושלים, אוקטובר 1984. 2 כרכים.

[Limor, Ora. THE DISPUTATION OF MAJORCA 1286: A CRITICAL EDITION AND INTRODUCTION. Dissertation - The Hebrew University of Jerusalem, October 1984. 2 Vols. (250, xvii; [31], 118 pp.)]

An anonymous Latin composition describing a series of disputations between an influential Genoese merchant, Ingheto Contaldo, and a few Jews, one of whom was a convert to Christianity. Found in 17 ms. versions, and two printed editions, this is the first known work presenting Jewish-Christian polemics on a lay level. The Jews criticize the militant missionary activities of the Mendicant Orders. The merchant's purpose was to convert the Jews, yet his account of the disputation reflects a cultural synthesis not totally conforming to official Church positions.

0140. סימונסון, שלמה. נוצרים נגד מתנצרים. עת-מול 9, 3 <53> (ינואר 1984) 6-8.

[Simonsohn, Shlomo. Christians against Conversos. EIT-MOL 9, 3 <53> (Jan 1984) 6-8.]

At first the Jews who converted to Christianity by force or persuasion in 1391 in Spain were well-treated. Persecution of the converts began in 1449 in Toledo. Despite royal and papal opposition, restrictions on the basis of "purity of blood" spread, and in the 16th century, under local pressures, the Church authorized the use of the Inquisition against converts.

0141. Abulafia, Anna Sapir. An Attempt by Gilbert Crispin, Abbot of Westminster, at Rational Argument in the Jewish-Christian Debate. STUDIA MONASTICA 26, 1 (1984) 55-74.

The late 11th century works of Gilbert Crispin, a pupil of Anselm of Canterbury, are characteristic of the transitory stage from the early type of Jewish-Christian disputation, where scriptural authority served as the main tool of argument, to the attempt to prove the truth of Christian doctrine through reason.

0142. Abulafia, Anna Sapir. Invectives against Christianity in the Hebrew Chronicles of the First Crusade. CRUSADE AND SETTLEMENT, ed. Peter W. Ebury. Cardiff: University College Cardiff Press, 1985. Pp. 66-72.

Hebrew chronicles describe the attack in 1096 on the Jewish communities along the Rhine and the Moselle (Speyer, Worms, Mainz, Cologne, Trier) and the Crusader massacre of those Jews who refused baptism. Many Jews committed suicide rather than fall into the Crusaders' hands. Draws attention to the hostile language used by the Jewish chroniclers to describe Christianity.

0143. Alcalá Galve, Angel. LOS ORIGENES DE LA INQUISICION EN ARAGON: S. PEDRO ARBUES, MARTIR DE LA AUTONOMIA ARAGONESA. Zaragoza: Diputación General de Aragón, 1984. 109 pp. (Colección "Temas de Historia Aragonesa," 1).

In relating the case of Pedro Arbués, states that the pretext for setting up the Inquisition was to investigate offenses and transgressions against the Church committed by Christians, but that the real goal was to combat a bourgeois, urban middle class made up largely of converts and Jews.

0144. Baquero Moreno, Humberto. Movimientos sociais antijudáicos em Portugal no século XV [Antisemitic Social Movements in Portugal in the 15th Century]. JEWS AND CONVERSOS: STUDIES IN SOCIETY AND THE INQUISITION, ed. Yosef Kaplan. Jerusalem: World Union of Jewish Studies; Magnes Press, Hebrew University, 1985. Pp. 62-73.

The idea that in Portugal relationships between Jews and Christians were peaceful is disputed. The socioeconomic roots of Jew-hatred may explain attempts of the masses to blame the conversos for the plague, but this social development was moderated by the conciliatory attitude of the kings of Portugal. Nevertheless, because of Church pressure, the Crown would not postpone the decree of expulsion in 1498.

0145. Beinart, Haim. La Inquisición española y la expulsión de los Judíos de Andalucía. JEWS AND CONVERSOS: STUDIES IN SOCIETY AND THE INQUISITION, ed. Yosef Kaplan. Jerusalem: World Union of Jewish Studies; Magnes Press, Hebrew University, 1985. Pp. 103-123.

The main explanation given by the Inquisition to justify the expulsion of the Jews of Andalusia in 1483 was the Jewish influence on conversos. Underlines the importance of this expulsion as a precedent for the general expulsion from Spain in 1492.

0146. Castaño González, Javier. Los Judíos medievales en el Principado de Asturias. EL OLIVO 9 <21> (Jan-June 1985) 27-62.

A history of the Jews of Asturias from the Visigothic period until the expulsion in 1492. Describes persecutions followed by relative calm, and the first segregationist decrees against the Jews in 1377, which caused an increasing exodus of Jews even before the expulsion.

0147. Ceballos Atienza, Antonio. La argumentación teológico-bíblica en la "Biblia Parva" de San Pedro Pascual. ESTUDIOS BIBLICOS 42, 1/2 (1984) 89-136.

A study of the anti-Jewish polemical work by the bishop of Jaén (end of the 13th century).

0148. Chazan, Robert. The Deeds of the Jewish Community of Cologne. JOURNAL OF JEWISH STUDIES 35, 2 (Fall 1984) 185-195.

Discussion of the account given by Hebrew chroniclers of the Crusader attacks on the Jews of Cologne in 1096. The Archbishop dispersed the Jews in outlying fortified towns, but this tactic did not prevent massacre by Crusaders. The Cologne chronicle is later than other chronicles and focuses more on the motif of Kiddush ha-Shem ("sanctification of the name" - deliberate martyrdom).

0149. Chazan, Robert. Maestre Alfonso of Valladolid and the New Missionizing. REVUE DES ETUDES JUIVES 143, 1/2 (Jan-June 1984) 83-94.

The polemical works of the apostate Alfonso of Valladolid (formerly Abner of Burgos, active in the mid-14th century) are an example of the "new missionizing." This movement, which began in the mid-13th century, presented arguments based on an appeal to abstract reason and on rabbinic literature, which became possible due to the appearance of apostates with knowledge of Jewish tradition. Abner's adept use of rabbinic texts to prove that the Messiah had already come had a demoralizing effect on the Jews despite attempts at rebuttal.

0150. Chazan, Robert. Polemical Themes in the "Milhemet Mitzvah." LES JUIFS AU REGARD DE L'HISTOIRE, ed. Gilbert Dahan. Paris: Picard, 1985. Pp. 169-184.

A study of Christian-Jewish polemic in the "Milhemet Mitzvah," written by R. Meir ben Simon of Narbonne in the mid-13th century, which reflects the rising power of the Church and its new missionizing efforts. Christian arguments are described and rebutted. R. Meir uses historical argument as well as rational proofs to show that Jesus could not be the Messiah.

0151. Edwards, John. The Conversos: A Theological Approach. BULLETIN OF HISPANIC STUDIES 62, 1 (Jan 1985) 39-49.

Outlines a "new and more comprehensive method of exploring the experience of Jewish Christians in medieval Spain," and their relationships with both Judaism and Christianity, as expressed in the disputations of the 14th century and viewed in terms of religious dialogue. Recently, researchers in the sociology of religion have begun to recognize religious experience as a factor in history. The author proposes to view the "converso" experience in this light.

0152. Edwards, John. Mission and Inquisition among Conversos and Moriscos in Spain, 1250-1550. PERSECUTION AND TOLERATION, ed. W.J. Sheils. Oxford: Blackwell, 1984. Pp. 139-151.

Summarizes efforts made to convert the Jews beginning in the 1240s-1250s, initiated by the friars and supported by the Crown, involving missionary preaching, formal disputations, and secular legislation. Concludes that these efforts largely failed - conversions took place due to social, political, and legal pressures, but not from religious conviction. Mass conversion occurred after the pogroms of 1391, and the Inquisition achieved the assimilation of about 80% of the Jewish population, the rest emigrating in 1492. Pp. 146-148 discuss missionizing activities amongst the Moslems in the 16th century.

0153. Elnecave, Nissim. 1391: Unos seis siglos atrás se produjo la más sangrienta hecatombe contra los Sefaradim. SEFARDICA 1, 1 (Mar 1984) 75-82.

An account of the Jewish communities in the kingdoms of medieval Spain. Surveys their way of life, traditions, synagogues, and the never-ending attacks on Jews from all classes of Spanish society. Includes a description of the pogroms of 1391, considered the beginning of the process leading to the expulsion.

0154. Friedman, Yvonne. Armenkultur und Literatur: Zur Entwicklung eines Motivs in der antijuedischen Polemik des 12. Jahrhunderts. KAIROS 26, 1/2 (1984) 80-88.

Traces developments that transformed the 12th-century anti-Jewish polemical literature of the Church into a "sub-culture" for the people, in plays, in paintings, and in sculpture.

0155. Geanokoplos, Deno John. BYZANTIUM. Chicago: University of Chicago Press, 1984. xxxix, 485 pp.

A collection of extracts from documents relating to Byzantine history and civilization. Pp. 265-269 contain sources on the status of the Jews as defined by the Theodosian Code, on an attempt by Leo VI (886-912) to impose Christianity on them, and an example of violent hostility toward the Jews in an accusation that they aided the Persian enemies of the Empire.

0156. Gil, Moshe. Dhimmi Donations and Foundations for Jerusalem. JOURNAL OF THE ECONOMIC AND SOCIAL HISTORY OF THE ORIENT 27, 2 (July 1984) 156-174.

Discusses and documents the fiscal oppression of the Jews of Jerusalem during the Muslim period, before the Crusades. The taxation of Jews in Jerusalem was harsher than elsewhere in the Muslim world.

0157. Ginzburg, Carlo. The Witches' Sabbat: Popular Cult or Inquisitorial Stereotype? UNDERSTANDING POPULAR CULTURE: EUROPE FROM THE MIDDLE AGES TO THE NINETEENTH CENTURY, ed. Stephen L. Kaplan. Berlin: Mouton, 1984. Pp. 39-51.

Criticizes the thesis of Norman Cohn that the Witches' Sabbat was an ancient negative stereotype projected onto Jews, early Christians and medieval heretics. This stereotype did exist, but was not threatening to society until the 14th century. Accusations of a demonic conspiracy to overthrow society were first made in 1321 against French lepers and Jews, and again in 1348 in the Western Alps region against the Jews.

0158. Gutwirth, Eleazar. The Jews in 15th Century Castilian Chronicles. JEWISH QUARTERLY REVIEW 74, 4 (Apr 1984) 379-396.

The Castilian chroniclers' attitudes toward Jews and conversos were neither antisemitic nor philosemitic; their chronicles were literary works and referred to Jews in the context of medieval stereotypes. Some chroniclers criticized the Jewish courtiers and financiers ("the Jew as bad adviser") while others put forward religious ideology as a justification for separation and expulsion.

0159. Landes, Richard Allen. THE MAKING OF A MEDIEVAL HISTORIAN: ADEMAR OF CHABANNES AND AQUITAINE AT THE TURN OF THE MILLENNIUM. Dissertation - Princeton University, 1984. 362 pp. Unseen. Includes anti-Judaism.

0160. Langmuir, Gavin I. Historiographic Crucifixion. APPROACHES TO JUDAISM IN MEDIEVAL TIMES, ed. David R. Blumenthal. Chico, CA: Scholars Press, 1984. Pp. 1-26. Also appeared in LES JUIFS AU REGARD DE L'HISTOIRE, ed. Gilbert Dahan. Paris: Picard, 1985. Pp. 109-127.

Examines the role of historiography in fabricating and perpetuating the charge of ritual murder in the case of the first such charge, made in 1150 by Thomas of Monmouth, five years after the death of William of Norwich. Thomas invented the accusation of Jewish crucifixion of the boy; the story spread rapidly and was adopted by medieval chroniclers. Jewish historians are blamed for failing to deny it completely, thus allowing modern non-Jewish writers to express theories giving Jews some responsibility for the crime.

0161. Langmuir, Gavin I. Thomas of Monmouth: Detector of Ritual Murder. SPECULUM 59, 4 (Oct 1984) 820-846.

Thomas of Monmouth's 12th century work, "The Life and Passion of Saint William the Martyr of Norwich," is a reconstruction of William's murder, and a defence of Thomas' contention that it was a ritual crucifixion by Jews. His aim was not so much to harm the Jews, but rather to enhance the glory of the Norwich monastery by converting William into a symbol of Christ. (See the preceding entry in regard to the historiography on this case.)

0162. Lowry, Martin J.C. Humanism and Anti-Semitism in Renaissance Venice: The Strange Story of "Decor Puellarum." LA BIBLIOFILIA 87, 1 (1985) 39-54.

Analysis of a work of secular piety printed by Nicholas Jenson in Venice, 1471, containing virulent antisemitism. Traces its origin to a Carthusian monastery linked with the local patrician elite and with humanist circles. Venetian humanism was not so liberal as was believed - intrigues against the Jews characterized this circle.

0163. Marco i Dachs, Lluis. LOS JUDIOS EN CATALUNA. Barcelona: Destino, 1985. 305 pp. In Catalan.

A history of the Jews in Catalonia. Records the discriminatory decrees and laws against Jews from their arrival in Spain until the expulsion, including the pogroms of 1391 and the establishment of the Inquisition. Includes documents, among them a complete list of survivors from various pogroms, a list of conversos, the edict of expulsion of the Jews of Aragon and Castile (1492) and an edict of expulsion by the Inquisitor of Valencia (1512).

0164. Miller, Dorothy Westerman. THE JEWS IN "PIERS PLOWMAN." Dissertation - City University of New York, 1984. 230 pp.

The 14th century English poet William Langland appears to have had positive attitudes towards the Jews. He may have met Jewish converts in the course of his work as a clerk in minor orders. "The quiet history of friendly relations...dispels the narrow, one-sided notion that the medieval Christian attitude toward the Jew was one of hostility only."

0165. Monsalvo Antón, José María. TEORIA Y EVOLUCION DE UN CONFLICTO SOCIAL: EL ANTISEMITISMO EN LA CORONA DE CASTILLA EN LA BAJA EDAD MEDIA. Madrid: Siglo XXI, 1985. 342 pp.

Discusses interpretations by various historians of antisemitism - historical, social, economic, religious - in the Middle Ages, followed by a comprehensive study of antisemitism in Castile during the 13th-15th centuries.

0166. Moses ben Nachman (Nachmanides). LA DISPUTE DE BARCELONE, SUIVI DU COMMENTAIRE SUR ESAIE 52-53. Trad. de l'hébreu par Eric Smilevitch. Archives du texte trad. du latin par Luc Ferrier. Lagrasse: Verdier, 1984. 101 pp.

The disputation of Barcelona took place in 1263 between R. Moses ben Nachman and the apostate Pablo Christiani. The circumstances of the disputation, and the new militancy and hostility towards Judaism on the part of the Church, are described in the introduction to this translation (pp. 1-20). The disputation focuses on the issue of whether Jesus was the Messiah. Includes translations of several Christian Latin texts describing the disputation, and orders by the King of Aragon relating to the disputation and to the destruction of the Talmud.

0167. Muzzarelli, Maria Giuseppina. EBREI E CITTA D'ITALIA IN ETA DI TRANSIZIONE: IL CASO DI CESENA DAL XIV AL XVI SECOLO. Bologna: CLUEB, 1984. 249 pp.

A sociological study of Jewish communities in central and northern Italy, and relations with the Christian population. Pp. 73-233 comprise a case study of the town Cesena in central Italy. Includes references to popular and clerical antagonism towards the Jews, particularly in the economic sphere.

0168. Orfali, Moises. Anthropomorphism in the Christian Reproach of the Jews in Spain (12th-15th Century). IMMANUEL 19 (Win 1984/85) 60-73.

In medieval anti-Jewish polemics the Jews were accused of desecrating and demeaning God by attributing to Him human qualities. The arguments were based on midrashim and aggadot which were interpreted literally rather than metaphorically. Cites the works of Agobard (Bishop of Lyon), Petrus Alfonsi, Raymond Martini, Geronimo de Santa Fe, Alfonso de Espina.

0169. Passerat, G. Les Juifs de Moissac au Moyen Age. BULLETIN DE LA SOCIETE ARCHEOLOGIQUE DE TARN ET GARONNE 109 (1984) 129-134.

The archives of the abbey of Moissac contain the text of a judgment from 1298 by the ruler of Quercy, Guy Caprais, ordering the expulsion of the Jews of Moissac in the wake of a similar order by Philippe le Bel (1296).

0170. Perez, Pierre. Histoire véridique d'un pape presque juif. TRIBUNE JUIVE 834 (31 Aug-6 Sept 1984) 26-27.

Sketches the story of Anacletus II, "the Jewish pope" (1130-1138), a scion of the Jewish Pierleoni family of Rome. His election was opposed by Innocent II who claimed the papacy from French exile, supported by Bernard of Clairvaux. Their opposition was based on Anacletus's Jewish descent.

0171. Pons, Antonio. LOS JUDIOS DEL REINO DE MALLORCA DURANTE LOS SIGLOS XIII Y XIV. Palma de Mallorca: Miguel Font Editor, 1984. 2 vols. (283; 339 pp.).

Vol. 1, pp. 98-103 include antisemitism and persecution of Jews in Majorca.

0172. Rahe, Thomas. Demographische und geistig-soziale Auswirkungen der Pest von 1348-1350. GESCHICHTE IN WISSENSCHAFT UND UNTERRICHT 35, 3 (Mar 1984) 125-144.

On pp. 134-138, "Judenpogrome," discusses the causes, the course and the results of the pogroms against the Jews of Europe during the period of the Black Death, 1348-1350.

0173. Riley-Smith, Jonathan. The First Crusade and the Persecution of the Jews. PERSECUTION AND TOLERATION, ed. W.J. Sheils. Oxford: B. Blackwell, 1984. Pp. 51-72.

Examines the connection between the Crusade to free Jerusalem and the attacks on the Jewish communities of the Rhineland in 1096. Motives for the massacres of the Jews included a desire to get supplies by extortion and looting, attempts to convert the Jews by force, and vengeance for the crucifixion. Although canon law opposed forced conversion and acts of vengeance against the Jews, the knights and nobles, and some preachers, used these themes to arouse enthusiasm for the Crusades.

0174. Talmage, Frank. Trauma at Tortosa: The Testimony of Abraham Rimoch. MEDIEVAL STUDIES 47 (1985) 379-415.

A commentary on the Psalms by Abraham Rimoch (15th century ms.) throws light on the intellectual atmosphere of Spanish Jewry at the time of the Disputation of Tortosa (1413-1414) in which Rimoch participated. In his Hebrew introduction to the commentary (given on pp. 412-413) Rimoch describes his personal history and the disputation, at which the Jews failed to formulate a response and many converted. His commentary also reflects despair and his belief that it is useless to engage in direct polemics with Christians; he attacks his fellow Jews for succumbing to conversion.

0175. Trautner-Kromann, Hanne. Sources of Jewish Polemics against Christianity in the Late Middle Ages. TEMENOS 20 (1984) 52-65.

A survey of various types of source material - accounts of disputations, Bible commentaries, philosophical and theological texts, homilies, responsa, letters. Jewish polemics against Christianity in the 13th century were a reaction to the anti-Jewish polemics of the 12th.

0176. Trost, Pavel. A Mock Report on the Prague Pogrom in 1389. SLAVICA HIEROSOLYMITANA 7 (1985) 239-240.

A short description of a gospel parody, "Passio Judaeorum Pragensium secundum Johannem rusticum quadratum," in which the story of the Prague pogrom of Easter 1389 is told in gospel phrases referring to the passion of Christ. The author of the work, probably a Czech clergyman, justifies the atrocities as revenge on the Jews for outraging the Host and, while mocking the mob of pogromists, praises their religious zeal.

0177. Wettinger, Godfrey. THE JEWS OF MALTA IN THE LATE MIDDLE AGES. Valletta, Malta: Midsea Books, 1985. x, 352 pp.

A study of the Jews of Malta and Gozo (combined population ca.500) in the 15th century. Although the Jews complained about official judicial persecution and ecclesiastical harassment (particularly on the part of the Inquisition), they held the status of "citizens" and were under the protection of the Sicilian Royal Chamber. The expulsion of 1492 took them by surprise and put an end to Jewish habitation of these islands.

0178. Wolff, Philippe. Quelques documents concernant les Juifs de Toulouse. LES JUIFS AU REGARD DE L'HISTOIRE, ed. Gilbert Dahan. Paris: Picard, 1985. Pp. 201-216.

Describes documents concerning the Jews of Toulouse in the 12th-14th centuries. Some instances of antisemitism in this period are given on pp. 204-205. Includes the documents in the Latin original.

0179. Wood, Diana. Infidels and Jews: Clement VI's Attitude to Persecution and Toleration. PERSECUTION AND TOLERATION, ed. W.J. Sheils. Oxford: Blackwell, 1984. Pp. 115-124.

Pope Clement VI (1342-1352) expressed a tolerant attitude toward the Jews. He believed in a close identification between the people of Israel and the Christian people. During 1348/49, when Jews were accused of causing the Black Death and were massacred by the thousands, Clement issued three papal bulls protecting the Jews and their property, and condemning the Flagellants who shed the blood of Jews. Clement VI admitted to hating the

Jews because they would not "accept the Faith and Salvation," but he was opposed to forced conversion of Jews.

0180. The World's First Government Issued Anti-Semitic Coin - 1149. THE SHEKEL 17, 4 (July/Aug 1984) 3.

Antisemitic money was invented in the 12th century in Halberstadt, Germany. Bishop Ulrich I (ca. 1149) issued a silver pfennig, probably for tax purposes, depicting the stoning of St. Stephen by the Jews.

THE EARLY MODERN PERIOD (1493-1788)

0181. אפטער, שמשון. יעקב שלום הערץ, דער היסטאריקער. די צוקונפט 90, 4/5 (מאי/יוני 1984) 146-148.

[Apter, Shimshon. Yaakov Shalom Hertz, the Historian. ZUKUNFT 90, 4/5 (May/June 1984) 146-148.]

Hertz's book "Di geshichte fun di Yidn in Ukraine" describes the period of the Chmielnicki massacres (1648), and refutes the charge, brought forth to justify the massacres, that the Jews leased Orthodox churches for their own use.

0182. בלקני, פנחס. רישומן של גזירות ת"ח-ת"ט במקורות עבריים. ספר בר-אילן [בית-ספר תיכון דתי בנתניה] 1 (1985) 186-203.

[Balkani, Pinchas. Impressions of the Pogroms of 1648-1649 in Hebrew Sources. SEFER BAR-ILAN (Religious High-School in Netanya) 1 (1985) 186-203.]

On the pogroms and the massacres of the Jews by the Ukrainian Cossacks, led by Bogdan Chmielnicki, as reflected in Jewish sources of the time.

0183. גולדברג, יעקב. המומרים בממלכת פולין-ליטא. ירושלים: מרכז זלמן שזר, 1985. 111, viii עמ'.

[Goldberg, Jacob. CONVERTED JEWS IN THE POLISH COMMONWEALTH. Jerusalem: Zalman Shazar Center, 1985. 111, viii pp.] With an English summary.

Analyzes the phenomenon of voluntary conversion of Jews to Catholicism in the Polish-Lithuanian kingdom during the 16th to 18th centuries. Describes Catholic missionary activity, Jewish motives for conversion, and the extent of the converts' integration in Christian society. Pp. 34-37 deal with the forced conversion of Jewish children, and pp. 67-69 with negative Christian attitudes toward the converts. Pp. 73-98 include documents in Polish with Hebrew translations.

0184. דויד, אברהם. לפרשת מותו של הגר יוסף סרלבו על קידוש השם. קרית ספר 59, 1 (ינואר 1984) 243-245.

[David, Avraham. The Martyrdom of the Proselyte Joseph Saralvo. KIRYAT SEFER 59, 1 (Jan 1984) 243-245.]

Joseph Saralvo, a Portuguese convert to Judaism, was burnt at the stake in 1583 in Rome. He and other Jews were arrested and tortured in Italy at the instigation of the Portuguese Inquisition which was incensed by the intensive proselytizing activities amongst the Portuguese marranos in Ferrara. Presents an account of Saralvo's martyrdom found in an ms.

0185. יעקבסון, חנה. עדות משלוניקי על עלילת-דם בלתי-ידועה ביוון בתחילת המאה השבע-עשרה. מאז ועד עתה: הרצאות הקתדרה (1977-1983), ערך צבי אנקורי. תל-אביב: אוניברסיטת תל-אביב, 1984. עמ' 67-72.

[Jacobsohn, Hanna. Testimony from Salonica on an Unknown Blood Libel in Greece in the Seventeenth Century. THEN AND NOW: ANNUAL LECTURES ON THE JEWS OF GREECE (1977-1983), ed. Zvi Ankori. Tel-Aviv: Chair for the History and Culture of the Jewry of Salonica and Greece, Tel-Aviv University, 1984. Pp. 67-72.]

At the beginning of the 17th century the Jews of Thebes were accused of a blood libel and were required to pay a large sum of ransom money. An account of this blood libel appears in a manuscript containing responsa, and describes the first blood libel known to have occurred in Greece. Other libels from that period occurring in Asia Minor are also described and attributed to anger and frustration of the populace under Ottoman rule.

0186. ירדני, מרים. הוגנוטים ויהודים בברנדנבורג ופרוסיה בסוף המאה ה-17 ובמאה ה-18. אומה ותולדותיה, חלק ב: העת החדשה, ערך שמואל אטינגר. ירושלים: מרכז זלמן שזר, 1984. עמ' 11-23.

[Yardeni, Miriam. Huguenots and Jews in Brandenburg and Prussia at the End of the 17th Century and in the 18th Century. NATION AND HISTORY: STUDIES IN THE HISTORY OF THE JEWISH PEOPLE, Vol. 2, ed. Shmuel Ettinger. Jerusalem: Zalman Shazar Center, 1984. Pp. 11-23.]

Surveys attitudes of Huguenot theologians, academics and historians towards the Jews. Both Huguenots and Jews, escaping from persecution, were welcomed in Brandenburg, where the indigent population had been decimated by the Thirty Years War. Some Huguenot sources express traditional Christian anti-Jewish views, but the general trend throughout the 18th century was toward appreciation and understanding. The most antisemitic views were expressed by J.H.S. Formey.

0187. לבל, ג'ני. הטרגדיה של יהודי בלגראד בשנת 1688. שבט ועם ה <י> (אוקטובר 1984) 110-128.

[Loebel, Jenny. The Tragedy of the Jews of Belgrade, 1688. SHEVET VE'AM 5 <10> (Oct 1984) 110-128.]

The occupation of Belgrade in 1688 by Austrian troops was a tragedy for the local Jewish community, most of whose members were imprisoned and ransomed for huge sums of money. Appeals of the community for help and other documents are included.

0188. רצהבי, יהודה. הגירוש למדבר. עת-מול ט, 3 <53> (ינואר 1984) 16-18.

[Ratzhaby, Yehuda. The Expulsion to the Desert. EIT-MOL 9, 3 <53> (Jan 1984) 16-18.]

The Jews of Yemen were expelled to the desert region of Mawza by the Imam al-Mahdi in 1679-1680. The Imam was apparently inspired by Caliph Omar's belief that there is no place for two religions in the Hejaz. Three-fourths of the Jews died, before the death of the Imam ended the banishment.

0189. Abramowicz, Léon. Les Juifs et les droits de l'homme sous la Revolution française: Quelques aspects de l'émancipation. JUDAISME ET DROITS DE L'HOMME, ed. Emmanuel Hirsch. Paris: Librairie des Libertés, 1984. Pp. 87-95.

Describes the situation of the Jews in France before and during the French Revolution, and the struggle for Jewish emancipation. Mentions difficulties in applying the anti-discriminatory laws: for example, in the Comtat Venaissin, Jews were still obliged to wear yellow hats a year and a half after the decree cancelling this law.

0190. Amaru, Betsy Halpern. Martin Luther and Jewish Mirrors. JEWISH SOCIAL STUDIES 46, 2 (Spr 1984) 95-102.

Rather than treating the changes in Luther's attitude to the Jews as a historical problem, suggests that they reflect his changing theological orientations. In Christian civilization "the Jew was a 'witness,' in positive terms, to the potential power of Christ, and in negative terms to the power of sin." These images of the Jew, or "Judenspiegel," reflecting their creator rather than the Jews themselves, were secularized in modern society.

0191. Ankori, Zvi. Giacomo Foscarini e gli Ebrei di Creta: Un riesame con una edicione degli "Ordine" sugli Ebrei. STUDI VENEZIANI 9 (1985) 67-183.

The "Ordine," an Italian corpus of laws and decrees, and the "Relacione," official reports of life in Crete during the 16th century, provide information on the activities and ideas of Giacomo Foscarini, the Italian Governor of Crete from 1574, who was accused of antisemitism by Johann W. Zinkeisen in his book "Geschichte des osmanischen Reiches in Europa" (Hamburg, 1840-63). Contends that Foscarini's antisemitic prejudice cannot be ignored, but it must be understood through objective analysis of his writings, such as "Against Promiscuity between Christians and Jews" and "Against the Employment of Christians in Jewish Homes."

0192. Arbell, Mordechai. "La Nación": Los judíos hispano-portugueses del Caribe. SEFARDICA 1, 1 (Mar 1984) 85-94.

Discusses the settlement of New Christians in Latin America. After being expelled from Brazil in 1654 by the Inquisition, they took refuge in the Caribbean area.

0193. Bietenholz, Peter G. Erasmus und die letzten Lebensjahre Reuchlins. HISTORISCHE ZEITSCHRIFT 240, 1 (Feb 1985) 45-66.

Deals with the correspondence between Christian humanists of the 16th century. Pp. 53-57 mention the anti-Jewish attitude of Erasmus of Rotterdam.

0194. Boehn, Guenther. HISTORIA DE LOS JUDIOS EN CHILE. VOL. 1: PERIODO COLONIAL. Santiago: Editorial Andrés Bello, 1984. xiv, 470 pp. An extract from the book appeared in SEFARDICA 1, 2 (Nov 1984) 43-49.

A detailed account of the career of Francisco Maldonado da Silva, a leader of the Chilean Jewish community, who was burnt at the stake in the "auto da fé" at Lima in 1639.

0195. Bromberg, Rachel Mizrahi. A propósito da "limpieza de sangue": A ligacão entre o poder e o racismo [Concerning "Purity of Blood": On the Link between Power and Racism]. O HEBREU 4 <46> (Jan 1984) 22-23.

Discusses the links between power and racism as reflected in the works of Maria Luiza Tucci Carneiro on the Portugese Statutes of Purity of Blood and their application against New Christians in Portugal and Brazil.

0196. Colafemmina, Cesare. The Jews of Reggio Calabria from the End of the XVth Century to the Beginning of the XVIth Century. LES JUIFS AU REGARD DE L'HISTOIRE, ed. Gilbert Dahan. Paris: Picard, 1985. Pp. 255-262.

A short description of the history of the Jews of Reggio, southern Italy, to which many Jews fled from Sicily after their expulsion in 1492. They suffered from Christian hostility due to economic or religious reasons. In 1510 Ferdinand the Catholic, as ruler of the Kingdom of Naples, expelled them again.

0197. Eisenbach, Artur. Postulat asymilacji Żydów i jego implikacje w dobie stanislawowskiej [The Proposal for Assimilation of the Jews and Its Implications in the Stanislaw Period]. BIULETYN ZYDOWSKIEGO INSTYTUTU HISTORYCZNEGO W POLSCE 131/132 (July-Dec 1984) 3-30.

Discusses the problem of the assimilation of Jews into Polish society during the reign of Stanislaw II (1764-

1772) as seen by educated Poles (among them Stanislaw Staszic) and Jews. Describes the antisemitism expressed by the Polish bourgeoisie and nobles, including stereotypes common during this period.

0198. Erling, Bernhard. Martin Luther and the Jews in the Light of His Lectures on Genesis. ECUMENICAL INSTITUTE FOR THEOLOGICAL RESEARCH YEARBOOK 1983/1984 (1984) 129-147. Appeared also in IMMANUEL 18 (Fall 1984) 64-78.

Examines Luther's polemical treatises against the Jews as well as his "Lecture on Genesis." Luther's primary charge against the Jews was their refusal to accept Jesus as the Messiah, a common argument at that time. Luther's violent use of language must be deplored and rejected, yet there are elements in his teachings which may facilitate religious pluralism.

0199. Foa, Anna. Il nuovo e il vecchio: L'insorgere della sifilide (1494-1530). QUADERNI STORICI 55 (Apr 1984) 11-34.

Using medical texts and chronicles, examines the reaction to the first appearance of syphilis in Europe in epidemic form. These reactions were patterned on the traditional attitude to leprosy, a symbolic scourge with a marked sexual meaning. Origin and blame were projected onto enemies, among them the Jews.

0200. Frey, Winfried. Passionsspiel und geistliche Malerei als Instrumente der Judenhetze in Frankfurt am Main um 1500. JAHRBUCH DES INSTITUTS DEUTSCHE GESCHICHTE 13 (1984) 15-59.

Two works of art - the local passion play and an altarpiece by Hans Holbein on the life of Christ - were used around 1500 to provoke hatred of the Jews in Frankfurt. The use of works of art for antisemitic purposes was not new; however, in this case, the anti-Jewish climate created by these works had an influence on the success of the apostate Johannes Pfefferkorn (1470-1522) in obtaining the consent of the Emperor and the local authorities to a missionary campaign among the Jews.

0201. Friedenberg, Daniel. Anti-Semitic Medals of Late Medieval Europe. THE SHEKEL 17, 4 (July/Aug 1984) 4-14. Excerpted from "Jewish Medals" (1970).

Almost all antisemitic medals of the period were of Germanic origin, the main type being the "Korn Jude." Issued in 1694-1696, and again in 1770-1773, it reflected periods of distress and high corn prices for which Jewish corn speculators were blamed. Other German antisemitic medals, such as the "Jud Suess" medal, are described, along with a single Belgian example. An unusual English medal reflects a price war over theater tickets in 1809.

0202. Gergely, Thomas. 1684-1984: Pour le tricentaire du Pourim de Padoue (dit de Buda). CENTRALE (BRUXELLES) 226 (Mar 1984) 10-11.

In 1684, the Jews of Padua were attacked because of rumors that the Jews of Buda had given aid to the Turks in their war against the Austrian and Venetian armies. The Jews of Padua were saved by the army and the town authorities from a pogrom. They instituted an annual day of thanksgiving - the Purim di Buda.

0203. Gilman, Sander L. Martin Luther and the Self-Hating Jews. MICHIGAN GERMANIC STUDIES 10, 1/2 (Spr-Fall 1984) 79-97. Unseen.

0204. Godin, André. L'antijudaïsme d'Erasme: Equivoques d'un modèle théologique. BIBLIOTHEQUE D'HUMANISME ET RENAISSANCE: TRAVAUX ET DOCUMENTS 47, 3 (Sept 1985) 537-553.

Describes the discussion which followed the publication of a booklet by Guido Kisch (1969) in which Erasmus was accused of hatred of the Jews and Judaism, mainly on the basis of his letters. Concludes that Erasmus's theological anti-Judaism had nothing in common with the violent antisemitism of Luther, or with racial antisemitism, but was a form of religious antagonism based on the conviction that after the appearance of Jesus Christ Judaism had no more significance.

0205. Halpérin, Jean; Sovik, Arne, eds. LUTHER, LUTHERANISM AND THE JEWS. Geneva: Lutheran World Federation, 1984. 80 pp. Unseen.

0206. Havilio, Harry. Origen y desaparición del criptojudaísmo en América. SEFARDICA 1, 1 (Mar 1984) 64-74.

Many converted Jews in the Iberian peninsula retained their Jewish practices in secret and eventually sought refuge in Latin America. The establishment of the Inquisition in America in the 16th century, accompanied by persecutions and pogroms, led to the dissolution of these communities.

0207. Horn, Maurycy. REGESTY DOKUMENTOW I EKSCERPTY Z METRYKI KORONNEJ DO HISTORII ZYDOW W POLSCE (1697-1795) [Abstracts of Documents and Excerpts from the Royal Registry Concerning the History of Jews in Poland (1697-1795)]. Vol. I: 1697-1763. Vol. II, pt. 1: 1764-1779. Wroclaw: Zaklad Narodowy im. Ossolinskich, 1984. ix, 165; 211 pp. Part of the above work, covering the years 1766-1780, appeared in the BIULETYN ZYDOWSKIEGO INSTYTUTU HISTORYCZNEGO W POLSCE 131/132 (1984) 159-182; 133/134 (1985) 133-155; 135/136 (1985) 103-118.

Includes material regarding restrictions imposed on the Jews.

0208. Ioly Zorattini, Pier Cesare. The Jews and the Inquisition of Aquileia and Concordia. JEWS AND CONVERSOS: STUDIES IN SOCIETY AND THE INQUISITION, ed. Yosef Kaplan. Jerusalem: Magnes Press, Hebrew University, 1985. Pp. 225-236.

Presents details of the Inquisition records for this area of Italy from the mid-16th to the end of the 18th century. A small number of cases dealt with converted Jews tried for Judaizing and for insulting the Catholic religion or church. The small number of cases and mild treatment of the Jews is attributed to the relative scarcity of Jews in the area and the secondary importance of their activities when compared with the problems of heresy and witchcraft.

0209. Ioly Zorattini, Pier Cesare, ed. PROCESSI DEL S. UFFIZIO DI VENEZIA CONTRO EBREI E GIUDAIZZANTI. Vol. 3: 1570-1572. Vol. 4: 1571-1580. Firenze: Leo S. Olschki, 1984-1985. 305; 425 pp. (Storia dell'Ebraismo in Italia: Studi e testi, V-VI. Sezione Veneta, 4-5). Vols. 1-2, covering the years 1548-1570, were published in 1980-1982.

Documents of trials conducted by the Inquisition in Venice against Jews, Marranos and New Christians. Emphasizes that the punishments meted out by this Tribunal were relatively light. The documents are in Italian, Latin and Portuguese.

0210. Link, Paul. My Encounters with Marranos in South America. JEWISH AFFAIRS 40, 9 (Sept 1985) 115-120.

Describes a visit to the former headquarters of the Inquisition in Lima, Peru, today a museum. Traces of persecution of the Marranos are still visible. In 1639 the Marrano community of Lima was liquidated in an auto-da-fé known as the "Day of the Grande."

0211. Lipiner, Elias. O cristão-novo: Mito ou realidade [The New Christian: Myth or Reality]. JEWS AND CONVERSOS: STUDIES IN SOCIETY AND THE INQUISITION, ed. Yosef Kaplan. Jerusalem: Magnes Press, Hebrew University, 1985. Pp. 124-138.

Examines the theories of A.J. Saraiva, as expressed in his book "Inquisicão e Cristãos-Novos" (see no. 225), regarding discrimination against and persecution of New Christians in Portugal during the 16th-18th centuries, which Saraiva claims was due to economic factors. Compares them with Sartre's theory of antisemitism.

0212. Medina, J.T. Los judios ante la Inquisición de las Islas Filipinas. HERENCIA JUDIA 31 (1984) 33-35.

A brief description of trials against Jews and New Christians in the Philippines during the 16th century.

0213. Meier, Kurt. Luthers Judenschriften als Forschungsproblem. THEOLOGISCHE LITERATURZEITUNG 110, 7 (July 1985) 485-492.

An historiographical survey dealing with Luther's antisemitism and the debate concerning the continuity of antisemitic thought from Luther to Hitler.

0214. Moulinas, René. Un cas particulier de l'histoire des Juifs du Pape en France: Les Juifs de Bédarrides, XVIe-XVIIe siècles. LES JUIFS AU REGARD DE L'HISTOIRE, ed. Gilbert Dahan. Paris: Picard, 1985. Pp. 267-281.

Describes the situation of the Jews in the areas under papal rule in France during the 16th-17th centuries. After the papal bull "Cum nimis absurdum" was issued by Pope Paul IV in 1555, the Jews were allowed to live only in ghettos. The towns of Bédarrides and Chateauneuf-du-Pape were exceptions as they were not politically dependent on the Pope. Jews lived there freely until 1694 when, as a result of activity by the Inquisition, they were obliged to move into ghettos.

0215. Nadav, Mordekhai. The Jewish Community of Nemyriv in 1648: Their Massacre and the Loyalty Oath to the Cossacks. HARVARD UKRAINIAN STUDIES 8, 3/4 (Dec 1984) 376-395. A revised and expanded version of the Hebrew, published in "Zion" 47 (1982).

Hebrew chronicles of the 17th century describe the massacre of Jews in Nemirov by the Cossacks. After efforts to buy their freedom failed, many Jews were murdered. A Polish source, the "Diary" of Boguslaw Maskiewicz, mentions a group of Jews who saved their lives by taking a loyalty oath to the Cossacks and retreating with the Polish forces who had briefly recaptured the town. These Jews may be identical to the forced converts described in the Hebrew chronicles. Gives translations of two of the chronicles.

0216. Novinsky, Anita. Cristianos nuevos: Un problema historiografico. SEFARDICA 1, 2 (Nov 1984) 51-67.

Describes different historical theories concerning the New Christians in Iberia and in Latin America. Some historians explain the Inquisition as a normal consequence of the existence of hostile, dissenting religious groups. New Christians were viewed by those in power as Catholic renegades. Other historians consider that the religious persecution and forced conversion of the Jews was abnormal, illegitimate and morally despicable. Saraiva (see no. 225) suggests that the New Christians were a myth invented by the Inquisition to stop the advance of the bourgeoisie.

0217. Novinsky, Anita. Sistema de poder y represión religiosa: Para una interpretación del fenómeno "Cristão-Novo" en el Brasil. SEFARDICA 1, 1 (Mar 1984) 17-24.

The Tribunal of the Spanish and Portuguese Holy Office (Inquisition) constitutes one of the most significant examples of religious manipulation in order to justify a power system. Religious racist ideology was extended to Brazil where the New Christians held important economic positions. The New Christians, accused of being heretics, finally assumed the "guilt" of Judaism.

0218. Oberman, Heiko A. THE ROOTS OF ANTI-SEMITISM IN THE AGE OF RENAISSANCE AND REFORMATION. Trans. by James I. Porter. Philadelphia: Fortress Press, 1984. xii, 163 pp. Originally published as "Wurzeln des Antisemitismus" (Berlin [West]: Severin und Siedler, 1981).

A study of the anti-Jewish attitudes of Christian theologians in the 16th century, particularly in Germany, in the perspective of historical development from medieval fanaticism to modern racism. Focuses on the views of Luther, Reuchlin, and Erasmus, while discussing other theologians as well (Calvin, Pfefferkorn, Zwingli, etc.). Even the Humanists, who spoke for tolerance and civil rights, supported the idea of a society free of Jews as advocated by Luther. Luther's anti-Judaism was strictly theological - he was not the father of modern antisemitism.

0219. Ouziel, Rachel. Brésil - des marranes aux chrétiens: Un effacement qui a duré trois siècles. NOUVEAUX CAHIERS 77 (Sum 1984) 50-57.

Traces the history of the New Christians of Brazil from the 16th to the 18th centuries. Despite economic success the New Christians faced hostility, rooted in medieval Christian prejudice, which was not wiped out by conversion. Denunciations to the Inquisition were common. After a short period of tolerance under Dutch rule (1630-1654), most were assimilated into Christian society, but antisemitic stereotypes persisted.

0220. Perry, Norma. Anglo-Jewry, the Law, Religious Conviction, and Self-Interest (1655-1753). JOURNAL OF EUROPEAN STUDIES 14, 1 <53> (Mar 1984) 1-23.

After 1655, Jews, mainly immigrants from Spain and Portugal, were allowed to enter London and to practice their religion, but were barred from the professions and from legal office. They could own but not inherit real estate through a process known as denization. Full property rights could be obtained through naturalization, which required conversion to Christianity.

0221. Pfisterer, Rudolf. Zwischen Polemik und Apologetik: Anmerkungen zu Veroeffentlichungen ueber Luthers Stellung zu den Juden. TRIBUENE 92 (1984) 99-124.

An historiographical survey of articles published in 1983 dealing with Martin Luther's attitude towards the Jews. Some historians draw a direct line from Luther to Hitler, while others tend to minimize the historical importance of Luther's antisemitism.

0222. Pluchon, Pierre. NEGRES ET JUIFS AU XVIIIE SIECLE: LE RACISME AU SIECLE DES LUMIERES. Paris: Tallandier, 1984. 313 pp.

Describes the social and juridical situation of Jews, Blacks and Mulattos in France and in its West Indian colonies in the 18th century. The Mendès-France Affair (ca. 1776), in which two slaves of a Jew demanded their liberty, was an occasion for vilification of Jews. The Encyclopedists were ambivalent, at best, about Jews, despite their professions of tolerance and equality.

0223. Reichrath, H. Luther und die Juden. PFAELZISCHES PFARRERBLATT 9 (1984) 137-144. Unseen.

0224. Rowan, Steven. Luther, Bucer and Eck on the Jews. SIXTEENTH CENTURY JOURNAL 16, 1 (1985) 79-90.

Analyzes the views of Martin Luther, Martin Bucer and Johann Eck on the Jews in the context of canon law, medieval custom and the politics of the Reformation. While Luther attacked the Jewish concept of righteousness through works as similar to the Catholic, the Catholics saw a resemblance between the Protestant and Jewish rejection of images, the Mass, and clerical celibacy.

0225. Saraiva, Antonio José. INQUISICAO E CRISTAOS-NOVOS [Inquisition and New Christians]. 5th ed. Lisboa: Editorial Estampa, 1985. 308 pp. (Imprensa Universitaria, 42). The first four editions appeared in 1969.

Presents the thesis that the Inquisition was established in Portugal in the 16th century by the upper classes who felt that they were being menaced, both materially and ideologically, by the new merchant bourgeoisie class, made up largely of New Christians. The present edition includes an appendix (pp. 211-291) on the polemic between the author and I.S. Révah (mainly letters and interviews published in the weekly "Diarío de Lisboa" in 1971). Révah accused Saraiva of libel and rejects the view that the Inquisition was a socio-economic phenomenon rather than an ethnic-religious one.

0226. Schmidt, Ephraïm. Een Maranen-proces te Antwerpen in de 16e eeuw over een gehouden joodse pasen [A Marrano Trial in 16th Century Antwerp, about a Jewish Passover Observance]. DE CENTRALE 185 (Apr 1984) 19-20.

In 1540 there were approximately twenty Marranos in Antwerp. In that year Emanuel Serano was tried by the Inquisition for holding a Passover Seder. He denied having committed the "crime," proffered various explanations, and was freed.

0227. Segre, Renata. Nuovi documenti sui Marrani d'Ancona (15-55-1559). MICHAEL 9 (1985) 130-233.

The election of Pope Paul IV in 1555 brought about a change in the status of the small community of Marranos in Ancona, Italy. Paul IV treated them as "apostates" and began persecutions - confiscation of goods, arrests, torture and trials. In 1556, 26 Marranos were burned at the stake. Pp. 160-232 contain documents.

0228. Simonsohn, Shlomo. Marranos in Ancona under Papal Protection. MICHAEL 9 (1985) 234-267.

Some recently discovered documents (given on pp. 243-267) have thrown light on the origins of the Marrano settlement in Ancona and the encouragement received from Popes Julius III and Paul III. The anti-Jewish policy of Paul IV, which resulted in the auto-da-fé of 1555-1556, is also discussed.

0229. Skoog, Age. Martin Luther en de Joden [Martin Luther and the Jews]. NES AMMIM LEZINGEN: GESPREKKEN IN ISRAEL 10, 4 (1984/1985) 22 pp.

A Dutch translation of a lecture held in English on 29 Feb. 1984. Discusses especially the reasons for Luther's change of attitude towards the Jews after 1530, from positive feelings to hatred: the unconvertability of the Jews, his unsuccessful dialogue with the rabbis, his fight against Christian sabbatarians, and traditional Christian anti-Jewish theology. Notes that although Luther's anti-Jewish writings were used by the Nazis for their own purposes, they have seldom been used against the Jews by most Lutherans.

0230. Stegemann, Ekkehard. Luthers Bibeluebersetzung und das juedisch-christliche Gespraech. EVANGELISCHE THEOLOGIE 44, 4 (July/Aug 1984) 386-405.

Analyzes the attitudes of Luther and other important Christian theologians of his time (Erasmus, Reuchlin) towards Jews and Judaism. Concludes that Luther's anti-Judaism resulted from his "Christianization" of the Old Testament.

0231. Tazbir, Janusz. Das Judenbild der Polen im 16.-18. Jahrhundert. ACTA POLONIAE HISTORICA 50 (1984) 29-57.

An examination of anti-Jewish stereotypes and attitudes in Poland in the 16th-18th centuries. The Jews were a large and closed group of aliens in the Polish state, a condition which gave rise to religious and economic antisemitism. Negative attitudes were also directed against other minorities in Poland.

0232. Toch, Michael. "Umb gemeyns nutz und nottdurfft willen": Obrigkeitliches und jurisdiktionelles Denken bei der Austreibung der Nuernberger Juden 1498/99. ZEITSCHRIFT FUER HISTORISCHE FORSCHUNG 11, 1 (1984) 1-21.

A detailed analysis of the economic motives behind the juridical acts taken by the city authorities of Nuremberg concerning the expulsion of the local Jews in 1498/9.

0233. Wistrich, Robert S. Martin Luther and the Jews. JEWISH QUARTERLY 31, 1 (Fall 1983/Win 1984) 37-40.

An examination of Luther's anti-Judaism and of Heiko Oberman's views (see no. 218). The latter "stressed that the intensity of Luther's anti-Judaism must be seen as an integral part of his struggle for the renewal of the Christian society and of the Church." Wistrich sees Luther's antisemitism as rooted in "the Gospels themselves, in early Pauline Christianity..."

THE MODERN PERIOD (1789-1985)

General

0234. אופנהיים, ישראל. תולדות יהודי פולין במאה ה-19 בראי ההיסטוריוגראפיה הפולנית של המאה ה-20. אומה ותולדותיה, חלק ב: העת החדשה, ערך שמואל אטינגר. ירושלים: מרכז זלמן שזר, 1984. עמ' 65-86.

[Oppenheim, Israel. The History of 19th Century Polish Jewry as Reflected in 20th Century Polish Historiography. NATION AND HISTORY: STUDIES IN THE HISTORY OF THE JEWISH PEOPLE, Vol. 2, ed. Shmuel Ettinger. Jerusalem: Zalman Shazar Center, 1984. Pp. 65-86.]

Surveys Polish historiography of the 19th and 20th centuries, but particularly the period between the World Wars. The historians concentrate on two spheres: the economic sphere, in which Jews are depicted as conspiring to exploit Polish farmers and landowners, to monopolize trade, and thereby to destroy Poland; the sphere of support, or lack thereof, for Polish nationalist aspirations, in which Jews are described as supporting the occupying powers against the national interest. Most of the writers believed that the solution to the "Jewish problem" is assimilation.

0235. בכרך, צבי. גזענות בשרות הפוליטיקה: מן המוניזם אל הנאציזם. ירושלים: הוצאת מאגנס, 1985. 182 עמ'.

[Bacharach, Zvi. RACISM - THE TOOL OF POLITICS: FROM MONISM TOWARDS NAZISM. Jerusalem: Magnes Press, 1985. 182 pp.]

Discusses the political development of racist ideology in Germany from the 19th century until the Nazi rise to power, and deals also with the Jewish reaction to antisemitism. Social Darwinism and the monistic idea, i.e. that one causal law governs nature, are the roots of racial ideas in Germany.

0236. ליפשיץ, משה. תולדות עם ישראל בדורות האחרונים: התנועה הלאומית. חלק א. תל-אביב: אור-עם, 1985. 242 עמ'.

[Lifshitz, Moshe. A HISTORY OF THE PEOPLE OF ISRAEL IN RECENT GENERATIONS: THE NATIONAL MOVEMENT. Part I. Tel-Aviv: Or-Am, 1985. 242 pp.]

A textbook for schoolchildren dealing with the history of Jewish nationalism and Zionism in the 19th and 20th centuries, up to 1945. Ch. 2 (pp. 12-20) deals with 19th century European antisemitism. Chs. 20-28 (pp. 169-242) deal with the Holocaust period.

0237. תיבון, אליעזר. הזיוף הגדול. עת-מול 9, 6 <56> (אוג 1984) 19-21.

[Tibbon, Eliezer. The Great Forgery. EIT-MOL 9, 6 <56> (Aug 1984) 19-21.]

Traces the history, since the French Revolution, of the belief in a Jewish conspiracy to overthrow society, and of the fraudulent "Protocols of the Elders of Zion," from its origins in a Russian attempt to accuse international Jewry of trying to overthrow the Tsarist regime and up to the Nazi period.

0238. Appel, John; Appel, Selma. JEWS IN AMERICAN GRAPHIC SATIRE AND HUMOR. Cincinnati, OH: American Jewish Archives, 1984. 23 pp.

Accompanies an exhibition from the authors' collection. An account of the development of Jewish stereotypes in caricatures from the late 19th century to the present. Includes many illustrations.

0239. Atlan, Liliane et al. LES JUIFS DANS L'HISTOIRE DE 1933 A NOS JOURS. Paris: PACEJ, 1984. 159 pp.

A textbook for schoolchildren, comprising a history of the Jews from 1933 to the present, including some material on earlier periods. Deals with antisemitism, relations between Christians and Jews, and especially the attitude of the Vatican towards the Jews between 1964-1983. (See also no. 1089.)

0240. Baker, Leonard. BRANDEIS AND FRANKFURTER: A DUAL BIOGRAPHY. New York: Harper and Row, 1984. vi, 567 pp.

See the index for references to antisemitism.

0241. Banki, Judith H. The Image of Jews in Christian Teaching. JOURNAL OF ECUMENICAL STUDIES 21, 3 (Sum 1984) 437-451.

A survey of content analysis in Protestant and Catholic textbooks since the inception of various studies beginning in the 1930s, due to a deep concern that "certain Christian teachings and preaching about Jews and Judaism represented one of the deep-seated and enduring sources of antisemitism."

0242. Berneri, Camillo. L'EBREO ANTISEMITA. Presentazione di Alberto Cavaglion. Traduzione di Rosa Zotto. Roma: Carucci, 1984. 115 pp. Originally published as "Le juif antisémite" (Paris: Vita, 1935).

A psychological study of Jewish self-hatred, which is explained by the inferiority complex and transference - i.e. hatred of those who represent what the person does not wish to be. Describes the cases of Otto Weininger, Benjamin Disraeli, and Karl Marx.

0243. Boutang, Pierre. MAURRAS: LA DESTINEE ET L'OEUVRE. Paris: Plon, 1984. 710 pp.

On the life and thought of Charles Maurras (1868-1952), the French writer, political activist and antisemite, editor of "L'Action Française," who was sentenced to life imprisonment after World War II for collaboration with the Nazis. Pp. 161-177 discuss the Dreyfus Affair.

0244. Bristow, Edward. History versus Memory: Jews and White Slavery. MOMENT 9, 4 (Apr 1984) 44-49.

Deals with the questions: "How widespread was the Jewish involvement? What did anti-Semites make of it? How did Jews respond to it?" Covers the period ca.1870-1930.

0245. Charles, Pierre. Les Protocoles des Sages de Sion. RENCONTRE - CHRETIENS ET JUIFS 18, 1 <77> (1984) 35-56. Reprint of an article which first appeared in the "Nouvelle Revue Théologique" 65 (1938).

A history of the publication and the dissemination of the "Protocols of the Elders of Zion." Compares the Protocols with the "Dialogue aux enfers entre Machiavel et Montesquieu" by Maurice Joly (1864), revealed in 1921 by the Times of London as the source of the Protocols.

Shows how the dialogue, a satire against the regime of Napoleon III, was clumsily reworked to provide evidence of a Jewish conspiracy.

0246. Daim, Wilfried. DER MANN, DER HITLER DIE IDEEN GAB: DIE SEKTIERERISCHEN GRUNDLAGEN DES NATIONALSOZIALISMUS. 2nd, rev. ed. Wien: H. Boehlaus Nachf., 1985. 316 pp.

A study of the life and ideas of the Austrian Joerg Lanz von Liebenfels (1874-1954), and his influence on Hitler's racist ideology. Discusses the racist "Order of the New Temple," founded by Lanz von Liebenfels in 1900, and his journal "Ostara."

0247. Dawidowicz, Lucy S. ON EQUAL TERMS: JEWS IN AMERICA, 1881-1981. New York: Holt, Rinehart and Winston, 1984. 194 pp. Revised version of an article which appeared in the "American Jewish Year Book," 1982 (pp. 3-98).

Pp. 37-41 refer to antisemitism during the Civil War and the rise in social discrimination during the 1870s and 1880s. Describes the foundation of organizations like the American Jewish Committee, the American Jewish Congress, and the ADL in the early 20th century to defend American Jews against antisemitism and to help persecuted Jews abroad. For antisemitism from 1920 to 1939, see pp. 86-94. For antisemitism during and since World War II, see the index.

0248. Dicker, Herman. AUS WUERTTEMBERGS JUEDISCHER VERGANGENHEIT UND GEGENWART. Gerlingen: Bleicher Verlag, 1984. 191 pp. Trans. from the English (see next entry).

0249. Dicker, Herman. CREATIVITY, HOLOCAUST, RECONSTRUCTION: JEWISH LIFE IN WUERTTEMBERG, PAST AND PRESENT. New York: Sepher-Hermon Press, 1984. xxii, 234 pp.

A history of the Jews in Wuerttemberg, from 1828 to 1945. Chs. 5-6 deal with antisemitism before the First World War and during the Third Reich, as well as Jewish reactions to it.

0250. Dietrich, Donald J. Modern German Catholic Antisemitism. FACE TO FACE 12 (Win 1985) 4-10. Also appeared in CHRISTIAN JEWISH RELATIONS 18, 2 (June 1985) 21-35.

An examination of the Catholic antisemitic milieu in Germany between 1870 and 1945. During the "Kulturkampf," the Catholic Center Party identified its liberal attackers with the Jews and became fiercely antisemitic. After 1879, with the alliance with the state, Catholic antisemitism was less blatant but helped to create an atmosphere in which Nazism became respectable. Neither the Church nor the Catholic parties supported the Nazi Party, but "they took no moral stand against its antisemitism." (See also no. 1231.)

0251. Diner, Dan. "Grundbuch des Planeten": Zur Geopolitik Karl Haushofers. VIERTELJAHRSHEFTE FUER ZEITGESCHICHTE 32, 1 (Jan 1984) 1-28.

A study of the theories of Karl Haushofer (1869-1946), an important German geopolitician. Pp. 6-10 describe his belief that Jews were responsible for urbanization and industrialization - i.e. for the contamination of nature. Nevertheless, he was a "traditional" antisemite, not a racist.

0252. Dinnerstein, Leonard. The Historiography of American Antisemitism. IMMIGRATION HISTORY NEWSLETTER 16, 2 (1984) 2-7. Unseen.

0253. Ettinger, Shmuel. The Position of Jews in Soviet Culture: A Historical Survey. JEWS IN SOVIET CULTURE, ed. Jack Miller. New Brunswick, NJ: Transaction Books, 1984. Pp. 1-21.

Notes that since Jews began to contribute to general Russian culture in the mid-19th century, their presence has elicited antisemitic reactions, which reached their height in Stalin's persecutions of Jewish writers and artists. Today, many nationalist writers continue to portray the Jews as corrupting Soviet society; some of them blame the Jews for the Revolution.

0254. Fontette, François de. SOCIOLOGIE DE L'ANTISEMITISME. Paris: Presses Universitaires de France, 1984. 127 pp. (Que sais-je?, 2194).

Examines the various definitions of a Jew in order to understand why the Jews have been persecuted and still suffer from antisemitism. Discusses Jewish existence in the Diaspora, the phenomenon of Jewish self-hatred, the Christian Church and antisemitism (especially the Vatican), antisemitism in the USSR, and anti-Zionism.

0255. Friedman, Milton. Capitalism and the Jews. ENCOUNTER 63, 1 (June 1984) 74-79.

The noted economist gives a two-fold explanation for the opposition of Jews to capitalism, despite their enormous debt to it. Firstly, during the 19th century the anti-capitalist Left supported emancipation. Secondly, they are subconsciously attempting to prove the fallacy of the antisemitic stereotype depicting the Jews as selfish and materialistic. In the author's view, Werner Sombart's "Die Juden und das Wirtschaftsleben" (1911), commonly considered antisemitic, is in fact pro-Jewish.

0256. Fubini, Guido. L'ANTISEMITISMO DEI POVERI. Firenze: Editrice la Giuntina, 1984. 100 pp.

A sociological study of antisemitism, particularly in the 20th century, viewed as a rejection of the Jews by different groups in society - Europeans, socialists (including discussion of Karl Marx), Soviets, fascists, Blacks, and others. Denies Antonio Gramsci's statement that antisemitism is nonexistent in Italy.

0257. Glazer, Nathan. Que "pèsent" les juifs dans la vie politique des Etats-Unis? NOUVEAUX CAHIERS 79 (Win 1984/1985) 30-37. "Trans. from the English, to be published in May 1985 in ANNALES DU C.R.A.A., 1984, Université de Bordeaux III" (unseen).

Discusses Jewish influence on American politics from the beginning of the 20th century up to the present. Includes issues such as the State Department's animosity towards Jews, the antisemitism of the 1920s, immigration restrictions in the 1930s-1940s. Concludes that today Jewish and US interests coincide more than ever before.

0258. Goldscheider, Calvin; Zuckerman, Alan S. THE TRANSFORMATION OF THE JEWS. Chicago: University of Chicago Press, 1984. 249 pp.

An analysis of modern Jewish society and politics, and their evolution from the 1780s until today. See pp. 136-153 for a discussion of political antisemitism.

0259. Grynberg, Henryk. PRAWDA NIEARTYSTYCZNA [The Unartistic Truth]. Berlin [West]: Ed. Archipelag, 1984. 145 pp.

Eight essays by a Polish Jewish writer who experienced the Holocaust as a child in Poland. Discusses antisemitism in general and in Poland. It is viewed as an irrational sentiment, the roots of which lie in the Christian attitude towards the Jews, caused by religious rivalry. Denies the existence of a special "Polish antisemitism." One essay discusses the reflection of the Holocaust in Polish literature.

0260. Hamerow, Theodore S. Cravat Jews and Caftan Jews. COMMENTARY 77, 5 (May 1984) 29-38. A German trans. appeared in VERSUNKENE WELT (see no. 288).

A survey of German Jewry in the 19th and 20th centuries, with emphasis on assimilation, the influx of the Ostjuden, and the development of racial antisemitism.

0261. Hanák, Péter, ed. ZSIDOKERDES, ASSZIMILACIO, ANTISZEMITIZMUS: TANULMANYOK A ZSIDOKERDESROEL A HUSZADIK SZASADI MAGYARORSZAGON [The Jewish Question, Assimilation, Antisemitism: Studies on the Jewish Question in 20th Century Hungary]. Budapest: Gondolat, 1984. 381 pp.

A collection of excerpts from the works of Hungarian writers (pp.17-114) and four essays - by Erik Molnár, István Bibó (pp. 135-294; see discussion by E. George in entry no. 656), Gyoergy Száraz, Péter Hanák.

0262. Hertzberg, Arthur. Zionism as Affirmative Action. HADASSAH MAGAZINE 66, 10 (June 1985) 22-25.

Zionism was an attempt to solve the problems of mounting antisemitism at the end of the 19th century, a form of "affirmative action" to end prejudice against Jews. Also discusses anti-Zionism.

0263. Hirsch, Emmanuel, ed. JUDAISME ET DROITS DE L'HOMME. Paris: Librairie des Libertés, 1984. 243 pp. (Bibliotheque des Droits de l'Homme et des Libertés Fondamentales. Collection Idéologies et Droits de l'Homme).

Papers given at a symposium held by the ADLF, Paris, 1983. Articles dealing with antisemitism: Léon Abramowicz: Les Juifs et les droits de l'homme sous la Révolution française: Quelques aspects de l'émancipation (87-95); Claude Tapia: La lutte des Juifs d'Afrique du Nord pour leur dignité (97-116); Serge-Allain Rozenblum: La violation des droits des Juifs en URSS (169-173); Jacques

Tarnero: Israël, cet obscur objet du délire (175-181); Carole Sandrel: Bernard Lazare, récupéré par les antisemites? (199-205).

0264. Hirschfeld, Magnus. Von Ursprung des deutschen Rassismus. TRIBUENE 95 (1985) 146-156.

An extract from the author's work "Racism" (of which only the English translation was published in London, 1938), dealing with the development of race theories in Western Europe during the 19th and 20th centuries, particularly those of German scientists in the 1920s (e.g. Hans Guenther, Ludwig Woltmann, I.F. Clauss, and F. Lenz). Traces the origins of their ideas in the writings of Houston Stewart Chamberlain and Arthur Gobineau. Pp. 155-156 contain comments on Hirschfeld's life and work.

0265. Holden, Matthew. Reflections on Two Isolated Peoples. JEWS IN BLACK PERSPECTIVES: A DIALOGUE, ed. Joseph R. Washington. Rutherford, NJ: Fairleigh Dickinson University Press, 1984. Pp. 181-211.

Analyzes the emergence of the Black-Jewish political alliance. As a result of their role in the Leo Frank case, the American Jewish leadership became involved in the anti-lynching movement of the 1920s. The inclusion of both groups in the New Deal coalition gave them an incentive to cooperate on issues of racial equality. However, with the rise of ethnocentrism, that part of the leadership which saw a point in cooperation has lost decisive influence. Calls for a better understanding of each side's fear of assault by racism or antisemitism.

0266. Isbister, J.N. FREUD: AN INTRODUCTION TO HIS LIFE AND WORK. Cambridge: Polity Press, 1985. xi, 318 pp.

An analysis of the actual facts of Freud's childhood and life experiences as opposed to the version presented by Freud himself. Views Freud's encounters with antisemitism, and his belief that antisemitism prevented him from receiving academic recognition, as a key to his ambition to "conquer Rome" (the Christian Church) and to his attacks on religion. Freud's relations with Jung were also affected by his belief in Jung's antisemitism.

0267. Jakubowski, Jackie. Revolutioner, omvaelvningar, krig och makthavare har avloest varandra men den gamla antisemitismen lever kvar [Revolts, Revolutions, Wars and Great Powers Have Passed but the Old Antisemitism Lives On]. JUDISK KROENIKA, Special nr. 2: "Judarna i Sovjet" (Apr 1984) 8-9.

Summarizes the history of antisemitism in Tsarist Russia and in the USSR, from the end of the 18th century through the 20th, showing that the Jews had no rights as a national minority and that the old Russian antisemitism still exists in the USSR today.

0268. Johnson, Paul. Marxism vs. the Jews. COMMENTARY 77, 4 (Apr 1984) 28-34.

Describes the tendency of intellectuals to be seduced by antisemitism, explained by their search for a radical explanation for the ills of society, and transmitted to the modern world via the French Enlightenment. Marx was influenced by French anti-capitalist antisemitism and German philosophical antisemitism. His early works attacked Jews as capitalists; later he widened his attack to the entire bourgeois class. "If Anti-Semitism is the socialism of fools, socialism is the Anti-Semitism of intellectuals." These ideas live on in Soviet anti-Zionism.

0269. Katz, Jacob. Lectures defectueuses de l'antisémitisme. SENS 36, 5/6 (May/June 1984) 203-214. Translated from "Commentary," July 1983.

Takes issue with three approaches used by historians to explain modern antisemitism: the socio-political, the psychoanalytic, and the emphasis on racial ideology. Modern antisemitism is a blend, and "any proper history of it must consist of a careful tracing of the processes whereby vestigial anti-Jewish beliefs, dating back to the Middle Ages, were successfully combined with a whole variety of modern ideologies." Mentions also the current tendency of historians to de-Judaize antisemitism by the universalization of the Holocaust.

0270. Kedward, H.R. Charles Maurras and the True France. IDEAS INTO POLITICS: ASPECTS OF EUROPEAN HISTORY 1880-1950, eds. R.J. Bullen, H. Pogge von Strandmann, A.B. Polonsky. London: Croom Helm; Totowa, NJ: Barnes and Noble, 1984. Pp. 119-129.

Discusses the thought of Maurras (1868-1952), the French nationalist writer and antisemite, in regard to what he termed the True France (the Monarchy) and Anti-France (the Republic). Describes his writings and activities during the 19th and 20th centuries - against Dreyfus, on the establishment of the Action Française, and his support for Pétain's Vichy government.

0271. Keilson, Hans. Linker Antisemitismus? DER DEUTSCHUNTERRICHT 37, 3 (1985) 69-86.

Examines the anti-Jewish and anti-Zionist attitudes of various left-wing thinkers, leaders, and movements from the 19th century up to the 1982 Lebanon war.

0272. Keller, Michael. Von Schwarz-Weiss-Rot zum Hakenkreuz: Zum Lebensweg von Ferdinand Dreher (1878-1945). WETTERAUER GESCHICHTSBLAETTER: BEIHEFT 1 (1984) 1-37.

On Ferdinand Dreher, a right-wing antisemite, the first director of the city archives in Friedberg, Hesse (1907-1945). He accused the Jews of responsibility for spreading materialism and bourgeois values, and for the German defeat in World War I. In 1933 he joined the Nazi party. Includes facsimiles from anti-Jewish pamphlets found amongst his papers.

0273. Kuehner, Hans. Rom und Jerusalem: Zwielichtige Israel-Politik des Vatikans. TRIBUENE 89 (1984) 62-75.

A survey of the Vatican's attitude towards the Zionist movement, from the time of Herzl and up to the massacre at Sabra and Shatila. Concludes that the Vatican's anti-Zionist stance stems from traditional anti-Judaism and antisemitism.

0274. Large, David C. Wagner's Bayreuth Disciples. WAGNERISM IN EUROPEAN CULTURE AND POLITICS, eds. David C. Large and William Weber. Ithaca, NY: Cornell University Press, 1984. Pp. 72-133.

A survey of the careers and intellectual contributions of members of the "Bayreuth Circle," from the first Bayreuth festival (1876) to the Nazi period. This group admired Wagner's confused and inconsistent social and political thought, including his antisemitism. Among those discussed is Houston Stewart Chamberlain, Wagner's son-in-law.

0275. Lévy, Albert. Racismes ou racisme. SENS 36, 5/6 (May/June 1984) 227-231.

Modern secular antisemitism adopted certain traditional Christian accusations. Progressively, this secularization led to racist antisemitism which dehumanized the Jews. The anti-immigrant racism now flourishing in France uses the immigrants as scapegoats, in the same way that antisemitic racism used Jews.

0276. Lindemann, Dirk. Richard Wagner: Twilight of the Nazi Spell. INDIANA SOCIAL STUDIES QUARTERLY 37, 3 (1984/1985) 64-76.

Suggests that the cultural and political influence of Richard Wagner on Nazism has been exaggerated. Many of his works were antithetical to fascism and were banned by the Nazis. Nevertheless, his antisemitism does provide a link to Nazi ideology.

0277. Littell, Franklin H. AMERICAN PROTESTANTISM AND ANTI-SEMITISM. Jerusalem: Hebrew University, Institute of Contemporary Jewry, Vidal Sassoon International Center for the Study of Antisemitism, Shazar Library, 1985. 51 pp. (Study Circle on World Jewry in the Home of the President of Israel, 7 Jan. 1985). Appeared also in Hebrew translation.

Reviews Protestant attitudes to Jews and Judaism in the 19th and 20th centuries, and discusses the place of the Jewish people and of a restored Israel in modern Christian thinking. The body of American Protestantism is founded on traditional teachings, and the bedrock of theological and cultural antisemitism still exists, although modified slightly over the years.

0278. Malino, Frances; Wasserstein, Bernard, eds. THE JEWS IN MODERN FRANCE. Hanover, NH: University Press of New England for Brandeis University Press, 1985. xii, 354 pp. (Tauber Institute Series, 4).

A collection of essays and papers, most of which were presented at a conference at Brandeis University, April 1983, on the encounter between Jews and French society since the Revolution. Essays dealing specifically with antisemitism: William B. Cohen; Irwin Wall: French Communism and the Jews (81-102); Zeev Sternhell: The Roots of Popular Anti-Semitism in the Third Republic (103-134);

Stephen A. Schuker: Origins of the "Jewish Problem" in the Later Third Republic (135-180); Patrice Higonnet: On the Extent of Anti-Semitism in Modern France (207-213); Pierre Birnbaum: Anti-Semitism and Anticapitalism in Modern France (214-223); Michael R. Marrus: Are the French Antisemitic? Evidence in the 1980s (224-242).

0279. LE MONOTHEISME CONTRE LE RACISME: Les actes du Colloque organisé le 29 mars 1981 par la Loge Saädia Gaon du B'nai B'rith. Paris: Union Française des Associations B'nai B'rith, 1984. 80 pp.

Lectures delivered at the symposium by Jews, Muslims, and Christians, dealing with problems of racism, including antisemitism.

0280. Moser, Jonny. Antisemitismus zwischen Doppeladler und Krukenkreuz. WIEN 1870-1930: TRAUM UND WIRKLICHKEIT, ed. Robert Waissenberger. Salzburg: Residenz Verlag, 1984. Pp. 64-70.

A survey of antisemitic activity and propaganda in various circles in Vienna, including the Catholic Church, political parties and, in the later period, the Nazi Party.

0281. Opitz, Reinhard. FASCHISMUS UND NEOFASCHISMUS. Frankfurt a.M.: Verlag Marxistische Blaetter, 1985. 537 pp. Unseen.

0282. Oren, Dan A. JOINING THE CLUB: A HISTORY OF JEWS AND YALE. New Haven, CT: Yale University Press, 1985. xiv, 440 pp. (The Yale Scene: University Series, 4).

Traces the history of Jews at Yale University from the 18th century to 1977, on the basis of archival records and interviews. The increase in social prejudice against Jews in the 1870s was also felt at Yale, especially as the Jews' intellectual achievements and academic preoccupations clashed with the Yale emphasis on social life and sports. Admissions procedures were liberalized during 1910-1920, but in 1923 an unofficial quota was imposed which lasted till the 1940s. Includes statistical tables on enrollment of Jews.

0283. O'Riordan, Manus. Anti-Semitism in Irish Politics. IRISH-JEWISH YEAR BOOK 34 (1984/1985) 15-27.

A survey of the strong antisemitic current in the Irish nationalist tradition. The founder of the nationalist Sinn Fein movement, Arthur Griffith, influenced by European and Afrikaner antisemitism at the end of the 19th century, published virulent attacks on the Jews in his "United Irishman" newspaper. Other leading Irish politicians demanded an alliance with Nazi Germany. The Irish fascist movement, the Blueshirts, and the religious antisemitism of Father Denis Fahey of the Holy Ghost Missionary Order continued to go unchecked, and influenced the Republican revival until the late 1950s.

0284. Poliakov, Léon. THE HISTORY OF ANTI-SEMITISM. VOL. 4: SUICIDAL EUROPE, 1870-1933. Trans. by George Klim. New York: Vanguard Press, 1985. xi, 422 pp. Originally published as "Histoire de l'antisémitisme: L'Europe suicidaire" (Paris: Calmann-Lévy, 1977).

Traces the rise of modern racist antisemitism from its origins in Germany, and the powerful impetus given to it in France during the Dreyfus Affair and in Russia at the time of the pogroms. The idea of the domination of the West by the Jews pervaded the European elite at the end of the 19th century and gradually spread to the masses as a result of the social and political crisis of World War I. Emphasizes the central role played by the idea of the Jewish conspiracy, not only in Germany but also in Western Europe, the USA, and the USSR during the First World War and the period of the Russian revolution, and traces links between Tsarist and Nazi antisemitism.

0285. Porter, Jack Nusan. Ukrainian-Jewish Relations Yesterday and Today. JOURNAL OF ETHNIC STUDIES 11, 4 (Win 1984) 117-123.

Describes efforts in the USA to initiate a dialogue between Jews and Ukrainians, Poles, and other Slavic groups. Second-generation Slavs tend to be less antisemitic, as second-generation Jews are less hostile to Slavs. Both groups also share a common enemy - Soviet Russia. Deeper understanding of the national and economic conflicts between Ukrainians and Jews gives a clearer picture of the origins of Ukrainian antisemitism and the reasons for collaboration of some Ukrainians with the Nazis. Describes recent research on these subjects.

0286. Preschel, Pearl Liba. THE JEWS OF CORFU. Dissertation - New York University, 1984. 186 pp.

Discusses the history of the Jews of Corfu from the 12th century till the destruction of the community during the Holocaust. The community was generally prosperous and enjoyed much freedom. In 1891, however, the Jews were accused of ritual murder, after which conditions deteriorated and many Jews emigrated.

0287. Radkau, Joachim. Richard Wagners Erloesung vom Faschismus durch die Emigration. EXILFORSCHUNG 3 (1985) 71-105.

Deals with the attitude of exiled German intellectuals (e.g. Thomas Mann, Theodor Adorno) towards the antisemitism of Richard Wagner. They tended to minimize the contribution of Wagner's antisemitism to Nazi ideology. Some of them even argued that the so-called direct line leading from Wagner's ideas to Nazism is an invention of Nazi propaganda, and that Wagner's antisemitism was a marginal and unimportant aspect of his work.

0288. Riedl, Joachim; Hofmann, Hans Peter, eds. VERSUNKENE WELT. Wien: Jewish Welcome Service, 1984. 242 pp.

Published as a catalog for three Jewish events taking place in Vienna in November-December 1984: an exhibition of photographs; an exhibition and study on Judaism and films; a symposium on "The World of Yesterday." Contains excerpts from Jewish literary works, and articles, some of which have appeared previously. Includes: Theodore S. Hamerow: Krawattenjuden und Kaftanjuden [Trans. from the English - see no. 260] (77-90); J. Riedl: Vor den Toten steht der Tod (109-118); J. Riedl: Geht doch in die Donau: Ueber den oesterreichischen Anteil am Holocaust (165-170); Jonathan Davis: Der unsichtbare Jude: Ueber das System des Antisemitismus in Film (195-197); Max Lippmann: Wollt ihr den totalen Film? Ueber die Darstellung juedischen Menschen im Film (198-204); J. Riedl; Marcel Ophuls: Schuldig! [An interview with Ophuls, discussing the Holocaust, antisemitism, and films] (205-214); Michael May: Antisemitismus heute (219-221).

0289. Riess, Stephen A. A Fighting Chance: The Jewish-American Boxing Experience, 1890-1940. AMERICAN JEWISH HISTORY 74, 3 (Mar 1985) 223-254.

The Jewish boxing tradition began in late 18th century London, where Jews boxed "to gain respect, achieve social mobility and counter invidious racial prejudices which stereotyped Jews as weak cowards." American Jewish immigrant youths had similar motives; boxing was an extension of self-defense against racial slurs and violence. See also Riess' introduction to this issue of "American Jewish History" (pp. 211-221).

0290. Roemer, Ruth. SPRACHWISSENSCHAFT UND RASSENIDEOLOGIE IN DEUTSCHLAND. Muenchen: Wilhelm Fink Verlag, 1985. 238 pp.

Deals with relations between philology and racist ideology in Germany. Ch. 11 (pp. 171-181), "Die Juden," deals with the anti-Jewish attitudes of various German philologists, from Jacob Grimm (early 19th century) up to the Nazi period.

0291. Rosenberg, Stuart E. THE NEW JEWISH IDENTITY IN AMERICA. New York: Hippocrene Books, 1985. xiv, 290 pp.

A survey of the influence of American life on the Jewish community from colonial times to the present. Part 3 (pp. 89-117), "Jews and Their Host Nations," discusses the origins of antisemitism, and whether America can succeed in transcending it where other nations have failed.

0292. Rothschild, Sylvia. A SPECIAL LEGACY: AN ORAL HISTORY OF SOVIET JEWISH EMIGRES IN THE UNITED STATES. New York: Simon and Schuster, 1985. 336 pp.

A history of Soviet Jewry from the Revolution to the 1970s, based on the oral testimony of 176 Soviet Jewish emigrés. Ch. 1 (pp. 27-57) deals with antisemitism and problems of Jewish identity. Ch. 2 (pp. 58-112) presents personal views of events, such as the euphoria after the Revolution, changed attitudes towards Jews under Stalin and during World War II, Stalin's purges, etc. Other chapters describe life in Soviet Russia, the second-class status of Jewish citizens, and the rise in Jewish consciousness which led to the emigration movement.

0293. Rubinstein, Hilary. Manifestations of Literary and Cultural Anti-Semitism in Australia, 1856-1946 (Part 2). MELBOURNE CHRONICLE 40 (Feb/Mar 1984) 2-4.

The blatant antisemitism of the Sydney "Bulletin" shows that cultural antisemitism existed in Australia although Australian Jews were seldom attacked as a group or as individuals. The "Bulletin" was obsessed with international Jewry, accused of plotting a financial conspiracy. The "Bulletin" printed antisemitic poems and cartoons; a sample of them is given here.

0294. Sessa, Anne Dzamba. At Wagner's Shrine: British and American Wagnerians. WAGNERISM IN EUROPEAN CULTURE AND POLITICS, eds. David C. Large, William Weber. Ithaca, NY: Cornell University Press, 1984. Pp. 246-277.

In this study of Wagner's influence in Britain and America up to World War II, his antisemitism is mentioned as having been particularly troublesome to his admirers. They tried to explain it away as an eccentricity. Wagner societies in these countries never took on the characteristics of a racist political cult.

0295. Sperber, Manès; Glaeser, Henri. Manès Sperber: Entretien avec Henri Glaeser. NOUVEAUX CAHIERS 76 (1984) 62-68.

A discussion of the popularity of totalitarian systems in the 19th and 20th centuries, and the phenomenon of antisemitism. Sees the key to these social phenomena in the psychology of man himself. A feeling of "angoisse" in every man gives rise to hatred. The diminution or lack of religious feeling brought about the search for a substitute "faith," the totalitarian regime.

0296. Velen, Victor A. Anti-Semitism and the Left. MIDSTREAM 31, 1 (Jan 1985) 8-12.

Antisemitism on the Left has existed since the time of the early Utopian Socialist Charles Fourier (1772-1837), who held that Jews personify the idea of commerce, the source of most social ills. Discusses also the antisemitic views of Pierre-Joseph Proudhon and Karl Marx. This trend has continued in the 20th century - for example, in the attitudes of the British Left towards Palestine and Israel, and in those of the German Socialists during the Weimar Republic.

0297. Volkov, Shulamit. Kontinuitaet und Diskontinuitaet im deutschen Antisemitismus 1878-1945. VIERTELJAHRSHEFTE FUER ZEITGESCHICHTE 33, 2 (Apr 1985) 221-244.

Argues that historians have tended to overstress the continuity between traditional and Nazi antisemitism, thereby neglecting novel elements in Nazi antisemitism, as well as the specific forms of antisemitic expression in the Second Empire.

0298. Washington, Joseph R., ed. JEWS IN BLACK PERSPECTIVES: A DIALOGUE. Rutherford, NJ: Fairleigh Dickinson University Press, 1984. 211 pp.

Selected papers from a symposium held by the University of Pennsylvania's Afro-American Studies program, March 1982, on relations between Jews and Blacks throughout the 20th century. Individual articles have been listed separately.

0299. Wechsler, Harold S. The Rationale for Restriction: Ethnicity and College Admission in America 1910-1980. AMERICAN QUARTERLY 36, 5 (Win 1984) 643-667.

An analysis of restrictions on the number of Jewish students in American colleges, examining the motives of the college authorities. Social acceptance or rejection of Jewish students by other students is described, based on excerpts from literary works.

0300. West, Richard. "Racism" and Anti-Semitism. THE SPECTATOR 252 <8113> (7 Jan 1984) 11-12.

A brief survey of the origin of the term "racism," and of antisemitism in the 19th and 20th centuries.

0301. Wheatcroft, Geoffrey. THE RANDLORDS. London: Weidenfeld and Nicolson, 1985. xix, 314 pp.

The story of the gold and diamond mining magnates of South Africa from the late 19th century to the present, many of whom were Jews. See the index for references to antisemitism in Europe and in South Africa, particularly during the period of the Boer War and the 1930s-1940s.

0302. Whitfield, Stephen J. VOICES OF JACOB, HANDS OF ESAU: JEWS IN AMERICAN LIFE AND THOUGHT. Hamden, CT: Archon Books, 1984. 322 pp.

Examines the Jewish experience in 20th century America. The four parts of the book deal with Jewish intellectual reactions to totalitarianism and the Holocaust, the history of American Jewry, the Jews in mass culture, and the Jews of the South. References to antisemitism occur throughout the book.

0303. Wistrich, Robert. HITLER'S APOCALYPSE: JEWS AND THE NAZI LEGACY. London: Weidenfeld and Nicolson, 1985. viii, 309 pp.

Argues that the annihilation of the Jewish people was the goal of the Nazi party from 1919 on, and that antisemitism was the central core of Adolf Hitler's creed and the main cause of the Second World War. Traces the origins of Hitler's apocalyptic war against the Jews to his background in pre-1914 Vienna. The Nazi themes have been picked up by Soviet, Arab and Islamic antisemitism disguised as "anti-Zionism." The Soviet Union today "presents a no less powerful source of antisemitism than Hitler's Third Reich in the 1930s and 1940s."

0304. Zoltai, Dénes. Wagner hier et aujourd'hui. NEOHELICON 11, 2 (1984) 43-63.

A response to the article by H. Zelinsky ("Neohelicon" 9, 1982) in which Wagner's antisemitism is described as the basis of a new religion of the arts which would have included the destruction of the Jews. Zoltai states that Wagner's antisemitism must be examined in the context of his times, and that he cannot be held reponsible for Nazi antisemitism and the Holocaust.

1789-1918: Europe

0305. אביהר, אליהו שמואל. השמדת-עם בתורות האנטישמיות של המאה ה-19. משואה 12 (אפריל 1984) 47-71.

[Avihar, Elijahu Shmuel. Genocide of a People According to the Teachings of Antisemitism of the 19th Century. MASSUAH 12 (Apr 1984) 47-71.]

Studies the theories of 19th century antisemitism in terms of historic responsibility for the genocide which took place in the 20th century. Surveys the influence of the French Revolution on antisemitism, the Napoleonic period, 1815 to 1848, Socialism, the development of race theory, and political antisemitism.

0306. אלכסנדר, גבריאל. ד"ר קארל לואגר, התנועה הנוצרית-
סוציאלית והיהודים בוינה של שלהי הקיסרות ההבסבורגית.
עבודת גמר לתואר מוסמך - האוניברסיטה העברית בירושלים,
החוג להיסטוריה, ספט' 1984. 126 עמ'.

[Alexander, Gabriel. DR. KARL LUEGER, THE CHRISTIAN SOCIAL PARTY, AND THE JEWS OF VIENNA AT THE END OF THE HABSBURG EMPIRE. M.A. thesis - Hebrew University of Jerusalem, Dept. of History, Sept. 1984. 126 pp.]

Covers the period 1897-1910, when Karl Lueger was mayor of Vienna and leader of the Christian Social Party. Focuses on the importance of antisemitism in the ideology of the party, and on the responses of the Jews.

0307. ביק (שאולי), אברהם. נצר משרשיו: מוצאו ועולמו היהודי של
קארל מארקס. תל אביב: הקיבוץ המאוחד, 1984. 96 עמ'.

[Bick (Shauli), Abraham. DEEP ARE THE ROOTS: GENEALOGY OF KARL MARX AND JUDAIC STRAIN IN HIS THOUGHT. Tel-Aviv: Hakibbutz HaMeuhad, 1984. 96 pp.]

Pp. 19-22 deal with Marx's essay "On the Jewish Question." Claims that Marx was in fact a defender of the Jews, and attacked them only as a symbol of a particular economic condition.

0308. בן-אורן, גרשון. מונטיפיורי ויהודי גרוזיה. פעמים 20
(1984) 69-76.

[Ben-Oren, Gershon. Montefiore and the Jews of Georgia. PE`AMIM 20 (1984) 69-76.]

In 1851 Moses Montefiore was informed of a blood libel the previous year against the Jews of Surami, Georgia. His intervention with Prince Vorontzev, the governor of Georgia, was unsuccessful. A private letter reveals that Vorontzev believed the charge and was active in the condemnation of seven Jews to penal servitude in Siberia. Anti-Jewish riots and blood libels in Georgia continued during the 1870s.

0309. טל, אוריאל. יהדות ונצרות ב'רייך השני'(1870-1914): תהליכים
היסטוריים בדרך לטוטאליטריות. הדפסה ב. ירושלים: הוצאת
מאגנס, האוניברסיטה העברית; יד ושם, 1985. 315 עמ'.

[Tal, Uriel. CHRISTIANS AND JEWS IN THE "SECOND REICH" (1870-1914): A STUDY IN THE RISE OF GERMAN TOTALITARIANISM. 2nd printing. Jerusalem: Magnes Press, Hebrew University; Yad Vashem, 1985. 315 pp.] Reprint of the 1969 ed. An English trans. appeared in 1975 (Ithaca: Cornell University Press).

A study of the attitudes of the German intelligentsia, and of Protestants and Catholics, towards Jews, and the development of antisemitic ideology, political parties and organizations in Germany. See particularly ch. 5 (pp. 175-235), "Christian and Anti-Christian Antisemitism," in which racist anti-Christian antisemitism is viewed as a secular transformation of Christian antisemitism, having absorbed the latter's terms, concepts, and attitudes.

0310. ליטוין, רנה; שלח, חזי, עורכים. מי מפחד מריכרד ואגנר; היבטים שונים של דמות שנויה במחלוקת. ירושלים: כתר, 1984. 349 עמ'.

[Litvin, Rina; Shelach, Hezi, eds. WHO'S AFRAID OF RICHARD WAGNER: ASPECTS OF A CONTROVERSIAL PERSONALITY. Jerusalem: Keter, 1984. 349 pp.]

A collection of articles, including ch. 3, "Wagner the Antisemite": Richard Wagner: Jewry in Music [trans. from the German] (203-218); Zvi Bacharach: Richard Wagner, the Anti-Humane Humanist (219-229); Otto Dov Kulka: Richard Wagner, from Democratic Radicalism to Racist Antisemitism (230-246).

0311. מאור, יצחק. "הסופות בנגב" כגורם להתעוררות התודעה הלאומית בקרב המשכילים היהודיים. דברי הקונגרס העולמי השמיני למדעי היהדות. ישיבות מרכזיות: תולדות עם ישראל. ירושלים: האיגוד העולמי למדעי היהדות, 1984. עמ' 1-12.

[Maor, Yitzhak. The "Sufot Banegev" as a Factor in the Rise of Nationalism among the Jewish Intelligentsia. PROCEEDINGS OF THE EIGHTH WORLD CONGRESS OF JEWISH STUDIES. PANEL SESSIONS: JEWISH HISTORY. Jerusalem: World Union of Jewish Studies, 1984. Pp. 1-12.]

Describes the antisemitism prevalent in Russia throughout the 19th century, culminating in the "Sufot Banegev," the pogroms in the south of Russia in 1881.

0312. מורגנשטרן, אריה. גזירת הגיוס לצבא הרוסי משנת 1827. ספר בר-אילן [בית-ספר תיכון דתי בנתניה] 1 (1985) 203-214.

[Morgenstern, Aryeh. The Decree on Recruitment to the Russian Army in 1827. SEFER BAR-ILAN [Religious High-School in Netanya] 1 (1985) 203-214.]

Surveys the anti-Jewish policies of the Tsars at the beginning of the 19th century, culminating in the "cantonist decree" of 1827, which imposed on the Jews a quota of children to be supplied annually as recruits for the army. Army service lasted 25 years, and began at age 18, although children were taken from age 12 for education at special institutions. The purpose of the decree was conversion and assimiliation of the Jews. Traces efforts of Western European Jewish leaders to cancel the decree. It remained in force until 1856.

0313. צימרמן, משה. האיש שהקדים את זומברט - לודולף הולסט. יהודים בכלכלה, ערך נחום גרוס. ירושלים: מרכז זלמן שזר, 1985. עמ' 245-256.

[Zimmermann, Moshe. The Man Who Preceded Sombart - Ludolf Holst. JEWS IN ECONOMIC LIFE, ed. Nachum Gross. Jerusalem: Zalman Shazar Center, 1985. Pp. 245-256.]

J.L. Holst (1756-1825), a conservative writer from Hamburg, analyzed the role of the Jews in the economic life of Hamburg at the beginning of the 19th century. He accused them of artificially increasing the demand for goods, which he saw as damaging to the state's economy. At the end of the 19th century, Sombart made use of Holst's views, without adopting his strongly anti-Jewish attitude.

0314. שריד, אברהם. ברנארד לאזאר - ממבשרי הציונות הסוציאליסטית. מאסף 15 (1985) 24-34.

[Sarid, Avraham. Bernard Lazare, a Herald of Socialist Zionism. ME'ASEF 15 (1985) 24-34.]

Deals with Bernard Lazare's attitudes towards the Jews and antisemitism, particularly as expressed in his book "L'Antisémitisme: Son histoire et ses causes" (1894). As a result of the Dreyfus Affair, he became a Zionist.

0315. Aberbach, Alan David. THE IDEAS OF RICHARD WAGNER: AN EXAMINATION AND ANALYSIS OF HIS MAJOR AESTHETIC, POLITICAL, ECONOMIC, SOCIAL AND RELIGIOUS THOUGHTS. Lanham, MD: University Press of America, 1984. x, 385 pp.

Deals with antisemitism in ch. 7 (pp. 267-308), "The Outmoded World of the Judaic-Christian Tradition." In "Das Judentum in der Musik" (1850) Wagner denied the capacity of Jews to have deep emotional feelings in music and art. Nevertheless, their financial power gave them influence in musical life. Despite the assistance he received from Jewish friends and patrons, the supposed threat posed to Germany by the Jews became an obsession for Wagner, and all his enemies were identified with the Jews. "Wagner's attitude toward Jews was remarkably inconsistent...anti-Jewish although not necessarily anti-Semitic..."

0316. Abramsky, Chimen. The Visits to Russia. THE CENTURY OF MOSES MONTEFIORE, eds. Sonia and V.D. Lipman. London: Oxford University Press, 1985. Pp. 254-265.

Surveys the anti-Jewish policies of Tsar Nicholas II, especially his decree of 1843 expelling Jews from the border area wih Prussia. In 1846 Moses Montefiore visited Russia in an attempt to have the decree repealed, but to no avail. The Tsar and his ministers did not conceal their hostility to the Jews and the determination to end the Jews' traditional way of life.

0317. Allen, Ann Taylor. SATIRE AND SOCIETY IN WILHELMINE GERMANY: "KLADDERADATSCH" AND "SIMPLICISSIMUS," 1890-1914. Lexington, KY: University Press of Kentucky, 1984. xiii, 264 pp.

A study of two satirical journals as a reflection of German history and culture of the times. See the index for references to Jews, including antisemitism, and particularly pp. 188-194, "The Jew: Pariah or Parvenu?"

0318. Andrews, Christopher. Secrets of the Kaiser. THE LISTENER 111 <2861> (7 June 1984) 10-11.

Recent research on Emperor Wilhelm II (1859-1941) of Germany, mainly by British and American historians, has thrown new light on his manic personality and obsessions, which included antisemitism. After his deposition (1918)

Wilhelm blamed his fate on "a Jewish conspiracy," and as early as 1919 advocated the extermination of the Jews.

0319. Barkai, Avraham. German-Jewish Migrations in the Nineteenth Century, 1830-1910. LEO BAECK INSTITUTE YEAR BOOK 30 (1985) 301-318.

Pp. 312-313 mention antisemitic restrictions in Germany which motivated Jewish emigration to the US until the 1870s, and the emigration from Austria after the 1848 pogroms.

0320. Behrendt, Bernd. ZWISCHEN PARADOX UND PARALOGISMUS: WELTANSCHAULICHE GRUNDZUEGE EINER KULTURKRITIK IN DEN NEUNZIGER JAHREN DES 19. JAHRHUNDERTS AM BEISPIEL AUGUST JULIUS LANGBEHN. Frankfurt a.M.: Lang, 1984. 559 pp.

Langbehn (1851-1907) was a German nationalist writer and popular philosopher. Discusses also his antisemitism. Unseen.

0321. Bensussan, Gérard. Rosa Luxembourg et la question juive. LES TEMPS MODERNES 472 (Nov 1985) 652-668.

Discusses the insistence of Rosa Luxemburg (1870-1919) that the "Jewish question" and Jewish nationality do not exist. She was frequently attacked by antisemites, both from the right and the left. She adopted Marx's attitude that antisemitism was essentially a class problem - the emancipation of society from exploitation. She refused to take part in the struggle over the Dreyfus Affair or against the pogroms in Russia.

0322. Berk, Stephen M. YEAR OF CRISIS, YEAR OF HOPE: RUSSIAN JEWRY AND THE POGROMS OF 1881-1882. Westport, CT: Greenwood Press, 1985. xvi, 231 pp. (Contributions in Ethnic Studies, 11).

Examines the causes of the pogroms in the south of Russia in 1881-1882 and the consequences for Russian Jewry. The reforms of Tsar Alexander II had partially removed restrictions on Jews and raised hopes for a solution of the Jewish question through integration. The pogroms, the failure of the government to suppress them, and the ambivalent reactions of the intelligentsia disappointed these hopes. The revolutionary movement welcomed the pogroms as "a bridge to the Revolution." The last part of the book describes Jewish responses to the pogroms (pp. 101-186).

0323. Blanchard, William H. Karl Marx and the Jewish Question. POLITICAL PSYCHOLOGY 5, 3 (Sept 1984) 365-374. Condensed from his book REVOLUTIONARY MORALITY (see the following entry).

Marx's "first paper on the Jewish question described the Jew as a greedy manipulator of money. A few years later he was still attacking greedy manipulators of money but his target had changed from the Jew to the capitalist." Marx's original hostility to capitalism, identified with Judaism, was perhaps stimulated by attempts of his "petty bourgeois" Jewish parents to restrain his extravagance. Jewishness and moneymaking were endowed with world significance as a threat to social justice.

0324. Blanchard, William. REVOLUTIONARY MORALITY: A PSYCHOSEXUAL ANALYSIS OF TWELVE REVOLUTIONISTS. Santa Barbara: ABC Clio Press, 1984. 281 pp. Unseen. (See the preceding entry.)

0325. Blejwas, Stanislaus A. Polish Positivism and the Jews. JEWISH SOCIAL STUDIES 46, 1 (Win 1984) 21-36.

Examines the attitude toward the Jews of the Polish Positivists in the 19th century, a liberal and patriotic group oriented toward modernization on a Western European model. They condemned antisemitism and favored Jewish equality. While criticizing the poor Jewish masses as anti-social, they assumed that by means of education and emancipation these Jews would assimilate within Polish society. However, assimilationism won little popular Jewish support.

0326. Burns, Michael Thornton. RURAL SOCIETY AND FRENCH POLITICS: BOULANGISM AND THE DREYFUS AFFAIR, 1886-1900. Princeton, NJ: Princeton University Press, 1984. xi, 249 pp. Based on the author's diss. - Yale University, 1981.

Investigates the minimal impact on the French rural population of the two major issues which "rocked" fin-de-siècle France - the extreme nationalism of Ernest Georges Boulanger and his followers, and the Dreyfus Affair with its accompanying antisemitism.

0327. Chevalier, Yves. Bernard-Lazare et l'antisémitisme. SENS 36, 7 (July 1984) 263-275.

Bernard-Lazare's view of antisemitism changed during the process of writing his work "L'Antisémitisme: Son histoire et ses causes" (1894), the first serious analysis of the problem. Initially he saw Jewish separatism as the cause of antisemitism, but while working on his book he became aware of external and more complex causes - religious, racial, political, and economic. In later works he no longer saw assimilation and socialism as a solution, and temporarily adopted Zionism.

0328. Chickering, Roger. WE MEN WHO FEEL MOST GERMAN: A CULTURAL STUDY OF THE PAN-GERMAN LEAGUE, 1886-1914. Boston: G. Allen and Unwin, 1984. xiv, 365 pp.

The Pan-Germans called for the consolidation of Germans throughout the world, and for the construction of a giant Central-European state, including areas of Russia and France - a policy which required general war. They were also at the forefront in promoting racist antisemitism in Imperial Germany.

0329. Cohen, Steve. Antisemitism, Immigration Controls and the Welfare State. CRITICAL SOCIAL POLICY 13 (Sum 1985) 73-92.

Immigration controls and racism are a central part of the ideology of the welfare state. Immigration controls facing Black people in Britain today originate in the institutionalized antisemitism of the early 20th century, often fostered by both capital and sections of the labor movement.

0330. Eloni, Yehuda. The Zionist Movement and the German Social Democratic Party, 1897-1918. STUDIES IN ZIONISM 5, 2 <10> (1984) 181-199.

Describes the debate in Zionist and non-Zionist Jewish organizations as to whether the Jews should take an organized stand in internal politics, in reaction to antisemitism. Zionists supported the Social Democratic Party in order to defeat the antisemitic parties, even though the SPD rejected Zionism and called for assimilation of the Jews. During the German revolution of 1918 the Zionists hoped that the socialists would change their position i.e. recognize the national rights of the Jewish people and help them to establish a homeland in Palestine.

0331. Engelmann, Hans. KIRCHE AM ABGRUND: ADOLF STOECKER UND SEINE ANTIJUEDISCHE BEWEGUNG. Berlin (West): Institut Kirche und Judentum, 1984. 185 pp.

Adolf Stoecker (1835-1909) was a demagogic preacher, an antisemite, and founder of the Christian Social Party. Unseen.

0332. Faehrmann, Willi. Die Buschhoff Affaere in Xanten. DAS BILD DES JUDEN IN DER VOLKS- UND JUGENDLITERATUR VOM 18. JAHRHUNDERT BIS 1945, ed. Heinrich Pleticha. Wuerzburg: Koenigshausen und Neumann, 1985. Pp. 127-139.

A report of the course of the blood libel trial in Xanten, Germany (1891-92) against Adolf Buschhoff, based on articles in contemporary newspapers, the protocol of the trial, and the Reichstag protocols.

0333. Fein, Yvonne. The Jewish Reactions and Responses to the Phenomenon of Anti-Semitism in Wilhelmine Germany, 1890-1914. MELBOURNE CHRONICLE 43 (Aug/Sept 1984) 2-4.

Examines the phenomenon as perceived by various historians, and discusses the Jewish reactions at the time.

0334. Ferenczi, Caspar. Nationalismus und Neoslawismus in Russland vor dem Ersten Weltkrieg. FORSCHUNGEN ZUR OSTEUROPAEISCHEN GESCHICHTE 34 (1984) 7-127.

Pp. 52-59 include discussion of the antisemitic views of the right-wing parties in Russia before the First World War, which were motivated by nationalism, racism, and socio-economic considerations. The Jews were accused of being cosmopolitans, capitalists, and socialists, and of using their international power to destroy Russia.

0335. Figes, Orlando. Ludwig Boerne and the Formation of a Radical Critique of Judaism. LEO BAECK INSTITUTE YEAR BOOK 29 (1984) 351-382.

The Jews' position within the Socialist movement was a difficult one due to the self-hatred of its Jewish members as well as to the movement's anti-Jewish tradition. The case of Ludwig Boerne shows that "it was also not uncommon for Jews to arrive at their socialism, both emotionally and intellectually, through a radical critique of 'Judaism' which then turned into a more general attack on bourgeois society."

0336. Gelfand, Toby. Le Professeur Germain Sée (1818-1896) et le "problème juif" dans la médecine à Paris. REVUE D'HISTOIRE DE LA MEDECINE HEBRAIQUE 38, 2 <153> (July 1985) 23-27.

Describes the career of Germain Sée, the first Jewish professor to enter the National Academy of Medicine in France, and the rise of French antisemitism at the end of the 19th century. Sée was attacked as a Jew in various literary works and in the press. He opposed the myth that Jews are especially prone to mental illness and thus dangerous to the French people.

0337. Gilman, Sander L. Karl Marx and the Secret Language of the Jews. MODERN JUDAISM 4, 3 (Oct 1984) 275-294.

Deals with Marx's Jewish self-hatred, especially in regard to the "language" of the Jews (i.e. their modes of expression, appearance, etc.), to his own swarthy appearance, and to the economic activities considered Jewish. Marx was torn between his identification with German, Christian culture which stigmatized Jews and Jewish traits, and his awareness that others saw him as a Jew. He thus felt a need to prove himself a non-Jew.

0338. Gilman, Sander L. Jews and Mental Illness: Medical Metaphors, Anti-Semitism, and the Jewish Response. JOURNAL OF THE HISTORY OF THE BEHAVIORAL SCIENCES 20, 2 (Apr 1984) 150-159.

A study of the belief, widespread from the late 18th century to the early 20th, that the Jews are psychopaths and degenerates, predisposed to mental illness.

0339. Goldstein, Jan. The Wandering Jew and the Problem of Psychiatric Anti-Semitism in Fin-de-Siècle France. JOURNAL OF CONTEMPORARY HISTORY 20, 4 (Oct 1985) 521-551.

Scientific study of the Jews began in the second half of the 19th century, but clashed with liberal opposition to singling them out. Jewish and Gentile doctors debated whether there was a specialized Jewish pathology. The founder of French psychiatry, Charcot, popularized the idea of a Jewish propensity to neurosis. His pupil, Henri Miege, tied it to "travelling insanity," a modern literalization of the legend of the "Wandering Jew." These ideas were exploited by antisemites like Drumont.

0340. González García, Isidoro. Los intelectuales españoles y la cuestion judía en la Europa de final del siglo XIX: La corriente liberal española. EL OLIVO 9 <21> (Jan-June 1985) 87-110.

An analysis of the Jewish question and antisemitism as reflected in public opinion and in the views of politicians and liberal intellectuals in Spain. Special emphasis is given to the attitudes of Emilio Castelar, Benito Perez Galdos and the "Institución Libre de la Enseñanza" circle.

0341. Green, Nancy L. LES TRAVAILLEURS IMMIGRES JUIFS A LA BELLE EPOQUE: LE "PLETZEL" DE PARIS. Paris: Fayard, 1985. 361 pp.

An account of the immigration of East European Jews to Paris at the end of the 19th century. Mentions antisemitism in Eastern Europe as a factor in Jewish emigration. The Dreyfus Affair had little effect on the attractions of France as a destination. Ch. 2 (pp. 61-94) describes the reaction of the antisemitic press to the arrival of the Jews. The French Jewish community feared that the influx would draw attention to Jews; however, they welcomed the evidence provided by the newcomers of the existence of a Jewish proletariat, to counter antisemitic claims that the Jews were capitalists and parasites.

0342. Gregor-Dellin, Martin. Erloesung dem Erloeser: Eine Betrachtung zu Richard Wagner. NEOHELICON 11, 2 (1984) 9-26.

Richard Wagner's antisemitism and racism is discussed on pp. 23-26 in the framework of a broader examination of his concept of redemption.

0343. Greive, Hermann. Zur multikausalen Bedingtheit des modernen Antisemitismus. JUDAICA 40, 3 (1984) 133-144.

Argues against one-factor analysis; modern antisemitism is caused by many factors - political, economic, social. Analyzes antisemitic agitation in Germany in 1878/79, aroused by Catholic circles and by Adolf Stoecker.

0344. Handler, Andrew. FROM THE GHETTO TO THE GAMES: JEWISH ATHLETES IN HUNGARY. New York: Columbia University Press, 1985. xii, 140 pp. (East European Monographs, 192).

Documents the contribution of Hungarian Jews to sporting achievements in Hungary in the 19th and 20th centuries. In the 19th century the Jews' interest in sports was part of a process of Magyarization and assimilation, despite antisemitism in Hungarian society. Successful Jewish athletes continued to face discrimination, malicious remarks, etc.

0345. Hawlik, Johannes. DER BUERGERKAISER: KARL LUEGER UND SEINE ZEIT. Wien: Herold-Verlag, 1985. 224 pp.

A biography of Karl Lueger (1844-1910), Mayor of Vienna from 1897 to 1910. Apart from his municipal and political activities, Lueger is well-known for his antisemitic ideas and propaganda, which were a means to achieve political power and not an essential part of his ideology (see pp. 194-201). Hitler was influenced not so much by these antisemitic ideas as by Lueger's political style and propaganda.

0346. Heid, Ludger. East European Jewish Workers in the Ruhr, 1915-1922. LEO BAECK INSTITUTE YEAR BOOK 30 (1985) 141-168.

The influx of East European Jews into the heavy industries of the Ruhr region aroused considerable antisemitic feeling. The local German-Jewish community assisted the migrants but feared this upsurge of antisemitism.

0347. Henig, Gerald S. San Francisco Jewry and the Russian Visa Controversy of 1911. WESTERN STATES JEWISH HISTORY 18, 1 (Oct 1985) 58-66.

Examines the role of the Jews of San Francisco in the Jewish campaign to abrogate the 1832 Russo-American Commercial Treaty, since Russia refused to give visas to American Jews. Unlike other California communities, the San Francisco leadership avoided mass rallies and preferred to lobby Congressmen and the local legislature. The treaty was abrogated but the censure of world opinion had little effect on the Russian government's treatment of Jews.

0348. Henriques, U.R.Q. Journey to Romania, 1867. THE CENTURY OF MOSES MONTEFIORE, eds. Sonia and V.D. Lipman. London: Oxford University Press, 1985. Pp. 230-253.

In 1867 antisemitism in Romania, encouraged by the virulently nationalistic press, was mainly social and economic. The government of Ion Bratianu adopted a policy of expulsion of Jews, and persecutions took place in Jassy and Galatz. Montefiore travelled to Romania to protest against this policy. While warmly received by the ruler, he was met by antisemitic crowds and his visit was ineffective.

0349. Hildermeier, Manfred. Die juedische Frage im Zarenreich: Zum Problem der unterbliebenden Emanzipation. JAHRBUECHER FUER GESCHICHTE OSTEUROPAS 32, 3 (1984) 321-357.

An anaysis of Tsarist policy towards the Jews from the 18th century till the outbreak of the First World War. At the beginning of the 20th century Tsarist Russia was, together with Romania, the only European country in which the Jews were not emancipated and suffered from legal, social and economic discriminaton and pogroms.

0350. Himmelfarb, Gertrude. The "Real" Marx. COMMENTARY 79, 4 (Apr 1985) 37-43.

A critique of Bruce Mazlish's book "The Meaning of Karl Marx" (see no. 368). The psychological analysis of Marx as a "humanist" thinker is criticized as simplistic and inadequate. Mazlish's claims that Marx was "not an anti-Semite as such" are unconvincing. The "humanism" of the early Marx cannot be reconciled with his antisemitism.

0351. Holmes, Colin. The Myth of Fairness: Racial Violence in Britain, 1911-1919. HISTORY TODAY 35 (Oct 1985) 41-45.

Mentions anti-Jewish riots in Tredegar, in strongly Protestant, strike-torn Wales in 1911, directed against Jewish-owned shops. During World War I, many Jews who were Russian or Polish subjects resisted conscription to fight as allies of the Tsar. In 1917, there was anti-Jewish rioting in Leeds and in the East End of London. However, none of this violence came from or was condoned by the state.

0352. Kampe, Norbert. Jews and Antisemites at Universities in Imperial Germany (I): Jewish Students - Social History and Social Conflict. LEO BAECK INSTITUTE YEAR BOOK 30 (1985) 357-394.

During the period 1871-1918, a Jewish educational elite emerged and strove to join the German "Bildungsbuergertum." The exclusion of Jews from academic and social life became a major student issue as a result of social conflict between upwardly mobile Jews, many of petty bourgeois origin, and Gentile students of the old elite at a time of crisis in the academic labor market. This crisis was blamed on the "over-representation" of Jewish students and other outsiders. Many German academics turned at this time from liberalism to conservatism and modern social antisemitism.

0353. Katz, Jacob. German Culture and the Jews. COMMENTARY 77, 2 (Feb 1984) 54-59.

A paper delivered at an International Conference on German Jewry, Clark University, Oct. 1983. Although 19th century German Jewry absorbed the surrounding culture, they never fully integrated but remained a sub-group in German society. They were great supporters of culture (literature, music, theater) but were considered socially inferior. The cultural antisemitism of the 19th century is discussed, with particular reference to Wagner.

0354. Katz, Jacob. HORS DU GHETTO: L'EMANCIPATION DES JUIFS EN EUROPE, 1770-1870. Trans. by J.F. Sené. Paris: Hachette, 1984. xxvii, 289 pp. Originally published as "Out of the Ghetto" (Cambridge, MA: Harvard University Press, 1973).

An analysis of the Jewish experience in Western Europe since the Emancipation. Discrimination against the Jews in pre-Emancipation society is also described. Discusses Gentile resistance to the integration of Jews in society as a result of the Christian antisemitic heritage, and socialist and romantic antisemitism.

0355. Katz, Jacob. "Die Juden sind unser Unglueck": Reflexionen ueber ein antisemitisches Schlagwort. TRIBUENE 92 (1984) 58-66.

Traces the formation of popular antisemitic slogans by leaders of antisemitic political parties, like Otto

Glogau and Adolf Stoecker, between 1870 and 1880. These slogans were adopted by a wide section of the population as a result of the economic, social and political crisis in Germany at this period.

0356. Kaufmann, Uri Robert. Swiss Jewry: From the "Jewish Village" to the City, 1780-1930. LEO BAECK INSTITUTE YEAR BOOK 30 (1985) 283-299.

Up to 1864-1866 most Swiss cantons did not allow Jews to migrate. The majority of Swiss Jews were restricted to rural communities, to the estates of minor foreign nobility. The political and social background for these restrictions are described on pp. 284-287, and the struggle for emancipation following international pressure on pp. 288-289.

0357. Kieniewicz, Stefan. Polacy i Żydzi w XIX w. [Poles and Jews in the 19th century]. POLITYKA 50 (Dec 1984) 8.

Describes Polish-Jewish relations in the period of the partitions of Poland (1795-1918). Touches on the problem of antisemitism in different parts of the Polish territories, especially areas under Russian and Austrian rule. Includes remarks on the Jew in Polish literature.

0358. Lambroza, Shlomo. Pleve, Kishinev and the Jewish Question: A Reappraisal. NATIONALITIES PAPERS 12, 1 (1984) 117-127.

Appointed Minister of the Interior in 1902 to suppress the rising discontent in Russia, Plehve had little sympathy for the oppressed Russian Jews. Contrary to myth, however, he was not linked to the Kishinev pogrom, and actually eased some anti-Jewish regulations after the pogrom.

0359. Lang, W.M. de. WEERKLANK VAN DE MORTARA-AFFAIRE IN NEDERLAND 1858-1859 [Echoes of the Mortara Affair in the Netherlands 1858-1859]. Dissertation - Amsterdam, 1984. Unseen. (See the following entry.)

0360. Lang, W.M. de. Weerklank van de Mortara-Affaire in Nederland [Echos of the Mortara Affair in the Netherlands]. STUDIA ROSENTHALIANA 19, 2 (Oct 1985) 159-173. Based on the author's dissertation (see the preceding entry).

Studies the reaction in the Netherlands to the abduction of Edgar Mortara by agents of the Papal government in 1858. Dutch Catholics - with the exception of S. Lipman, a Catholic journalist converted from Judaism - supported the Papal refusal to return the child to his Jewish parents. Dutch Protestants were not concerned with the fate of the Jewish child, and rather saw the case as an opportunity to attack the Catholic Church.

0361. Le Rider, Jacques. DER FALL OTTO WEININGER: WURZELN DES ANTIFEMINISMUS UND ANTISEMITISMUS. Wien: Loecker-Verlag, 1984. 292 pp.

An analysis of Otto Weininger's ideas as an example of the 19th century anti-enlightenment tradition in which "modern" anti-feminism and antisemitism are rooted. Ch. 9 (pp. 189-220) discusses Weininger's antisemitic views as expressed in his book "Geschlecht und Charakter" (1903).

0362. Lombarès, Michel de. L'AFFAIRE DREYFUS. Paris: Charles-Lavauzelle, 1985. 224 pp.

An account of the Dreyfus Affair, giving details of further evidence supporting the author's thesis that neither Dreyfus nor Esterhazy were traitors to France. This theory was first presented in his book "L'Affaire Dreyfus, la clef du mystère" (Paris: R. Laffont, 1972).

0363. Lonsbach, Richard Maximilian. FRIEDRICH NIETZSCHE UND DIE JUDEN: EIN VERSUCH. 2nd ed. Bonn: Bouvier, 1985. 102 pp.

Reprint of the first edition (Stockholm, 1939), with an epilogue by Heinz Robert Schlette (pp. 91-100) describing the life of the author. Lonsbach (1890-1974) was born as R.M. Cahen in Germany, emigrated in 1937 to Switzerland, and published under a pseudonym. The book analyzes Nietzsche's attitude towards the Jews, stressing pro-Jewish views in contrast to Nazi antisemitism.

0364. Lowenstein, Steven M. Governmental Jewish Policies in Early Nineteenth Century Germany and Russia: A Comparison. JEWISH SOCIAL STUDIES 46, 3/4 (Sum/Fall 1984) 303-320.

Examines why similar measures adopted by both governments in relation to the Jews had very differing results. Tsar Nicholas I adopted German policies of integration, such as encouraging Jews to engage in agriculture, organizing Jewish communal bodies, military conscription, and secular education. In Germany these measures were progressive, whereas in Russia they were oppressive because they were ruthlessly forced upon the Jews, they carried no promise of legal equality, and their purpose was to convert the Jews or to exclude them from Russian society.

0365. Lunn, Kenneth. Immigrants and British Labour's Response. HISTORY TODAY 35 (Nov 1985) 48-52.

Deals with Jewish immigration to Britain before World War I. Jews were accused of taking jobs away from the British, undercutting wages, and creating an alien culture. Antisemitic stereotypes suggested that Jews represented the archetypal capitalist, sought to be owners rather than employees, and were unenthusiastic trade unionists. However, trade union hostility, though widespread, was short-lived.

0366. Markish, Simon. Vjaceslav Ivanov et les Juifs. CAHIERS DU MONDE RUSSE ET SOVIETIQUE 25, 1 (Jan-Mar 1984) 35-47.

Discusses the attitude towards the Jews of Vjaceslav Ivanov (1866-1949), a pre-revolutionary Russian poet, who stated that antisemitism is anti-Christian. Compares Ivanov's attitudes to those of his mentor Dostoevsky and others.

0367. Maurer, Trude. Medizinalpolizei und Antisemitismus. JAHRBUECHER FUER GESCHICHTE OSTEUROPAS 33, 2 (1985) 205-230.

Deals with the German policy of closing the eastern border to immigration of "Ostjuden" (Jews from Eastern Europe) during the First World War. This policy resulted from antisemitic stereotypes describing the eastern Jews as dirty, a health hazard, and swindlers in trade.

0368. Mazlish, Bruce. THE MEANING OF KARL MARX. Oxford: Oxford University Press, 1984. viii, 188 pp.

A "close textual analysis" of the life and work of Karl Marx, emphasizing that his thought took the form of a secular religion, deeply affected by his Christian upbringing. Supports the research trend seeing a unity between the thought of the young, "humanist" Marx and the later "scientific" thinker. Marx's early essay, "On the Jewish Question," is dealt with in ch. 6 (pp. 70-77). In presenting Judaism as a synonym for capitalism, Marx echoes antisemitic stereotypes, perhaps influenced by self-hatred. In the process, he reached fruitful insights about society and history.

0369. Méchoulan, Henri. La cédule de 1802 ou le dernier soubresant de l'anti-judaïsme espagnol d'état. REVUE DES ETUDES JUIVES 143, 3/4 (July-Dec 1984) 373-376.

Discusses the cedula of 1802 which excluded Jews from the categories of foreigners encouraged to enter and to settle Spain. In 1816 a decree was issued renewing the cedula. This was one of the last measures of official religious racism in Europe in the 19th century.

0370. Nord, Philip G. Three Views of Christian Democracy in "Fin de Siècle" France. JOURNAL OF CONTEMPORARY HISTORY 19, 4 (Oct 1984) 713-727.

The three currents of (Catholic) Christian Democratic thought in the 1890s were: traditionalist, republican-progressive, and nationalist-antisemitic. The latter appealed to the lower middle-classes and the small business community. Discusses the "Union Nationale" founded by the abbé Garnier and the "Union Fraternelle du Commerce et de l'Industrie" founded by Léon Harmel.

0371. Orbach, Alexander. THE RUSSIAN-JEWISH LEADERSHIP AND THE POGROMS OF 1881-1882: THE RESPONSE FROM ST. PETERSBURG. Pittsburgh, PA: University of Pittsburgh, Russian and East European Studies Program, 1984. 37 pp. (Carl Beck Papers in Russian and East European Studies, 308).

Examines different Russian Jewish solutions to antisemitism, such as "Zionism," mass emigration to the West, and integration of Jews into Russian society. Describes the anti-Jewish attitudes of Tsar Alexander III and his Minister of the Interior N.P. Ignatiev in their contacts with the Jewish notables of St. Petersburg who lobbied for the full integration of Russian Jewry during and after the pogroms of 1881-82.

0372. Pierrard, Pierre. Le "complot juif" selon Drumont. L'HISTOIRE 84 (Dec 1985) 32-34, 37.

Describes the events of 1 May 1891 in Fourmies, France, when authorities ordered the shooting of workers who were planning to demonstrate. In 1892, Edouard Drumont published "Le Secret de Fourmies" in which he "explains" that this shooting was the work of a Jewish conspiracy.

0373. Poliakov, Léon. HISTORIA DEL ANTISEMITISMO: LA EMANCIPACION Y LA REACCION RACISTA. Trad. del francés de Elena Rotés. Barcelona: Muchnik Editores, 1985. 311 pp. Originally published as "Histoire de l'antisémitisme: De Voltaire à Wagner" (Paris: Calmann-Lévy, 1968).

Discusses antisemitism in the 19th century in France, Germany, Great Britain, and Russia.

0374. Pollak, Michael. VIENNE 1900: UNE IDENTITE BLESSEE. Paris: Ed. Gallimard-Julliard, 1984. 220 pp.

Includes a chapter on antisemitism in Vienna at the end of the 19th century (pp. 75-107). The decline of liberalism and the development of the nationalist and Christian-Social movements brought in their wake waves of antisemitism. Quotes fragments dealing with antisemitism from Arthur Schnitzler's autobiography. Also discusses Herzl's Zionist ideas and the Jewish reaction to them.

0375. Polonsky, Antony. Political Anti-Semitism in Britain before the First World War. STUDIA NAD FASZYZMEM I ZBRODNIAMI HITLEROWSKIMI 9 (1985) 67-87.

Political antisemitism in Britain at this period was produced by the interaction of the large immigration of East European Jews, the development of European political antisemitism, and political and social crises. Immigrant Jews were criticized for causing low wages and for unwillingness to assimilate, but violent incidents were few. The Aliens Act restricting their entry was passed in 1905. Among intellectuals, the group linked to Hilaire Belloc, Cecil Chesterton and G.K. Chesterton linked Jews to financial scandal. Leo Maxse saw the Jews as tools of Germany, and the left-wing J.A. Hobson accused Jewish speculators of dragging Britain into the Boer War.

0376. Pozzi, Regina. Alle origini del razzismo contemporaneo: Il caso di Ernest Renan. RIVISTA DI STORIA CONTEMPORANEA 4 (Oct 1985) 497-520.

Traces the philosophy of Ernest Renan (1823-1892), the French philologist and historian of religion, as seen in his writings and lectures. In some of his works, e.g. "Histoire generale des langues sémitiques," Renan tried to prove the superiority of the Indo-European nations over the Semitic ones by linguistic analysis. Discusses the ties between this work and the racial antisemitism developing in late 19th century France. However, in other works, Renan underlined the importance of the Jewish contribution to the idea of justice; these works had an influence on socialism.

0377. Prinz, Arthur. JUDEN IM DEUTSCHEN WIRTSCHAFTSLEBEN: SOZIALE UND WIRTSCHAFTLICHE STRUKTUR IM WANDEL 1850-1914. Ed. Avraham Barkai. Tuebingen: Mohr, 1984. ix, 202 pp. (Schriftenreihe wissenschaftlicher Abhandlungen des Leo Baeck Instituts, 43).

Ch. 3 (pp. 67-92), entitled "Industrialisierung und Gruenderkrise 1871-1874," contains a section on political antisemitism.

0378. Rathenau, Walther. WALTHER RATHENAU - INDUSTRIALIST, BANKER, INTELLECTUAL AND POLITICIAN: NOTES AND DIARIES 1907-1922. Ed. Hartmut Pogge von Strandmann. Trans. Caroline Pinder-Cracraft. Oxford: Clarendon Press, 1985. xv, 346 pp.

Includes the assimilated German Jewish politician's ambivalent attitude towards Judaism, and his opposition to conversion, viewed as a concession to the official policy of discrimination. He saw assimilation and the fight for equality as the solution to the Jewish problem.

0379. Rosenman, Stanley. A Psychohistorical Source of Psychoanalysis: Malformed Jewish Psyches in an Immolating Setting. ISRAEL JOURNAL OF PSYCHIATRY AND RELATED SCIENCES 21, 2 (1984) 103-116.

Presents the reactions of assimilated Jews to rejection by German society during the 19th century from a psychoanalytical point of view. Their reactions were often based on delusions due to their need for acceptance and love from the host society, e.g. blaming themselves for antisemitism, or viewing it as an atavism that Gentile society would outgrow. The trauma of persecution created a victim consciousness - a need to repeat calamities. Psychoanalysis was created as an attempt to repair this psychological damage and to redeem the Gentiles from antisemitism.

0380. Rosenthal, Bernice Glatzer. Wagner and Wagnerian Ideas in Russia. WAGNERISM IN EUROPEAN CULTURE AND POLITICS, eds. David C. Large and William Weber. Ithaca, NY: Cornell University Press, 1984. Pp. 198-245.

A study of Wagner's influence on Russian culture from the 1890s to the 1920s. Pp. 223-225 discuss Russian figures who adopted Wagner's ideas on the Jewish question - for example, Vol'fing (Emil Medtner, 1872-1936), who repeated the themes of Wagner's "Jewry in Music," claiming that Jews were always alien to the folk spirit of the nations in which they lived; he maintained that to doubt the contribution of the Jews to civilization did not imply antisemitism.

0381. Rotenstreich, Nathan. JEWS AND GERMAN PHILOSOPHY: THE POLEMICS OF EMANCIPATION. New York: Schocken Books, 1984. viii, 266 pp.

Discusses the encounter between German philosophy and Judaism in the 18th and 19th centuries, focusing on the Hegelian and Kantian systems, and analyzes their negative evaluation of Judaism. Explores also the views of Schopenhauer and Nietzsche, and Jewish responses.

0382. Sandrel, Carole. Bernard Lazare, récupéré par les antisémites? JUDAISME ET DROITS DE L'HOMME, ed. Emmanuel Hirsch. Paris: Librairie des Libertés, 1984. Pp. 199-205.

Bernard Lazare's book "L'Antisemitisme: Son histoire et ses causes" (1894) has been used by antisemites against the Jews. Describes Bernard Lazare's life, Zionist activities, and other works, in order to prove that he later changed his opinions and should not be regarded as a traitor to the Jewish people.

0383. Scham, Alan M. Emile Zola and French Anti-Semitism. MIDSTREAM 30, 10 (Dec 1984) 52-55.

Excerpted from the author's work-in-progress "Emile Zola: Life of a Rebel." It was Zola who was ultimately responsible for having Dreyfus recalled from Devil's Island for a new trial at Rennes in 1899. Zola blamed the Catholic Church for deliberately promoting an overt policy of antisemitism.

0384. Schoeps, Julius H. Ritualmordbeschuldigung und Blut-aberglaube: Die Affaere Buschhoff im niederrheinischen Xanten. KOELN UND DAS RHEINISCHE JUDENTUM, eds. Jutta Bohnke-Kollwitz et al. Koeln: J.P. Bachem, 1984. Pp. 286-300.

Ritual murder accusations against Jews were widespread in Germany between 1880-1900. One example was the blood libel of Xanten, where a Jewish butcher, Adolf Buschhoff, was tried for the ritual murder of a five-year-old child in June 1891. Describes the event, the course of the trial, and the responses of antisemites to the acquittal.

0385. Simon, L. Bernard-Lazare: Etait-il vraiment un prophète? SENS 36, 7 (July 1984) 251-262.

A sketch of Bernard Lazare's life. As a young man he was antisemitic and xenophobic. He later played a role in the defense of Dreyfus and joined Herzl in the beginnings of the Zionist organization.

0386. Smolarski, Henri. Enlèvement à Bologne. TRIBUNE JUIVE 892 (1-7 Nov 1985) 14-17.

An account of the unsuccessful intervention of Moses Montefiore in the case of the kidnapping of Edgar Mortara by papal authorities in 1858.

0387. Stern, Edith. Gerichtsmedizinische Bezuege zu dem Ritualmordprozess von Tiszaeszlár, Ungarn, 1882-83. MONATSSCHRIFT FUER KRIMINOLOGIE UND STRAFRECHTSREFORM 67, 1 (1984) 38-47.

Deals with medical testimony given during the ritual murder trial in Tiszaeszlár, Hungary (1882-1883), the first time medical science was used in a court.

0388. Suchy, Barbara. Antisemitismus in den Jahren vor dem Ersten Weltkrieg. KOELN UND DAS RHEINISCHE JUDENTUM, eds. Jutta Bohnke-Kollwitz et al. Koeln: J.P. Bachem, 1984. Pp. 252-286.

A study of antisemitism in the lower Rhineland before the First World War. Claims that political antisemitism did not strike deep roots in this region, but antisemitism on the level of everyday life was widespread, as found in pamphlets, posters, articles, popular poems and books.

0389. Szordykowska, Barbara. Kwestia żydowska w Rosji w latach 1905-1907 [The Jewish Question in Russia in the Years 1905-1907]. BIULETYN ZYDOWSKIEGO INSTYTUTU HISTORYCZNEGO W POLSCE 129/130 (Jan-June 1984) 3-14.

Discusses the situation of the Jews in Russia before and during the first Russian revolution. Anti-Jewish legislation since 1791 and the pogroms at the end of the 19th-early 20th centuries are described. During the 1905 revolution, there was a tendency towards recognition of the principle of civic equality for Jews, but without concrete effect.

0390. Szordykowska, Barbara. Problematyka żydowska w rosyjskiej Dumie Państwowej w latach 1907-1912 [The Jewish Problem in the Russian Duma in the Years 1907-1912]. BIULETYN ZYDOWSKIEGO INSTYTUTU HISTORYCZNEGO W POLSCE 131/132 (July-Dec 1984) 71-82.

Describes the Jewish question as reflected in discussions of the Duma based on protocols of the meetings and articles from the press. The discussions concerned the participation of Jews in the army and the laws of the Pale of Settlement which restricted the Jews' movements, and reflect the growth of antisemitic and chauvinistic attitudes in the Duma after 1907.

0391. Toury, Jacob. Troubled Beginnings: The Emergence of the Oesterreichisch-Israelitische Union. LEO BAECK INSTITUTE YEAR BOOK 30 (1985) 457-475.

The rise of modern antisemitism in Austria did not provoke any outcry from Viennese Jewry until the young District Rabbi, Joseph Samuel Bloch, rose in 1882 to attack the silence of Jewish liberals and to call for Jewish self-help. Bloch's denunciations of August Rohling, author of "Der Talmudjude," brought him popularity and a seat in the Reichsrat. In 1884 he founded a newspaper, the "Oesterreichische Wochenschrift," which fought antisemitism. The Oesterreichisch-Israelitische Union, founded in 1885/6, failed to fulfil Bloch's hopes to establish an ethnic religious Jewish pressure group.

0392. Vigne, Eric; Gauchet, Marcel. Entretien: Le démon du soupçon. L'HISTOIRE 84 (Dec 1985) 48-56.

An interview with the political scientist Gauchet on the subject of conspiracy theories and their origins. On pp. 54-56 he refers to the Jewish conspiracy and the "Protocols of the Elders of Zion."

0393. Vincenzi, Christopher. The Aliens Act 1905. NEW COMMUNITY 12 (Sum 1985) 275-284.

The Aliens Act of 1905 in Great Britain was intended to restrict Jewish immigration which was said to reduce wages and cause overcrowding. Unseen.

0394. Wank, Solomon. A Case of Aristocratic Antisemitism in Austria: Count Aehrenthal and the Jews, 1878-1907. LEO BAECK INSTITUTE YEAR BOOK 30 (1985) 435-456.

Count Alois Lexa von Aehrenthal (diplomat and Austrian Foreign Minister, 1906-1912), as a young official, held moderate reformist conservative views. He expressed vague antisemitism but never subscribed to radical antisemitic party politics. When the monarchic and aristocratic political order was threatened by revolutionary forces, Aehrenthal became an arch-conservative and absolutist - social and political disturbances were no longer explained by structural problems and social forces, but by a Jewish conspiracy.

0395. Wassermann, Henry; Franz, Eckhart G. "Kauft nicht bei Juden": Der politische Antisemitismus des spaeten 19. Jahrhunderts in Darmstadt. JUDEN ALS DARMSTAEDTER BUERGER, ed. E.G. Franz. Darmstadt: Eduard Roether Verlag, 1984. Pp. 123-136.

Describes political antisemitism during the Second Empire in Germany, resulting from the crisis of 1873. Antisemitic parties and organizations, like the Agrarian Movement of Otto Boeckel and the German Reform Union, organized mass meetings and spread antisemitic propaganda in the press.

0396. Weinberg, David. "Heureux comme Dieu en France": East European Jewish Immigrants in Paris, 1881-1914. STUDIES IN CONTEMPORARY JEWRY 1 (1984) 26-54.

Discusses the East European Jews' organizational, economic, political, and cultural activities. Mentions the reactions to their influx by antisemites such as Edouard Drumont, and the Jewish reactions to the Dreyfus Affair.

0397. Werner, Eric. Juden um Richard und Cosima Wagner. OESTERREICHISCHE AKADEMIE DER WISSENSCHAFTEN: PHIL.-HIST. KLASSE: ANZEIGER 121, 1-9 <1984> (1985) 131-169.

Deals with the attitude of Richard Wagner to various Jewish musicians, e.g. Meyerbeer, Halévy, Hermann Levi. Traces Wagner's antisemitism to three sources: nationalism, anarchism and, only at the end of his life, racism.

0398. Wertheimer, Jack. Jewish Lobbyists and the German Citizenship Law of 1914: A Documentary Account. STUDIES IN CONTEMPORARY JEWRY 1 (1984) 140-162.

The leaders of German Jewry were concerned about the fairness of procedures concerning acquisition or loss of citizenship and were "convinced that state officials routinely discriminated against Jews." In 1913, when the Reichstag deliberated over a new Reich and State Citizenship Law, German Jewry lobbied actively on behalf of Jewish interests.

0399. Wessling, Berndt Wilhelm. MEYERBEER: WAGNERS BEUTE - HEINES GEISEL. Duesseldorf: Droste Verlag, 1984. 308 pp.

This biography of the German-Jewish composer Meyerbeer (1767-1864) discusses his relations with Richard Wagner. Wagner's hatred for the successful Meyerbeer was the immediate cause for writing his antisemitic pamphlet "Das Judentum in der Musik" (1850).

0400. Zelinsky, Hartmut. Der Kapellmeister Hermann Levi und seine Stellung zu Richard Wagner und Bayreuth, oder der Tod als Gralsgebiet. JAHRBUCH DES INSTITUTS FUER DEUTSCHE GESCHICHTE: BEIHEFT 6 (1984) 309-351.

Examines the relationship between the German-Jewish conductor Hermann Levi (1839-1900) and Richard and Cosima Wagner. Despite Levi's great admiration for Wagner's works and his willingness to conduct the first performance of "Parsifal," Wagner had hesitations about letting a Jew conduct this Christian work. Describes the antisemitic potential of "Parsifal" - the emphasis on "pure blood" and the non-Jewish image of Jesus - which had a strong influence on Hitler.

1789-1918: The Islamic World

0401. שתדלנותו המדינית של משה מונטיפיורי למען קהילות ישראל במזרח. פעמים 20 (1984).

[The Activity of Sir Moses Montefiore (1784-1885) on Behalf of Sephardi and Oriental Jewry. PE`AMIM 20 (1984).]

This issue of the journal includes four articles dealing with efforts by Montefiore and by European Jewish organizations to ease the plight of the Jews in Arab lands, particularly in the wake of a rash of blood libel accusations such as that in Damascus (1840) and in Safi, Morocco (1863). Includes excerpts from the Montefiore Diaries. The articles: Moshe Ma'oz: The Background of the Damascus Blood Libel (29-36); David Kushnir: The Firman of the Ottoman Sultan [Abdul-Majid] Rejecting Blood Libels against the Jews (37-45); Michel Abitbol: Montefiore's Mission on Behalf of the Jews of Morocco (46-54); Amnon Netzer: Montefiore and the Jews of Persia (55-68).

0402. Allouche-Benayoun, Joelle. Mémoires juives et acculturation à la France: A propos de femmes juives d'Algérie. TRACES 9/10 (1984) 54-67.

Pp. 64-65 discuss antisemitism in Algeria and humiliations suffered in the 19th century before the arrival of the French.

0403. Karagila, Zvi. Sur l'activité diplomatique européenne lors de l'Affaire de Damas. REVUE DES ETUDES JUIVES 144, 4 (Oct-Dec 1985) 369-375.

Presents three documents (two letters and a note addressed to the Pasha of Egypt) written in French in 1840, found in the archives of the Russian consulate in Egypt, discussing the blood libel in Damascus and the persecution of the Jews there.

0404. Lipman, Sonia; Lipman, V.D., eds. THE CENTURY OF MOSES MONTEFIORE. Oxford: Oxford University Press, 1985. 448 pp. (Littman Library of Jewish Civilization).

Includes the following articles on antisemitism: Tudor Parfitt: "The Year of the Pride of Israel": Montefiore and the Damascus Blood Libel of 1840 (131-148); K.D. Barnett: A Diary That Survived: Damascus 1840 (149-170); David Littman: Mission to Morocco, 1863-1864 (171-229).

0405. Miège, J.L., ed. LES RELATIONS INTERCOMMUNAUTAIRES JUIVES EN MEDITERRANEE OCCIDENTALE, XIIE-XXE SIECLES: Actes du Colloque international... Sénanque, mai 1982. Paris: Centre National de la Recherche Scientifique, 1984. 299 pp.

The following articles discuss antisemitism in Algeria and Morocco in the 19th century: Michael M. Laskier: Anglo-French Jewish Organizations and Morocco Jewry 1862-1900 (129-140); Régine Goutalier: Le "Sémaphore" de Marseille et le décret Crémieux (180-186); Carol Iancu: Les Juifs d'Algérie et de France pendant la crise antijuive algérienne 1897-1898: Correspondance inédite de Simon Kanouï (187-202).

0406. Tapia, Claude. La lutte des Juifs d'Afrique du Nord pour leur dignité. JUDAISME ET DROITS DE L'HOMME, ed. Emmanuel Hirsch. Paris: Librairie des Libertés, 1984. Pp. 175-181.

Describes the situation of the Jews in North Africa before French colonization, and the "dhimma" system which gave religious liberty to Jews and Christians but imposed humiliating laws as well. The French colonial authorities' attitude to the Jews was also ambiguous, and included some discriminatory measures. Describes methods used by the Jews in their struggle for emancipation.

0407. Vincent, Andrew. The Jew, the Gipsy and El-Islam: An Examination of Richard Burton's Consulship in Damascus and his Premature Recall, 1868-1871. JOURNAL OF THE ROYAL ASIATIC SOCIETY 2 (1985) 155-173.

The British Orientalist Richard Burton wrote a violently antisemitic essay in 1872 on his return from Damascus. It was published posthumously in 1898, in censored form, as part of his "The Jew, the Gipsy and El-Islam." Burton believed that his recall was engineered by the Jews of

Damascus, whose dubious financial dealings he had refused to protect, and who had used the influence of important British Jews against him.

1789-1918: Latin America

0408. Aizemberg, Isidoro. Coro: La primera comunidad judía de América Latina contemporanea. SEFARDICA 1, 2 (Nov 1984) 9-20.

The first Jewish community in independent Latin America was established in Coro, Venezuela in 1824 by a group from Curaçao, led by David Hohebed. Hohebed held various official posts, and opposed the despotic and antisemitic attitudes of Father Yepes.

0409. Boehn, Guenther. LOS JUDIOS EN EL PERU DURANTE EL SIGLO XIX. Santiago: Universidad de Chile, 1985. 184 pp.

A history of the Jews in Peru, beginning with the arrival of the converted Jews of Spanish or Portuguese origin. They were persecuted by the Inquisition at the trial of Lima (1639). Some of them were condemned and burned at the stake. The difficulties of Jews faced with the deep rejection of a prejudiced Catholic society are described. In 1869, antisemitic outbursts again spread in Lima owing to economic problems blamed on Jewish bankers.

1789-1918: South Africa

0410. Shain, Milton. From Pariah to Parvenu: The Anti-Jewish Stereotype in South Africa, 1880-1910. JEWISH JOURNAL OF SOCIOLOGY 26, 2 (Dec 1984) 111-127.

Traces the development of an anti-Jewish stereotype in journalism, caricatures, and theatrical productions, sparked by the influx of East European Jews after 1880. The Jew was depicted as physically repulsive, depraved and dishonest. The image of the crooked cosmopolitan Jewish financier (exemplified by the characters of "Hoggenheimer" and "Goldenstein" in drama and cartoons) became embedded in South African ethnic mythology.

1789-1918: The USA and Canada

0411. Borden, Morton. JEWS, TURKS AND INFIDELS. Chapel Hill, NC: University of North Carolina Press, 1984. xi, 163 pp.

Discusses the political and social status of Jews in America during the 19th century. Religious liberty was guaranteed, but many continued to define America as a Christian nation. Non-Christians should have freedom of worship, but no right to participate in government. Many states restricted office to Christians or to Protestants. Also discusses attempts to ensure equal treatment for Jewish citizens of the US in countries discriminating against Jews, such as Switzerland (pp. 82-96).

0412. Cohen, Naomi Wiener. Antisemitic Imagery: The Nineteenth-Century Background. JEWISH SOCIAL STUDIES 47, 3/4 (Sum/Fall 1985) 307-311.

A paper read at the Annual Meeting of the Conference on Jewish Social Studies, 6 May 1984. Describes popular antisemitic images recurrent in 19th-century America: the Jew as Christ-killer, the Jew as Shylock, and the Jew as eternal alien.

0413. Cohen, Naomi Wiener. ENCOUNTER WITH EMANCIPATION: THE GERMAN JEWS IN THE UNITED STATES 1830-1914. Philadelphia: Jewish Publication Society of America, 1984. xiv, 407 pp.

Includes discussion of social discrimination, negative stereotypes and ideological antisemitism in the USA (and in Europe) and Jewish responses (see pp. 222-285).

0414. Fels, Tony. Religious Assimilation in a Fraternal Organization: Jews and Freemasonry in Gilded-Age San Francisco. AMERICAN JEWISH HISTORY 74, 4 (June 1985) 369-403.

A study of the complex social processes of Jewish integration in the Masonic fraternity in San Francisco (1870-1900) based on social motivation and convergence of religious outlook. Pp. 399-402 deal with residual Jewish-Protestant "ethnic antipathies" and accusations of anti-semitism in Masonic lodges.

0415. Feuer, Lewis S. America's First Jewish Professor: James Joseph Sylvester at the University of Virginia. AMERICAN JEWISH ARCHIVES 36, 2 (Nov 1984) 152-202.

A biographical essay on the career of J.J. Sylvester (1814-1897), a brilliant British Jewish mathematician appointed as professor at the University of Virginia in 1842. The appointment of a Jew was attacked by the local Protestant press. In 1845, Sylvester was forced to resign following a violent clash with a student, possibly provoked by antisemitism. Later, as the first professor of mathematics at Johns Hopkins (1877-1883), he attacked antisemitism in American universities.

0416. Goodman, Abram Vossen. America's Dreyfus Case: My Father's Fight to Free Leo Frank. REFORM JUDAISM 14, 1 (Fall 1985) 12-13.

An account of the role played by the author's father in attempts to arouse public opinion in Boston in 1913-1915 to prevent the execution of Leo Frank (see next entry). At his instigation, the newspaper "Boston Traveler" took part in the campaign and attempted to prove Frank's innocence.

0417. Gralnick, William A. Leo Frank: Pardon Denied. REFORM JUDAISM 12, 4 (Sum 1984) 6-7.

In 1915, Leo Frank, a New York Jew living in Atlanta, was tried, convicted, and sentenced to death by hanging for the murder of a 14-year-old Black girl, Mary Phagan, whose body was found in the basement of the factory where he worked. The affair unleashed a storm of antisemitic sentiment. After the trial, the factory janitor confessed to the crime. The governor of Georgia commuted the death sentence in expectation of a retrial. But a group of vigilantes lynched Frank. The Atlanta Jewish community recently appealed to the State Pardon and Paroles Board for a posthumous pardon.

0418. Livingstone, David N. Science and Society: Nathaniel S. Shaler and Racial Ideology. INSTITUTE OF BRITISH GEOGRAPHERS: TRANSACTIONS 9, 2 (1984) 181-210.

Discusses the racist theories of Nathaniel S. Shaler (1841-1906), American geologist and professor at Harvard. He believed Jews were part of "America's race problem." Antisemitism "was not a manifestation of religious intolerance... [but] reflected man's deep instinctual reaction to ethnic differences."

0419. Rome, David. Early Anti-Semitism: The Holy Land; Tardivel. CANADIAN JEWISH ARCHIVES 34 (1985) 159 pp. (Anti-Semitism, VI).

This series (see the next two entries as well) consists of excerpts from Canadian books and from the press of the 19th and early 20th centuries, with connecting text. Pp. 1-41 discuss works on the Holy Land, including references to the miserable plight of the Jews due to their refusal to accept Jesus as the Messiah. Pp. 42-64, "The Politics of Racism," trace the beginning of blatant antisemitism in Canada, from ca. 1885 to the present. Pp. 65-152 deal with the case of Jules-Paul Tardivel, a leader of "the militant and extremist movements within Quebec church and politics," who disseminated his nationalistic and antisemitic views through his weekly journal "La Vérité," founded in 1881. Tardivel died in 1905, but his son Paul carried on in his footsteps for another 18 years.

0420. Rome, David. Early Anti-Semitism: The Imprint of Drumont. CANADIAN JEWISH ARCHIVES 35 (1985) 118 pp. (Anti-Semitism, VII).

The antisemitism of Edouard Drumont (1844-1917), French journalist and antisemitic leader, had great influence in Canada due to his access to French Canadians through the religious press, especially "Action Sociale Catholique." He himself saw Quebec as a pristine image of France, uncorrupted by Jews. His books were widely read despite doubts as to his loyalty to the Church. Also covers various antisemitic campaigns waged by the French Canadian Catholic press with no specific links to Drumont (e.g. repetition of ritual murder charges, and demands to revive medieval anti-Jewish legislation).

0421. Rome, David. Early Anti-Semitism: The Voice of the Media. Part I. CANADIAN JEWISH ARCHIVES 33 (1984) 121 pp. (Anti-Semitism, V).

The deeply antisemitic character of the Quebec French-language press, deriving from the influence of the Catholic Church, was expressed in attacks on the Jews, including accusations of a conspiracy of Jews and Freemasons, anti-immigrant propaganda, attacks on the Talmud, etc. Pp. 52-79 describe the visits of Sarah Bernhardt to

Canada, especially her visit to Quebec in 1905, which was met with Church-inspired hostility.

0422. Trachtenberg, Henry Manuel. "THE OLD CLO' MOVE": ANTI-SEMITISM, POLITICS, AND THE JEWS OF WINNIPEG, 1882-1921. Dissertation - York University, 1984.

The Jews of Winnipeg had a two-fold response to the widespread antisemitism of the period: to preserve their religious and cultural values, and to engage in politics as a defense mechanism. This political activity is here described and analyzed. Unseen.

0423. Walden, Daniel. Reflections on Columbus' "Medine": The Myth and the Reality of the Jewish Immigrants' New World, 1880-1915. MODERN JEWISH STUDIES ANNUAL 5 [=YIDDISH 5, 4] (Fall 1984) 5-13.

On p. 9, discusses the fact that the vision of America as the "goldeneh medine" was frequently marred by anti-semitic incidents and genteel prejudice.

1919-June 1945: General

(Includes philosophical and psychological studies in the aftermath of the Holocaust)

0424. אקשטין, בנימין. מאוטהאוזן: מחנה ריכוז וכליון. ירושלים: יד ושם, 1984. 370 עמ'.

[Eckstein, Benjamin. MAUTHAUSEN: CONCENTRATION AND ANNIHILATION CAMP. Jerusalem: Yad Vashem, 1984. 370 pp.]

A detailed account of the establishment and operation of the Mauthausen camp in Austria from 1938 to 1945, and the various aspects of life in the camp. Ch. 1 (pp. 5-35) describes the background to the establishment of the concentration camps in general. Pp. 201-211 relate how Mauthausen prisoners were put to death at the nearby euthanasia center in Hartheim. Describes also camps connected with Mauthausen, such as Ebensee and Gusen.

0425. גילברט, מרטין. מסע אחרון: גורל היהודים באירופה הנאצית. תל-אביב: עם עובד, 1984. 200 עמ'.

[Gilbert, Martin. FINAL JOURNEY: THE FATE OF THE JEWS IN NAZI EUROPE. Tel Aviv: Am Oved, 1984. 200 pp.] Translated from the English (London: G. Allen and Unwin, 1979).

Combines descriptions of Nazi policy formulation with history of events and personal accounts by Jews.

0426. מאדאיטשעק, טשעסלאוו. טייל פראגן פארבונדענע מיטן גענאציד-פראבלעם איבער יידן אין היטלער-אייראפע. בלעטער פאר געשיכטע 22 (1984) 241-252.

[Madajczyk, Czeslaw. Some Questions Connected with the Problem of the Genocide of the Jews in Hitler's Europe. BLETER FAR GESZICHTE 22 (1984) 241-252.] Translated from Polish. With English and Polish summaries.

Raises three points for consideration by historians: 1) The connection between the plan to exterminate the Jews and the plan to dispose of the Slavic peoples, positing that responsibility for both lay with the SS, i.e. Himmler; 2) The term "genocide" is too general and should be replaced by the Jewish term "holocaust" when discussing Hitler's actions and plans to wipe out entire races; 3) The fact that concentration and extermination camps were placed in Poland is not due to Polish antisemitism but rather to geographic strategy.

0427. פקנהיים, אמיל. השואה כארוע חסר תקדים בהיסטוריה, בפילוסופיה ובתיאולוגיה. דעת 15 (קיץ 1985) 121-129.

[Fackenheim, Emil. The "Shoa" as a Novum for History, Philosophy and Theology. DAAT 15 (Sum 1985) 121-129.] To be published in English in "A Handbook of Jewish Theology," eds. A.A. Cohen, P. Mendes-Flohr.

The "Shoa" (Holocaust) as a unique event poses questions for the historian, the philosopher, and the theologian. Explanations such as "racist madness" are not sufficient. The event requires a new and unprecedented response - the sanctification of life rather than martyrdom and death.

0428. קולקה, אוטו דב; גוטמן, ישראל, עורכים. מאנטישמיות מודרנית ל"פתרון סופי": לקט מאמרים. ירושלים: מרכז זלמן שזר, 1984. 284 עמ'. (סוגיות בתולדות עם ישראל).

[Kulka, Otto Dov; Gutman, Yisrael, eds. FROM MODERN ANTISEMITISM TO "THE FINAL SOLUTION": SELECTED STUDIES. Jerusalem: Zalman Shazar Center, 1984. 284 pp. (Issues in Jewish History).]

A collection of Hebrew articles, all of which appeared previously in various books and periodicals. The authors: Ben-Zion Dinur, Shmuel Ettinger, Nathan Rotenstreich, Jacob Talmon, Yisrael Gutman, Otto Dov Kulka, Uriel Tal, Daniel Carpi, Leni Yahil, Saul Friedlaender, Yehuda Bauer, Jacob Katz.

0429. ריגנר, גרהארט מ. הכנסיות ו"הפתרון הסופי." גשר 110 (אביב 1984) 13-23.

[Riegner, Gerhart M. The Churches and the "Final Solution." GESHER 110 (Spr 1984) 13-23.]

A lecture delivered at a symposium in Jerusalem, 1982. Describes contacts with Catholic and Protestant Church leaders during 1940-1943 to try to save Jews, based on personal experiences and recollections of the author, who was a representative of the World Zionist Congress in Geneva. He describes the attitudes of the clergy as positive, but they did not do enough because they did not understand the extent of the catastrophe.

0430. Abrams, Alan. SPECIAL TREATMENT: THE UNTOLD STORY OF HITLER'S THIRD RACE. Secaucus, NJ: Lyle Stuart, 1985. 261 pp.

An account of the experiences of the "Mischlinge" (half-Jews, and Jews in mixed marriages) under the Nazi regime, in Germany and in occupied Europe. Many of them were able to survive the Holocaust as a result of loopholes in the racial laws. Ch. 9 (pp. 185-206) emphasizes the phenomenon of "antisemitic Jews" who justified or assisted Nazi persecution of their own people - e.g. the Verband Nationaldeutscher Juden.

0431. Aly, Goetz; Roth, Karl Heinz. DIE RESTLOSE ERFASSUNG: VOLKSZAEHLEN, IDENTIFIZIEREN, AUSSONDERN IM NATIONALSOZIALISMUS. Berlin: Rotbuch Verlag, 1984. 157 pp.

Ch. 3 (pp. 55-91), "Die Judenstatistik," deals with statistics collected by the Nazi regime on the Jews in Germany and in the occupied territories, and their reflection of Nazi racial policy.

0432. Arad, Yitzhak. "Operation Reinhard": Extermination Camps of Belzec, Sobibor and Treblinka. YAD VASHEM STUDIES 16 (1984) 205-239. Appeared simultaneously in Hebrew. A shorter version, in Yiddish, appeared in BLETER FAR GESZICHTE 22 (1984) 171-181.

Describes the planning and construction of these three camps during the first half of 1942 - the sizes of the camps and the gas chambers, the number of personnel involved, the logistics of transportation of the Jews, the problems which arose while carrying out the exterminations (gas chambers too small, technical breakdowns, how to dispose of the bodies and the victims' belongings, etc.). These three camps were all liquidated by November 1943; a total of 1,700,000 victims were gassed and incinerated, including the majority of the Jewish population of the General Government (Poland).

0433. Bauer, Yehuda. The Place of the Holocaust in Contemporary History. STUDIES IN CONTEMPORARY JEWRY 1 (1984) 201-224.

Analyzes the uniqueness of the Holocaust which lies in "the totality of its ideology and of its translation of abstract thought into planned, logically implemented total murder." Defines the difference between "genocide" and "holocaust" with reference to cases in history and to various views put forward by historians. Concludes that studying the Holocaust will give us a better understanding of Jewish history - of what happened and why - and may help to retain a sense of moral values in a cynical world.

0434. Berghahn, Marion. GERMAN-JEWISH REFUGEES IN ENGLAND: THE AMBIGUITIES OF ASSIMILATION. London: Macmillan, 1984. ix, 294 pp.

A discussion on German-Jewish identity, based on interviews with German and Austrian Jewish refugees who emigrated to England in the 1930s. Ch. 1 (pp. 21-46) discusses the emancipation period and mentions the problem of antisemitism and its place in German culture. Ch. 3 (pp. 47-74) describes the Nazi period. Personal encounters with antisemitism show that, for many, the 1920s were worse than the 1930s, and Austria worse than Germany. For antisemitism in Britain, see the index.

0435. Browning, Christopher R. FATEFUL MONTHS: ESSAYS ON THE EMERGENCE OF THE FINAL SOLUTION. New York: Holmes and Meier, 1985. ix, 111 pp.

Examines Nazi Jewish policy in fall 1941-spring 1942, and suggests a shift away from a Hitlerocentric focus to study the views and actions of middle- and lower-echelon Germans involved in the destruction process. The author defines himself as a "moderate functionalist" in ch. 1 (pp. 8-38), "The Decision Concerning the Final Solution." Pp. 39-85 describe the participation of the Wehrmacht and the SS in the destruction of the Jews of Serbia.

0436. Carsten, F.L. BRITAIN AND THE WEIMAR REPUBLIC: THE BRITISH DOCUMENTS. London: Batsford Academic and Educational Ltd., 1984. viii, 343 pp.

See the index for references to antisemitism in Germany and among British diplomats.

0437. Celnikier, Feliks. Pojecie Zyda w doktrynie i hitlerowskim prawodawstwie [The Concept of the Jew in Hitlerian Doctrine and Legislation]. STUDIA NAD FASZYZMEM I ZBRODNIAMI HITLEROWSKIMI 9 (1985) 207-277.

An analysis of those paragraphs of the laws, decrees, and regulations of the Third Reich (in Germany from 1933, and in the occupied territories of Poland, the USSR, France and Belgium during the War) which dealt with the problem of defining a Jew. Concludes that there was no single definition. Also deals with the influence of Houston Stewart Chamberlain on Hitler's doctrine.

0438. Chadwick, Owen. The Pope and the Jews in 1942. PERSECUTION AND TOLERATION, ed. W.J. Sheils. Oxford: B. Blackwell, 1984. Pp. 435-472.

Purposes to clarify what the Vatican and Pope Pius XII knew and what they did not know regarding the Nazi plan to exterminate the Jews. Based on Vatican documents and the diary of the British envoy, d'Arcy Osborne, claims that the Vatican (specifically the Secretary of State, Cardinal Maglione, and the Pope) did not have a network of informants, and knew no more than did the Western powers. When information began to come through regarding atrocities and mass exterminations, at first it was not believed and later it was decided to keep the policy of silence. Faults the Pope for remaining silent.

0439. Charny, Israel W., ed. TOWARD THE UNDERSTANDING AND PREVENTION OF GENOCIDE: PROCEEDINGS OF THE INTERNATIONAL CONFERENCE ON THE HOLOCAUST AND GENOCIDE. Boulder, CO: Westview Press, 1984. xix, 396 pp.

A selection of papers delivered at the conference in Tel-Aviv, June 1982. Many of the contributions dealing with genocide in general analyze the Holocaust as an example and also discuss antisemitism. Partial contents: Monty Penkower: From Holocaust to Genocides (129-136); Ronald Aronson: Societal Madness: Impotence, Power and Genocide (137-153); I. W. Charny: Genocide and Mass-Destruction: A Missing Dimension in Psychopathology (154-174); Alice L. Eckardt: Power and Powerlessness: The Jewish Experience (183-196); Dieter D. Hartmann: Compliance and Oblivion: Impaired Compassion in Germany for the Victims of the Holocaust (197-201); Frances G. Grossman: A Psychological Study of Gentiles Who Saved the Lives of Jews during the Holocaust (202-216); Luba K. Gurdus: German Expressionism Heralding Genocide and the Holocaust (223-231); Chester L. Hunt: A Critical Evaluation of the Resistance of German Protestantism to the Holocaust (241-254); A.Roy Eckardt: The Holocaust and ("Kiveyachol") the Liberation of the Divine Righteousness (255-264); Alan L. Berger: Holocaust: The Pedagogy of Paradox (265-277).

0440. Cohen, Steven Arthur; Kniesmeyer, Joke et al. THE WORLD OF ANNE FRANK/ DIE WERELD VAN ANNE FRANK. Amsterdam: Anne Frank Stichting (Uitgeverij Bert Bakker), 1985. 230 pp. In English and Dutch.

An album describing the life of Anne Frank and her family. Explains the background to the family's story: the persecution of the Jews in Germany, antisemitic propaganda, the Holocaust in Holland, etc. Emphasizes the choices faced by the Dutch people - to resist, collaborate or remain passive. Also mentions anti-Zionism and antisemitism today.

0441. Cohen, Yerachmiel [Richard]. Problems of Western European Jews in the 20th Century: A Comparative Study of Danzig and Paris. DANZIG - BETWEEN EAST AND WEST: ASPECTS OF MODERN JEWISH HISTORY, ed. Isadore Twersky. Cambridge, MA: Harvard Univ. Press, 1985. Pp. 19-35.

Compares the responses of the Jewish community leadership in Danzig and in Paris to the antisemitism of the 1920s and 1930s. The greater integration of East European Jews in Danzig helped to maintain unity; Paris Jewry remained divided until 1943, when the Jewish leadership abandoned its faith in the French liberal tradition as defender of the Jews. The Danzig leadership, however, recognized early on that their German liberal orientation was a weak protection and was able to fight antisemitism when possible, and to save most of the community by collective emigration in 1938.

0442. Conway, John S. The Vatican and the Holocaust: A Reappraisal. MISCELLANEA HISTORIAE ECCLESIASTICAE 9 (1984) 475-489.

The decision of the Vatican to publish a selection of documents on the Holocaust period, "Actes et documents du Saint Siège relatifs à la seconde guerre mondiale," has made possible a reassessment of papal policy. Vatican impotence resulted from the Pope's stance of "pessimistic neutrality," the lack of will or resources for a major campaign to help the Jews, and the obstructiveness of Allied and Axis governments. When intervention did occur, it delayed or reduced but could not prevent deportations.

0443. Dossa, Shiraz. Hannah Arendt on Eichmann: The Public, the Private, and Evil. REVIEW OF POLITICS 46, 2 (Apr 1984) 163-182.

Defends Hannah Arendt against the charge that she was a "self-hating Jewess" and related charges evoked by her book "Eichmann in Jerusalem" (1963). Arendt's judgments made sense in terms of her political theory and its suppositions, especially her distinction between the public and private domains and her views of self-interest, morality, and totalitarianism. One reason for "misreading" Arendt was her "raising questions about something... considered canonical: the image of the Jew as victim."

0444. Dreifuss, Gustav. Victims and Victimizers. SHDEMOT 21/22 (Win 1984) 121-126.

The author, a psychotherapist in Israel, presents a psychological interpretation of the evil unleashed in the Holocaust. "The victimizer and the victim are two aspects of the same archetype: an active (aggressive) and a passive (suffering) side." Every person has within him both aspects, and it is essential for man to become aware of this in order to combat evil.

0445. Ezorsky, Gertrude. Hannah Arendt's View of Totalitarianism and the Holocaust. PHILOSOPHICAL FORUM 16, 1/2 (Fall 1984/Win 1985) 63-81.

Criticizes Arendt's views of both the Nazi perpetrators and their victims as expressed in her works "The Origins of Totalitarianism" and "Eichmann in Jerusalem." Shows that these views support her theory but do not comply with the actual facts. Eichmann was a criminal and a murderer, and not the banal and trivial bureaucrat described by Arendt.

0446. Fein, Helen. ACCOUNTING FOR GENOCIDE: NATIONAL RESPONSES AND JEWISH VICTIMIZATION DURING THE HOLOCAUST. Chicago: University of Chicago Press, 1984. xxi, 468 pp. A paperback version of the New York: Free Press, 1979 ed.

Described as an "application of historical sociology, not a work of conventional history," the work assesses why the destruction of the Jews was not uniformly effective throughout Europe. Three factors determined Nazi success - the extent of German control, the activity of national resistance movements, and the extent of antisemitism in the pre-war period. Part 1 (pp. 3-194) discusses the will of the Germans to annihilate the Jews, and its origins; the role of the Allies, the European neutrals, and the Church in failing to prevent the Holocaust; and conditions in the occupied countries. Part 2 deals mainly with the responses of the Jews.

0447. Fouilloux, Etienne. Le Vatican entre Hitler et Staline. L'HISTOIRE 70 (Sept 1984) 34-42.

In a discussion of the differences in Vatican policy towards Nazi Germany and Stalinist Russia during the 1930s, emphasizes that the Vatican's conciliatory attitude towards Germany arose from the hope of reaching a Concordat with the regime. Refers to Pius XI's failure to condemn the persecution of the Jews, though he declared that racial antisemitism is inadmissible.

0448. Goldhagen, Daniel. The "Cowardly" Executioner: On Disobedience in the SS. PATTERNS OF PREJUDICE 19, 2 (Apr 1985) 19-32.

SS men who showed signs of cowardice or of emotional distress were invalided out of their units, in contrast to the popular misconception that those who refused to participate in the killing were executed or were sent to concentration camps. Discusses the question of whether or not their refusal was based on sympathy for the fate of the Jews.

0449. Hamerow, Theodore S. The Hidden Holocaust. COMMENTARY 79, 3 (Mar 1985) 32-42.

A somewhat obscured aspect of the Holocaust is that the destruction of the Jewish community had considerable support throughout Europe. In the West, politicians and historians acknowledge that large numbers of non-Germans supported the annihilation of the Jews, but in the East the view is held that the Holocaust was the work of the Germans and that the great majority of Eastern Europe was opposed to the antisemitism of the Third Reich.

0450. Hirsch, Herbert. Why People Kill: Conditions for Participation in Mass Murder. INTERNATIONAL JOURNAL OF GROUP TENSIONS 15, 1-4 (1985) 41-57.

Describes three conditions for "guilt-free massacre" as exemplified by Nazism and the Holocaust - the cultural, the psychological and the political. The cultural conditions involved antisemitic Nazi propaganda and mythology, including the dehumanizing stereotype of the Jew. The psychological conditions involved unquestioning obedience to authority. The above are part of the process of political socialization, in which a population and its leaders justify acts of destruction, as did the Nazis, without feeling guilt.

0451. Jaeckel, Eberhard; Rohwer, Juergen, eds. DER MORD AN DEN JUDEN IM ZWEITEN WELTKRIEG: ENTSCHLUSSBILDUNG UND VERWIRKLICHUNG. Stuttgart: Deutsche Verlags-Anstalt, 1985. 252 pp.

Based on papers delivered at the Stuttgart Conference, May 1984. Includes: E. Jaeckel: Die Entschlussbildung als historisches Problem (9-18); Saul Friedlaender: Vom Antisemitismus zur Ausrottung (18-61); Karl A. Schleunes: Nationalsozialistische Entschlussbildung und die Aktion T4 (70-84); Helmut Krausnick: Hitler und die Befehle an die Einsatzgruppen im Sommer 1941 (88-107); Alfred Streim: Zur Eroeffnung des allgemeinen Judenvernichtungsbefehls gegenueber den Einsatzgruppen (107-120); Raul Hilberg: Die Aktion Reinhard (125-137); Wolfgang Scheffler: Chelmno, Sobibor, Belzec und Majdanek (145-152);

Gitta Sereny: Treblinka (157-161); Yehuda Bauer: Auschwitz (164-174); Andreas Hillgruber: Der geschichtliche Ort der Judenverfolgung (213-225).

0452. Jaffé, Aniela. C.C. Jung und der Nationalsozialismus. ANALYTISCHE PSYCHOLOGIE 16, 1 (Jan 1985) 66-77.

On Carl Jung's attitude to Nazism and the question of his alleged antisemitism. (See also next entry.)

0453. Kirsch, James. Jungs sogenannter Antisemitismus. ANALYTISCHE PSYCHOLOGIE 16, 1 (Jan 1985) 40-65.

Discusses Jung's alleged antisemitism in the light of his relationship with Freud. (See also preceding entry.)

0454. Knox, MacGregor. Conquest, Foreign and Domestic, in Fascist Italy and Nazi Germany. JOURNAL OF MODERN HISTORY 56, 1 (Mar 1984) 1-57.

Compares the world views and political programs of Mussolini and Hitler. On the place of Jews in Hitler's race theory, see pp. 11-14, 20-22; on the 1938 racial laws in Italy and the Church's protest, p. 48; on Nazi actions against the Jews, pp. 52-56.

0455. Kogon, Eugen et al. LES CHAMBRES A GAZ, SECRET D'ETAT: UNE DOCUMENTATION. Trans. Henry Rollet. Paris: Editions de Minuit, 1984. 299, xx pp. Originally published as "Nationalsozialistische Massentoetungen durch Giftgas" (Frankfurt a.M.: S. Fischer Verlag, 1983).

A collection of documents published in response to the "revisionist historians" who deny the reality of the gas chambers as part of the Nazi death machine used against Jews and non-Jews.

0456. Krausnick, Helmut. HITLERS EINSATZGRUPPEN: DIE TRUPPE DES WELTANSCHAUUNGSKRIEGES, 1938-1942. Frankfurt a.M.: Fischer Taschenbuch Verlag, 1985. 395 pp.

A history of the mass murders carried out in the Nazi-occupied territories of Eastern Europe by the Einsatzgruppen during the years 1939-1942. Argues that these troops believed they were fighting an ideological war against Bolshevism and the Jews. The regular German army was also directly involved in the murder actions, influenced by the same ideas.

0457. Lang, Berel. The Concept of Genocide. PHILOSOPHICAL FORUM 16, 1/2 (Fall 1984/Win 1985) 1-18.

Describes the characteristic features of genocide - the explicit intention to destroy a race, or a cultural or religious group - taking the Nazi actions against the Jews as the most explicit example. Discusses its consequences in the history and practice of ethics.

0458. Lepoutre, Marcel. Pie XII et les Juifs. REVUE DES DEUX MONDES (May 1984) 310-319.

Defends Pope Pius XII against the charge that he was indifferent or hostile to the fate of the Jews during the Holocaust.

0459. Lifton, Robert Jay. Medicalized Killing in Auschwitz. PSYCHOANALYTIC REFLECTIONS ON THE HOLOCAUST, eds. Steven A. Luel, Paul Marcus. Denver, CO: University of Denver; New York: Ktav, 1984. Pp. 11-34.

A study of Nazi doctors, particularly those who were in Auschwitz, based on interviews conducted in Germany and Austria with 28 former Nazi doctors. Examines their motivations for killing, and their ideological belief that they were performing a healing function in the name of a higher bioethical principle - mass murder as a healing and cleansing process.

0460. Mendelsohn, John. The Holocaust: Records in the National Archives on the Nazi Persecution of the Jews. PROLOGUE 16, 1 (Spr 1984) 22-39.

A description of records in the US National Archives, including German state papers, Nuremberg trial records, the files of the German-American Bund, records of the US Army in occupied Germany, an Auschwitz file, audio-visual records, etc.

0461. Mueller-Hill, Benno. TOEDLICHE WISSENSCHAFT: DIE AUSSONDERUNG VON JUDEN, ZIGEUNERN UND GEISTESKRANKEN, 1933-1945. Reinbek bei Hamburg: Rowohlt, 1984. 187 pp.

A study of the behavior of doctors, scientists, and researchers who participated in Nazi operations to exterminate the undesirable groups - Jews, gypsies, and the mentally ill.

0462. Papazian, Pierre. A "Unique Uniqueness"? MIDSTREAM 30, 4 (Apr 1984) 14-18. Was the Holocaust Unique? Responses to Pierre Papazian (by Y. Bauer, L.S. Dawidowicz, A.R. and A.L. Eckardt, H. Fein, G.M. Kren and L.H. Rappoport, N. Levin, D.A. Rustow). Ibid. 19-25.

Papazian, an Armenian, argues against the uniqueness of the Holocaust, in that the Armenian massacres were also acts of genocide, as well as other acts of mass murder in this century. He quotes from the works of various writers who respond here by stating that it was basically not the act of genocide which was unique but the reason for it - the racial ideology.

0463. Ray, John J.; Kiefl, Walter. Authoritarian and Achievement Motivation in Contemporary West Germany. JOURNAL OF SOCIAL PSYCHOLOGY 122, 1 (Feb 1984) 3-19.

A psychological study in 1982 of 136 residents of Munich was compared with results of studies in the USA, Australia and South Africa. The German respondents' scores for authoritarian personality were within the Western range. The authors therefore reject the existence of a "German authoritarian personality as an explanation for Nazism, as tyranny has been the normal human method of government." The Holocaust, too, can be explained as part of the European tradition of antisemitism, due to factors like the Jews' exclusivity, and religious enmity towards them, and not as a solely German phenomenon.

0464. Reese, William L. Christianity and the Final Solution. PHILOSOPHICAL FORUM 16, 1/2 (Fall 1984/Win 1985) 138-147.

Asserts that "the Holocaust will not have completed its work until Christians have accepted responsibility" for antisemitism and ultimately for the Final Solution. Asks why, in Vichy France, Hitler's orders were carried out almost before they were given; in the Vatican, Pope Pius XII remained passive in the face of knowledge of ongoing Jewish slaughters; in later stages of the war the Allies were unable to direct a single raid against the railway lines leading into the concentration camps. The answer is Christian antisemitism.

0465. Rotenstreich, Nathan. Can Evil Be Banal? PHILOSOPHICAL FORUM 16, 1/2 (Fall 1984/Win 1985) 50-62.

Refutes Hannah Arendt's theory of the banality of evil as expressed in her book "Eichmann in Jerusalem." Argues with points in her book, citing page numbers from the 1963 edition. States that "evil cannot be banal precisely because it presupposes deliberation and planning."

0466. Sayen, Jamie. EINSTEIN IN AMERICA: THE SCIENTIST'S CONSCIENCE IN THE AGE OF HITLER AND HIROSHIMA. New York: Crown Publishers, 1985. 340 pp.

See index for references to antisemitism experienced at various points in Einstein's life, in Germany and in the United States.

0467. Silvain, Gérard. LA QUESTION JUIVE EN EUROPE, 1933-1945. Paris: J.C. Lattès, 1985. 419 pp.

A collection of photographs and documents reflecting the persecution of the Jews in Europe during this period. Most of the material relates to France (pp. 20-250) and to Germany (pp. 252-324) and the background to the Holocaust, rather than to the events of the Holocaust itself. Includes Nazi and other antisemitic propaganda, and documents on the isolation of the Jews and their exclusion from society (e.g. "aryanization" of businesses).

0468. Tar, Zoltán; Marcus, Judith. Two Theories of Fascism and Society: Georg Lukács and Emil Lederer. STATE, CULTURE AND SOCIETY 1, 1 (Fall 1984) 61-75.

Compares the perspectives on fascism and Nazism of Lukács and Lederer. Both focused on the superstructure - the realm of politics, ideology and mass psychology - rather than on the economic infrastructure, and both disregarded the "Jewish question."

0469. Westbrook, Robert B. The Responsibility of Peoples: Dwight Macdonald and the Holocaust. HOLOCAUST STUDIES ANNUAL 1 <1983> (1984) 35-68.

New York intellectuals found it difficult to formulate a response to the Holocaust during the 1940s-50s. One of the few who did was Dwight Macdonald, owner and editor of the journal "Politics." In his March 1945 article "The Responsibility of Peoples," Macdonald dealt with the question of responsibility for the Final Solution. Macdonald spoke for individual responsibility rather than collective guilt, but went on to draw a picture of modern society which is so tightly organized and mechanized that the individual becomes powerless. Following reactions to his article, he later posited collective political guilt of the German people, as opposed to moral guilt.

0470. Wilhelm, Hans-Heinrich. Zur Haltung der Kirchen waehrend des Ostfeldzuges: Widerstand oder Kollaboration? ZEITGESCHICHTE 13, 2 (Nov 1985) 39-52.

An analysis of the attitudes of the various Churches (Catholic, Lutheran, Orthodox) to Nazi acts during the war on the eastern front. Concludes that, with some exceptions, the Churches did not resist Nazi war crimes, including the mass murder of the Jews by the Einsatzgruppen, due to their anti-Bolshevism and traditional antisemitism.

1919-1945: Australia

0471. Blakeney, Michael. AUSTRALIA AND THE JEWISH REFUGEES, 1933-1948. Sydney: Croom Helm, 1985. 335 pp.

Australian reluctance to accept Jewish refugees before and during World War II was connected to traditional immigration policies intended to ensure a "White Australia" and barring "genetically undesirable races." Traces the history of cultural and intellectual antisemitism in Australia, often originating in Britain, and of Social Darwinist and right-wing nationalist ideas and their influence on immigration policies before and after 1933. Unemployment caused by the Depression (and often blamed on Jewish financial machinations) aroused fears of being swamped by hordes of Jewish refugees. The official Jewish community acquiesced in these fears. As a result, only 7500 refugees reached Australia before 1941. Even after the war, the public and press opposed entry of the Jewish refugees.

0472. Blakeney, Michael. Australia and the Jewish Refugees from Central Europe: Government Policy 1933-1939. LEO BAECK INSTITUTE YEAR BOOK 29 (1984) 103-133.

Describes Australia's restrictive immigration policy from the 1920s through 1943, including the role of racism and antisemitism. Pp. 112-119 are devoted to the Evian

Conference (July 1938) and reactions of the press and public opinion when Australia refused to take in more refugees. Kristallnacht and its repercussions are discussed - Australia made some concessions to ease its policy, but the outbreak of war in 1939 put an end to refugee immigration.

0473. Blakeney, Michael. The Julius Stone Affair, 1940-41: A Tang of Antisemitism. QUADRANT 29, 5 <211> (May 1985) 45-49.

In 1941, the appointment of Professor Julius Stone to a Chair in Law at the University of Sydney was rescinded. Opposition to the appointment was political but "assumed an anti-Semitic garb." After a public outcry, Stone was reinstated. This affair was a reflection of the deteriorating status of the Jews in Australia from the 1930s on.

0474. Carr-Gregg, Charlotte; Maclean, Pam. "A Mouse Nibbling at a Mountain": The Problem of Australian Refugee Policy and the Work of Camilla Wedgwood. AUSTRALIAN JOURNAL OF POLITICS AND HISTORY 31, 1 (1985) 49-60.

Examines the contribution of Camilla Wedgwood, the anthropologist, to the settlement of German refugees in Australia. Shows her attempts to influence government policy, which was based on antisemitic prejudice against the Jews as a non-assimilable, parasitic group.

0475. Rutland, Suzanne D. Australian Responses to Jewish Refugee Migration before and after World War II. AUSTRALIAN JOURNAL OF POLITICS AND HISTORY 31, 1 (1985) 29-48.

A survey of Australian immigration policy from 1933 to 1947. Although several officials were sympathetic to the needs of the refugees, and despite Australia's need for increased population, the public was indifferent or hostile. The government feared an influx of lower-class Jews which would arouse racial tensions. Jewish organizations pressed for the admittance of selected "useful citizens." In the post-war period the number of Jewish DPs allowed entry was restricted due to the outcry that Australia was being used as a "dumping-ground for Jews."

1919-1945: Germany

(Includes historiographical and psychological studies of Nazism and of Hitler)

0476. בנארי, יהודה. תנועת ההתנגדות היהודית למשטר הנאצי בראשיתו. האומה 74/75 (אביב/קיץ 1984) 56-62.

[Benari, Yehuda. The Jewish Movement of Opposition to the Nazi Regime at Its Beginning. HA-UMMA 74/75 (Spr/Sum 1984) 56-62.]

On the role played by Jabotinsky and the Revisionist movement in the boycott of German goods in response to the Nazi boycott of Jewish shops and businesses in 1933. Jabotinsky understood the Nazi danger and sought to expand the boycott movement and use it to bring down the Nazi regime. The Transfer Agreement between Germany and the Jewish Agency dealt a death blow to the boycott and to Jewish economic opposition to the Nazis.

0477. בנקיר, דוד. המפלגה הקומוניסטית הגרמנית ויחסה לאנטישמיות ברייך השלישי, 1933-1938. יהדות זמננו 2 (1984) 131-151.

[Bankier, David. The German Communist Party and Antisemitism in the Third Reich, 1933-1938. YAHADUT ZEMANENU 2 (1984) 131-151.]

The KPD (Kommunistische Partei Deutschlands) viewed antisemitism as a functional tool of dictatorial capitalism, and Nazi antisemitism as no different than other varieties, out to harm only poor, lower-class Jews. However, following the riots of November 1938 (Kristallnacht), the Party launched a more extensive propaganda campaign against antisemitism.

0478. בנקיר, דוד. השאלה היהודית במאבק בין מגמות ההתמסדות והרדיקליזציה ברייך השלישי, 1934-1935. אומה ותולדותיה, חלק ב: העת החדשה, ערך שמואל אטינגר. ירושלים: מרכז זלמן שזר, 1984. עמ' 357-371.

[Bankier, David. The Jewish Question in the Struggle between the Trends towards Establishment and towards Radicalization in the Third Reich, 1934-1935. NATION AND HISTORY: STUDIES IN THE HISTORY OF THE JEWISH

PEOPLE, Vol. 2, ed. Shmuel Ettinger. Jerusalem: Zalman Shazar Center, 1984. Pp. 357-371.]

A study of the period July 1934 to September 1935, based on secret public opinion reports, shows a decline in popular support for National Socialism, even to the point of apathy and resistance. There were two trends in Nazism - towards political establishment, represented by the government and towards radical agitation, represented by the SA. Antisemitism was the factor that could unify these trends and rally the masses to support Nazi ideology. The Nuremberg Laws were enacted for this purpose in September 1935, making the radical views part of government policy.

0479. גוטמן, ישראל. בעלטה ובמאבק: פרקי עיון בשואה ובהתנגדות היהודית. ירושלים: ספרית פועלים, 1985. 285 עמ׳.

[Gutman, Yisrael. STRUGGLE IN DARKNESS: STUDIES IN HOLOCAUST AND RESISTANCE. Jerusalem: Sifriat Poalim, 1985. 285 pp.]

Ch. 1 (pp. 11-46) deals with the characteristics of Nazi antisemitism - its racial ideology. Describes the similarities and differences between that and antisemitism as it was manifested throughout the centuries.

0480. יחיל, לני. היטלר, היהודים והשואה: עצמת האידיולוגיה ומגבלות הפסיכוהיסטוריה. הדואר 64, 17 (8 מרס 1985) 265-268; 64, 18 (15 מרס 1985) 282-285.

[Yahil, Leni. Hitler, the Jews and the Holocaust: The Power of Ideology and the Limitations of Psychohistory. HADOAR 64, 17 (8 Mar 1985) 265-268; 64, 18 (15 Mar 1985) 282-285.]

With reference to the book by Fred Weinstein, "The Dynamics of Nazism" (1980), the author criticizes the methodology of psycho-history. Psycho-sociological explanations for the rise of Nazism in Germany tend to reduce the importance of antisemitic ideology.

0481. לאופר, רחל. השתקפות מדיניות ההשמדה בהיסטוריוגרפיה הגרמנית בשנות הששים: ניתוח השוואתי של שלוש גישות. יהדות זמננו 2 (1984) 99-128.

[Laufer, Rachel. The Extermination of the Jews in the German Historiography of the Sixties: A Comparative

Analysis of Three Approaches. YAHADUT ZEMANENU 2 (1984) 99-128.]

Analyzes the theses of Martin Broszat, Ernst Nolte, and Karl Dietrich Bracher. Broszat emphasizes changes in the structure of government during the Nazi period; Nolte concentrates on Nazi racial ideology and its implementation. Bracher's thesis is a combination of the two: the anti-Jewish policy was based on Nazi ideology, but the implementation of the Final Solution was possible due to the structure of the regime.

0482. מרגליות, אברהם. מגמות ודרכים במאבקה הכלכלי של יהדות גרמניה בתקופת הרדיפות הגזעיות. אומה ותולדותיה, חלק ב: העת החדשה, ערך שמואל אטינגר. ירושלים: מרכז זלמן שזר, 1984. עמ' 339-355.

[Margaliot, Abraham. Ways and Means in the Economic Struggle of German Jewry in the Period of Racial Persecution. NATION AND HISTORY: STUDIES IN THE HISTORY OF THE JEWISH PEOPLE, Vol. 2, ed. Shmuel Ettinger. Jerusalem: Zalman Shazar Center, 1984. Pp. 339-355.]

From 1933 to 1937 the Nazi government enacted various laws restricting Jewish economic activity, but the Jews were allowed to organize self-help projects, which are here described. Boycotts and harassment of Jews was not official government policy, but took place on the Nazi Party or local government level. Academics, lawyers, doctors, scientists, and clerks suffered more than did businessmen; the Nazis were sensitive to international repercussions. But in 1938 the aryanization process was intensified and the self-help system ceased operation.

0483. קולקה, אוטו דב. תגובות הכנסיות ברייך השלישי לגירוש היהודים והשמדתם לאור דו"חות סודיים של השלטון. אומה ותולדותיה, חלק ב: העת החדשה, ערך שמואל אטינגר. ירושלים: מרכז זלמן שזר, 1984. עמ' 385-398.

[Kulka, Otto Dov. Reactions of the Churches in the Third Reich to the Deportations and Extermination of the Jews in the Light of Secret Government Reports. NATION AND HISTORY: STUDIES IN THE HISTORY OF THE JEWISH PEOPLE, Vol. 2, ed. Shmuel Ettinger. Jerusalem: Zalman Shazar Center, 1984. Pp. 385-398.]

A study of reports on public opinion, prepared by the security services and various government and party authorities during the years 1939-1945, reveals general indifference to the fate of the Jews on the part of the German population and the Churches, and widespread knowledge of the extermination operation in the East. Some reaction is noted in 1943 - by the general population which feared acts of retaliation, and by some clergymen on moral and humane grounds - but these protests disappeared in 1944, perhaps because the public became used to the idea of the liquidation of Jews; the lack of protest on the part of the Churches was due to their heritage of anti-Judaism.

0484. שוהם, שלמה גיורא. וולהאלה, גולגתא ואושוויץ. זמנים 17
(חורף 1985) 4-21.

[Shoham, Shlomo Giora. Valhalla, Calvary and Auschwitz. ZMANIM 17 (Win 1985) 4-21. Appeared in English in THE JERUSALEM QUARTERLY 35 (Spr 1985) 87-100.]

Explains Nazi antisemitism and the Holocaust in terms of a clash between the Jewish "participant" social character (guided by law and moral principle) and the Teutonic "separant" character. When the Nazis rejected Christianity as a Jewish imposition on the free German spirit, the "separant" forces erupted violently, and especially against the Jews.

0485. שטנגל, יהושע אלכסנדר. מלחמת העולם השנייה: מלחמת השמדה.
תל-אביב: ביתן, 1985. 221 עמ'.

[Stengel, Yehoshua Alexander. THE SECOND WORLD WAR: WAR OF ANNIHILATION. Tel Aviv: Bitan, 1985. 221 pp.]

Pp. 114-163 deal with Nazi racist antisemitism and the implementation of the Final Solution. Supports the "intentionalist" theory that already in the 1920s Hitler planned the extermination of the Jews.

0486. Aberbach, David. Hitler's Politics and Psychopathology: An Interpretation. ENCOUNTER 65, 3 <378> (Sept/Oct 1985) 74-77.

Accounts for Hitler's psychological hold on the German people. Traces his personal history and the psychological sources of his antisemitism. Concludes that Hitler projected his own perversity and "despicable" weakness onto the Jews, and transformed himself into the all-powerful savior with whom his people identified.

0487. Ammon, Guenther. The Dynamics of Holocaust. DYNAMISCHE PSYCHIATRIE 17, 5/6 (1984) 404-415.

A paper delivered at a symposium on "Psychodynamics of the Holocaust," Haifa, 1984. Discusses the brutality and inhumanity of the Nazi power structure, and the reasons for the lack of action taken by the German people as a whole to save the Jews. Followed by an interview by Yaacov Friedler (pp. 416-418) in which Ammon stated that the most criminal thing done to the Jewish people was not the physical harm that they suffered, but the dehumanization that destroyed the core of their personalities.

0488. Aronson, Shlomo. Die dreifache Falle: Hitlers Judenpolitik, die Alliierten und die Juden. VIERTELJAHRSHEFTE FUER ZEITGESCHICHTE 32, 1 (Jan 1984) 29-65.

Deals with the origins and development of Hitler's "Final Solution." Stresses that Hitler regarded himself first and foremost as a politician, and one should therefore view his policy towards the Jews in the perspective of his political aims, strategies and tactics.

0489. Atsmony, David. Antisemitic Paper Money. SHEKEL 17, 4 (July/Aug 1984) 19-21. Reprinted from "The Currency Collector" 7, 4 (1966).

After World War I, banknotes in Germany became valueless, and they were used to incite antisemitism. They were over-printed with scurrilous slogans by antisemitic organizations, including by the Nazi party, especially before the 1922-1923 Reichstag elections. Municipalities also issued antisemitic notes.

0490. Bar-On, A. Zvie. Measuring Responsibility. PHILOSOPHICAL FORUM 16, 1/2 (Fall 1984/Win 1985) 95-109.

Deals with the question of collective guilt, or who was responsible for implementing the Final Solution. Presents the views of three Germans: Adolf Eichmann, who said that his superiors, and ultimately Hitler, were responsible; Guenter Grass, who said that all Germans were responsible, whether guilty of commission or of omission; Karl Jaspers, who defined four categories - criminal guilt, political guilt, moral and metaphysical guilt. Concludes that the notion of collective guilt can justifiably be applied to the German people, qualified by the different kinds of guilt described above.

0491. Bessel, Richard. Political Violence and the Nazi Seizure of Power. HISTORY TODAY 35 (Oct 1985) 8-14.

Analyzes the role played by political violence, mostly directed towards the Left, in destroying opposition to the Nazi takeover in 1933. Violence towards the Jews erupted in March and April with attacks on Jewish-owned shops and the officially organized boycott of April 1st. Protests abroad and lack of popular support ensured that this campaign was never repeated.

0492. Black, Edwin. THE TRANSFER AGREEMENT: THE UNTOLD STORY OF THE SECRET AGREEMENT BETWEEN THE THIRD REICH AND JEWISH PALESTINE. New York: Macmillan, 1984. xvi, 430 pp.

The international boycott movement against German goods arose spontaneously in Feb. 1933 as a response to Nazi antisemitic actions. On April 1st Hitler declared an anti-Jewish boycott in Germany, amounting to a "systematic economic pogrom." World Jewry staged mass protest marches and rallies. The world boycott of German goods in 1933 might have brought down Hitler's regime, but it was made ineffectual by the Transfer Agreement between the Zionist Organization and the Third Reich, operative from Fall of 1933 until 1941. The complexities and ramifications of the boycott movement and the Transfer Agreement are described.

0493. Black, Peter R. ERNST KALTENBRUNNER: IDEOLOGICAL SOLDIER OF THE THIRD REICH. Princeton, NJ: Princeton University Press, 1984. xiv, 348 pp.

A biography of the Austrian-born Nazi leader, head of the RSHA from 1943 to 1945, hanged at Nuremberg in Oct. 1946. Includes discussion of antisemitism in his family, in his educational experiences, and in Austria.

0494. Blackburn, Gilmer W. EDUCATION IN THE THIRD REICH. Albany, NY: State University of New York Press, 1985. viii, 217 pp.

See the index for references to antisemitism.

0495. Bock, Gisela. Racism and Sexism in Nazi Germany: Motherhood, Compulsory Sterilization and the State. WHEN BIOLOGY BECAME DESTINY: WOMEN IN WEIMAR AND NAZI GERMANY, eds. Renate Bridenthal, Atina Grossman, Marion Kaplan. New York: Monthly Review Press, 1984. Pp. 271-296.

A revised version of an essay which appeared in "Signs: Journal of Women in Culture and Society" 8, 3 (1983). Emphasizes the use of eugenics or "race hygiene" and the control of procreation by the Nazis to prevent the birth of the "socially or racially unfit." Those sterilized included social deviants and the mentally ill, as well as Jews and gypsies.

0496. Bosch, Manfred. ALS DIE FREIHEIT UNTERGING: EINE DOKUMENTATION UEBER VERWEIGERUNG, WIDERSTAND UND VERFOLGUNG IM DRITTEN REICH IN SUEDBADEN. Konstanz: Suedkurier, 1985. 352 pp.

Pp. 277-325 deal with the persecution of the Jews in south Baden.

0497. Brickman, William. Nazi Negation at Nuremberg: The Racial Laws of 1935 and German Education. WESTERN EUROPEAN EDUCATION 17, 2 (Sum 1985) 3-15.

A survey of Nazi racist theory and an account of the Nuremberg Laws and their effect on German research and education. Describes some Nazi textbooks. Includes lengthy notes and bibliography.

0498. Browning, Christopher R. A Reply to Martin Broszat Regarding the Origins of the Final Solution. SIMON WIESENTHAL CENTER ANNUAL 1 (1984) 113-132. A revised English version of a paper published in the "Vierteljahrshefte fuer Zeitgeschichte" 29, 1 (Jan 1981).

Agrees with Broszat's refutation ["Vierteljahrshefte fuer Zeitgeschichte" 25, 4 (1977)] of David Irving's claim that the Final Solution took place without Hitler's approval. However, whereas Broszat argues that there was no single decision to murder, the mass murder developing out of "a series of separate killing actions in 1941-1942," Browning believes that Hitler "ordered..., incited or solicited, the preparation of an extermination plan in the summer of 1941."

0499. Busch, Eberhard. Karl Barth und die Juden 1933-34, auch ein Beitrag zu einem umstrittenen Aspekt der "Theologischen Erklaerung" von Barmen. JUDAICA 40, 3 (Sept 1984) 158-175.

Deals with the silence of the Barmen Synod of the Protestant Church (May 1934) regarding Nazi antisemitism. After examining the theological declaration of the Synod, composed mainly by Karl Barth, concludes that although the word Jew is not mentioned, one should regard this declaration as indirectly taking a position in favor of the Jews.

0500. Calic, Edouard. HEYDRICH: L'HOMME CLEF DU IIIE REICH. Paris: Ed. Robert Laffont, 1985. 356 pp.

Traces the career of Reinhard Heydrich, chief of the RSHA (Reich Security Main Office), who engineered the "Final Solution," the extermination of the Jews.

0501. Carr, William. A Final Solution? Nazi Policy towards the Jews. HISTORY TODAY 35 (Nov 1985) 30-36.

A popular account of the historical controversy over the relative importance of Hitler's antisemitism and of conflicting elements in the regime in determining Nazi policy towards the Jews. Antisemitic legislation is presented as an outlet for agitation by rank-and-file Nazis. It is "questionable" whether Hitler's threats in 1939 imply the existence of a plan to destroy the Jews physically. Reviews the arguments of "intentionalist" and "structuralist" historians.

0502. Cocks, Geoffrey. PSYCHOTHERAPY IN THE THIRD REICH: THE GOERING INSTITUTE. New York: Oxford University Press, 1985. 326 pp.

See the index for references to antisemitism.

0503. Denkler, Horst; Laemmert, Eberhard, eds. "DAS WAR EIN VORSPIEL NUR ...": BERLINER COLLOQUIUM ZUR LITERATURPOLITIK IM "DRITTEN REICH." Berlin (West): Akademie der Kuenste, 1985. 210 pp. (Schriftenreihe der Akademie der Kuenste, 15).

A collection of articles dealing with the persecution of writers and scientists, mostly Jewish, in the Third Reich. Most of the articles focus on the bookburning of 10 May 1933, which was not a spontaneous act but rather planned and carried out by the faculty and students of German universities. Includes articles by Leo Loewenthal, George L. Mosse, Gerhard Sauder, Klaus Vondung, Hans-Dieter Schaefer, Hubert Orlowsky, Wolfgang Emmerich.

0504. Denzler, Georg; Volker, Fabricius. DIE KIRCHEN IM DRITTEN REICH. Vol. 1-2. Frankfurt a.M.: Fischer Taschenbuch Verlag, 1984. 222; 287 pp.

Examines the reactions of the Churches in Germany to the Nazi regime and its methods of terror. Concludes, in contrast to some historians' contentions, that the Churches did not constitute political resistance movements. A chapter in vol. 1 (pp. 133-158) deals with the attitudes of the Churches towards the persecution and extermination of the Jews. Vol. 2 contains primary sources.

0505. Derwiński, Zdzislaw Andrzej. "Piast" wobec Hitlera i nazizmu (1931-1934) ["Piast" vis-à-vis Hitler and Nazism (1931-1934)]. SLASKI KWARTALNIK HISTORYCZNY SOBOTKA 2 (1984) 219-233.

About the negative attitude of "Piast," the weekly of the Polish Peasant Party (Stronnictwo Ludowe), towards Hitler and Nazism. The weekly criticized Hitler's foreign policy, and emphasized the similarity between fascism, communism, and antisemitism in Germany.

0506. Dipper, Christof. The German Resistance and the Jews. YAD VASHEM STUDIES 16 (1984) 51-93. Appeared simultaneously in Hebrew. Trans. from the German ("Geschichte und Gesellschaft" 9, 1983).

A study of the German resistance to the Nazi regime - the Left (socialists, communists), the Right (military, bureaucrats), and the Churches - shows that the Reich's anti-Jewish measures were not a major concern for any of these groups. Analyzes statements by members of these groups regarding the "Judenpolitik."

0507. Ehrlich, Ernst Ludwig. Katholische Kirche und Judentum zur Zeit des Nationalsozialismus: Eine geschichtliche Erfahrung und eine Herausforderung an uns. JUDAICA 40, 3 (Sept 1984) 145-157.

From his experience in Berlin as an eyewitness to the deportations of the Jews (1941-43), and from written sources of the same period, the author analyzes the attitude of the Catholic Church towards the destruction of Berlin Jewry. He concludes that the traditional anti-Jewish positions of the Church reduced its resistance potential; it barely opposed the deportations.

0508. Engelmann, Bernt. GERMANY WITHOUT JEWS. Toronto: Bantam Books, 1984. 380 pp. Originally published as "Deutschland ohne Juden" (Muenchen: Schneekluth, 1970).

Discusses the Jewish emigration from Germany, and the extermination by Hitler of those who remained, in an effort to measure the losses Germany suffered as a direct result of the Holocaust, and the role Nazi antisemitism played in Germany's defeat in World War II. See especially ch. 9, "Anti-Semitic Pipe Dreams."

0509. Ericksen, Robert P. THEOLOGIANS UNDER HITLER: GERHARD KITTEL, PAUL ALTHAUS AND EMANUEL HIRSCH. New Haven, CT: Yale University Press, 1985. x, 245 pp.

A study of three German Protestant theologians who supported Hitler and Nazism. Deals with antisemitism mainly in the case of Gerhard Kittel (pp. 28-78), who joined the Nazi party in 1933 and lent his expertise on Jewish matters to Nazi institutions and to a propaganda magazine published by Goebbels. In his post-war self-defense Kittel claimed that he did not participate in Nazi anti-Jewish policy and had even made private protests.

0510. Finzen, Asmus. AUF DEM DIENSTWEG: DIE VERSTRICKUNG EINER ANSTALT IN DIE TOETUNG PSYCHISCH KRANKER. Rehburg-Loccum: Psychiatrie-Verlag, 1984. 133 pp.

Deals with two transports of Jewish psychiatric patients from a sanatorium near Hannover to an unknown destination in 1940. They were never heard from again. This case was part of the "euthanasia program," conducted from December 1939 through 1941, in which incurable patients were murdered in gas chambers or by inoculation. This program was the forerunner to the mass extermination of the Jews.

0511. Fleming, Gerald. HITLER AND THE FINAL SOLUTION. With an introduction by Saul Friedlaender. Berkeley, CA: University of California Press, 1984. xxxvi, 219 pp. Originally published as "Hitler und die Endloesung" (Wiesbaden: Limes, 1982).

Fleming's main aim is to refute the revisionist thesis that Hitler was not aware of the Final Solution (at least not before 1943) which was initiated by Himmler and local SS commanders. Using British, American, German and Soviet archives, he shows that Hitler deliberately planned and personally ordered the extermination of the Jews. This evidence supports the view of historians who see a direct relation between Hitler's ideology, especially his antisemitism, and Nazi policies.

0512. Fox, John P. The Final Solution: Intended or Contingent? The Stuttgart Conference of May 1984 and the Historical Debate. PATTERNS OF PREJUDICE 18, 3 (July 1984) 27-39.

Describes the Conference proceedings (see above, no. 451) in which leading historians discussed the question whether Hitler had planned the Final Solution from the start and directly ordered its execution, or whether it evolved in response to a particular set of cirumstances.

0513. Fox, John P. Nazi Germany and German Emigration to Great Britain. EXILE IN GREAT BRITAIN: REFUGEES FROM HITLER'S GERMANY, ed. Gerhard Hirschfeld. Leamington Spa: Berg, 1984. Pp. 29-62.

Examines the factors (i.e. the enactment of Nazi policy based on racist ideology) which caused nearly 400,000 Germans to emigrate in the period 1933 to 1940/41, most of them Jews, and the deterioration of Anglo-German relations due to Nazi treatment of the Jews and Britain's protests. Officials of Nazi organizations in Britain tried to stamp out opposition to the regime abroad by harassing the emigrés.

0514. Fraenkel, Ernst. DER DOPPELSTAAT: RECHT UND JUSTIZ IM "DRITTEN REICH." Frankfurt a.M.: Fischer Taschenbuch Verlag, 1984. 256 pp.

The author, a lawyer in Germany till 1938, analyzes the misuse of law and justice in Nazi Germany against those who were considered enemies of the State, especially Jews. Emphasizes the dual nature of the Nazi state - the contradiction between the apparent preservation of law and norms, and the actual acts of the government.

0515. Friedlaender, Saul. From Anti-Semitism to Extermination: A Historiographical Study of Nazi Policies toward the Jews and an Essay in Interpretation. YAD VASHEM STUDIES 16 (1984) 1-50. Appeared simultaneously in Hebrew.

An analysis of historical studies published since the end of the war, divided into two categories: global interpretations of Nazism, which are either based on German history, on the concept of fascism, or viewed as a facet of totalitarianism; and interpretations of Nazi antisemitism, in which two opposing positions have evolved - "intentionalism" and "functionalism." For an earlier presentation of the issues discussed here, see the author's introduction to Gerald Fleming's "Hitler and the Final Solution" (above, no. 511).

0516. Friedman, Herbert A. A Look at Anti-Semitic Propaganda on German Inflation Money. THE SHEKEL 17, 4 (July/Aug 1984) 35-42. Reprinted excerpts from "Coins," Sept. 1968.

Maintains that it is impossible to catalogue all of the antisemitic types of money issued in the 1920s, but a few general categories can be used: legitimate government bills, Notgeld, tokens, and money-like documents.

0517. Friedrich, Arnold, ed. ANSCHLAEGE: 220 POLITISCHE PLAKATE ALS DOKUMENTE DER DEUTSCHEN GESCHICHTE 1900-1980. Ebenhausen bei Muenchen: Langewiesche-Brandt, 1985. 220 pp.

A collection of 220 political posters reflecting German history from 1900 to 1980, including Nazi antisemitic propaganda posters.

0518. Gamm, Hans-Jochen. Wie sich die Bilder gleichen. TRIBUENE 93 (1985) 82-92.

Analyzes the stereotypes and the attitudes behind the anti-Turkish jokes circulating in contemporary Germany. Compares these with the anti-Jewish jokes of the pre-Holocaust period. (See also no. 564.)

0519. Ginzel, Guenther Bernd. JUEDISCHER ALLTAG IN DEUTSCHLAND 1933-1945. Duesseldorf: Droste Verlag, 1984. 252 pp.

A collection of documents and photographs about Jewish life in Germany during the Nazi period. Includes material relating to the racial laws, discrimination against and violence towards Jews, Nazi propaganda posters and caricatures, and the Holocaust.

0520. Goebel, Klaus. Fahnen, Feiern und Parolen: Nationalsozialistische Propaganda in Wuppertal. WUPPERTAL IN DER ZEIT DES NATIONALSOZIALISMUS, ed. Klaus Goebel. Wuppertal: Peter Hammer Verlag, 1984. Pp. 9-25.

An illustrated article, dealing with Nazi propaganda in Wuppertal between 1924 and 1945. Focuses on Josef Goebbels, who began his career as an agitator in Wuppertal. The local Nazis, under the powerful leadership of the Gauleiter Alfred Strassweg, used various means, such as speeches, parades, posters, broadcasts, and even statistics, in the service of their propaganda in which racist antisemitism played a central role.

0521. Goeldel, Denis. MOELLER VAN DEN BRUCK (1876-1925), UN NATIONALISTE CONTRE LA REVOLUTION: CONTRIBUTION A L'ETUDE DE LA "REVOLUTION CONSERVATRICE" ET DU CONSERVATISME ALLEMAND DU XXE SIECLE. Frankfurt a.M.: Lang, 1984. xi, 614 pp. (European University Studies, Series 3: History and Allied Studies, vol. 211).

A study of a German conservative thinker during the Weimar period. See pp. 470-472, "La question de l'antisémitisme chez Moeller."

0522. Gordon, Sarah. HITLER, GERMANS AND THE "JEWISH QUESTION." Princeton, NJ: Princeton University Press, 1984. xiv, 412 pp.

Examines the role played by antisemitism in the rise of Hitler to power in Germany and in the process leading to the Holocaust. Statistical data on Nazi party members and voting patterns, including their church affiliation, show the extent of the popular appeal of antisemitism. Challenges the accepted view that older, male, Protestant, middle-class Germans tended to be antisemitic whereas blue-collar workers were immune. Gestapo records from the Duesseldorf area are used to show which groups and institutions, including the Churches, opposed the persecution of Jews.

0523. Hamburger, Ernest; Pulzer, Peter. Jews as Voters in the Weimar Republic. LEO BAECK INSTITUTE YEAR BOOK 30 (1985) 3-66.

Based on the draft of a work by Ernest Hamburger, translated after his death and edited for publication by Peter Pulzer, and using the latter's own research on electoral behavior in the Weimar Republic. In the post World War I period most Jews supported the German Democratic party (DDP) which was thus attacked as an international, decadent "Judenpartei." The party officially opposed antisemitism but conservative elements feared identification with the Jews. The German Volkspartei (DVP), under Stresemann, opposed antisemitism, but he had to fight antisemitic tendencies within the party.

0524. Hanson, John H. Nazi Culture: The Social Uses of Fantasy as Represson. PSYCHOANALYTIC REFLECTIONS ON THE HOLOCAUST, eds. Steven A. Luel, Paul Marcus. Denver, CO: University of Denver; New York: Ktav, 1984. Pp. 35-51.

A psycho-historical examination of the origins, nature, and purpose of Nazi culture - the myths, the psychopathic symbols, Nazi propaganda, and the "sociopathic tendencies and genocidal inclinations" in German society.

0525. Hartmann, Dieter D. Anti-Semitism and the Appeal of Nazism. POLITICAL PSYCHOLOGY 5, 4 (Dec 1984) 635-642.

Recent research has tended to minimize the underlying hostility of German society toward Jews. The upper and middle classes supported Hitler for reasons of self-interest, but many also sympathized with Nazi antisemitism. Widespread disapproval of violence against Jews did not preclude compliance with a legal policy of exclusion. There was a general willingness to dehumanize Jews and to condone their "disappearance."

0526. Hauner, Milan L. A German Racial Revolution? JOURNAL OF CONTEMPORARY HISTORY 19, 4 (Oct 1984) 669-687.

Defines Hitler's racist views and Nazi ideology as a "racial revolution," with racial war as the prime mover, directed against all non-Aryans, but particularly against Jews.

0527. Heinonen, Reijo. Antijudaism och antisemitism i den tyska kyrkokampen: Ett bidrag till ansvarsproblemet i den teologiska judaistiken [Anti-Judaism and Antisemitism in the German Churches' Struggle: A Contribution to the Problem of the Responsibility of Theologians]. NORDISK JUDAISTIK 6, 2 (1985) 84-93. With a German summary.

Deals with the passive attitude of the Catholic and Lutheran Churches towards the anti-Jewish policy of the Nazis, and analyzes the theological concepts of the Lutheran Church. Also focuses on the Christian study of Judaism during the 1920s and '30s, which was anti-Jewish in character.

0528. Henning, Kai; Kestler, Josef. Die Rechtsstellung der Juden. STAATSRECHT UND STAATSRECHTLEHRE IM DRITTEN REICH, ed. Ernst-Wolfgang Boeckenfoerde. Heidelberg: C.F. Mueller Juristischer Verlag, 1985. Pp. 191-211.

An analysis of the legal status of the Jews in Nazi Germany, showing use of the legal system in the service of Nazi racist policy.

0529. Henry, Frances. VICTIMS AND NEIGHBORS: A SMALL TOWN IN NAZI GERMANY REMEMBERED. Foreword by Willy Brandt. South Hadley, MA: Bergen and Garvey, 1984. x, 201 pp.

An examination of economic and social relations between Germans and Jews in a small town in the Rhineland, fictionally named "Sonderburg," from the beginning of the 20th century to the Holocaust. Before 1933, Jews were comfortably integrated into local society, though they suffered from some antisemitism. With the growth of Nazi persecution, some local citizens refused to discriminate against and oppress their neighbors and employers. Others were active Nazis. Counters the myth of "total complicity" of the German people.

0530. Herf, Jeffrey. The Engineer as Ideologue: Reactionary Modernists in Weimar and Nazi Germany. JOURNAL OF CONTEMPORARY HISTORY 19, 4 (Oct 1984) 631-648.

Studies the reconciliation of romantic traditions of German nationalism with modern technology as expressed by engineers, leaders in the right-wing politics of Weimar Germany and in the Nazi party. Their propaganda stated that it was the Nordic race which was meant to develop technology, not the Jews, who represented materialism, capitalism, parasitism - i.e. the antithesis of culture.

0531. Herf, Jeffrey. REACTIONARY MODERNISM: TECHNOLOGY, CULTURE AND POLITICS IN WEIMAR AND THE THIRD REICH. Cambridge: Cambridge University Press, 1984. xii, 251 pp. Based on the author's dissertation - Brandeis University, 1981.

Includes discussion on the transformation of anti-capitalist rhetoric to anti-Jewish rhetoric. See index for references to antisemitism, and especially ch. 6, "Werner Sombart: Technology and the Jewish Question."

0532. Hildebrand, Klaus. THE THIRD REICH. Trans. by P.S. Falla. London: George Allen and Unwin, 1984. x, 184 pp. Originally published as "Das Dritte Reich" (Muenchen: R. Oldenbourg, 1979).

Concentrates on the political history of the Third Reich. See the index for antisemitism.

0533. Himmelfarb, Milton. No Hitler, No Holocaust. COMMENTARY 77, 3 (Mar 1984) 37-43.

"Anti-Semitism was a necessary condition for the Holocaust, it was not a sufficient condition. Hitler was needed." Contends that traditional Christian antisemitism was not responsible for the Holocaust - Hitler was, and he was anti-Christian as well as an antisemite.

0534. Hirsch, Martin; Majer, Diemut; Meinck, Juergen, eds. RECHT, VERWALTUNG UND JUSTIZ IM NATIONALSOZIALISMUS: AUSGEWAEHLTE SCHRIFTEN, GESETZE UND GERICHTSENTSCHEIDUNGEN VON 1933 BIS 1945. Koeln: Bund-Verlag, 1984. 590 pp.

Ch. 1 deals with the Weimar Republic and includes two sections on antisemitism in the judicial system. The rest of the book covers the period of the Third Reich, including anti-Jewish legislation and racist ideology.

0535. Holzer, Jerzy. Geneza narodowego socjalizmu [The Genesis of National Socialism]. PRZEGLAD HISTORYCZNY 75, 4 (1984) 747-759.

Contains some remarks on the importance of antisemitism in Nazi ideology.

0536. Hoos, Hans-Helmut. Zur Geschichte der Friedberger Juden 1933-1942. WETTERAUER GESCHICHTSBLAETTER. BEIHEFT 1 (1984) 37-105. Unseen.

0537. Jaeckel, Eberhard. HITLER IN HISTORY. Hanover, NH: University Press of New England for Brandeis University Press, 1984. 115 pp. (Series from the Tauber Institute for the Study of European Jewry, 3).

Four lectures delivered at Brandeis University in Sept.-Oct. 1983, with an additional chapter summarizing the author's views. Argues that Hitler planned in the 1920s to wage war to acquire "Lebensraum" for the German people, but also to exterminate the Jews, and that he deceived the German people who admired him with childlike devotion, and who would not believe that he "knew" about the atrocities being committed. He ruled Germany as a monocrat - all vital political decisions were made by him alone. His power rested in his ability to play differing and opposing interest groups against each other.

0538. Jell-Bahlsen, Sabine. Ethnology and Fascism in Germany. DIALECTICAL ANTHROPOLOGY 9, 1-4 (June 1985) 313-335.

An analysis of the reasons for the absence in Germany of anthropology as a discipline based on the idea of a universal humanity. Describes the development of ethnology in 19th century Germany, and the exploitation by the Nazis of the discipline's racist ideas. Debates between ethnographers in the 1930s caused them to split into two schools, both of which were racist and antisemitic.

0539. Johann, Ernst; Franz, Eckhart G. Duestere Vorzeichen: Unterschwelliger und offener Antisemitismus in den Jahren der Weimarer Republik. JUDEN ALS DARMSTAEDTER BUERGER, ed. E.G. Franz. Darmstadt: Eduard Roether Verlag, 1984. Pp. 143-148.

Anti-Jewish propaganda was disseminated in Darmstadt during the Weimar period mainly by nationalistic groups of students; the universities and high schools became centers of antisemitism. In the early thirties, the local Nazi parties were dominant in spreading antisemitic propaganda.

0540. Kahn, Lothar. The Nuremberg Laws: Prelude to Murder. CONGRESS MONTHLY 52, 6 (Sept/Oct 1985) 10-12.

The promulgation of the Nuremberg Laws in September 1935 marked a decision by Hitler to proceed full force against the Jews and to force them out of the political and social life of Germany. The American press condemned the laws, but failed to realize their significance in stamping the Jews as inferior beings.

0541. Kamenetsky, Christa. CHILDREN'S LITERATURE IN HITLER'S GERMANY: THE CULTURAL POLICY OF NATIONAL SOCIALISM. Athens, OH: Ohio University Press, 1984. xv, 359 pp.

Traces the impact of systematic Nazi censorship of school libraries, reading curriculums, and publications for children. Works by Jewish writers, or which dealt favorably with Jews, were banned, and the depiction of negative Jewish stereotypes was encouraged.

0542. Kaplan, Marion. Sisterhood under Siege: Feminism and Anti-Semitism in Germany, 1904-1938. WHEN BIOLOGY BECAME DESTINY: WOMEN IN WEIMAR AND NAZI GERMANY, eds. Renate Bridenthal, Atina Grossman, Marion Kaplan. New York: Monthly Review Press, 1984. Pp. 174-196.

German-Jewish women suffered from discrimination both as Jews and as women within German society. In 1904, the Juedischer Frauenbund (League of Jewish Women) was founded. Cooperation with the German feminist movement on women's issues, and against antisemitism, continued throughout the Weimar period, though "subterranean currents" of antisemitism were felt even then. After 1933, however, there was little solidarity between German and Jewish women. The JFB played an important part in sustaining the community until its dissolution in 1938.

0543. Kater, Michael H. Everyday Anti-Semitism in Prewar Nazi Germany: The Popular Bases. YAD VASHEM STUDIES 16 (1984) 129-159. Appeared simultaneously in Hebrew.

Presents examples of antisemitic incidents during the Weimar Republic and in the 1930s. Antisemitism on the grass-roots level existed in Germany from the Middle Ages on - it was not an invention of the Nazi regime. Anti-Jewish actions during the years 1933-1938 - restrictive legislation and discriminatory measures - often arose on popular demand, and the many acts of violence perpetrated by the SA had popular support.

0544. Kater, Michael H. Professoren und Studenten im Dritten Reich. ARCHIV FUER KULTURGESCHICHTE 67, 2 (1985) 465-489.

Analyzes reactions of professors and students to the Nazi regime, including attitudes towards the persecution of Jewish academics in the spring of 1933. Agrees basically with the thesis that neither the professors nor the students opposed Nazism until the war was clearly lost.

0545. Kershaw, Ian. The Hitler Myth. HISTORY TODAY 35 (Nov 1985) 23-29.

Describes Hitler's popular image and its eager acceptance by the German public, including the perception of Hitler as fanatically committed to ruthless action against "the enemies of the people." Antisemitism, however, was a less prominent issue in the Nazi party's electoral success than has often been presumed. After 1933, Hitler was careful not to be associated with unpopular pogrom-type excesses.

0546. Kren, George M. Psychohistory, Psychobiography and the Holocaust. PSYCHOHISTORY REVIEW 13, 1 (Fall 1984) 40-45.

"Austrian and German culture made available to Hitler an antisemitic ideal which would serve as the form through which Hitler's pathology expressed itself... [The] connection between Hitler's psychological development and his antisemitism, more than any other factor, accounts for its intensity and obsessional quality."

0547. Kudlien, Fridolf. AERZTE IM NATIONALSOZIALISMUS. Koeln: Kiepenheuer und Witsch Verlag, 1985. 311 pp.

Deals with the roles and functions of physicians in the Nazi regime - their participation in the Nazi establishment as well as their resistance to the regime, the expulsion of Jewish doctors from medical institutions, and medical crimes in the concentration camps.

0548. Kulka, Otto Dov. Die Deutsche Geschichtsschreibung ueber den Nationalsozialismus und die "Endloesung": Tendenzen und Entwicklungsphasen 1924-1984. HISTORISCHE ZEITSCHRIFT 240, 3 (June 1985) 599-640. Appeared in English as "Major Trends and Tendencies in German Historiography on National Socialism and the 'Jewish Question' (1924-1984)," in the LEO BAECK INSTITUTE YEAR BOOK 30 (1985) 215-242.

Distinguishes three periods in German historiography on Nazism and the Holocaust: 1) 1924-1944, in which the political struggles of the time predominate, and antisemitism is presented as a political ploy; 2) 1945-1960, characterized by almost total silence on the "Jewish question" and emphasizing the fall of the Weimar Republic and the structure of the totalitarian state; 3) 1960-1984, focusing on the conflict between the "intentionalist" and the "structuralist" schools. Concludes that the time is ripe for a synthesis of these approaches.

0549. Kulka, Otto Dov. Die Nuernberger Rassengesetze und die deutsche Bevoelkerung in Lichte geheimer NS-Lage- und Stimmungsberichte. VIERTELJAHRSHEFTE FUER ZEITGESCHICHTE 32, 4 (Dec 1984) 582-624.

An analysis of the German population's reactions to the Nuremberg Laws (1935), based on the monthly reports of the SD and the Gestapo. The attitudes expressed by the interviewees are divided into four categories: 1) Approval of the Laws as a way to regulate the Jews' position in society; 2) Approval by extreme antisemites as legitimation for the use of terror tactics; 3) Opposition and criticism by a minority of the population, often motivated by foreign policy considerations; 4) General antisemitic reactions throughout the country. Concludes that the development of Nazi anti-Jewish policy was influenced and encouraged by the antisemitic reactions described in these reports.

0550. Lang, Jochen von. DER ADJUTANT: KARL WOLFF, DER MANN ZWISCHEN HITLER UND HIMMLER. Muenchen: Herbig, 1985. 428 pp.

A biography of Karl Wolff (1900-1984), SS-General and liaison officer between Hitler and Himmler. As an enthusiastic believer in Nazi racist ideology, and as a high-ranking officer in the Waffen-SS, he probably took part in the Final Solution, or at least had knowledge of it, although this has never been proven.

0551. Lapide, Pinchas. JEDER KOMMT ZUM VATER: BARMEN UND DIE FOLGEN. Neukirchen-Vluyn: Neukirchener Verlag, 1984. 66 pp. Ch. 1 (pp. 7-34), entitled "Barmen ohne Juden: Eine Defizitanzeige," appeared in English as "No Balm in Barmen? A Jewish Debit Account" in the ECUMENICAL REVIEW 36, 4 (Oct 1984) 423-436, and in the JOURNAL OF THEOLOGY FOR SOUTHERN AFRICA 50 (Mar 1985) 37-51.

The Barmen declaration, passed at the first Synod of the German Confessing Church in May 1934, was directed against Nazi appropriation of Christian symbols and beliefs, and against "German Christians" who adopted the racist ideology. It failed to mention Christianity's debt to Judaism, or the persecution of the Jews, and included an Aryan paragraph banning pastors and Church officials of "non-Aryan" parentage.

0552. Lebzelter, Gisela. Die "Schwarze Schmach": Vorurteile, Propaganda, Mythos. GESCHICHTE UND GESELLSCHAFT 11, 1 (1985) 37-58.

Describes the racist propaganda, widespread in the Rhineland, against Black soldiers who were part of the French occupation forces during and after World War I. Pp. 53-55 show how the concepts and methods of this propaganda were incorporated by Hitler and the Nazis for use against the Jews.

0553. Levine, Herbert S. The Jewish Leadership in Germany and the Nazi Threat in 1933. GERMAN NATIONALISM AND THE EUROPEAN RESPONSE, 1890-1945, eds. Carole Fink et al. Norman, OK: University of Oklahoma Press, 1985. Pp. 181-206.

Defends the response of the German Jewish leadership to the first Nazi measures against the Jews in 1933 as based on concern for immediate Jewish interests. Official Nazi policy towards the Jews had not yet been formulated; conservative forces in Germany feared foreign reactions to anti-Jewish violence, whereas Nazi followers demanded practical measures against the Jews. Many German Jews assumed that they would find a way to cooperate with the regime and continue to live in Germany with restricted rights and economic opportunities.

0554. Lewin, Ronald. HITLER'S MISTAKES. London: Leo Cooper, in association with Secker and Warburg, 1984. v, 186 pp.

Purports "to consider Hitler's career objectively, without the deforming intrusion of moral judgements, to evaluate... the ends at which he aimed and the means that he employed." See the index for references to Jews and to the Final Solution.

0555. Lockot, Regine. ERINNERN UND DURCHARBEITEN: ZUR GESCHICHTE DER PSYCHOANALYSE UND PSYCHOTHERAPIE IM NATIONALSOZIALISMUS. Frankfurt a.M: Fischer Taschenbuch Verlag, 1985. 386 pp.

A history of psychoanalysis and psychotherapy under the Nazi regime. Challenges the common thesis regarding the "liquidation" of this profession by the Nazis. Although Jewish psychoanalysts were forced to stop their practice, and many had to leave Germany, the psychoanalytical institutions continued to function.

0556. McInnis, Raymond G. Adolf Hitler's "Mein Kampf": Origin, Impact, Criticism and Sources. REFERENCE SERVICES REVIEW 13, 1 (Spr 1985) 15-24.

Summarizes the contents of "Mein Kampf," in which the Jews are defined as destroyers of civilization; the publishing history of the book; its origins, which are bound up with the origins of Nazism (including the role of antisemitism); the impact of the book on Germans and non-Germans; and criticism both contemporary and recent. Includes a list of sources on "Mein Kampf," Hitler and Nazism.

0557. Majer, Diemut. "Racial Inequality" and the Nazification of the Law in Nazi Germany. ISRAEL YEARBOOK ON HUMAN RIGHTS 14 (1984) 111-119.

The nazification of the law consisted of a shift of the existing legal order, which was based on equality, toward the principle of "ethnic inequality." This was done indirectly, by interpreting or perverting the existing law so that it would conform with Nazi ideology.

0558. Marabini, Jean. LA VIE QUOTIDIENNE A BERLIN SOUS HITLER. Paris: Hachette, 1985. 248 pp.

A description of everyday life in Berlin from 1933 to 1945. The book, written by a historian and journalist, includes references to the Nuremberg Laws, antisemitic demonstrations, and "Kristallnacht."

0559. Maurer, Trude. The East European Jew in the Weimar Press: Stereotype and Attempted Rebuttal. STUDIES IN CONTEMPORARY JEWRY 1 (1984) 176-198.

The Ostjuden in Germany proved an ideal target for every form of antisemitic agitation. The "center and conservative parties tended to join in the hounding of the Ostjude, although with a less obsessive perspective than that shown by the overtly antisemitic volkisch camp. Only on the Left were there movements ready to raise their voice - by no means unanimously or loudly - in defense of the immigrants and of a measure of immigration."

0560. Meyer, Enno. GESCHICHTE DER DELMENHORSTER JUDEN 1695-1945. Oldenburg: Heinz Holzberg Verlag, 1985. 125 pp. (Oldenburger Studien, 26).

Pp. 49-93 deal with the period 1914-1945, including antisemitism and the fate of the local Jews under the Nazi regime.

0561. Michalka, Wolfgang, ed. DAS DRITTE REICH: DOKUMENTE ZUR INNER- UND AUSSENPOLITIK. Vol. 1-2. Muenchen: Deutscher Taschenbuch Verlag, 1985. 342; 434 pp.

Vol. 1, pp. 150-173 and vol. 2, pp. 232-267 include documents relating to Nazi antisemitic policy culminating in the "Final Solution."

0562. Mosse, George L. Bookburning and the Betrayal of German Intellectuals. NEW GERMAN CRITIQUE 31 (1984) 143-155.

Discusses the burning, on the night of 10 May 1933, of 20,000 books in Berlin and over 2,000 in other large cities of the Reich, the symbolic prelude to the subsequent ban on publication and library circulation of books by Jews and by German and foreign writers who were not in line with "Nazi culture." It was the academics who were responsible, not the "Volk" or illiterate people. The incident is viewed in the framework of the development of German culture and society.

0563. Mueller, Gerhard Ludwig. Theologie und Ideologie: Bonhoeffer und die Anfaenge der Bekennenden Kirche 1933. CATHOLICA 38, 2 (1984) 135-150.

The German Protestant theologian Dietrich Bonhoeffer opposed Nazi racist legislation concerning Jews who had converted to Christianity. Bonhoeffer's early opposition to Nazism had an important influence on the 1934 Barmen Declaration.

0564. Nierenberg, Jess. "Ich moechte das Geschwuer loswerden": Tuerkenhass in Witzen in der Bundesrepublik Deutschland. FABULA 25, 3/4 (1984) 229-240.

Compares present-day German hatred of the Turks, as expressed in jokes, to antisemitism during the Third Reich and the negative folkloristic attitudes then adopted against the Jews. (See also no. 518.)

0565. Noakes, J.; Pridham, G., eds. NAZISM 1919-1945. VOL. 2: STATE, ECONOMY AND SOCIETY 1933-1939: A DOCUMENTARY READER. Exeter: University of Exeter, 1984. 195-608 pp. (Exeter Studies in History, 8).

Ch. 23 (pp. 521-567), entitled "Antisemitism 1933-39," comprises historical narrative interspersed with extracts from documents, and deals with the 1933 terror, boycott, and discriminatory legislation; the 1935 Nuremberg Laws; antisemitic propaganda and the popular response; Jewish policy in 1936/37; the radicalization of antisemitism in 1937/38; Kristallnacht and its repercussions; SS policy in 1938/39.

0566. Ossietzky, Carl von. RECHENSCHAFT: PUBLIZISTIK AUS DEN JAHREN 1913-1933. Hrsg. von Bruno Freix. Frankfurt a.M.: Fischer Taschenbuch Verlag, 1984. 329 pp.

A collection of articles written between 1913-1933 by Carl von Ossietzky (1889-1938), German publicist and pacifist. The article entitled "Antisemiten" (pp. 207-218) appeared in "Die Weltbuehne," 19 July 1932. For Ossietzky, antisemitism is connected to nationalism. He rejects the mystical and organic interpretation of the word "Volk" (nation) which aroused antisemitic feelings in Germany.

0567. Paetzold, Kurt, ed. VERFOLGUNG, VERTREIBUNG, VERNICHTUNG: DOKUMENTE DES FASCHISTISCHEN ANTISEMITISMUS 1933-1942. Frankfurt a.M.: Roederberg-Verlag, 1984. 362 pp.

A documentation of the persecution of Jews under the Nazi regime - from the day when Hitler came to power (Jan 1933), through the Nuremberg Laws (1935) and "Kristallnacht" (Nov 1938), to the Wannsee Conference (Jan 1942) at which it was decided to implement the Final Solution.

0568. Pentzlin, Heinz. DIE DEUTSCHEN IM DRITTEN REICH. Stuttgart: Seewald Verlag, 1985. 222 pp.

Describes the various attitudes of the Germans towards the Nazi regime and its actions from the point-of-view of the author, then a journalist. Pp. 165-191 deal with reactions of the German population to the persecution of the Jews.

0569. Pflug, Guenther, ed. DIE JUEDISCHE EMIGRATION AUS DEUTSCHLAND 1933-1941: DIE GESCHICHTE EINER AUSTREIBUNG. Eine Ausstellung der Deutschen Bibliothek, Frankfurt am Main, unter Mitwirkung des Leo-Baeck Instituts, New York. Frankfurt a.M.: Buchhaendler-Vereinigung, 1985. 324 pp.

A catalog of an exhibition on Jewish emigration from Germany, 1933-1941. Includes material regarding Nazi anti-Jewish measures, especially legislation.

0570. Piccolo, Sergio. J.P. Goebbels e la propaganda nazionalsocialista: Proposte per una nuova chiave di lettura attraverso testi e discorsi. STORIA CONTEMPORANEA 15, 3 (June 1984) 443-461.

Deals with Goebbels and his approach and contributions to Nazi propaganda. Views his antisemitism as arising in large part from rejection as a poet by Jewish publishers and intellectual jealousy and rivalry vis-à-vis Jews.

0571. Piotrowski, Bernard. W SLUZBIE RASIZMU I BEZPRAWIA "UNIWERSYTET RZESZY" W POZNANIU (1941-1945) [In the Service of Racism and Lawlessness: The "Reichsuniversitaet" in Poznan (1941-1945)]. Poznań: Wydawnictwo Naukowe Uniwersytetu im. A. Mickiewicza, 1984. 175 pp.

An account of the scientific, educational and political propaganda activities of the German fascist university founded in Poznan (German Posen) in April 1941. Describes methods used in the social sciences and natural sciences faculties to prove the superiority of the German race over the Jews, Slavs, and others.

0572. Psychoanalysis and the Holocaust: A Roundtable. PSYCHOANALYTIC REFLECTIONS ON THE HOLOCAUST, eds. Steven A. Luel, Paul Marcus. Denver, CO: University of Denver; New York: Ktav, 1984. Pp. 207-229.

Proceedings of a discussion which took place on 2 May 1982, between the editors and four psychoanalysts: Martin S. Bergmann, Sidney Furst, Frances G. Grossman, Martin Wangh. Includes discussion on the psychology of antisemitism, of Nazi leaders, including Hitler, and of the German people as accomplices or bystanders.

0573. Reinharz, Jehuda. The Zionist Response to Antisemitism in Germany. LEO BAECK INSTITUTE YEAR BOOK 30 (1985) 105-140.

Historians studying the Zionist press have concluded that the Zionist movement did not respond to antisemitism in Germany in the Weimar period. The author maintains that Zionists were far from complacent, but cooperation with the Centralverein - recognized experts in defense activity but the Zionists' "assimilationist" opponents - seemed to them impossible. By 1932, the Zionists admitted that Palestine could not solve the immediate problem, and they offered mainly psychological and moral help.

0574. Richards, Pamela Spence. "Aryan Librarianship": Academic and Research Libraries under Hitler. JOURNAL OF LIBRARY HISTORY 19, 2 (Spr 1984) 231-258.

Describes the Nazi impact on academic and research libraries in Germany and occupied lands. Mentions the expulsion of Jews from German academic life, the fate of the Jewish libraries and Judaica collections, and the establishment of the Library for Research on the Jewish Question in Frankfurt am Main.

0575. Richards, Pamela Spence. German Libraries and Scientific and Technical Information in Nazi Germany. THE LIBRARY QUARTERLY 55, 2 (Apr 1985) 151-173.

The effects of the Nuremberg Laws on German libraries, and the attempt to exclude non-German, Jewish-influenced research from them, are discussed on pp. 157-160.

0576. Roth, John K. How to Make Hitler's Ideas Clear? PHILOSOPHICAL FORUM 16, 1/2 (Fall 1984/Win 1985) 82-94.

Describes Hitler's world view, his interpretation of the laws of nature - that life is an eternal struggle, that racial and cultural purity are essential for survival and excellence, and that the Jew is the fundamental enemy. The Final Solution evolved from wish to reality as Hitler gained power, but periods of ambivalence caused people to misinterpret his intentions.

0577. Saldern, Adelheid von. MITTELSTAND IM DRITTEN REICH: HANDWERKER, EINZELHAENDLER, BAUERN. Frankfurt a.M.: Campus-Verlag, 1985. 401 pp.

Pp. 202-207 discuss the attitudes of the artisans, the traders, and the peasants towards the Jews - the latter were relatively less antisemitic because the Jews did not present any economic competition in their sphere. The artisans' organizations were actively antisemitic.

0578. Scheffler, Wolfgang. Rassenfanatismus und Judenverfolgung. DEUTSCHLAND 1933: MACHTZERFALL DER DEMOKRATIE UND NATIONALSOZIALISTISCHE "MACHTERGREIFUNG," eds. Wolfgang Treue, Juergen Schmaedeke. Berlin (West): Colloquium Verlag, 1984. Pp. 16-44.

A lecture delivered at an international conference in Bonn, Jan. 1983. Argues that a direct line leads from Hitler's antisemitic views and actions during the 1920s and '30s to the Final Solution, thus supporting the "intentionalist thesis," and describes the various stages in the plan to destroy European Jewry.

0579. Schoenberner, Gerhard, ed. ARTISTS AGAINST HITLER: PERSECUTION, EXILE, RESISTANCE. Bonn: Inter Nationes, 1984. 72 pp.

A collection of articles on the resistance of German artists (in the plastic and performing arts) to Nazism, both in Germany and in exile. Mentions the persecution of Jewish artists, actors, etc. On pp. 59-62, describes the Nazi battle against "degenerate" Jewish art.

0580. Schreiber, Gerhard. HITLER-INTERPRETATIONEN 1923-1983: ERGEBNISSE, METHODEN UND PROBLEME DER FORSCHUNG. Darmstadt: Wissenschaftliche Buchgesellschaft, 1984. xi, 393 pp.

An historiographical survey of approximately 1500 works written between 1923-1983 dealing with Hitler's thoughts and deeds. See pp. 103-127, "Antisemitismus und Rassismus." Pp. 337-366 contain a bibliographical guide.

0581. Schwarzwaelder, Herbert. BREMEN IN DER NS-ZEIT (1933-1945). Hamburg: Hans Christians Verlag, 1985. 952 pp. (Geschichte der freien Hansestadt Bremen, 4).

Pp. 73-76, 312-320, 463-464 deal with the Nazi anti-Jewish policy in Bremen, and with the extermination of the local Jews.

0582. Showalter, Dennis E. "A Tidal Wave of Degeneracy": National Socialism and Cultural Politics in Nuernberg, 1923-33. SOUTH ATLANTIC QUARTERLY 83, 3 (Sum 1984) 283-296.

The Nazi campaign to purify German culture from decadent (i.e. modern, progressive, Jewish) influences is exemplified in Nuremberg, particularly in the virulent antisemitic diatribes of Julius Streicher and his newspaper "Der Stuermer."

0583. Siemsen, Carl. Anti-Semitic Emergency Notes: A Sequel. THE SHEKEL 17, 4 (July/Aug 1984) 22-27. Reprinted from "The Currency Collector" 8, 3 (1967).

In the politically turbulent years after World War I, colorfully illustrated subject money notes were printed in Germany for sale to collectors. Lists examples of the antisemitic "emergency money."

0584. Sierpowski, Stanislaw. Dylematy mniejszościowe Ligi Narodów [The Minorities Dilemma of the League of Nations]. PRZEGLAD ZACHODNI 3 (1984) 25-59; 5/6: 13-45.

The second part of this article describes discussions at the 14th session of the League of Nations (1933) on the Jewish problem in Germany. The German representative denied the right of this forum to discuss the issue as it was a special "racial problem" (pp. 32-34).

0585. Sombart, Nicolaus. Spaziergaenge mit Carl Schmitt. MERKUR 38, 2 <424> (1984) 191-201.

Describes a conversation which took place after the outbreak of the Second World War between the author and Carl Schmitt (1888-1983?), the German political and legal theorist, known as the "Crown Jurist" of the Third Reich. Schmitt contended that the Jews invented race theory and that they conspire to conquer the world, basing his views on Disraeli's novel "Tancred."

0586. Sonn, Naftali Herbert; Berge, Otto. SHICKSALSWEGE DER JUDEN IN FULDA UND UMGEBUNG. Fulda: Druck Art, 1984. 233 pp.

A history of the community from the end of the 18th century through 1942. The persecution and extermination of Jews under the Nazi regime is discussed at length.

0587. Staub, Ervin. The Psychology of Perpetrators and Bystanders. POLITICAL PSYCHOLOGY 6, 1 (Mar 1985) 61-85.

Explores psychological sources, social conditions and cultural preconditions that contribute to a government's fostering of genocide, mass murder, and other acts of violence against a subgroup. The behavior of bystanders can influence government policy. Hitler's propaganda, together with an existing antisemitic base in Germany, caused the people afflicted with economic woes to blame the Jews.

0588. Stern, Joseph Peter. HITLER: LE FUEHRER ET LE PEUPLE. Paris: Flammarion, 1985. 308 pp. Originally published as "Hitler: The Fuehrer and the People" (London: Fontana/Collins, 1975).

Describes the growth of the Hitler myth and the fascination which Hitler had for people. Analyzes the themes and propaganda methods used by Hitler, based on his book "Mein Kampf" and on his speeches (including his attacks on the Jews). Deals especially with his language - the phraseology of sacrifice, of nature, and of prophecy. For material relating to Nazi laws against the Jews, see pp. 159-174.

0589. Suchy, Barbara. The Verein zur Abwehr des Antisemitismus (II): From the First World War to Its Dissolution in 1933. LEO BAECK INSTITUTE YEAR BOOK 30 (1985) 67-103.

Part I of this article (LBIYB 28, 1983) covers the period from the founding of the "Abwehrverein" (a joint Jewish/Gentile effort to fight antisemitism) in 1890 in Berlin to the First World War. Part II discusses the organization's leaders (especially Georg Gothein, chairman from 1909 to 1933), and its problems of finance and membership, based on analysis of the Abwehrverein's bulletin. Examines attitudes of Jews, Christians, and religious and political groups to the organization, whose work had a predominantly defensive character involving much apologetics. The Abwehrverein was liquidated in July 1933 after carrying on "a futile battle [against antisemitism] for more than four decades."

0590. Tal, Uriel. On Modern Lutheranism and the Jews. LEO BAECK INSTITUTE YEAR BOOK 30 (1985) 203-213.

In the political and economic crises of the 1920s, the German Lutheran Church feared liberalism as well as right-wing radicalism. Leaders of the anti-Nazi trend (later the Confessional Church), many of whom later defended Jewish rights, equated Judaism (especially Zionism) with Nazism, claiming that both rejected salvation through Christ and exalted materialism, narrow ethnic nationality, and secular political messianism. This view was influenced by Luther's anti-Judaism and traditional antisemitic ideas.

0591. Taylor, Simon. PRELUDE TO GENOCIDE: NAZI IDEOLOGY AND THE STRUGGLE FOR POWER. London: Duckworth, 1985. xii, 228 pp.

A sociological study of the evolution of Nazi ideology from 1919 to 1933, analyzing Nazi propaganda and election leaflets and showing how big business and political interests manipulated public opinion and blamed social ills on the Jews. Pp. 197-222, "Ideology and Genocide," examine "why such an irrational ideology eventually became the expression of a particular social consciousness." Concludes that the German middle classes, in economic crisis, turned to an irrational explanation of their problems - the Jewish conspiracy. This belief was essential to Nazism, and salvation was possible only by elimination of the Jews.

0592. Toussaint, Ingo. DIE UNIVERSITAETSBIBLIOTHEK FREIBURG IM DRITTEN REICH. 2nd rev. ed. Muenchen: K.G. Saur, 1984. xiv, 272 pp.

Includes the effect of Nazi persecution on the fate of Jews connected with the library - the personnel, readers, booksellers, and owners of private libraries in Freiburg.

0593. Troeger, Joerg, ed. HOCHSCHULE UND WISSENSCHAFT IM DRITTEN REICH. Frankfurt a.M.: Campus-Verlag, 1984. 188 pp.

A collection of articles dealing with the connections and cooperation between National Socialism and the German scientific community. Shows that science, and scientists from various disciplines (especially engineers and physicians), played an important role in serving the Nazi regime and its anti-Jewish policy.

0594. Turner, Henry Ashby. GERMAN BIG BUSINESS AND THE RISE OF HITLER. New York: Oxford University Press, 1985. xxi, 504 pp.

German big business before 1933 did not, on the whole, support Hitler and his political program. Antisemitism was regarded by German business circles with distaste as a vulgar and plebian phenomenon and the Nazis had to play it down. Nazi attacks on Jewish "finance capitalism" are mentioned.

0595. Vischer, Wilhelm. Témoignage d'un contemporain. REVUE D'HISTOIRE ET DE PHILOSOPHIE RELIGIEUSES 64, 2 (1984) 117-122.

The author, who taught Old Testament studies in Germany during the early 1930s, describes the circumstances surrounding the Barmen Declaration of 1934, in which he tried without success to introduce a passage condemning Nazi persecution of the Jews.

0596. Wagener, Otto. HITLER - MEMOIRS OF A CONFIDANT. Ed. by Henry Ashby Turner. Trans. by Ruth Hein. New Haven, CT: Yale University Press, 1985. xxvi, 333 pp. Originally published as "Hitler aus naechster Naehe" (Frankfurt a.M.: Ullstein, 1978).

An account by Otto Wagener, Chief of Staff for the SA, later head of the Economic Policy Section of the Nazi Party 1929-1933, of his conversations with Hitler, reconstructed from memory in 1946. For specific statements about Jews, see the index.

0597. Watson, George. Was Hitler a Marxist? ENCOUNTER 63, 5 (Dec 1984) 19-25.

Between 1913-1914, and during his time in Landsberg prison (1923-1924), Hitler read Marxist literature. Argues that Hitler found Marxism "indispensable" and was much influenced by it. Marx "publicly declared that whole nations as well as whole classes would have to be exterminated."

0598. Weckbecker, Arno. DIE JUDENVERFOLGUNG IN HEIDELBERG 1933-1945. Heidelberg: C.F. Mueller Juristischer Verlag, 1985. 286 pp.

A history of the persecution of the Jews in Heidelberg during the Nazi era. Describes the rise of the local Nazi party and its antisemitism before 1933, anti-Jewish legislation relating to the expulsion of Jews from public and economic life, the "Kristallnacht" pogrom, and the deportations during the war.

0599. Weckbecker, Arno. Die Judenverfolgung in Heidelberg 1933-1945: Ein Ueberblick. HEIDELBERG UNTER DEM NATIONALSOZIALISMUS, eds. Joerg Schadt, Michael Caroli. Heidelberg: C.F. Mueller Juristischer Verlag, 1985. Pp. 399-467.

Surveys the organization of the Jewish community in Heidelberg, and gives a detailed description (with statistical data) of the discrimination, persecutions, and deportations of the 1696 Jews of Heidelberg.

0600. Wicke, Peter. Sentimentality and High Pathos: Popular Music in Fascist Germany. POPULAR MUSIC 5 (1985) 149-158.

Examines the influence on German popular music of the Reichskulturkammer (Reich Chamber of Culture). On pp. 151-153, describes the "dejudification" process by which Jewish composers and performers were expelled from the profession. "Jewish" music, e.g. jazz, was described as Negro music seen through the eyes of New York Jews; it was a major economic competitor with German music.

0601. Wilhelm, Hans-Heinrich. The Holocaust in National-Socialist Rhetoric and Writings: Some Evidence against the Thesis That before 1945 Nothing Was Known about the "Final Solution." YAD VASHEM STUDIES 16 (1984) 95-127. Appeared simultaneously in Hebrew.

Historians searching for "secret" sources to prove who knew about the Final Solution have overlooked clear and "open" evidence - the public speeches and writings of Nazi leaders. Discusses two works as examples: an editorial by Josef Goebbels in the widely-distributed newspaper "Das Reich," 9 May 1943 (quoted here almost in full), and a pamphlet by Robert Ley, "Pesthauch der Welt" ("Pestilential Miasma of the World"), published in 1944 in Dresden. Millions of readers, then, knew that the Final Solution was in progress, unless they claim "selective perception" as an argument for lack of awareness.

0602. Wolgast, Eike. Die geistige Gleichschaltung als Bestandteil der nationalsozialistischen Machtergreifung 1933. HEIDELBERGER JAHRBUECHER 28 (1984) 41-57.

The last part of this article (pp. 50-55) discusses the attitudes of German university professors and students towards the expulsion of their Jewish colleagues from the universities; most of them supported the Nazi anti-Jewish policy.

0603. Zedek, Moshe. Demystifying the Holocaust. ISRAEL HORIZONS 32, 3/4 (Mar/Apr 1984) 3-5, 31.

Speaks against the contention that the Holocaust is "unknowable" and "cannot be understood." Explains the rise of the Nazis to power as a logical development of political and economic conditions, and antisemitism as the Nazis' inevitable tool.

1919-1945: The Islamic World

0604. לוי, אבנר. הפרעות ביהודי תראקיה, 1934. פעמים 20 (1984) 111-132.

[Levi, Avner. The Anti-Jewish Pogrom in Terakia, 1934. PE`AMIM 20 (1984) 111-132.]

Describes the pogrom (looting, beatings, and intimidation with intent to expel the Jews) in 1934 in Thrace (European Turkey), when 3,000 of the 13,000 Jewish inhabitants fled the area. Discusses the background to this event - Turkish nationalism, the influence of Nazi propaganda, and particularly C.R. Atilhan and his antisemitic newspaper "Millî Inkilâp." Finally, the central government condemned and put a stop to this harassment.

0605. Allali, Jean-Pierre. Le pogrom de Constantine. TERRE RETROUVEE 952 (Oct 1984) 22.

Marks 50 years since the pogrom on 5 August 1934.

0606. Attal, Robert. Le pogrom de Constantine du 5 août 1934. TRACES 11 (1984) 62-73.

The Muslim population of Constantine, Algeria, provoked by French antisemitic propaganda, assaulted the Jews on August 3rd-5th, 1934. Gives the background to French antisemitism in Algeria and describes the pogrom.

0607. Ayoun, Richard. A propos du pogrom de Constantine (août 1934). REVUE DES ETUDES JUIVES 144, 1-3 (Jan-Sept 1985) 181-186.

Since 1929, Jewish-Muslim confrontations were recurrent in Constantine as a result of economic crisis, the rise of Algerian nationalism, and antisemitic propaganda from Palestine and Syria, influenced by Nazi and French right-wing ideas. Describes the pogrom which broke out after rumors spread that the Jews were burning mosques and killing Muslims. 23 Jews were killed, hundreds injured, and houses and shops destroyed. Anti-Jewish violence broke out in other towns of the area, indicating premeditation. Suggests the possibility of collusion by the authorities.

1919-1945: The USA and Canada

0608. מלצר, יהודית. אנטישמיות אצל כהני-הדת בצבא ארה"ב (בימי מלחמת העולם השנייה). הדואר 64, כה (17 מאי 1985) 403-404.

[Meltzer, Judith. Antisemitism amongst the Chaplains in the U.S. Armed Forces (during World War II). HADOAR 64, 25 (17 May 1985) 403-404.]

Translated from the English, and part of a broader research work carried out by the author, based on material from the JWB archives and the personal collections of Jewish chaplains. Describes a number of antisemitic incidents involving Christian chaplains.

0609. קאופמן, מנחם. לא-ציונים באמריקה במאבק על המדינה, 1939-1948. ירושלים: הספריה הציונית על-יד ההסתדרות הציונית העולמית, 1984. יב, 413, xxiii עמ'. (סידרת מחקרים של המכון ליהדות זמננו, האוניברסיטה העברית בירושלים).

[Kaufman, Menahem. NON-ZIONISTS IN AMERICA AND THE STRUGGLE FOR JEWISH STATEHOOD, 1939-1948. Jerusalem: Hassifriya Haziyonit, 1984. 413, xxiii pp. (Series of

Studies of the Institute of Contemporary Jewry, Hebrew University of Jerusalem).] With an English summary.

Includes references to the role of antisemitism, which was on the rise in the US in the 1930s and early 1940s, as a determinant in the attitudes and policies of Jewish non-Zionist groups.

0610. Ashkenas, Bruce. A Legacy of Hatred: The Records of a Nazi Organization in America. PROLOGUE 17, 2 (Sum 1985) 93-106.

An illustrated article on the activities of the German American Bund (1933-1941) based on records held by the US National Archives which reflect the antisemitic and pro-Nazi propaganda of the Bund and American reactions to it. Concludes that the majority of Americans, even fascists, saw the Bund as a foreign aberration and that it had little appeal for most German-Americans. The Bund archive also contains a unique file on anti-Nazi organizations.

0611. Capeci, Dominic J. Black-Jewish Relations in Wartime Detroit: The Marsh, Loving, Wolf Surveys and the Race Riot of 1943. JEWISH SOCIAL STUDIES 47, 3/4 (Sum/Fall 1985) 221-242.

Spurred by interracial tensions and rising antisemitism, Blacks attacked and looted Jewish shops on Hastings Street in Detroit on 20 June 1943. Describes surveys conducted by sociologist Donald C. Marsh and associates during the winter of 1942/43 on Black/Jewish customer-merchant attitudes, and a follow-up survey in fall 1944 to measure the effects of the riot. The results showed that "black antagonisms stemmed from socioeconomic factors rather than antisemitism per se."

0612. Davies, Alan; Nefsky, Marilyn Felcher. The United Church and the Jewish Plight during the Nazi Era, 1933-1945. CANADIAN JEWISH HISTORICAL SOCIETY JOURNAL 8, 2 (Fall 1984) 55-71.

Irving Abella and Harold Troper, in "None is Too Many" (Random House, 1982), accused the Canadian churches of silence on the fate of the Jews during the Nazi era. In fact, the attitude of the United Church was more complex. While some Germanophile, Volkisch ideas were expressed in the Church journal "New Outlook," the editorial line condemned Nazi policy. Several activists called for the admission of Jewish refugees to Canada, and in 1937 Church institutions and some local presbyteries began to act on this issue. However, the Church as a body failed to react to the horrors of the Holocaust because they could not believe the reports.

0613. Eisen, George. The Voices of Sanity: American Diplomatic Reports from the 1936 Berlin Olympiad. JOURNAL OF SPORT HISTORY 11, 3 (1984) 56-78.

Confidential diplomatic reports from Berlin and Vienna, found in the US National Archives, show that though aware of the discriminatory practices aimed at Jewish athletes, no American political leader voiced opposition to US participation in the Olympics.

0614. Falk, Gerhard. The Reaction of the German-American Press to Nazi Persecutions, 1933-1941. JOURNAL OF REFORM JUDAISM 32, 2 (Spr 1985) 12-23.

A survey of the views of 14 German-language newspapers, as presented in the "Buffalo Volksfreund," shows general sympathy for Hitler and Nazi antisemitic policies until America's entry into the war.

0615. Feldman, Egal. Reinhold Niebuhr and the Jews. JEWISH SOCIAL STUDIES 46, 3/4 (Sum/Fall 1984) 293-302.

Reinhold Niebuhr (1892-1971), the American Protestant theologian, was one of the first to direct attention to the rising wave of antisemitism in Nazi Germany and to make efforts to bring about US intervention in the war. Niebuhr admitted that the roots of antisemitism lie in the sacred sources of Christian belief, and was strongly opposed to the Christian proselytizing of Jews. He also assisted American Zionists and criticized British policy in 1946-47.

0616. Finger, Seymour Maxwell. AMERICAN JEWRY DURING THE HOLOCAUST. New York: Holmes and Meier, 1984. Various pagings.

The report of the American Jewish Commission on the Holocaust on the response of American Jewry to the Holocaust. Refers in passing to the role of antisemitism in the US in shaping that response, and to the failure of US Jews to distinguish between traditional antisemitism and Nazism.

0617. Fleischman, Harry. Norman Thomas and the Jews. JEWISH FRONTIER 52, 1 (Jan 1985) 8-10.

Norman Thomas (1884-1968), the Protestant minister and Socialist leader, expressed great sympathy for the Jews suffering from antisemitism. Thomas fought to open America's doors to Jewish refugees during World War II.

0618. Glass, William R. Fundamentalism's Prophetic Vision of the Jews: The 1930s. JEWISH SOCIAL STUDIES 47, 1 (Win 1985) 63-76.

A study of US Christian fundamentalist writings from the 1930s shows that their view of the Jews was shaped by their understanding of Biblical prophecy and the role to be played by the Jews in their millennial scheme. Both the return to Zion and the rise of antisemitism in Europe were interpreted as signs of the imminent return of Christ. Antisemitism should not be actively opposed, except by prayer and relief; since it was due to the divine rejection of the Jews, it was to be combatted by evangelism. Failure to condemn Nazi antisemitic policies also reflected a greater concern with fighting communism.

0619. Harper, Jimmy. Alabama Baptists and the Rise of Hitler and Fascism, 1930-1938. JOURNAL OF REFORM JUDAISM 32, 2 (Spr 1985) 1-11.

Fundamentalist antisemitic attitudes influenced Southern Baptist thought and encouraged an initially favorable attitude towards Hitler and fascism. Though officially condemning antisemitism, Alabama Baptists repeated German slurs. Their attitudes were molded by racial and religious prejudice against minorities, approval of Hitler as an anticommunist and an apparently moral, upright figure, and the influence of traditional antisemitism.

0620. Helling, Rudolf A. A SOCIO-ECONOMIC HISTORY OF GERMAN-CANADIANS: THEY, TOO, FOUNDED CANADA. Wiesbaden: Franz Steiner Verlag, 1984. 156 pp. (Vierteljahrschrift fuer Sozial- und Wirtschaftsgeschichte, Beiheft 75).

A general history of the German community in Canada. In 1933, the Nazi government in Berlin began to organize and propagandize German-Canadians. German-language newspapers published antisemitic pieces. When refugees from Nazism, Jews and others, arrived during World War II, Canadian officials seemed oblivious to the moral and ideological issues involved.

0621. Higham, Charles. AMERICAN SWASTIKA. Garden City, NY: Doubleday, 1985. xxvii, 332 pp.

A study of the connections between Americans and Nazis from the 1930s until after World War II. "Documents the covert activities of Nazi collaborators in the Senate and in the hierarchy of the Catholic Church... the protection of Nazi mass murderers by members of the Roosevelt and other administrations." Father Coughlin and Senator Burton K. Wheeler, leader of the "America First" movement which opposed US intervention in World War II, were supported financially and politically by Germany. Many Americans accepted the identification of Jews with Communism, which was viewed as a greater evil than Nazism. Describes activities of the German-American Bund.

0622. Kolodny, Ralph L. Catholics and Father Coughlin: Misremembering the Past. PATTERNS OF PREJUDICE 19, 4 (Oct 1985) 15-25.

Progressive Catholic historians have attempted to minimize the support of American Catholics for Father Charles Coughlin, the populist antisemitic broadcaster. However, evidence shows that many Catholics who felt threatened by anti-clerical movements in Spain and in the USSR turned to right-wing movements. Coughlin's broadcasts and newspapers popularized the "Protocols of the Elders of Zion," and the Christian Front, a group of supporters, attacked Jews physically. Coughlin also received support from important figures in the Catholic hierarchy.

0623. Kraut, Alan M.; Breitman, Richard D.; Imhoof, Thomas W. The State Department, the Labor Department, and German Jewish Immigration, 1930-1940. JOURNAL OF AMERICAN ETHNIC HISTORY 3, 2 (Spr 1984) 5-38.

The Hoover administration reduced immigration from Europe far below the level allowed by the Immigration Act of 1924. Throughout the 1930s, State Department officials controlled the distribution of visas. Secretary of Labor Frances Perkins sought special consideration for refugees and an increase in immigration from Germany. This engendered a struggle between the State Department and the Labor Department, from which State emerged in 1940 with near complete jurisdiction over visa policy. The matter of antisemitism in the State Department and in the Foreign Service (among consuls) is also discussed.

0624. Lewis, David Levering. Henry Ford's Anti-Semitism and its Repercussions. MICHIGAN JEWISH HISTORY 24, 1 (1984) 3-10. Unseen.

0625. Lewis, David Levering. Parallels and Divergencies: Assimilationist Strategies of Afro-American and Jewish Elites from 1910 to the Early 1930s. JOURNAL OF AMERICAN HISTORY 71, 3 (Dec 1984) 543-564.

Examines the collaboration of the elite groups of the Jewish and Black communities - wealthy established German Jews and educated Northern Blacks - in fighting antisemitism and racism. Both Southern Black migrants and East European Jewish immigrants met vicious discrimination. Their leadership tried to counter it with legal battles for equality, fighting racism in art and literature, and an ideology of integration through assimilation - strategies that were far-removed from the daily problems of ordinary Blacks and Jews.

0626. Lewis, David Levering. Shortcuts to the Mainstream: Afro-American and Jewish Notables in the 1920s and 1930s. JEWS IN BLACK PERSPECTIVES: A DIALOGUE, ed. Joseph R. Washington. Rutherford, NJ: Fairleigh Dickinson University Press, 1984. Pp. 83-87.

Discusses the intensive activity of American Jewish public figures on behalf of American Blacks during this period. Blacks and Jews share "not a similar heritage but an identical adversary - a species of white gentile." The Black and Jewish leaderships, who combined to fight against racism and antisemitism, shared an ideology of equality through assimilation and integration.

0627. Lipstadt, Deborah E. The American Press and the Persecution of German Jewry: The Early Years 1933-1935. LEO BAECK INSTITUTE YEAR BOOK 29 (1984) 27-55.

Studies the American press's reactions to Nazi antisemitism, and analyzes the manner in which the news was presented to the public. Antisemitic persecutions were an important but certainly not central element of foreign press reports, and evoked more interest during the early periods of Nazi rule than it did in subsequent years.

0628. Maga, Timothy P. The Quest for a Generous America: Varian Fry and the Refugee Cause 1940-1942. HOLOCAUST STUDIES ANNUAL 1 <1983> (1984) 69-87.

Describes the efforts of Varian Fry, a New York writer, to assist refugees, mainly Jewish, in unoccupied France. Fry, sent by the Emergency Rescue Committee of the American Friends of German Freedom to rescue intellectuals and political refugees, was hampered by the uncooperative attitudes of the American government, and especially the consulate which did all in its power to prevent Jewish immigration. When despite America's entry into the war strict quotas were not relaxed, Fry publicly attacked Roosevelt's government.

0629. Michael, Robert. America and the Holocaust. MIDSTREAM 31, 2 (Feb 1985) 13-16.

Surveys the attitudes of the American population, of government officials (including President Roosevelt), and of the Churches towards Jews during the Holocaust period. Their view was that of a negative stereotype, based on theological, mythological antisemitism, manifested by discrimination and indifference laced with hostility. They were not interested in saving European Jewry from the Holocaust.

0630. Morgan, Ted. FDR: A BIOGRAPHY. New York: Simon and Schuster, 1985. 830 pp.

See index for Roosevelt's attitude to the Jewish refugee problem during the 1930s and 1940s, and the influence of antisemitism on his administration.

0631. Ogles, Robert M.; Howard, Herbert H. Father Coughlin in the Periodical Press, 1931-1942. JOURNALISM QUARTERLY 61, 2 (Sum 1984) 280-286, 363.

During the 1930s Coughlin became a major media figure with his famous radio broadcasts. However, his attacks on the Jews and his support for Hitler finally made him unacceptable and in 1942 he was effectively silenced. Examination of the coverage of Coughlin's activities in seven major journals, and statistical analysis of references in them to major themes of his career (among them antisemitism and pro-Nazism), show that the press took a generally negative attitude towards Coughlin.

0632. Shapiro, Edward S. The Approach of War: Congressional Isolationism and Anti-Semitism, 1939-1941. AMERICAN JEWISH HISTORY 74, 1 (Sept 1984) 45-65.

At a time when the desire of most Jews for intervention in European politics was opposed to that of most Americans to avoid such involvement, the Jews could easily be accused of disloyalty. Surveys the background and thinking of a small group of Senators and Congressmen who accused Jewish bankers of conspiring to drag the US into war. Hollywood, generally believed to be controlled by Jews, was said to be whipping up war hysteria. These Congressmen, often from agrarian states, were influenced by the Populist-Progressive tradition and believed that big business and the Jews had engineered America's entry into World War I.

0633. Shapiro, Edward S. The World Labor Athletic Carnival of 1936: An American Anti-Nazi Protest. AMERICAN JEWISH HISTORY 74, 3 (Mar 1985) 255-273.

After a campaign for a US boycott of the 1936 Berlin Olympics failed, the pro-boycott faction of the American Athletics Union and the Jewish Labor Committee held a World Labor Athletic Carnival in New York to protest German antisemitic sporting policy and the International Olympic Committee's acquiescence to it. The movement for workers' sports failed, but it helped the pro-boycott faction to depose their opponent Avery Brundage from the AAU. He became an outspoken antisemite.

0634. Shapiro, Warren. Some Implications of Clark Wissler's Race Theory. MANKIND 15, 1 (Apr 1985) 1-17.

A recent attempt to place the American anthropologist Clark Wissler (1870-1947) in a central position in the history of anthropology ignores his blatant racism, expressed not only in scholarly circles but also in his work for the US government. He gave "scientific" status to the 1924 Immigration Act which preferred "Nordic" immigrants and reduced the quotas of others. Although he was not specifically anti-Jewish, Wissler bears responsibility for use of the Act to prevent the admission of Jewish refugees into the US.

0635. Strum, Harvey. Fort Ontario Refugee Shelter, 1944-1946. AMERICAN JEWISH HISTORY 73, 4 (June 1984) 398-421.

Discusses the Fort Ontario (Oswego) Refugee Shelter and US policy towards refugees during World War II, shaped by a climate of antisemitism.

0636. Strum, Harvey. Henry Stimson's Opposition to American Jews and Zionism. PATTERNS OF PREJUDICE 18, 4 (Oct 1984) 17-24.

Henry Stimson disliked Jews but was offended by blatant antisemitism and appalled by German persecution of the Jews. However, as an opponent of Jewish immigration since the 1920s, Stimson persuaded Roosevelt not to set up refugee camps in the US. After the war he perceived US Jewry's demand for a Jewish state and denazification of Germany as hostile to US interests.

0637. Wyman, David S. THE ABANDONMENT OF THE JEWS: AMERICA AND THE HOLOCAUST, 1941-1945. New York: Pantheon Books, 1984. xv, 444 pp.

A study of the failure of the USA to carry out a major rescue effort to save the Jews of Europe, due to the hostility of the State Department to Jewish immigration; the lack of cooperation from Roosevelt and his administration who feared an influx of Jews; the lack of strong public pressure on account of antisemitism and anti-immigrant attitudes; and the indifference of Americans in general, including the mass media and the Churches, to the Holocaust. Provides new evidence for the personal responsiblity of President Roosevelt. Cites the failure of American Jewish organizations to make an effective response.

1919-1945: The USSR and Eastern Europe

0638. ארד, יצחק. המדיניות ודרכי הביצוע של "הפתרון הסופי" בליטא. יהדות ליטא, עורך: לייב גרפונקל. כרך 4: השואה, 1941-1945. תל-אביב: איגוד יוצאי ליטא בישראל, 1984. עמ' 39-47.

[Arad, Yitzhak. The Policy and Implementation of the "Final Solution" in Lithuania. LITHUANIAN JEWRY, ed. Leib Garfunkel. Vol. 4: The Holocaust, 1941-1945. Tel-Aviv: Igud Yots'ei Lita b'Israel, 1984. Pp. 39-47.]

Defines three periods in the German implementation of their anti-Jewish policy: June-December 1941, in which 173-177,000 Jews were exterminated by Einsatzgruppen and by Lithuanians who organized pogroms and mass murders; January 1942-July 1943, in which Jewish work-power was exploited, along with selective extermination actions; August 1943-July 1944, when those who could work were put in concentration camps and the rest were murdered.

0639. באדנר, רוברט. החקלאות היהודית בפולין בראי "דער יידישער
לאנדווירט" (1933-1939). גלעד 7/8 (1985) 141-160.

[Badner, Robert. Jewish Agriculture in Interwar Poland as Reflected in "Der Yiddisher Landwirt" (1933-1939). GAL-ED 7/8 (1985) 141-160.]

A study of Jewish farmers, based on articles in the Polish-Yiddish journal "Der Yiddisher Landwirt" published in Lvov from 1933 to 1939. Although, between the two World Wars, rural Polish Jews experienced pogroms, anti-Jewish propaganda, and anti-Jewish legislation, they identified totally with the Polish state and failed to see the coming Holocaust.

0640. בנק, חיים. אנטישמיות בין שכנינו בברזיב. ספר זכרון -
קהילת ברזיב (בז׳וזוב), ערך אברהם לויטה. תל-אביב: יוצאי
בז׳וזוב והסביבה, 1984. עמ׳ 50-51.

[Bank, Chaim. Antisemitism among Our Neighbors in Brzozów. A MEMORIAL TO THE BRZOZOW COMMUNITY, ed. Avraham Levite. Tel Aviv: Survivors of Brzozów, 1984. Pp. 50-51.]

Describes antisemitic incidents, and pogroms, in the town of Brzozów and in Poland during the 1930s.

0641. גאר, יוסף. פרטים על חורבן ליטא בדו"חות של "עוצבות
המבצע," ב"דו"ח ואלטר שטאלקר" וב"רשימה המסכמת" של קרל
יגר. יהדות ליטא, עורך: לייב גרפונקל. כרך 4: השואה,
1941-1945. תל-אביב: איגוד יוצאי ליטא בישראל, 1984.
עמ׳ 21-26.

[Gar, Joseph. Details on the Destruction of Lithuanian Jewry in the Reports of the "Einsatzgruppen," in the "Walter Stahlecker Report" and in the "Summary Report" of Karl Jaeger. LITHUANIAN JEWRY, ed. Leib Garfunkel. Vol. 4: The Holocaust, 1941-1945. Tel-Aviv: Igud Yots'ei Lita b'Israel, 1984. Pp. 21-26.]

The reports were written by the Reich Security office from the end of June 1941 to 24 April 1942, based on reports from the field, excerpts of which are given here relating to the extermination of the Jews, along with excerpts from the reports of SS Commanders Walter Stahlecker and Karl Jaeger.

0642. גרפונקל, לייב. חשבוננו עם הליטאים. יהדות ליטא, עורך: לייב גרפונקל. כרך 4: השואה, 1941-1945. תל-אביב: איגוד יוצאי ליטא בישראל, 1984. עמ' 48-60.

[Garfunkel, Leib. Our Account with the Lithuanians. LITHUANIAN JEWRY, ed. Leib Garfunkel. Vol. 4: The Holocaust, 1941-1945. Tel-Aviv: Igud Yots'ei Lita b'Israel, 1984. Pp. 48-60.]

Describes Lithuanian antisemitism during the years of independence (1919-1940), during the Soviet occupation (1940/41), and particularly after the German occupation in June 1941 when Lithuanians collaborated in the mass extermination of the Jews.

0643. דראזדאווסקי, מאריאן מ. די באציונג פון דער פוילישער רעגירונג פונעם גענעראל וולאדיסלאוו שיקארסקי צו דער טראגעדיע פון די פוילישע יידן. בלעטער פאר געשיכטע 22 (1984) 113-132.

[Drozdowski, Marian M. The Attitude of General Wladyslaw Sikorski's Polish Government towards the Tragedy of the Polish Jews. BLETER FAR GESZICHTE 22 (1984) 113-132.] Trans. from Polish. With English and Polish summaries. Appeared in English in ACTA POLONIAE HISTORICA 52 (1985) 147-170.

Describes efforts by Sikorski and the Polish government-in-exile to inform the world about the plight of the Jews in Poland between 1939 and 1943, and aid given to the Jews by the Polish underground.

0644. נוסבאום, קלמן. והפך להם לרועץ: היהודים בצבא העממי הפולני בברית-המועצות. תל-אביב: אוניברסיטת תל-אביב, המכון לחקר התפוצות, 1984. 380 עמ'.

[Nussbaum, Klemens. A STORY OF AN ILLUSION: THE JEWS IN THE POLISH PEOPLE'S ARMY IN THE USSR. Tel-Aviv: Tel-Aviv University, Diaspora Research Institute, 1984. 380 pp.]

Deals with efforts made by Polish Jews living in the USSR during World War II to join the Polish brigades. These Jews, who joined the Polish army for ideological motives and played an important role in its military activities, faced the discriminatory policy of Polish military authorities, including an attempt to impose a "numerus clausus" for Jews, especially during the creation of the units commanded by General Anders.

0645. נוסבאום, קלמן. "לגיון יהודי" או אחיזת עיניים? שבות 10 (1984) 47-54.

[Nussbaum, Klemens. "Jewish Legion" or Delusion? SHVUT 10 (1984) 47-54.]

During World War II, when a Polish army was established in the USSR under the command of General Anders, a proposal was made to organize a separate "Jewish legion." Polish military circles supported the plan because they wanted to carry out a selection in the military units in order to exclude the Jews, whom they considered to be an undesirable element.

0646. פרעקער, טערעסא. פוילישע קאטוילישע אינטעליגענץ לגבי דער טראגעדיע פון פוילישע יידן. בלעטער פאר געשיכטע 22 (1984) 133-148.

[Prekerowa, Teresa. Polish Catholic Intelligentsia and the Tragedy of the Polish Jews <Exemplified by the Activities of Two Catholic Underground Organizations - the "Front Odrodzenia Polski" and "Unia">. BLETER FAR GESZICHTE 22 (1984) 133-148.] With English and Polish summaries.

The "Unia" was a militant political Christian-Democratic organization, whereas the FOP was non-political, and devoted to social and educational problems. Describes the ideology and activities of the FOP in helping Jews, in contrast to conservative Catholic bodies who evinced antisemitism. The "Unia" called on its members to help Jews individually, but not collectively as did the FOP. This attitude towards Jews changed after the war, when the old negative stereotypes of the Jew resurfaced.

0647. רדליך, שמעון. תדמית היהודים בעיניהם של לא-יהודים בצבא הסובייטי בתקופת מלחמת העולם השניה. שבות 11 (1985) 97-104.

[Redlich, Shimon. The Image of the Jews as Perceived by Non-Jews in the Soviet Army during the Second World War. SHVUT 11 (1985) 97-104.]

Based on testimonies of 80 Soviet POWs captured and interrogated by German intelligence units in 1944/45 and documented on microfilm at the U.S. National Archives. The image is extremely negative; Jews are perceived as parasites, evading army service, being responsible for the war, having powerful positions in the USSR hierarchy, serving as NKVD agents, and identifying with the policy of extermination of their own people.

0648. Ancel, Jean. Plans for Deportation of the Rumanian Jews and Their Discontinuation in Light of Documentary Evidence (July-October 1942). YAD VASHEM STUDIES 16 (1984) 381-420. Appeared simultaneously in Hebrew.

In September 1942 the Romanian Prime Minister approved plans for the deportation of Romania's Jews to Belzec extermination camp. The Jewish underground leadership, learning about the plan from the Nazi press and from Romanian officials, organized a petition in protest. The US government warned that if deportations are carried out "measures shall be taken against Rumanians living in America." The American protest made a strong impression on Romania's ruling circles; also, they did not wish to become a puppet state of Germany. Therefore, despite official approval of the German plan, it was not implemented. Pp. 391-420 contain documents.

0649. Ardeleanu, Ion et al. TEROAREA HORTHYSTO-FASCISTA IN NORD-VESTUL ROMANIEI, SEPTEMBRIE 1940-OCTOMBRIE 1944 [Horthyist-Fascist Terror in North-West Romania, September 1940-October 1944]. Bucharest: Editura Politică, 1985. 340 pp.

Deals with the occupation of the northwest part of Romania by the Hungarian regime of Miklós Horthy and its treatment of the Romanian population. Includes information on the Jewish population (pp. 176-195) - conditions in concentration camps, acts of terror, lack of food, forced labor, etc. After Germany's occupation of Hungary in 1944, the terror increased. On the Final Solution in Transylvania, see pp. 249-295.

0650. Benvenisti, David. At the Deep Roots of That Unique Phenomenon - the Salvation of the Bulgarian Jews. SOCIAL, CULTURAL AND EDUCATIONAL ASSOCIATION OF THE JEWS IN THE PEOPLE'S REPUBLIC OF BULGARIA ANNUAL 19 (1984) 133-142.

Explains the failure of fascism and Nazism in Bulgaria, due to Bulgarian resistance to antisemitism.

0651. Cohen, Asher. Continuity in the Change: Hungary, 19 March 1944. JEWISH SOCIAL STUDIES 46, 2 (Spr 1984) 131-144.

Examines the negative attitudes of politicians, intellectuals, and the general population in Hungary towards the Jews during the inter-war period, which facilitated the swift deportation of Hungarian Jewry, most of them to Auschwitz, after the German occupation in March 1944. The Jews believed that they had successfully assimilated into Hungarian society, and were not equipped to help themselves in 1944.

0652. Cohen, David. The Monarcho-Fascist Establishment, Nazi Germany and the Jewish Problem in Bulgaria. SOCIAL, CULTURAL AND EDUCATIONAL ASSOCIATION OF THE JEWS IN THE PEOPLE'S REPUBLIC OF BULGARIA ANNUAL 19 (1984) 63-83.

An account of anti-Jewish measures by the "fascist monarchic" regime in Bulgaria during World War II, from a communist point of view, charging that the regime cooperated with the Nazis in attempts to deport the Jews.

0653. Dagan, Avigdor, ed. THE JEWS OF CZECHOSLOVAKIA. Vol. 3. Philadelphia: Jewish Publication Society of America; New York: Society for the History of Czechoslovak Jews, 1984. xii, 700 pp.

This volume concludes a trilogy on the history of Czechoslovakia's Jews from 1918 to 1948. Vol. 3 covers the Holocaust years and the attempts to rebuild Jewish communal life in Bohemia, Moravia, and Slovakia after World War II. See the index for references to antisemitism.

0654. Dushkov, Zhidovar. On Some Problems of Anti-Semitism in Bulgaria in the Years of the Second World War. SOCIAL, CULTURAL AND EDUCATIONAL ASSOCIATION OF THE JEWS IN THE PEOPLE'S REPUBLIC OF BULGARIA ANNUAL 19 (1984) 143-149.

An explanation, in communist terms, of Bulgarian fascist antisemitism, described as a German import, motivated by economic competition and an attempt to divert the attention of the working classes.

0655. Erez, Zvi. The Jews of Budapest and the Plans of Admiral Horthy, August-October 1944. YAD VASHEM STUDIES 16 (1984) 177-203. Appeared simultaneously in Hebrew.

Describes Horthy's negotiations with the Allies, particularly the Soviets, to arrange a secret surrender so that Hungary would be occupied by the Russians rather than the Germans. In October the Germans foiled these plans, aided by the antisemitic Hungarian Arrow Cross Party. Discusses Horthy's attitude toward the Jews - he wanted to save them because he thought they were important to the Allies, and partly for humane reasons - and the attitude of the Allied Powers, who were indifferent.

0656. George, Emery. István Bibó, "The Jewish Question in Hungary": A Review Essay. CROSS CURRENTS 4 (1985) 47-57.

Bibó's article, written in 1948, was reprinted in the original Hungarian in "Zsidókérdés, asszimiláció, antiszemitizmus," ed. by Péter Hanák (see no. 261). George describes the article, covering the inter-war period and post-World War II, including anti-Jewish legislation in Hungary and the failure of the Churches to aid the Jews during the Holocaust, and compares it with his own experiences. Bibó's discussion of the nature of antisemitism (religious, economic, psychological) is compared with that of Sartre.

0657. Glatz, Ferenc, ed. AZ 1944 EV HISTORIAJA [The Year 1944 in History]. Budapest: Lapkiado Vallalat, 1984. 175 pp.

An anthology marking the fortieth anniversary of the German occupation of Hungary in 1944, including articles, documents and photographs dealing with the persecution of the Jews and the Holocaust. Includes some material on antisemitism in Hungary during the inter-war period.

0658. Grinberg, Maria. Robotniczy Kongres walki przeciwko antysemityzmowi (z dziejów żydowskiego ruchu zawodowego) [The Workers' Congress to Combat Antisemitism (from the History of the Jewish Syndicalist Movement)]. BIULETYN ZYDOWSKIEGO INSTYTUTU HISTORYCZNEGO W POLSCE 129/130 (Jan-June 1984) 39-60.

Discusses antisemitism in Poland in the 1930s and the struggle against it by the socialists, the left-wing intelligentsia, Polish trade unionists, and the Jewish population. Describes a proposal to organize a Workers' Congress to Combat Antisemitism, supported by the Polish Communist Party and some Jewish parties. However, the Congress did not take place.

0659. Hillgruber, Andreas. Der Ostkrieg und die Judenvernichtung. "UNTERNEHMEN BARBAROSSA": DER DEUTSCHE UEBERFALL AUF DIE SOWJET UNION 1941, eds. Gerd R. Ueberschaer, Wolfram Wette. Paderborn: Schoening, 1984. Pp. 219-234.

Deals with the extermination of the Jews living in the Russian-occupied territories, in the context of the German invasion of Russia and the war in the East. Analyzes the connection between Nazi anti-Communist and racist ideology and the Final Solution.

0660. Iancu, Carol. Les associations et mouvements de jeunesse juifs sionistes en Europe de l'Est avant la Seconde Guerre Mondiale: Le cas de la Roumanie. MOUVEMENTS DE JEUNESSE CHRETIENS ET JUIFS, eds. Gérard Cholvy et al. Paris: Editions du Cerf, 1985. Pp. 301-311.

Views antisemitism as one of the factors motivating the establishment of Zionist youth organizations in Romania before World War II.

0661. Karády, Viktor. Les juifs de Hongrie sous les lois antisémites: Etude d'une conjoncture sociologique, 1938-1943. ACTES DE LA RECHERCHE EN SCIENCES SOCIALES 56 (Mar 1985) 3-30.

Studies the antisemitic legislation in Hungary and the reaction of the Jewish population (with statistical data on economic status, degree of assimilation, etc.). Concludes that the reaction was weak and marked by continued confidence that official institutions would protect them from German demands, even as the antisemitic laws were being passed.

0662. Kawalec, Krzysztof. Obóz narodowy wobec sukcesu hitlerowców [The National Movement vis-à-vis Hitler's Success]. SLASKI KWARTALNIK HISTORYCZNY SOBOTKA 2 (1984) 235-246.

Discusses the diversified attitudes of the national movement in Poland (Endecja and other parties) between 1931-1934 towards Hitler's success. Some of them were anti-German and antisemitic at the same time; their antisemitism was not racial, but political and economic. However, extremists were fascinated by the Nazi ideas. Mentions the antisemitic and racist journal "Rozwój."

0663. Kovács, Mária M. Luttes professionnelles et antisémitisme: Chronique de la montée du fascisme dans le corps médical hongrois, 1920-1944. ACTES DE LA RECHERCHE EN SCIENCES SOCIALES 56 (Mar 1985) 31-44.

The rise of antisemitism in Hungary after World War I was reflected in intensified competition between Jewish and non-Jewish doctors, and in the struggle between an organization of right-wing doctors (MONE) and a liberal section of the Medical Federation. Even after the anti-Jewish legislation of 1938/39, which limited the proportion of Jewish doctors in the Federation, the government applied the laws in a liberal manner so as not to disrupt the health services. This policy ended with the German invasion in March 1944.

0664. Kozminski, Maciej. National Consciousness and Stereotypes in the Hungarian-Slovakian Borderland Area after the First World War. ACTA POLONIAE HISTORICA 50 (1984) 157-198.

In this study of competition between rival Hungarian and Czech nationalisms, accusations against the Jews of untrustworthiness and opportunism are described (pp. 186-187). In Slovakia they were accused of representing Hungarian interests and seen as agents of Magyarization; in Hungary they were accused of disloyalty when registering their nationality as Jewish.

0665. Krakowski, Shmuel. Holocaust in the Polish Underground Press. YAD VASHEM STUDIES 16 (1984) 241-270. Appeared simultaneously in Hebrew.

During the war years hundreds of underground papers were published in Poland, representing some eighty political parties and organizations. Offers excerpts from the most important papers, reflecting the positions of these Polish groups vis-à-vis the Jews. Concludes that the Holocaust did not change their attitudes - those who supported equal rights for all continued to do so, and those who were antisemitic before remained so.

0666. Levin, Dov. FIGHTING BACK: LITHUANIAN JEWRY'S ARMED RESISTANCE TO THE NAZIS, 1941-1945. Trans. by Moshe Kohn and Dina Cohen. Foreword by Yehuda Bauer. New York: Holmes and Meier, 1985. xvi, 298 pp. Originally published as "Lohamim ve-omdim al nafsham" (Jerusalem: Yad Vashem; Hebrew University, Institute of Contemporary Jewry, 1974).

An account of resistance to the Nazis in four major ghettos in Lithuania after 1941, and of Jews who had fled to the Soviet Union and formed the Lithuanian Division of the Soviet Army. Gives the background to the deterioration of relations between Jews and non-Jews in Lithuania during the 1930s and the period of Soviet rule (1940-41) which led to the active participation of the Lithuanians in the mass murder of the Jews. See the index for antisemitism and discrimination against Jews in the Lithuanian Division and in partisan units. Based on documents, newspaper reports, memoirs and interviews with survivors.

0667. Malia, Martin. Wiecznie powracajaca Polska [Poland's Eternal Return]. ZESZYTY HISTORYCZNE 70 (1984) 3-29. Translated from the English.

An essay on the history of Poland containing some remarks on Polish-Jewish relations between the two World Wars and on antisemitism (pp. 18-20).

0668. Mendelsohn, Ezra. Recent Work on the Jews in Inter-War East Central Europe: A Survey. STUDIES IN CONTEMPORARY JEWRY 1 (1984) 316-337.

A survey of post-World War II historiography dealing with Poland, Czechoslovakia, Hungary, Romania, and the Baltic States, including the subject of antisemitism. Includes extensive bibliographical notes (pp. 329-337).

0669. Michel, Henri. ET VARSOVIE FUT DETRUITE. Paris: Albin Michel, 1984. 455 pp.

A history of Poland from 1939 to 1946. On antisemitism in Poland and the situation of the Jews in Warsaw during World War II, see ch. 2 (pp. 69-103), "Varsovie sous l'occupation allemande."

0670. Mierzyński, Roman. Stosunek PPS do Hitlera i narodowego socjalizmu [The Attitude of the PPS to Hitler and National Socialism]. SLASKI KWARTALNIK HISTORYCZNY SOBOTKA 2 (1984) 205-217.

Discusses the critical attitude of the Polish Socialist Party (PPS) toward Hitler and National Socialism in the years 1932-1934 on the basis of articles published in the party's review "Robotnik." Analyzes fascist ideology, including antisemitism, as seen by socialist activists in this period in Poland.

0671. Mrożek, Slawomir. Nos [A Nose]. KULTURA 7/8 (July/Aug 1984) 37-45.

Describes antisemitic incidents in Poland from the writer's schooldays before the Second World War. Refers also to relations between Jews and Poles during the War.

0672. Polonsky, Antony. Roman Dmowski and Italian Fascism. IDEAS INTO POLITICS: ASPECTS OF EUROPEAN HISTORY 1880-1950, eds. R.J. Bullen, H. Pogge von Strandmann, A.B. Polonsky. London: Croom Helm, 1984. Pp. 130-146.

Dmowski (1864-1939) was the principle ideologist of the Polish Right. In the 1920s he espoused the ideas of Italian fascism, gravely underestimating the German threat to Poland. He was a rabid antisemite, arguing that the Jewish presence in Poland had prevented the emergence of a Polish middle class. He was convinced that the Jews dominated European politics, and that this would inevitably cause a violent anti-Jewish reaction.

0673. Rosenthal, David. Polish Jewry between the Wars. MIDSTREAM 30, 4 (Apr 1984) 40-45.

Describes Jewish life in the political, cultural, and economic spheres, and Polish discrimination against the Jews in those spheres.

0674. Sabev, Teodor. L'Eglise orthodoxe bulgare et la question juive. MISCELLANEA HISTORIAE ECCLESIASTICAE 9 (1984) 83-89.

Describes the fight of the Bulgarian Orthodox Church to save Bulgarian Jews during the Second World War. Church authorities strongly opposed a projected government law which would discriminate against Jews; the opposition was successful, and the Bulgarian Jews were saved.

0675. Seidmann, David. L'EXISTENCE JUIVE DANS L'OEUVRE DE PANAIT ISTRATI. Paris: Nizet, 1984. 118 pp.

Panait Istrati (1884-1935), a Romanian and French writer, was accused of antisemitism by the communists in the 1930s because of his critical attitude towards Jewish communists in the Soviet Union. Jews in Romania also attacked him because he published articles in a journal connected with the Iron Guard. Describes his life, his relations with Jews, and his literary work, and denies the accusation of antisemitism.

0676. Szakály, Sándor. A hadsereg és a zsidótoervények az ellenforradalmi Magyarországon [The Army and the Jewish Laws in Counter-Revolutionary Hungary]. VALOSAG 9 (1985) 94-101.

At the time of the anti-Jewish legislation of 1938/39, which fixed quotas for Jews in the professions and in the economic sphere, there was no antisemitism among veteran army officers and in the army command. Between 1941 and 1945 the army accepted the official line on the Jewish question, but execution of the laws depended on the individual commander. Antisemitism had a destructive effect on the army and on military discipline.

0677. Tec, Nechama. Sex Distinctions and Passing as Christians during the Holocaust. EAST EUROPEAN QUARTERLY 18, 1 (Mar 1984) 113-123.

This study of 308 Polish Jews and their 563 Polish rescuers, based on memoirs and interviews, attempts to determine whether sex (i.e. being male or female) was a variable in the Jews' success at passing as Christians or in the Christians' reactions to them. The results show no significant difference.

0678. Wapiński, Roman. Ksztaltowanie sie w Polsce w latach 1922-1939 pogladów na ruchy faszystowskie w Europie [The Formation of Views in Poland on Fascism in Europe during the Period 1922-1939]. STUDIA NAD FASZYZMEM I ZBRODNIAMI HITLEROWSKIMI 9 (1985) 89-125.

On pp. 112-113, mentions the positive interest of the Polish National Democratic Party (Endecja) in German fascist antisemitism.

0679. Weisser, Michael R. A BROTHERHOOD OF MEMORY: JEWISH LANDSMANSCHAFTEN IN THE NEW WORLD. New York: Basic Books, 1985. xiii, 303 pp.

Refers to pogroms in Eastern Europe as a factor in emigration to the US, especially the 1919-1920 pogroms in the Ukraine. Ch. 4 (pp. 112-139) describes the relief mission of the JDC in 1920 and the money raised by landsmanschaften for it. Ch. 6 describes similar efforts after World War II.

0680. Zipold-Materkowa, Grażyna. Hitler i faszyzm na lamach "Wiadomości Literackich" [Hitler and Fascism in "Wiadomości Literackie"]. SLASKI KWARTALNIK HISTORYCZNY SOBOTKA 2 (1984) 337-347.

Discusses the critical and clear-sighted reaction of the Polish literary journal "Wiadomości Literackie" to Hitler and fascism in the period 1933-1939, especially that of one of its columnists, the Polish poet Antoni Slonimski. Also discusses antisemitism in Germany as reflected in this journal.

1919-1945: Western Europe

0681. אורוול, ג'ורג'. מדוע אני כותב ועוד מסות. תרגם אפרים ברוידא. תל-אביב: עם עובד, 1984. 189 עמ'.

[Orwell, George. WHY I WRITE, AND OTHER ESSAYS. Trans. by Ephraim Broide. Tel-Aviv: Am Oved, 1984. 189 pp.]

The essay "Antisemitism in Britain" (pp. 65-78), originally published in the "Contemporary Jewish Record," April 1945, deals with antisemitism in Britain during the Second World War. Claims that the war caused an increase in antisemitic feeling although individuals would not admit to being antisemites, and that antisemitism is an expression of belief in the superiority of one's own nation. The way to "cure" antisemitism is by fighting the "nationalistic disease."

0682. אלמוג, שמואל. התפתחותה של השאלה היהודית באנגליה בתום מלחמת העולם הראשונה. ציון 50 (1985) 397-431.

[Almog, Shmuel. The Development of the Jewish Question in England at the End of World War I. ZION 50 (1985) 397-431.]

The First World War and the revolutions in Eastern and Central Europe increased antisemitic attitudes in Britain. The image of the Jew as revolutionary, and the fear that the Communist revolution might spread to Britain, played an important role in this antisemitic wave. However, the pluralism of British society, its democratic institutions and its tolerance towards other religions prevented antisemitism from spreading.

0683. אנגל, דוד. הבריחה ההפגנתית של חיילים יהודיים מהצבא הפולני באנגליה בשנת 1944: פרשה ביחסים בין אנגלים, פולנים ויהודים בתקופת מלחמת העולם השנייה. יהדות זמננו 2 (1984) 177-207.

[Engel, David. The Desertion of Jewish Soldiers from the Polish Army in Britain in 1944: An Episode in the Relations between the British, the Poles and the Jews during World War II. YAHADUT ZEMANENU 2 (1984) 177-207.]

As a result of antisemitism, approximately one-third of the Jewish soldiers serving in the Polish Army in Britain deserted at the beginning of 1944. The first two groups of deserters were absorbed into the British Army, and the third was promised work in British military installations (this was not implemented for technical reasons).

0684. כהן, ירחמיאל. יהודים ונוצרים בצרפת בתקופת מלחמת-העולם השנייה: ניסיון מתודולוגי. אומה ותולדותיה, חלק ב: העת החדשה, ערך שמואל אטינגר. ירושלים: מרכז זלמן שזר, 1984. עמ' 373-384.

[Cohen, Yerachmiel (Richard). Jews and Christians in France during the Second World War: A Methodological Experiment. NATION AND HISTORY: STUDIES IN THE HISTORY OF THE JEWISH PEOPLE, Vol. 2, ed. Shmuel Ettinger. Jerusalem: Zalman Shazar Center, 1984. Pp. 373-384.]

Studies the French Jewish establishment's attitudes in the perspective of Christian attitudes towards three issues: Pétain during the first few months of his regime; foreign Jews in France; the selections for deportation in summer 1942. Concludes that Jews and Catholics welcomed Pétain as the savior of France; that Jews and Christians felt the government had a right to place restrictions on foreigners; and that each group, in drawing up lists of deportees, tried to save their own people.

0685. מארוס, מיכאל ר. וישי בטרם וישי: מגמות אנטישמיות בצרפת בשנות ה-30. זמנים 14 (חורף 1984) 42-51.

[Marrus, Michael R. Vichy before Vichy: Antisemitic Currents in France during the 1930s. ZMANIM 14 (Win 1984) 42-51.] Originally published as "Vichy avant Vichy" in "H-Histoire" 3 (Nov 1979); appeared in English in the "Wiener Library Bulletin" 33 (1980).

The antisemitism of the 1930s accompanied a much wider tide of xenophobia; the most potent charge against the Jews was that they were foreigners. Strains of anti-Jewish thought or policy turned up amongst the Right, the Catholics, the neo-socialists, the pacifist Left and even elements of the Communist movement. Describes quotas and statutes initiated against foreigners, and political and economic accusations against the Jews, as precursors to Vichy policy.

0686. Adler, Jacques. FACE A LA PERSECUTION: LES ORGANISATIONS JUIVES A PARIS DE 1940 A 1944. Paris: Calmann-Lévy, 1985. 329 pp. A translation and adaptation of "The Jews of Paris and the Final Solution: Communal Responses and Internal Conflicts 1940-1944" (Dissertation - Melbourne, no date).

The antisemitic persecution of Jews in Paris during the War stemmed from the policies of the Nazis and of the Vichy government. Examines the responses of the various communal bodies - the official UGIF, the Consistoire, the immigrant political groups and welfare institutions. An appendix (pp. 275-302) contains official documents relating to the Vichy government's anti-Jewish policy.

0687. Allen, Louis. Jews and Catholics. VICHY FRANCE AND THE RESISTANCE: CULTURE AND IDEOLOGY, eds. Roderick Kedward, Roger Austin. London: Croom Helm, 1985. Pp. 73-87.

Concludes that Vichy antisemitism "is consciously an 'anti-judaïsme d'état' claiming roots in the Catholic past of France." The French Catholic Right developed a moral theology of antisemitic measures designed to exclude the Jews from French life. The Statut des Juifs of October 1940, a French initiative approved by the Vatican, adopted a racial definition of Jews. Only the deportations of French Jews aroused some Church protests. Post-war rethinking has not yet brought about a fundamental change in Jewish-Catholic relations in France.

0688. Aronsfeld, C.C. Reminiscences on a Bicentenary: The London Times and Hitler. JEWISH AFFAIRS 40, 2 (Feb 1985) 17-19 and MIDSTREAM 31, 4 (Apr 1985) 39-41.

Argues that the Times' most disastrous error was its misjudgment of Hitler. This was due not to indifference regarding antisemitism but more to the fact that the truth "defied belief."

0689. Assouline, Pierre. 1944-1945: L'EPURATION DES INTELLECTUELS. Bruxelles: Ed. Complexe, 1985. 175 pp. (La Mémoire du siècle, 44).

Discusses the purge of intellectuals, writers, and journalists who collaborated with the Germans during the occupation of France. Describes the trials of Henri Béraud, Robert Brasillach, and other intellectuals, and mentions their anti-communist and anti-Jewish activities.

0690. Birnbaum, Pierre. Attaques antisémites contre Pierre Mendès France. PIERRE MENDES FRANCE ET LE MENDESISME, eds. François Bédarida, Jean-Pierre Rioux. Paris: Fayard, 1985. Pp. 175-182.

The antisemitic attacks on Mendès France from the beginning of his career in the 1930s have hardly received any attention. The right of Mendès France, as well as Léon Blum, to represent Frenchmen was constantly being questioned. In 1938 the virulently antisemitic fascist press described him as a member of a Jewish conspiracy against France. Attacks continued during World War II and his premiership in the 1950s.

0691. Brewer, John D. The British Union of Fascists and Anti-Semitism in Birmingham. MIDLAND HISTORY 9 (1984) 109-122.

Focuses on local branches of the BUF rather than on the leadership and argues that while the BUF as a whole was antisemitic, there were varying local levels of commitment and activity. Describes the West Midlands branch, centered in Birmingham, which was never strong and contrasts it to the success of Oswald Mosley, the fascist leader, in whipping up antisemitism in the East End of London.

0692. Brewer, John D. Looking Back at Fascism: A Phenomenological Analysis of BUF Membership. SOCIOLOGICAL REVIEW 32, 4 (Nov 1984) 742-760.

Interviews with 15 former members of the British Union of Fascists were conducted within a methodological framework, assuming bias due to the lapse of time and to later negative connotations of fascism. Non-members characterized fascists as violent, dictatorial, and rabidly antisemitic. The ex-members explained their past by rationalizing that fascism had claimed to solve their personal crises and the crisis facing Britain, which they blamed on social conditions, unemployment, and the Jews.

0693. Brewer, John D. MOSLEY'S MEN: THE BRITISH UNION OF FASCISTS IN THE WEST MIDLANDS. Aldershot: Gower, 1984. xii, 159 pp.

An analysis of support for the BUF during the 1930s, with special reference to the West Midlands. Based on interviews with 15 former members, with descriptive statistical analyses and case studies. Mentions the role played by antisemitism in support for the movement. Not all supporters were antisemites and some even left the movement in protest against antisemitism. Ch. 7 (pp. 104-115), "The Birmingham BUF Branch and Anti-Semitism," compares antisemitic activity in Birmingham with other centers of fascist activity.

0694. Chauvy, Gérard. LYON 40-44. Paris: Plon, 1985. 424 pp.

Ch. 16 deals with the situation of the Jews in Lyons during the Second World War. Describes the activities of the "Service de l'aryanisation économique," which confiscated Jewish property.

0695. Cohen, Asher. "Pour les Juifs": Des attitudes philosémites sous Vichy. PARDES 1 (1985) 138-149.

Describes the opposition of a part of the non-Jewish French population to the antisemitism of the Vichy government as reflected in letters written to the authorities by individuals or organizations.

0696. Defrasne, Jean. L'OCCUPATION ALLEMANDE EN FRANCE. Paris: Presses Universitaires de France, 1985. 127 pp.

See ch. 7 for details of the Nazi terror, and in particular pp. 87-88 for the rise of antisemitism.

0697. Fleck, Christian et al. GRENZFESTE DEUTSCHER WISSENSCHAFT: UEBER FASCHISMUS UND VERGANGENHEITSBEWAELTIGUNG AN DER UNIVERSITAET GRAZ. Hrsg. vom Verein Kritische Sozialwissenschaft und Politische Bildung. Graz: Verlag fuer Gesellschaftskritik, 1985. 162 pp.

A collection of articles dealing with fascism and antisemitism in Graz, Austria, and particularly at the University, from the 1920s to 1945.

0698. Fleury, Alain. "LA CROIX" ET L'ALLEMAGNE DE 1930 A 1940. Dissertation - University of Tours, June 1984.

The French Catholic newspaper, "La Croix," founded in 1883, was known for its violently antisemitic positions. Unseen.

0699. Frank, Joseph. French Intellectuals between Wars. DISSENT 31, 1 (Win 1984) 103-108.

Taking as his reference point the recent book by H.R. Lottman, "The Left Bank" (Boston, 1982), the author discusses the ideas and actions of intellectuals adhering to the Left and the Right, particularly after the Nazi occupation of France, including antisemites such as Robert Brasillach, Drieu La Rochelle, and Céline.

0700. Garneri, Giuseppe. TRA RISCHI E PERICOLI: FATTI E TESTIMONIANZE NEL PERIODO DELLA RESISTENZA, DELLA LIBERAZIONE E DELLA PERSECUZIONE CONTRO GLI EBREI. 2nd ed. Pinerolo: Ed. Alzani, 1985. 180 pp.

Documents aid given by the Church to the persecuted in Italy, based on archival material and other documentary sources. Pp. 111-168 describe aid given to the Jews by Catholic priests and nuns and their protests against Nazi antisemitic propaganda.

0701. Goldman, Aaron. The Resurgence of Antisemitism in Britain during World War II. JEWISH SOCIAL STUDIES 46, 1 (Win 1984) 37-50.

Although the violent Jew-baiting of the fascists won few adherents during the 1930s, a more subtle antisemitism was gaining ground in Britain, such as disagreeable literary stereotypes, middle-class professional antipathy and social discrimination against "alien" Jews. In 1942 a campaign of rumors and leaflets, partly Nazi-inspired, accused the Jews of profiteering and draft-dodging, and described the war as a "Jewish war." The National Council for Civil Liberties, with church and trade union figures, pushed for strong government action against antisemitism.

0702. Goodstein, Judith R. The Rise and Fall of Vito Volterra's World. JOURNAL OF THE HISTORY OF IDEAS 45, 4 (Oct-Dec 1984) 607-617.

Paper presented at a colloquium at Brandeis University, 1982. Vito Volterra was a member of a circle of distinguished Italian mathematicians, all Jewish. When Mussolini established the fascist Accademia d'Italia, Volterra and other members of his circle signed Benedetto Croce's manifesto against the politicization of science. No Jews were appointed to Mussolini's Academy even before the racial laws of 1938. As a result of the laws, those Jewish scientists who had not already lost their posts were dismissed.

0703. Halls, Bill. Catholicism under Vichy: A Study in Diversity and Ambiguity. VICHY FRANCE AND THE RESISTANCE: CULTURE AND IDEOLOGY, eds. Roderick Kedward, Roger Austin. London: Croom Helm, 1985. Pp. 133-146.

While Catholicism was an important source of political and social support for the Vichy regime, and Catholics played a key role in promulgating the 1940 Statut des Juifs, their influence diminished as German control of Vichy increased. The Church hierarchy and the intelligentsia were deeply divided between Pétainist antisemites and anti-collaborationists, some of whom joined the Resistance or protested against persecution of the Jews. Three of the four French cardinals supported Pétain; their attitude to the deportations was ambiguous.

0704. Hirschfeld, Gerhard, ed. EXILE IN GREAT BRITAIN: REFUGEES FROM HITLER'S GERMANY. Leamington Spa: Berg; Atlantic Highlands, NJ: Humanities Press, for the German Historical Institute, London, 1984. iv, 314 pp. Originally published as "Exil in Grossbritannien: Zur Emigration aus dem nationalsozialistischen Deutschland" (Stuttgart: Klett-Cotta, 1983).

A collection of articles on the experiences of German Jews who took refuge in Britain between 1933 and 1939 as a result of Nazi anti-Jewish policies. Several articles mention British antisemitic attitudes towards the refugees and their influence on government policy. Includes articles by Francis L. Carsten, John P. Fox (see above, no. 513), Bernard Wasserstein, Anthony Glees, Lothar Kettenacker, Conrad Puetter, Michael Seyfert, John Willett, Herbert Loebl, Rainer Koelmel, Marion Berghahn.

0705. Klarsfeld, Serge. VICHY-AUSCHWITZ: LE ROLE DE VICHY DANS LA SOLUTION FINALE DE LA QUESTION JUIVE EN FRANCE. Vol. 2: 1943-1944. Paris: Fayard, 1985. 411 pp. Vol. 1: 1942 was published in 1983.

Emphasizes the differences between antisemitic ideologies in Germany and in France. Describes the anti-Jewish initiatives of Vichy, especially against Jewish refugees in France. The opposition of the clergy contributed to a reduction in the number of deportations. Pp. 193-401 contain documents, maps, and statistical tables.

0706. Kriegel, Annie. REFLEXIONS SUR LES QUESTIONS JUIVES. Paris: Hachette, 1984. 633 pp. (Collection Pluriel).

A collection of essays, one of which (pp. 29-58) discusses the policy of the French Communist party towards Jews during the Nazi occupation and the Holocaust, and a pamphlet written by Communist intellectual G. Politzer on antisemitism. The Communists condemned antisemitism not out of sympathy for the Jews but because they viewed it as a political obstacle.

0707. Leneman, Esther. Entretien avec Zeev Sternhell. TRACES 8 (1984) 64-72.

An interview following the publication of Sternhell's book "Ni droite, ni gauche: L'idéologie fasciste en France" (Paris: Ed. du Seuil, 1983). Sternhell says that fascism does not necessarily give rise to antisemitism.

For many French fascists during the 1930s, antisemitism was a political instrument which they adopted for opportunistic reasons. In Italy, Jews were acceptable in the fascist vision of an organic society, but antisemitism was an essential element of Nazism.

0708. Lindstroem, Ulf. FASCISM IN SCANDINAVIA, 1920-1940. Stockholm: Almqvist and Wiksell International, 1985. vii, 196 pp.

Gives the reasons for fascism's lack of electoral appeal in Scandinavia, despite the Depression. Pp. 55-59 discuss the minor role played by antisemitism and racism in a very homogeneous society. While concepts of race biology were popular, racial prejudice was a marginal issue and could not draw a mass following.

0709. Lipschitz, Chaim U. FRANCO, SPAIN, THE JEWS, AND THE HOLOCAUST. Ed. by Ira Axelrod. New York: Ktav, 1984. 237 pp.

Despite antisemitic statements uttered by Franco, and despite Nazi-influenced antisemitism in Spain, thousands of Jews were saved during the Holocaust period by fleeing from France into Spain. Franco is also credited with a direct role in saving about 250,000 Sephardic Jews in the Balkans. Studies the historical events and Franco's attitudes and ambivalence, concluding that there is no clear explanation for Franco's actions.

0710. Longuechaud, Henri. "CONFORMEMENT A L'ORDRE DE NOS CHEFS ...": LE DRAME DES FORCES DE L'ORDRE SOUS L'OCCUPATION 1940-1944. Paris: Plon, 1985. 226 pp.

Describes the collaborationist politics of the Vichy government's repression of anti-German, pro-English or Gaullist sympathizers. For antisemitic policies and measures, see pp. 63-65.

0711. Lottman, Herbert R. PETAIN - HERO OR TRAITOR: THE UNTOLD STORY. New York: W. Morrow, 1985. 444 pp.

A biography of Marshal Henri-Philippe Pétain, premier of the French Vichy government from 1940-1944. For references to his antisemitic views, and antisemitism in France before and during the Vichy regime, see the index.

0712. Manning, A.F. The Dutch Catholics under German Occupation. MISCELLANEA HISTORIAE ECCLESIASTICAE 9 (1984) 196-223.

The attitude of the Dutch Catholic population towards the German occupiers was determined by the stand of the bishops, who generally tried to avoid collaboration. However, p. 204 describes how in Sept.-Oct. 1942 they agreed to bar Jews from Catholic libraries and reading rooms under threat that if they disobeyed, the State grant for the libraries would be withheld. Mentions protests by the Church against deportation of the Jews.

0713. Mason, Henry L. Testing Human Bonds within Nations: Jews in the Occupied Netherlands. POLITICAL SCIENCE QUARTERLY 99, 2 (1984) 315-343.

Refers to Helen Fein's thesis that the Holocaust tested the bonds between Jews and gentiles in the occupied countries. A comparison with Denmark, where solidarity with the Jews was maintained and almost all of them were saved, shows that Danish gentiles and Jews resisted the process of segregation which in the Netherlands destroyed the ties between the Dutch and their Jewish fellow citizens. Indifference, bureaucratic legalism and the failure of the Churches to adopt a strong stand contributed to Nazi success in the Netherlands.

0714. Mehlman, Jeffrey. LEGS DE L'ANTISEMITISME EN FRANCE. Paris: Denoël, 1984. 196 pp. Originally published as "Legacies of Antisemitism in France" (Minneapolis: University of Minnesota Press, 1983).

Four essays presenting the views of French thinkers and writers regarding Jews, as an indication of the antisemitic attitudes prevalent among French intellectuals prior to and during the Second World War. The essays discuss Maurice Blanchot and his political articles written for the journal "Combat"; Jacques Lacan's psychoanalytic critiques of Léon Bloy and Freud; Jean Giraudoux's attitudes as expressed in his own works and in his criticism of Racine's biblical plays; André Gide's "antisemitic page" in his "Journal" (1914), and his satire "Les Caves du Vatican."

0715. Mondszain, Marie-Josée Baudinet. Juif - face et profil. TRACES 9/10 (1984) 170-182.

Discusses caricatures of the Jews in the Nazi period and why they took the form they did. Refers mainly to documents distributed in France in 1940. Examples of caricatures are given on pp. 179-181.

0716. Morand-Deviller, Jaqueline. Louis-Ferdinand Céline und die Politik. WIDERSTAND, FLUCHT, KOLLABORATION: LITERARISCHE INTELLIGENZ UND POLITIK IN FRANKREICH, ed. Juergen Siess. Frankfurt a.M.: Campus Verlag, 1984. Pp. 141-173.

Pp. 145-150 deal with the antisemitic views of Céline. Rejects the biographical explanations of his antisemitism and suggests that its roots lie in Céline's "pacifism" (his opposition to World War I for which he held the Jews responsible) and in his revolt against the decadence of his times which led him to racism and nationalism.

0717. Muray, Philippe. CELINE. Paris: Denoël, 1984. Unseen. Published previously by Ed. du Seuil, 1981 (237 pp.).

See interview of Muray by François Lagarde, "Le siècle de Céline," in L'INFINI 8 (Fall 1984) 31-40, including discussion of the book and of Céline's antisemitism.

0718. Neugebauer, Wolfgang, ed. WIDERSTAND UND VERFOLGUNG IN WIEN 1934-1945: EINE DOKUMENTATION. VOL. 3: 1938-1945. 2nd ed. Wien: Oesterreichischer Bundesverlag, 1984. 555 pp. The first edition appeared in 1975.

A collection of documents with explanatory texts. On Nazi persecution of the Jews in Vienna, including antisemitic legislation, pogroms, deportation and extermination, see pp. 194-326 (ed. by Jonny Moser) and 344-348. Pp. 504-519 contain documents regarding Christians who helped Jews.

0719. Pedatella, R. Anthony. Italian Attitudes toward Jewry in the Twentieth Century. JEWISH SOCIAL STUDIES 47, 1 (Win 1985) 51-62.

Historically, the Italian people's attitudes toward the Jews were little affected by antisemitism. Despite the racial purity laws adopted under German pressure in 1938, Italy resisted German measures denying Jews their rights and protected Jews during the Holocaust. Mussolini opposed Zionism insofar as it was pro-British, but willingly collaborated with the Revisionists. However, he feared "international Zionism." He followed a philosemitic line during the 1920s-1930s, and his antisemitism after 1938 was purely opportunistic.

0720. Pedatella, R. Anthony. The Italians Are Looking Better Than Ever. JEWISH FRONTIER 52, 4 (Apr 1985) 10-14, 29-30.

The role played by Italians during the Holocaust in saving Jews, and the non-cooperation of the Italian authorities with their own and German racial legislation, is rooted in the Italian national character which is individualistic and resists authority, and in the integration of Jews in Italian society. The racial legislation of 1938 marked a fundamental rupture between fascism and the Italian bourgeoisie.

0721. Rajsfus, Maurice. L'AN PROCHAIN LA REVOLUTION: LES COMMUNISTES JUIFS IMMIGRES DANS LA TOURMENTE STALINIENNE 1930-1945. Paris: Mazarine, 1985. 361 pp.

A study of the Jewish communists in France and their participation in the political struggles of this period. Ch. 8 includes discussion of the antisemitism of French communist leaders (based on an interview with Arthur and Lise London). Appendix 9 (p. 317) includes a document from 1943 dealing with antisemitism in the USSR.

0722. Ramati, Alexander. DER ASSISI UNTERGRUND: ASSISI UND DIE NAZI-BESETZUNG NACH DEM BERICHT VON PATER RUFINO NICCACCI. Trans. Utta Roy-Seifert. Muenchen: L. Roitman, 1984. 204 pp. Originally published as "The Assisi Underground: The Priests who Rescued Jews" (New York: Stein and Day, 1978) and "While the Pope Kept Silent: Assisi and the Nazi Occupation as Told by Rufino Niccacci" (London: G. Allen and Unwin, 1978).

Based on the memoirs of Father Niccacci, an organizer and operator of the network of priests who rescued Jews in Assisi.

0723. Simon, Walter B. OESTERREICH 1918-1938: IDEOLOGIEN UND POLITIK. Wien: Boehlau, 1984. 183 pp.

A socio-political study of political parties and their ideologies in the Austrian Republic, 1918-1938. The antisemitic positions of some of the parties are mentioned, attributed to Jewish prominence in the economy, culture, and the professions.

0724. Sturm, Hubert. HAKENKREUZ UND KLEEBLATT: IRLAND, DIE ALLIIERTEN UND DAS "DRITTE REICH" 1933-1945. Vol. 1-2. Frankfurt a.M.: Peter Lang, 1984. 326; 353 pp.

An analysis of the complicated relations between Ireland and Nazi Germany. Ch. 10 (pp. 134-151) deals with reactions of the Irish government and population to the anti-Jewish policy of the Nazis from 1933 to 1945.

0725. Szafran, A.W. Aspects psychologiques de l'antisémitisme chez les écrivains fascistes. ACTA PSYCHIATRICA BELGICA 84, 3 (May/June 1984) 273-283.

Examines the works of Louis-Ferdinand Céline, Lucien Rebatet, Robert Brasillach and Pierre Drieu La Rochelle. One possible explanation for their antisemitism is narcissistic disturbance of the personality. The racist attitudes of these writers are also explained by their lack of empathy.

0726. Thurlow, Richard. Anti-Nazi Antisemite: The Case of Douglas Reed. PATTERNS OF PREJUDICE 18, 1 (Jan 1984) 23-34.

Douglas L. Reed (1895-1976), Central European correspondent of the Times until 1938, was opposed to Hitler's Nazism but supported Otto Strasser's views. He believed in the conspiracy theory of history, whose agents were communists and Zionists. He became famous before the war because of his writings warning against Hitler's Nazism and Britain's appeasement policy. After the war he wrote a number of antisemitic works.

0727. Veillon, Dominique. LA COLLABORATION: TEXTES ET DEBATS. Paris: Librairie Générale Française, 1984. 480 pp.

A collection of documents and articles which appeared in the French press between 1940 and 1944 dealing with collaboration with the Nazis. In pt. 5 (pp. 227-288), antisemitism and anti-communism are discussed as important ideologies which, it was believed at the time, justified collaboration.

0728. Voigt, Klaus. Gli emigrati in Italia dai paesi sotto la dominazione nazista: Tollerati e perseguitati (1933-1940). STORIA CONTEMPORANEA 16, 1 (Feb 1985) 45-87.

Jews emigrated to Italy because of the traditional lack of antisemitism in this country. The situation changed with Mussolini's racial laws (imposed in September 1938) which obliged "foreign" Jews to leave Italy. Most of them went to Palestine and North or South America.

0729. Webber, G.C. Patterns of Membership and Support for the British Union of Fascists. JOURNAL OF CONTEMPORARY HISTORY 19, 4 (Oct 1984) 575-606.

Examines the BUF in the 1930s in regard to two questions: how many people joined the movement and from what levels of society. Pp. 596-597 discuss the movement's antisemitic policy.

0730. Weinzierl, Erika. ZU WENIG GERECHTE: OESTERREICHER UND JUDENVERFOLGUNG, 1938-1945. Koeln: Styria-Verlag, 1985. 224 pp.

An analysis of the attitudes of Austrians towards the tragic fate of the Austrian Jews during the years 1938-1945. The positions of the Churches are discussed at length. Imputes the lack of popular solidarity with Austrian Jews to the deep antisemitic traditions in the country. Includes documents.

0731. Wilson, Keith M. The "Protocols of Zion" and the "Morning Post," 1919-1920. PATTERNS OF PREJUDICE 19, 3 (July 1985) 5-14.

A behind-the-scenes account of the publication of a series of articles based on the "Protocols of the Elders of Zion" in 1920, in the conservative British newspaper "Morning Post." The editor, H.A. Gwynne, believed that social unrest in Britain, and Bolshevism, were manifestations of a centuries-old Jewish conspiracy against society. He decided to publish the articles despite responsible opinions that they were a fraud.

0732. Wiltschegg, Walter. DIE HEIMWEHR: EINE UNWIDERSTEHLICHE VOLKSBEWEGUNG. Muenchen: Oldenbourg Verlag, 1985. 400 pp.

A history of the Austrian fascist movement "Die Heimwehr" in the inter-war period. See pp. 264-266: "Antisemitismus."

0733. Zamojski, Jan. Rezonans powstania w getcie warszawskim wśród spoleczności żydówskiej we Francji (1943-1944) [Reactions to the Uprising in the Warsaw Ghetto in the Jewish Community in France (1943-1944)]. DZIEJE NAJNOWSZE 1 (1984) 127-148.

The first part of the article describes the Jewish community in France before the Second World War. The influx of Eastern European immigrants provoked antisemitism, and they also met with hostility from well-established French Jews. Discusses the nature of antisemitism in France during this period.

July 1945-1985: General

General Works

0734. אטינגר, שמואל; אגמון, יעקב. על הסטוריה והסטוריונים. יהדות זמננו 2 <1984> (1985) 47-59.

[Ettinger, Shmuel; Agmon, Yaakov. On History and Historians. YAHADUT ZEMANENU 2 <1984> (1985) 47-59.]

Transcription of a radio interview on 30 Jan. 1982 with the historian Shmuel Ettinger, on general historical problems and the nature of Jewish history. He also discussed whether antisemitism today is growing or retreating, and the reasons for the success of antisemitic propaganda (pp. 56-57).

0735. אטינגר, שמואל; באואר, יהודה; לוי, ברנארד אנרי. אנטישמיות היום. ירושלים: מרכז ההסברה, 1984. 19 עמ'. (כנסים).

[Ettinger, Shmuel; Bauer, Yehuda; Lévy, Bernard Henri. ANTISEMITISM TODAY. Jerusalem: Central Office of Information, 1984. 19 pp.]

Three lectures delivered at conferences organized in Sept. and Dec. 1983. Ettinger speaks about antisemitism and anti-Zionism amongst young people in the Western world, the danger being in the superficiality of their culture. Bauer discusses the different types of antisemitism now prevalent in the USSR, in the USA, and in Western Europe. Lévy discusses the new antisemitism which takes the form of attacks against Israel.

0736. פערשטענדיק, מ. "פארברעכן און שטראף"-לאזיקייט. מעלבורנער בלעטער 41 (אפריל-מאי 1984) 2-5.

[Fershtendik, M. "Crime and Punishment"-Leniency. MELBOURNE CHRONICLE 41 (Apr/May 1984) 2-5.]

The fact that Nazi war criminals were not duly punished for their heinous deeds (by the Allied powers, and later by the German government) has had a direct impact on present-day terrorism, and mass murders and antisemitism on the part of neo-Nazis, revisionist historians, and left-wing anti-Zionists, all of whom fear no punishment.

0737. קרפ, דוד. האנטישמיות - סכנה לחברה המערבית. הדואר 65, 1 (1 נוב 1985) 11-12.

[Karp, David. Antisemitism - a Danger to Western Society. HADOAR 65, 1 (1 Nov 1985) 11-12.]

A report on an international symposium organized by the Vidal Sassoon International Center for the Study of Antisemitism in New York, Oct. 1985. The speakers warned against ignoring the activities of neo-Nazis and other extreme racist groups, and stressed that these groups, together with the intense anti-Zionist campaign led by the Soviet Union, are dangerous for Western society and democracy as a whole.

0738. Abzug, Robert H. INSIDE THE VICIOUS HEART: AMERICANS AND THE LIBERATION OF NAZI CONCENTRATION CAMPS. New York: Oxford University Press, 1985. xii, 192 pp.

Descriptions of events in various camps mention the American soldiers' failure to identify with the victims, accepting the German view of them as sub-human. This process intensified in the D.P. camps where Jews were often regarded as rabble and held in harsh conditions; antisemitic incidents also occurred. Attempts to convey the camp experience to the US public through visits and films are described.

0739. Arnold, Caroline; Silverstein, Herma. ANTI-SEMITISM: A MODERN PERSPECTIVE. New York: Julian Messner, 1985. 224 pp.

Focuses on major events since World War II that characterize antisemitism in the modern world. Gives a short history of antisemitism, and describes Nazism and the Holocaust, antisemitism in various countries since the war, and attempts to combat antisemitism.

0740. Bauer, Yehuda. Anti-Semitism Today: A Fiction or a Fact? MIDSTREAM 30, 8 (Oct 1984) 24-31. Appeared in Portuguese in HERANCA JUDAICA 61 (June 1985) 47-52.

While a wave of antisemitism engulfs the world, Jewish groups are pre-occupied with the marginal threats of neo-Nazism and terrorism. The main threats to the Jewish people today are Soviet propaganda, which focuses on the "world Zionist conspiracy," attacks against the Jewish religion, and accusations of Zionist-Nazi collaboration; Arab antisemitism, influenced by Western thought and traditional Islamic anti-Judaism; and antisemitism disguised as anti-Zionism.

0741. Bauer, Yehuda. ANTISEMITISM TODAY: MYTH AND REALITY. Jerusalem: Hebrew University, Institute of Contemporary Jewry, Vidal Sassoon International Center for the Study of Antisemitism; Shazar Library, 1985. 43 pp. (Study Circle on World Jewry in the Home of the President of Israel, 30 January 1984). Appeared simultaneously in Hebrew.

Emphasizes that the main danger in the current wave of antisemitism lies in three areas - Soviet antisemitism; the Third World, especially Arab and Moslem antisemitism; and antisemitism in the guise of anti-Zionism or virulent opposition to Israel and Israeli policies.

0742. Bauer, Yehuda. Modern Antisemitism. NES AMMIM LEZINGEN: GESPREKKEN IN ISRAEL 11, 3 (1985) 4-21.

Analyzes antisemitism in the USSR, in the Arab world and in the West, including anti-Zionism and Holocaust denial. Discusses the roots of antisemitism. States that all forms of antisemitism are based on Christian models, although some antisemites are also anti-Christian.

0743. Becker, Jillian. THE PLO: THE RISE AND FALL OF THE PALESTINE LIBERATION ORGANIZATION. New York: St. Martin's Press, 1984. xi, 303 pp.

Includes information on PLO funds delivered to neo-Nazi groups and the propaganda campaign leading to the UN resolution equating Zionism with racism.

0744. Belotserkovsky, Vadim. Solzhenitsyn Speaks: Undoing the West in the Soviet Union. THE NATION 240, 10 (16 Mar 1985) 289, 306, 308.

Soviet dissidents, led by Solzhenitsyn and his circle, spread anti-American and anti-Western propaganda in the USSR. Among this type of propaganda are antisemitic broadcasts by Radio Liberty, including an antisemitic passage from Solzhenitzyn's "August 1914." (See also no. 747.)

0745. Bradlow, Frank R. The Consequences of the Second World War for the Jews of the World. JEWISH AFFAIRS 40, 9 (Sept 1985) 42-56.

Surveys the immediate reaction of the Jewish people and the rest of the world to V.E. Day and the end of the war. Few people understood the enormity of the Holocaust. The South African press did not even mention the fate of the Jews. The Holocaust had some positive effects - the awakening of the Christian conscience and a decrease in antisemitism in the democratic countries. Describes the persistence of antisemitism in the USSR.

0746. Eitinger, Leo, ed. THE ANTISEMITISM IN OUR TIME: A THREAT AGAINST US ALL. Oslo: The Nansen Committee, 1984. 161 pp.

The proceedings of the First International Hearing on Antisemitism, Oslo, June 1983. Consists of the Oslo Declaration condemning the resurgence of antisemitism and anti-Zionism, amended versions of the papers given at the hearing, and a shortened version of the discussion. Contents: Yehuda Bauer: The Most Ancient Group Prejudice: Antisemitism (13-19); Erika Weinzierl: Religious Antisemitism (20-27); Reinhard Ruerup: Emancipation and Antisemitism (28-37); L. Eitinger: Antisemitism - "Only" a Psychological Reaction to a Minority (38-46); Per Ahlmark: Sweden and the New Antisemitism (63-69); Gregory Freiman: Antisemitism in the Soviet Union as Experienced by a

Refusenik (70-74); Bela Vago: Communist Antisemitism: The Case of Romania and Hungary (75-85); Immanuel Jakobovits: Antisemitism Today: Some Jewish Perspectives (91-97); Léon Poliakov: The Fascination with the Jew (104-108); Joergen Schliemann: The Hidden Antisemitism (109-113); Giuliana Limiti: Antisemitism at UNESCO (114-124); Jean Halpérin: Antisemitism as a Challenge (125-129); Elie Wiesel: Concluding Remark (136-140).

0747. Heuvel, Katrina vanden. The Muzzled Dissident: No Free Speech at Radio Liberty. THE NATION 241, 19 (7 Dec 1985) 612-615.

Discusses the case of Vadim Belotserkovsky, a Jewish dissident who was dismissed for publicizing charges of antisemitism against Radio Liberty, the US-backed Russian emigré station in Munich (see no. 744). Surveys the history of Radio Liberty since its founding in 1951 and the struggle between earlier emigrés, mostly Russian nationalist, Orthodox, and anti-democratic and the more liberal, mainly Jewish "third wave" of the 1970s. Reagan's appointments to the station management have released the constraints on the extreme nationalist emigrés.

0748. Hux, Samuel. Anti-Semitism, Anyone? How "Polite" Anti-Semitism Has Become a Fashionable Flaw. MOMENT 10, 8 (Sept 1985) 59-62.

Describes a superficial attitude towards antisemitism found in some cultural circles in America today, taking as an example the memoirs of Ingeborg Day, "Ghost Waltz" (Viking Press, 1980). The daughter of an Austrian Nazi, Day is a US citizen and a journalist who states that she hates all Jews, is nauseated by chassidim, and cannot abide gefilte fish. The acceptance of "polite" antisemitism is connected with anti-Zionism.

0749. Levi della Torre, Stefano. Fine del dopoguerra e sintomi antisemitici. RIVISTA DI STORIA CONTEMPORANEA 13, 3 (1984) 437-455.

Deals with the problem of antisemitism in Europe, the USA, the USSR, and the Third World following the creation of the State of Israel. Discusses the political context of the new hostility, including reactions to the Lebanon War and antisemitism in the guise of anti-Zionism. Also discusses Holocaust denial.

0750. Levi della Torre, Stefano. Nuove forme della giudeofobia. LA RASSEGNA MENSILE DI ISRAEL 50, 5-8 (May-Aug 1984) 249-280.

Analyzes contemporary forms of antisemitism such as revisionism (Holocaust denial), the increase of publications against Israel and the Jews and, during the War in Lebanon, a revival of theological antisemitism in some Catholic circles. Discusses the political context of this new hostility.

0751. McMurtry, John. Fascism and Neo-Conservatism: Is There a Difference? PRAXIS INTERNATIONAL 4, 1 (Apr 1984) 86-102.

Compares Nazi fascism with neo-conservatism in the 1970s and 1980s, particularly in the USA and Central and South America. Enumerates eight points for a positive comparison, one of them being anti-communism. "This logic of anti-communism is, at bottom, the logic of anti-semitism writ large. In Nazi Germany and in post-coup 1970s Argentina, the two are made explicitly coterminous."

0752. McRoy, James J. Youth Reflect on Hitler: A Cross-National Study. SOCIAL EDUCATION 49, 6 (Sept 1985) 545-552.

Content analyses of 2000 essays written by British and US high school students in 1978, on the subject "What I have heard about Adolf Hitler," compared with results from surveys held in West Germany in 1977, show a superficial knowledge of the subject. The fifty variables analyzed included: German anti-Semitism, the Holocaust, Genocide, the Nuremberg racial laws, Kristallnacht. Concludes that students must be taught the historical context of Nazism and the Holocaust, and that Holocaust curriculum guides should include discussion of the psychology and the historical roots of antisemitism.

0753. Nelson, Lars-Erik. Anti-Semitism and the Airwaves. FOREIGN POLICY 60 (Win 1985/86) 180-196.

After the elimination in 1982 of pre-broadcast review procedures, many complaints were received about antisemitic and anti-democratic broadcasts by Radio Liberty. Analysis of five sample programs showed that the complaints were justified. Suggests transferring the station to the USA.

0754. Parin, Paul. "The Mark of Oppression": Ethnopsychoanalytische Studie ueber Juden und Homosexuelle in einer relative permissiven Kultur. PSYCHE 39, 3 (Mar 1985) 193-219.

An ethnopsychoanalytic study of Jews and homosexuals revealed similarities in the psychic constitution of these groups, explained by encounters with discrimination during adolescence.

0755. Pfisterer, Rudolf. Neue Zentren der Judenfeindschaft. TRIBUENE 96 (1985) 126-139.

Since 1945 the main threat of antisemitism comes from the Left rather than the Right, expressed mainly through the anti-Zionist agitation of the Soviet Union, the New Left and the Arab states, using lies, disinformation and the falsification of history.

0756. Philips, Michael. Racist Acts and Racist Humor. CANADIAN JOURNAL OF PHILOSOPHY 14, 1 (Mar 1984) 75-96.

A theoretical study, arguing that racist humor is equivalent to a racist act. Discusses jokes, cartoons, and stereotypes, including some about Jews.

0757. Roth, Stephen J. New Fears and Forebodings: The State of Antisemitism. SURVEY OF JEWISH AFFAIRS 1 <1982> (1984) 173-191.

A survey of antisemitism in 1982. Despite the rise in the number of terrorist attacks on Jews, and media hostility towards Israel during the Lebanon war, the panic reaction of many Jews was unjustified. Government-sponsored antisemitism, "the most dangerous form," is rare outside the Soviet or Arab camps. Right-wing extremist groups remain marginal, but their inclination towards terrorism is dangerous. The new intellectual Right, e.g. GRECE in France and the ultra-conservatives in the USA, forms a potential threat. Analyzes Holocaust denial, and antisemitic elements in anti-Israel publications.

0758. Roth, Stephen J. Ten Years after Helsinki and the Ottawa Human Rights Stalemate. INSTITUTE OF JEWISH AFFAIRS: RESEARCH REPORT 6 (Sept 1985) 12 pp.

By signing the Helsinki Final Act the Soviets agreed to an international yardstick for human rights which both the West and Soviet dissidents could invoke. At the Human Rights Experts' Conference in Ottawa (May-June 1985) the USA and the UK denounced official state antisemitism in the USSR, disguised as anti-Zionism. The Soviets retaliated with claims of antisemitism in Western countries.

0759. Sachar, Howard M. DIASPORA: AN INQUIRY INTO THE CONTEMPORARY JEWISH WORLD. New York: Harper and Row, 1985. xiv, 539 pp.

A survey of the Jewish world since the Holocaust, not including Israel and the USA. See the index for antisemitism in each country.

0760. Schulweis, Harold. Antisemitism, Malignant Obsession. MOMENT 10, 6 (June 1985) 60-62.

When antisemitism and the fear of it are allowed to shape one's concept of Judaism, then that aspect of Jewish tradition which sees the gulf between the Jews and the rest of the world as biologically determined becomes dominant, engendering feelings of despair and isolation. Calls on Jews to return to the tradition of involvement with the non-Jewish world.

0761. Taguieff, Pierre-André. Typologies, racisations, antisémitismes. TRACES 9/10 (1984) 137-154.

Discusses what and who is a Jew, the identification of antisemitism with anti-Zionism, the stand of the extreme right, and the Jewish stereotype.

0762. Wal, Bauco van der. The Anne Frank Center: The Evolution of a Holocaust Memorial into an Educational Institution. MORAL EDUCATION FORUM 10, 3/4 (Fall/Win 1985) 54-61.

The author, director of the Center (founded in 1957), explains the purposes of the institution. Antisemitism is a typical expression of racism, anti-humanism and anti-democratic thought, and can best be fought by supporting equality and democracy. In the 1970s, antisemitism seemed a matter of the past, but today the Center warns against the resurgence of neo-Nazism and fascism and their appeal to young people.

0763. Weil, Frederick. The Variable Effects of Education on Liberal Attitudes: A Comparative-Historical Analysis of Anti-Semitism Using Public Opinion Survey Data. AMERICAN SOCIOLOGICAL REVIEW 50, 4 (Aug 1985) 458-474.

A positive relationship between higher levels of educational attainment and social and political liberalism (especially tolerance) has been found in many studies. Recent findings indicate that this effect is not universal but varies according to nationality. The existence of "enlightened" views in a population depends on the length of time a country has had a liberal regime and on its degree of religious heterogeneity. This hypothesis was tested in relation to antisemitism in West Germany, France, Austria, and the USA, from 1959 to 1984.

Christian-Jewish Relations (In a specific country, see that country)

0764. רש, יהושע. הותיקן ומדינת ישראל: נתוני-יסוד להערכת-המצב. כיוונים 22 (פבר 1984) 71-83.

[Rash, Yehoshua. The Vatican and the State of Israel: Basic Facts for Situation-Evaluation. KIVUNIM 22 (Feb 1984) 71-83.]

Discusses reasons for the Vatican's refusal to recognize the State of Israel, one of them being theological - the belief that the Jews' dispersion is due to their refusal to accept Jesus as the Messiah. Revision of this belief would be a radical step for the Catholic Church. Vatican Council II has helped change attitudes towards Jews, but not towards the State of Israel.

0765. Amson, Fabienne; Gruber-Ejnes, Pascale. Du génocide à la coexistence. REGARDS 146 (26 Sept/9 Oct 1985) 22-23, 25.

Describes attempts at reconciliation between Jews and Christians after the Holocaust. Meetings and discussions are held in order to understand one another and to fight antisemitism. After the Vatican's "Nostra Aetate" declaration (1965) some liturgical texts hostile to Jews were changed.

0766. Brockway, Allan R. The Pastor, the Church and the Jewish People. CHRISTIAN JEWISH RELATIONS 17, 4 (Dec 1984) 11-21.

This paper, by the World Council of Churches Programme Secretary for Christian-Jewish Relations, was read at a seminar for the clergy of the Lutheran diocese of Stockholm, Oct. 9, 1984. "Active resistance to antisemitism is a continuing demand upon the Church, one that becomes ever more compelling when we Christians hear from Jews about the subtle ways antisemitism creeps into even the most `enlightened' Christian practice."

0767. Busi, Frederick. The Pope and the PLO. MIDSTREAM 30, 2 (Feb 1984) 25-30.

Explains the background for the meeting between Pope John Paul II and Arafat in 1982 in terms of the Vatican's historical anti-Jewish and anti-Zionist stance.

0768. Cohn-Sherbok, Dan. Jews and Judaism in Christian Education. CHRISTIAN JEWISH RELATIONS 18, 2 (June 1985) 3-7.

A survey of changes in Christian teaching about Jews and Judaism as shown in the Summer 1984 issue of the "Journal of Ecumenical Studies" (see nos. 775, 789, 935). Concludes that considerable progress has been made in Christian education, but "in the Jewish classroom little has been done to reassess Christians and Christianity."

0769. "The Common Bond": Commentary and Reaction. CHRISTIAN JEWISH RELATIONS 18, 3 (Sept 1985) 55-76.

The text of the 1985 "Notes for Preaching and Teaching" of the Catholic Church, called "The Common Bond: Christians and Jews," together with comments by Norman Solomon and a statement of the International Jewish Committee on Interreligious Consultations expressing dissatisfaction with the Notes. The proposed teaching on the rejection of Jesus by the Jews, on the Church's historical responsibility for antisemitism, and on the Holocaust are criticized as inadequate.

0770. Decourtray, Albert. The Christian Responsibility. CHRISTIAN JEWISH RELATIONS 17, 3 (Sept 1984) 25-29.

Extracts from an address delivered by the Archbishop of Lyons, April 1984, to mark the 40th anniversary of the Conseil Représentatif des Institutions Juives de France. States that antisemitism is a psychological and moral injustice, rooted in prejudice which leads to discrimination and rejection of the other. Christians should struggle against anti-Judaism through love and prayer.

0771. Dolęgowska-Wysocka, Miroslawa. Antysemityzm katolicki raz jeszcze [Catholic Antisemitism Once More]. ARGUMENTY 7 (1985) 5. Unseen.

0772. Eckardt, A. Roy. Antisemitism Is the Heart. CHRISTIAN JEWISH RELATIONS 17, 4 (Dec 1984) 43-51. Appeared in the Oct. 1984 issue of THEOLOGY TODAY as part of a Colloquy for Jews and Christians.

Calls for Christian understanding and acceptance of the Jews on their own terms in this age of post-Holocaust theology. Unfortunately, antisemitism endures, with age-old Christian prejudices and accusations voiced against the Jews, along with anti-Israel and anti-Zionist sentiments. The Church should accept responsibility and ask forgiveness for the harm it has caused the Jews, and dedicate itself to an all-out war against antisemitism.

0773. Etchegaray, Roger. Judaïsme et christianisme. FRANCE-ISRAEL INFORMATION 105 (Jan 1984) 21-22. An English translation, with a response by Leon Klenicki, appeared in the ADL BULLETIN (Feb 1984). A Portuguese translation, with Klenicki's response, appeared in HERANCA JUDAICA 56 (Mar 1984).

An address delivered by the Archbishop of Marseilles to the Synod of Bishops, Rome 1983. He called for a two-fold mission of reconciliation and penance in recognition of the bond linking Judaism and Christianity.

0774. Evdokimov, Michel. Réaction d'un orthodoxe. SENS 37, 10/11 (Oct/Nov 1985) 320-322.

The writer, an Orthodox priest, comments on the Catholic Church's recent declarations on relations with the Jews from an Orthodox standpoint. He mentions that in parishes where the liturgy has been translated into modern languages, anti-Jewish expressions have been eliminated. Antisemitism must also be eliminated from Church teaching.

0775. Fisher, Eugene J. Research on Christian Teaching Concerning Jews and Judaism: Past Research and Present Needs. JOURNAL OF ECUMENICAL STUDIES 21, 3 (Sum 1984) 421-436.

Surveys recent studies of American Catholic textbooks and teaching materials in regard to the image of Jews and Judaism expressed in them. Lists negative themes and stereotypes still embedded in Christian catechetical material, and presents themes for positive relationship and dialogue between Christians and Jews.

0776. Fisher, Eugene J. Twenty Years after Vatican II: The Church Is Still Struggling to Define Its Relationship with the Jewish People. B'NAI B'RITH INTERNATIONAL JEWISH MONTHLY 100, 2 (Oct 1985) 20-25.

An assessment of the origins and results of the "Nostra Aetate" declaration. The ambiguity of the declaration was deliberate; the Church wanted a doctrinal statement transcending debate. It has since been clarified by explicit condemnations of antisemitism and an explanation of the role of the Holocaust in Christian-Jewish relations. The "Notes for the Correct Presentation of Jews and Judaism in Preaching and Catechesis" should clear up remaining misunderstandings about anti-Jewish statements in the Gospels.

0777. Gottschalk, Alfred. From the Kingdom of Night to the Kingdom of God: Jewish-Christian Relations and the Search for Religious Authenticity after the Holocaust. CONTEMPORARY JEWRY: STUDIES IN HONOR OF MOSHE DAVIS, ed. Geoffrey Wigoder. Jerusalem: Hebrew University, Institute of Contemporary Jewry, 1984. Pp. 235-245.

Since the Holocaust, there has been a need to rethink Jewish and Christian theology, particularly the latter after centuries of anti-Jewish teaching and preaching. Significant advances have been made by both the Protestant and Catholic Churches, but mainly on the level of theological debate, and not on the lay level where attitudes have changed very little.

0778. Klein, Charlotte. Guidelines 1967-1982: A Preliminary Balance Sheet. CHRISTIAN JEWISH RELATIONS 17, 1 (Mar 1984) 30-36.

Discusses guidelines issued by various Christian Churches redefining the relationship between Jews and Christians.

0779. Landau, Lazare. Vingt ans après le Concile. SENS 37, 10/11 (Oct/Nov 1985) 323-332.

After the Holocaust, the French historian Jules Isaac devoted his life to the study of the origins of antisemitism and concluded that a false interpretation of the Gospels had given rise to the Church's "teaching of contempt," responsible for persecution of the Jews. Isaac's pressure on the Catholic Church contributed to the Vatican II declaration on the Jews. The Protestant Churches made similar declarations in 1948 and 1961. Surveys various catechisms, textbooks and documents in which the influence of these declarations is felt.

0780. Levin, Nora. Whither Christian-Jewish Dialogue? JUDAISM 33, 2 (Spr 1984) 233-239. Reprinted in CHRISTIAN JEWISH RELATIONS 17, 2 (June 1984) 35-42.

The ongoing post-Holocaust dialogue has had little effect on Christian day by day preaching, teaching, or liturgy. Currently, intense hostility towards Israel is often intermixed with old ingrained anti-Jewish feeling. Opposes dialogue in strictly theological terms, and calls for dialogue in terms of "human community and human history."

0781. Liebster, Wolfram. Holocaust und Tradition der Kirche. TRIBUENE 96 (1985) 164-173.

Since the Holocaust, Christianity has undergone a deep theological crisis reflected in the controversy over the decisions of the Rhineland Synod (Jan. 1980) concerning the renewal of relations between Jews and Christians, which put forward a new non-antisemitic interpretation of the New Testament and the place of the Jews in Church history. The legitimacy of these decisions has been attacked.

0782. Luthériens et Juifs: De nouvelles relations. LES NOUVEAUX CAHIERS 77 (Sum 1984) 47-49.

The International Jewish Committee on Interreligious Consultations organized a meeting in Stockholm (July 1983) with the Lutheran World Federation. The declarations of both the Lutheran and the Jewish participants are presented here. The Lutherans state that the violent verbal attacks made by the Protestant Reformers against the Jews cannot be excused, but that Luther was not a racial, nationalistic or political antisemite.

0783. Nostra Aetate - Twenty Years Later: A Landmark in Jewish-Christian Relations. FACE TO FACE 12 (Fall 1985) 49 pp.

Speeches and papers presented at a colloquium held in Rome, April 1985, to celebrate the 20th anniversary of the Vatican II declaration, dealing with its historical importance, its implications for Jewish-Christian relations, and its influence on theology. The participants: Eugene J. Fisher, Ronald B. Sobel, Pope John Paul II, Nathan Perlmutter, Joseph L. Lichten, Johannes Willebrands, Thomas P. Stransky, Leon Klenicki, Jorge Mejia, Marcel J. Dubois, David Novak, Theodore Freedman, Edward H. Flannery, Charles Angell.

0784. "Nostra Aetate" Twenty Years On: A Symposium. CHRISTIAN JEWISH RELATIONS 18, 3 (Sept 1985) 5-54.

Jewish and Christian scholars, rabbis and clergymen discuss the effects of the "Nostra Aetate" declaration on Christian relations with Judaism. The declaration cleared the Jews of the charge of deicide, condemned antisemitism and called for its removal from the teachings of the Church. The text of the declaration, together with the 1975 guidelines and suggestions for its implementation, are appended.

0785. Notas para una correcta presentación de Judíos y Judaísmo en la predicación y la catéquesis de la iglesia católica. CRITERIO 58 <1948> (July 1985) 376-381.

A Spanish translation of the Catholic Church's "Notes for the Correct Presentation of Jews and Judaism...," a comment on the Nostra Aetate declaration, aimed towards a comprehensive teaching of Judaism in order to avoid antisemitism and racism.

0786. Ribière, Germaine. Le peuple juif au présent. RENCONTRE - CHRETIENS ET JUIFS 18 <78> (1984) 5-8; 19 <79/80> (1985) 5-64.

An account of the development of Christian-Jewish dialogue since the Conference of Seelisberg in 1947 at which five commissions were established to fight antisemitism and eradicate it from Christian teaching. Discusses the role played by Jules Isaac. The progress of the Catholic Church in applying the principles of the "Nostra Aetate" declaration is assessed. Pp. 28-64 include the texts of the "10 points of Seelisberg," the Bad Schwalbach theses and the various declarations of the Catholic Church, and a paper by Jules Isaac on the Christian roots of antisemitism ("L'Antisémitisme a-t-il des racines chrétiennes") delivered at the Sorbonne on 15 December 1959.

0787. Schuessler Fiorenza, Elisabeth; Tracy, David, eds. THE HOLOCAUST AS INTERRUPTION. Edinburgh: T. and T. Clark, 1984. xi, 88 pp. (Concilium, 175). Appeared in French as LE JUDAISME APRES AUSCHWITZ (Paris: Beauchesne, 1984). 139 pp. (Concilium, 195).

A collection of articles on the implications of the Holocaust for theology, especially Christian theology, which in the past legitimized the dehumanization of inferior groups. Some articles are listed separately.

0788. Unger, Gérard. Dialogue judéo-chrétien: Echange fructueux ou miroir de soi? TRIBUNE JUIVE 892 (1-7 Nov 1985) 18-21.

Despite the reservations of some Jewish observers, the recent "Notes for Preaching and Teaching" of the Catholic Church are a positive development marked by new theological approaches. Many anti-Jewish teachings are eliminated but the Church has not yet taken responsibility for the growth of antisemitism.

0789. Vernoff, Charles Elliott. After the Holocaust: History and Being as Sources of Method within the Emerging Interreligious Hermeneutic. JOURNAL OF ECUMENICAL STUDIES 21, 4 (Fall 1984) 639-663.

One of the themes discussed is that, since the Holocaust, sensitive Christians feel that it is morally imperative to change Christianity's relationship toward the Jews, given Nazism's roots in Christian antisemitism.

0790. Willebrands, Johannes. Vatican II and the Jews: Twenty Years Later. CHRISTIAN JEWISH RELATIONS 18, 1 (Mar 1985) 16-30. Appeared in French in SENS 37, 10/11 (Oct/Nov 1985) 303-316. Extracts appeared in Polish in TYGODNIK POWSZECHNY 22 (2 June 1985) 5, 7.

A slightly shortened text of the Cardinal Bea Memorial Lecture delivered 10 March 1985. Sums up the achievements of the Vatican Council, among them the promulgation of a new theological vision of Jews and Judaism. The Church no longer teaches that the Jews committed "deicide" or are an "accursed" people. These changes must be incorporated into everyday life and Church teachings.

Nazi War Crimes Trials and War Criminals

0791. קארפינאוויטש, א. די אייביקע ווונד (ארום דער פראגע צו ברענגען צו משפט נאצישע פארברעכערס). פאלק און ציון 56 (יאנואר/פבר 1984) 13-14.

[Karpinovitch, A. The Eternal Wound (On the Question Whether to Bring Nazi War Criminals to Trial). FOLK UN ZION 56 (Jan/Feb 1984) 13-14.]

Contends that Nazi war criminals should not be tried in Israel because it is the world's responsiblity to punish them.

0792. קורן, יצחק; כהן, חיים; זמיר, יצחק. מדינת ישראל וענישת פושעי מלחמת העולם השניה. ירושלים: הקונגרס היהודי העולמי, 1984. 14 עמ'.

[Korn, Yitzhak; Cohn, Haim H.; Zamir, Yitzhak. THE STATE OF ISRAEL AND PUNISHMENT OF WORLD WAR II WAR CRIMINALS. Jerusalem: World Jewish Congress, 1984. 14 pp.]

Papers delivered at a symposium held in Jerusalem on 2 October 1983, discussing whether Israel should or should not bring war criminals to trial. The pros and cons are considered.

0793. שאפירא, ראובן. ישראל-פאליציי אויף די שפורן פון נאציס. פאלק און ציון 56 (יאנואר/פבר 1984) 14-15, 29.

[Shapira, Reuven. Israel's Police on the Nazis' Tracks. FOLK UN ZION 56 (Jan/Feb 1984) 14-15, 29.]

0794. Astor, Gerald. THE "LAST" NAZI: THE LIFE AND TIMES OF DR. JOSEPH MENGELE. New York: Donald I. Fine, 1985. xii, 305 pp.

Describes the life of Josef Mengele, his background, his activities during World War II and at Auschwitz, his escape and life in hiding in Latin America. Contends that the body found in Brazil in 1985 was probably that of Mengele, and dismisses claims of the existence of a powerful ODESSA network helping war criminals. However, Mengele was helped by the South American German community with its Nazi sympathies, and by the moral indifference of the world.

0795. Beattie, John. THE LIFE AND CAREER OF KLAUS BARBIE: AN EYEWITNESS RECORD. London: Methuen, 1984. 228 pp.

A biography of the former chief of the Gestapo in Lyons, based on interviews with people who knew him in Germany, France, and Bolivia. Describes his escape after the War with US aid, the hunt for him by Beate Klarsfeld, and his extradition to France in 1982.

0796. Bower, Tom. KLAUS BARBIE: BUTCHER OF LYONS. London: Michael Joseph, 1984. 255 pp.

A detailed account of Barbie's career, especially about his escape after the war and the hunt for him in South America until his extradition to France in February 1983.

0797. Casamayor. NUREMBERG 1945: LA GUERRE EN PROCES. Paris: Stock, 1985. 202 pp.

An account of the Nuremberg trials based on the protocols, by the French writer and jurist who was one of the prosecutors.

0798. Charny, Israel W. Genocide: The Ultimate Human Rights Problem. SOCIAL EDUCATION 49, 6 (Sept 1985) 448-452.

In his studies of Nazi war criminals, the author found that many of them present a claim of self-defense - that the victims were an inferior species who threatened their identity or their racial or religious purity. Denial of genocide by the perpetrators is common, including Holocaust denial, and they are opposed to discussion and commemoration of the events. Calls for an "early warning system" to warn against possible genocide.

0799. Diamond, Sander A.; Riemschneider, Ernst G. Albert Speer - "des Teufels Architekt." FRANKFURTER HEFTE 39, 8 (1984) 52-61.

Deals with the attitude of Albert Speer, architect of the Third Reich and Minister for Munitions and Supply, towards Hitler, the Holocaust and other subjects related to his activities within the Nazi regime. The authors, who interviewed him, do not believe his claim that he knew nothing about the Holocaust.

0800. Evleth, Donna. The Papon Case: Anti-Semitism in the Resistance? THE NATION 238, 14 (14 Apr 1984) 443-445.

Maurice Papon is accused of having aided in the deportation of 1690 Jews from Bordeaux between 1942 and 1944. Papon, a former member of the Resistance and Minister of the Budget under Pres. Giscard d'Estaing, in World War II served as secretary-general of the prefecture of Bordeaux under the Vichy government. He has been indicted to stand trial for "crimes against humanity."

0801. Friedlander, Henry. The Judiciary and Nazi Crimes in Postwar Germany. SIMON WIESENTHAL CENTER ANNUAL 1 (1984) 27-44.

The Allies moved to denazify the German judicial system after 1945, but this was difficult because "over 90% of all judicial officials had belonged to the Nazi party." The number of Nazi war crimes trials and the severity of punishment declined from the 1950s on. The German public has been increasingly indifferent and even hostile. Some judicial authorities are commended for their investigative activities and for compilation of indictments.

0802. Friedrich, Joerg. DIE KALTE AMNESTIE: NS-TAETER IN DER BUNDESREPUBLIK. Frankfurt: Fischer Taschenbuch Verlag, 1984. 431 pp.

Traces the fate of 200,000-300,000 Nazi war criminals in the Federal Republic of Germany. Describes their efforts to integrate in post-war German society, and the efforts to bring some of them to trial. Concludes that one cannot accuse the FRG of "denial of the past."

0803. Gruber, Ruth. One-Woman Army. HADASSAH MAGAZINE 67, 4 (Dec 1985) 30-35.

Describes the work of Beate Klarsfeld in hunting down Nazi war criminals, and denouncing Communist and Arab antisemitism. In 1978 the Beate Klarsfeld Foundation was established in New York to publish documents on the Holocaust. She and her husband Serge have published books on the Jews deported from France, which will be used in the trial of Klaus Barbie.

0804. Harthoff, Bernhard. Von Judenjaegern und ihren Treibern. TRIBUENE 95 (1985) 20-26.

A description of the war crimes trial taking place in Bonn of Graf Modest Alfred Leonard von Korff who was the SD-commander in Châlons-sur-Marne, France.

0805. Hausner, Gideon. ITELET JERUZSALEMBEN: AZ EICHMANN-PER TOERTENETE. [Trans.]: Péter Balabán. Budapest: Europa Koenyvkiadó, 1984. 722 pp. Originally published as "Justice in Jerusalem" (New York: Harper & Row, 1966).

An account, by the prosecutor, of Adolf Eichmann's trial in Jerusalem, 1961.

0806. Haymann, Emmanuel. Le bourreau de Drancy traqué à Damas. TRIBUNE JUIVE 894 (15-21 Nov 1985) 10-15.

Describes the case of Aloïs Brunner, one of Eichmann's assistants, who organized the deportation of Jews from Salonika and from Nice. From 1943, he was head of the concentration camp of Drancy, and was responsible for the deportation of 150,000 Jews to Auschwitz. Since 1954, he has been living in Damascus, and was identified by Beate and Serge Klarsfeld in 1980.

0807. Hey, Bernd. NS-Gewaltverbrechen, Wissenschaft und Oeffentlichkeit: Anmerkungen zu einer interdisziplinaeren Tagung ueber die Vergangenheitsbewaeltigung. GESCHICHTE IN WISSENSCHAFT UND UNTERRICHT 35, 2 (Feb 1984) 86-91.

Report of an interdisciplinary meeting in Tutzing, Germany dealing with Nazi crimes, the attitudes toward them in post-war Germany and the war crimes trials.

0808. Heydecker, Joe J.; Leeb, Johannes. DER NUERNBERG PROZESS: NEUE DOKUMENTE, ERKENNTNISSE UND ANALYSEN. Vol. 1-2. Koeln: Kiepenheuer und Witsch, 1985. 582 pp. in 2 vols.

A collection of published material from the Nuremberg Trials, mainly from the protocols.

0809. Holtzman, Elizabeth. Mengele and the World's Indifference. JEWISH FRONTIER 52, 4 (Apr 1985) 5-6, 29.

The author, who took part in an attempt to bring Josef Mengele to justice, charges the US government with indifference to this issue and calls on US Jews to pressure the government to act. Condemns the fact that war criminals faced with deportation find considerable support in the US.

0810. Holtzman, Elizabeth. United States Ties to Nazi War Criminals. PIONEER WOMAN 29, 1 (Jan/Feb 1984) 3-4.

Brooklyn District Attorney Elizabeth Holtzman calls for a thorough examination of the role of the US government in aiding, protecting and collaborating with Nazi war criminals after World War II.

0811. Hoyos, Ladislas de. BARBIE. Paris: R. Laffont, 1984. 311, [27] pp.

A detailed report on the activites of Klaus Barbie during World War II and in South America, and on the preparations for his trial in France.

0812. Hunt, Linda. US Coverup of Nazi Scientists. BULLETIN OF THE ATOMIC SCIENTISTS 41, 2 (Apr 1985) 16-24. Unseen.

0813. Iyer, Pico. The Great Mengele Mystery. TIME 125, 25 (24 June 1985) 8-14.

Describes the discovery in Brazil of remains alleged to be those of Josef Mengele; also his career and life in South America after the war and some background regarding his war crimes.

0814. Lang, Jochen von. EICHMANN: L'INTERROGATOIRE. Paris: Pierre Belfond, 1984. Trad. par Jean-Marie Argelês. 309 pp. Originally published as "Das Eichmann-Protokoll" (see the next entry).

0815. Lang, Jochen von. DAS EICHMANN-PROTOKOLL: TONBANDAUFZEICHNUNGEN DER ISRAELISCHEN VERHOERE. Frankfurt a.M.: Ullstein, 1985. 276 pp.; 68 pp. of documents. First published in 1982 (Berlin: Wolf Jobst Siedler Verlag).

The protocols of Eichmann's interrogation by Israeli police captain Avner Less, from May 1960 to February

1961, prior to the trial which took place in April. (See the preceding entry for the French translation.)

0816. Lichtenstein, Heiner. IM NAMEN DES VOLKES? EINE PERSOENLICHE BILANZ DER NS-PROZESSE. Koeln: Bund Verlag, 1984. 232 pp.

Having observed many Nazi war-crimes trials since 1959, the author describes 15 cases. The aim of the book is to acquaint the public with lesser-known criminals.

0817. Lichtenstein, Heiner. Nazi-Unterschlupfe in Lateinamerika: Verschlungene Fluchtwege, Diktatoren als Freunde und Helfer. TRIBUENE 95 (1985) 116-122.

Traces the flight of four leading Nazi war criminals (Josef Mengele, Klaus Barbie, Walter Rauff and Franz Stangl) to South American countries, and stresses the help they received from the local dictators.

0818. Linklater, Magnus; Hilton, Isabel; Ascherson, Neal. THE FOURTH REICH: KLAUS BARBIE AND THE NEO-FASCIST CONNECTION. London: Hodder and Stoughton, 1984. 352 pp. Published in the US as THE NAZI LEGACY: KLAUS BARBIE AND THE INTERNATIONAL FASCIST CONNECTION (New York: Holt, Rinehart and Winston, 1985).

Describes the war-time and post-war career of Klaus Barbie. Two sections deal with his crimes against the Jews: pp. 45-54 - the segregation and terrorization of the Jews of Amsterdam prior to their deportation in the summer of 1942; pp. 106-115 - deportations of Jews from Lyons, where Barbie was Gestapo chief.

0819. MacPherson, Malcolm. THE LAST VICTIM: ONE MAN'S SEARCH FOR PIETER MENTEN, HIS FAMILY'S FRIEND AND EXECUTIONER. London: Weidenfeld and Nicolson, 1984. 310 pp. Published in the US as THE BLOOD OF HIS SERVANTS (New York: Times Books, 1984).

Bibi Krumholz, who emigrated from Poland to Palestine in 1935 (where he changed his name to Haviv Kanaan), discovered after the War that his childhood friend Pieter Menten had been an SS-officer and had commanded the squad which murdered the Jews of their village and stole their wealth. Menten reemerged after the War as a respected millionaire in Holland. Recounts Krumholz's struggle to find Menten, collect evidence of his crimes, and bring him to trial. In 1977, Menten was sentenced to ten years' imprisonment.

0820. Marnham, Patrick. Waiting for Barbie. HARPER'S MAGAZINE 271 <1627> (Dec 1985) 53-59.

The lack of enthusiasm of most citizens of Lyons for the trial of war criminal Klaus Barbie is due mainly to their fears of revelations about French collaboration with the Nazis. Many Jews deported by Barbie were denounced by French informers.

0821. Nazis Alive and Well in Canada. JEWISH DEFENDER 1, 2 (Sum 1984) 2-3.

Discusses Nazi war criminals living in Canada - "as many as 1000" according to a former West German official.

0822. Paris, Erna. L'AFFAIRE BARBIE: ANALYSE D'UN MAL FRANCAIS. Trad. par Amale Naccache. Paris: Ed. Ramsay, 1985. 320 pp. Originally published as UNHEALED WOUNDS: FRANCE AND THE KLAUS BARBIE AFFAIR (Methuen, 1985).

Tells the story of the delay in bringing Klaus Barbie to trial. Describes the personality of Jacques Vergès, Barbie's defense lawyer, and his ties with the pro-Nazi Swiss banker François Genoud, both of whom are involved in anti-Zionist propaganda activities. Describes the growth of racism in France in recent years and the popularity of Le Pen's "Front National," which has created an unfavorable atmosphere for the expected trial.

0823. DER PROZESS GEGEN DIE HAUPTKRIEGSVERBRECHER VOR DEM INTERNATIONALEN MILITAERGERICHTSHOF, NUERNBERG, 14. NOVEMBER 1945 - 1. OKTOBER 1946. Vol. 1-13. Muenchen: Delphin Verlag, 1984. 15, 316 pp. Unseen.

A 13 volume photo offset edition of the 23 volume edition published in Nuremberg in 1947. See the companion volume by Christian Zentner (no. 840).

0824. Renz, Ulrich. Vor Gericht "nichts aufregendes": Von den Schwierigkeiten NS-Verbrechen zu ahnden. TRIBUENE 95 (1985) 16-20.

Cites several cases of war criminals brought to trial this year in West Germany who received light sentences, indicating the difficulties involved in punishing these criminals.

0825. Rosenkranz, Herbert. NS-Kriegsverbrecher vor Gericht. TRIBUENE 96 (1985) 106-119.

Deals with legal and historical aspects of the Nuremberg Trials, analyzes and defines in legal terms the nature of war crimes in general and Nazi war crimes in particular, and the question of obedience or resistance to criminal military orders.

0826. Rosenthal, Ludwig. "THE FINAL SOLUTION TO THE JEWISH QUESTION," MASS-MURDER OR HOAX? AN EVALUATION OF THE EVIDENCE IN THE TRIAL OF THE MAJOR WAR CRIMINALS BEFORE THE INTERNATIONAL MILITARY TRIBUNAL AT NUREMBERG FROM NOVEMBER 14, 1945 TO OCTOBER 1, 1946. Trans. by Regina Lackner. Berkeley, CA: Institute for the Righteous Acts, Judah L. Magnes Memorial Museum, 1984. viii, 145 pp. Originally published as "'Endloesung der Judenfrage': Massenmord oder 'Gaskammerluege'?" (Darmstadt: Darmstaedter Blaetter, 1979).

A collection of excerpts from the confessions of Nazi war criminals tried at Nuremberg, published for the purpose of inculcating awareness of the Holocaust in the German population, particularly for history teachers and students.

0827. Ruzie, David. Les procès de Nuremberg et les persécutions raciales. YOD 21 (1985) 33-64.

Summarizes the organization of the Nuremburg Trials, the charges brought against the Nazi war criminals, and the verdicts.

0828. Ryan, Allan A. QUIET NEIGHBORS: PROSECUTING NAZI WAR CRIMINALS IN AMERICA. San Diego, CA: Harcourt Brace Jovanovich, 1984. xii, 386 pp.

Thousands of war criminals were admitted to the USA following World War II, particularly as a result of the Displaced Persons Act of 1948 which was deliberately designed to discriminate against Jews and to favor anti-communist Balts and Ukrainians. In 1950, after protests, the Act was amended. In the late 1970s, the Office of Special Investigations was established in the Justice Department, headed by the author, in order to track down wanted criminals and bring them to trial. Describes some important cases, for instance, those of John Demjanjuk and Andrija Artukovic, and US involvement in the escape of Klaus Barbie.

0829. Saidel, Rochelle G. THE OUTRAGED CONSCIENCE: SEEKERS OF JUSTICE FOR NAZI WAR CRIMINALS IN AMERICA. Albany, NY: State University of New York Press, 1984. 260 pp.

A series of interviews with and profiles of Americans who have protested against the presence of Nazi war criminals and collaborators in the USA and who are engaged in efforts to have them brought to trial. Among those interviewed are Elizabeth Holtzman, Allan Ryan (see the preceding entry), and Charles R. Allen, who has exposed Nazism and racism in the US in articles on the American Nazi Party and the Ku Klux Klan. Criticizes American policy after World War II which allowed entry to these criminals and Jewish failure to protest.

0830. Samuels, Shimon. Der "belgische Barbie": Die ADLEF und die Aufdeckung der Verbelen-Affaere. B'NAI B'RITH JOURNAL 30 (May 1984) 32-33.

Describes the discovery by the ADL of war crimes committed in Belgium by Robert P.J. Verbelen. After the war he settled in Vienna and was given protection by the US army. In 1965 he was tried in Vienna for his war crimes and acquitted. Now new evidence and witnesses have been found.

0831. Schnapper, Dominique et al. Barbie: Procès à l'oubli. LES NOUVEAUX CAHIERS 76 (Spr 1984) 1-54.

Thirteen short articles about Klaus Barbie, about Gestapo actions in Lyons and vicinity, 1942-1944, and about Barbie's attorney, Jacques Vergès and his antisemitism.

0832. Scott, Peter Dale. Why No One Could Find Mengele: Allan Dulles and the German S.S. THE THREEPENNY REVIEW 23 (Fall 1985) 16-18.

Josef Mengele was captured in 1945 and identified as a Nazi war criminal; nevertheless, he escaped to Latin America. It is now known that the SS networks were preserved for anti-communist activities as the result of an agreement between Allan Dulles of the OSS (precursor of the CIA) and SS criminals who were granted immunity.

Evidence indicates that Mengele was assisted by the OSS and the Vatican escape line.

0833. Skriver, Ansgar. Nordamerika als Nazi-Asyl. TRIBUENE 95 (1985) 101-116.

Many Nazi war criminals, including scientists and collaborators from Eastern Europe, settled after the war in the USA and Canada. It is difficult to bring them to trial because the authorities are not cooperative, especially in Canada. Some of these former Nazis are also active in producing Holocaust denial propaganda.

0834. Steinbach, Peter. Zur Auseinandersetzung mit nationalsozialistischen Gewaltverbrechen in der Bundesrepublik Deutschland: Ein Beitrag zur deutschen politischen Kultur nach 1945. GESCHICHTE IN WISSENSCHAFT UND UNTERRICHT 35, 2 (Feb 1984) 65-85.

A survey of the Nazi war crimes trials in West Germany, from the Nuremberg Trials to the present. Contends that the trials are important because they help to fight Holocaust denial propaganda.

0835. Tusa, Ann; Tusa, John. THE NUREMBERG TRIAL. New York: Atheneum, 1984. 519 pp. First published by London: Macmillan in 1983, with a paperback ed. in 1984.

A detailed, day-by-day account of the Nuremberg Trials, referring to antisemitism especially in connection with the trials of Alfred Rosenberg and Julius Streicher.

0836. Weiser Varon, Benno. Mengele and the Nazi Hunters. MIDSTREAM 31, 8 (Oct 1985) 27-33.

The author, Israeli representative in Paraguay 1968-1972, describes his experiences in connection with the hunt for Josef Mengele. He, like many others, believed that Mengele was in Paraguay, protected by the regime. Israel had not pressed to find him, since Paraguay's support at the UN was regarded as paramount. German authorities, however, could have traced Mengele through ties with his family in Germany.

0837. Weiser Varon, Benno. The Nazis' Friends in Rome. MIDSTREAM 30, 4 (Apr 1984) 10-13.

Discusses the Vatican's involvement in the escape of Nazis and war criminals, with particular reference to Bishop Alois Hudal, Pope Pius XII, and Pope Paul VI.

0838. Wiedemann, Erich. "Sechs millionen, da kann ich nur lachen": Ueber die weltweite Jagd nach dem Auschwitz-Arzt Josef Mengele. DER SPIEGEL 39, 17 (22 Apr 1985) 28-53.

Describes efforts made by various people and organizations throughout the world to apprehend Josef Mengele and bring him to trial, from the early 1960s until 1985.

0839. Wiesenthal, Simon. Der Umgang mit NS-Prozessen in der Bundesrepublik Deutschland. SCHATTEN DER VERGANGENHEIT: DEUTSCHE UND JUDEN HEUTE, ed. Andreas Wojak. Guetersloh: Guetersloher Verlagshaus Mohn, 1985. Pp. 43-54.

Deals with war crimes trials in the Federal Republic of Germany, emphasizing the objective and subjective difficulties involved in punishing the Nazi war criminals.

0840. Zentner, Christian. DER NUERNBERGER PROZESS: DOKUMENTATION, BILDER, ZEITTAFEL. Muenchen: Delphin Verlag, 1984. 128 pp. Unseen.

Accompanies the 13 volume edition of the protocols of the Nuremberg Trials (see no. 823).

Neo-Nazism, Holocaust Denial, and Popularization of Nazism (In a specific country, see that country)

0841. גוטמן, ישראל. השואה: זיכרון והכחשה. סקירה חודשית 32, 6
(31 יולי 1985) 24-32.

[Gutman, Yisrael. The Holocaust: Remembrance and Denial. SKIRA CHODSHIT 32, 6 (31 July 1985) 24-32.]

Surveys aspects of Holocaust remembrance, particularly in modern-day historiography. On pp. 29-32, discusses neo-Nazism and Holocaust denial, claiming that although the persons engaged in these activities are few in number, there is a lot of money supporting them, mostly coming from former Nazis.

0842. וידאל-נאקה, פייר. האמנם אייכמן של נייר? זמנים 18/19 (קיץ 1985) 110-124.

[Vidal-Naquet, Pierre. Eichmann - A Paper Tiger? ZMANIM 18/19 (Sum 1985) 110-124.]

A polemic against revisionist historians who deny the Holocaust, particularly Robert Faurisson. Takes issue with and quotes extensively from the book by Serge Thion, "Vérité historique ou vérité politique? Le dossier de l'affaire Faurisson" (Paris: La Vieille Taupe, 1980) in which Thion argues for an objective evaluation of Faurisson's claims.

0843. פיגא, ישראל. נעא-נאציזם אין די דעמאקראטישע לענדער. קולטור און לעבן 19, 1 <87> (פעב 1985) 10-12.

[Figa, Yisrael. Neo-Nazism in the Democratic Countries. KULTUR UN LEBN 19, 1 <87> (Feb 1985) 10-12.]

Points to the existence of Neo-Nazi persons, groups and publications in the US, Canada and West Germany today and to the protection of Nazi war criminals by the US and the USSR after World War II.

0844. Friedlaender, Saul. KITSCH UND TOD: DER WIDERSCHEIN DES NAZISMUS. Aus dem franzoesischen von Michael Grendacher. Muenchen: Carl Hanser Verlag, 1984. 119 pp. See the description in the next entry.

0845. Friedlaender, Saul. REFLECTIONS OF NAZISM: AN ESSAY ON KITSCH AND DEATH. Trans. by Thomas Weyr. New York: Harper and Row, 1984. 141 pp. Originally published as "Reflets du Nazisme" (Paris: Ed. de Seuil, 1982). (See the preceding entry for the German translation.)

An analysis of the "new discourse" on Nazism as reflected in recent films (e.g. Fassbinder, Syberberg), novels (e.g. Steiner, Tournier) and biographies (e.g. Speer), in which the worst aspects of Nazism are neutralized. Historians, too, distort the images of Hitler and Nazism, and the image of the Jew, whether they are revisionists who deny the Holocaust or Marxists who minimize the role of antisemitism and the Final Solution in Nazi ideology. Studying the present-day phenomenon sheds light on the hold that Nazism and Hitler had on the popular imagination in Germany during the Nazi era.

0846. Greene, Wallace. The Holocaust Hoax: A Rejoinder. JEWISH SOCIAL STUDIES 46, 3/4 (Sum/Fall 1984) 263-276.

A refutation of the allegations of the "Journal of Historical Review" and other revisionist publications which claim that the Holocaust was a myth and that a conspiracy exists to prevent that truth being known. Brings evidence from captured German documents. "A staggering array of documents" is available tracing every stage in the building and operation of the extermination camps.

0847. Gutman, Yisrael. DENYING THE HOLOCAUST. Jerusalem: Hebrew University, Institute of Contemporary Jewry, Vidal Sassoon International Center for the Study of Antisemitism; Shazar Library, 1985. 40 pp. (Study Circle on World Jewry in the Home of the President of Israel, 13 May 1984). Appeared simultaneously in Hebrew.

The essence of the denial is directed against Zionism and Israel, though the thrust of the assault is directed against the entire Jewish people; it seeks to delegitimize the Jews and Zionism by identifying them with racism. Discusses the development of the Holocaust denial phenomenon - the methods, the motives, the leaders, the audience, and the Jewish reaction.

0848. Kulka, Erich. Fighting Distortions and the Denials of the Holocaust. THE VOICE OF AUSCHWITZ SURVIVORS IN ISRAEL: FORTY YEARS AFTER, ed. Shira Nahari. Jerusalem: Public Committee in Israel of Survivors of Auschwitz, 1985. Pp. 13-37. Published simultaneously in German as "Vierzig Jahre danach."

Traces the history of Holocaust denial, and describes a number of publications by neo-Nazi or extreme right-wing authors.

0849. Rosenfeld, Alvin. IMAGINING HITLER. Bloomington, IN: Indiana University Press, 1985. xx, 121 pp.

"Nazism... has been lifted from its historical base and transmuted into forms of entertainment and political bad faith. What a generation ago stood before us as a historical and moral scandal of unprecedented proportions is today a source of light-hearted amusement, popular distraction, pornographic indulgence and antisemitic slander." Analyzes the myth of Hitler's survival, realistic fictional works about Hitler, literary treatments of the Holocaust, and misuse of the Holocaust to debase the image of the Jew.

0850. Rosenfeld, Alvin. Where Hitler Lives Again: Pop Culture Finds a New Hero. DISSENT 32, 2 <139> (Spr 1985) 219-225.

Modern-day popularization of Hitler and the Nazis, and trivialization of the Holocaust, create a "blurring of distinctions between Nazis and Jews and, at its most politically pernicious, a willed equation of the two." Describes this phenomenon in literature, in the arts, and in politics. The popularization of Hitler means a perpetuation of the worst occurrence in history and the danger that it may happen again.

Anti-Zionism and Anti-Israel

0851. ראובני, יעקב. התקשורת במערב ומלחמת לבנון: הערות ולקחים בשולי הויכוח. גשר 110 (אביב 1984) 44-49.

[Reuveny, Jacob. The Western Media and the War in Lebanon: Some Observations and Lessons. GESHER 110 (Spr 1984) 44-49.]

Discusses the anti-Israel and antisemitic results of the media coverage of the Lebanon War as expressions of Israel's overexposure to the media in the "electronic age." Suggests that Israel counter such antagonistic propaganda in future by keeping a low profile vis-à-vis the media and by better information campaigns.

0852. שפרינצק, אהוד. אנטי-ציונות: מדה-לגיטימציה לדה-הומניזציה. כיוונים 25 (נוב 1984) 43-54.

[Sprinzak, Ehud. Anti-Zionism: From Delegitimation to Dehumanization. KIVUNIM 25 (Nov 1984) 43-54.] Appeared in English trans. in FORUM ON THE JEWISH PEOPLE, ZIONISM AND ISRAEL 53 (Fall 1984) 1-12; in French in SILLAGES 11 (Sum 1985) 43-60; in Spanish in RUMBOS 11 (Dec 1984) 5-20.

Criticizes the simplistic description of anti-Zionism as traditional antisemitism in modern form; it is rather a deliberate process of political delegitimation, and in extreme form - dehumanization. Since the UN "Zionism= Racism" resolution, Israel is considered as a racist state which has no right to exist. There is a threat to the legitimacy of Zionism in Western political culture, and a danger in the creation of a new "racist Zionist" stereotype. Argues for a long-range information campaign aimed at intellectuals, as a preventive measure.

0853. Améry, Jean. RADICAL HUMANISM: SELECTED ESSAYS. Ed. and trans. by Sidney Rosenfeld and Stella P. Rosenfeld. Bloomington, IN: Indiana University Press, 1984. xi, 144 pp.

The essay entitled "Antisemitism on the Left" (pp. 37-51) attacks the Left for expressing antisemitic sentiments in anti-Israel and anti-Zionist writings. The essay appeared previously in "Dissent" (Win 1982). The German original appeared in "Merkur" 30 (June 1976).

0854. El asalto a los derechos humanos: Simposium. HERENCIA JUDIA 32 (1985) 9-20.

Translation of the proceedings of a meeting organized by International B'nai B'rith and the WJC, which took place at the US State Department in Dec. 1984, in order to discuss the equation of Zionism with racism. Includes contributions by Elliot Abrahams, Tommy Kohn, Daniel P. Moynihan (see no. 871), Meir Rosenne, Marshall Breger (see no. 857), Jeane Kirkpatrick.

0855. Bernards, Reena. Nairobi Revisited. NEW OUTLOOK 28, 10/11 <250/251> (Oct/Nov 1985) 13-15.

Describes attempts to counter anti-Zionist attacks at the UN Nairobi Conference for Women. Following preliminary meetings of Jewish women in New York with Arab-American and Black women, the New Jewish Agenda suggested guidelines for Israeli-Palestinian dialogue, condemning the "Zionism is racism" equation and opposing all forms of racism and antisemitism.

0856. Blum, Yehuda Z. Anti-Semitism at the United Nations. ADL BULLETIN 40, 3 (Mar 1984) 1, 11-13. Appeared in Dutch in ISRAEL: ORGAAN VAN HET GENOOTSCHAP NEDERLAND-ISRAEL 5 (Apr 1984) 15.

The edited text of a letter addressed to UN Secretary-General Javier Perez de Cuellar deploring the UN's "upsurge of anti-Semitism which converted the world body, to its lasting shame, into one of the foremost contemporary forums of international anti-Semitism."

0857. Breger, Marshall J. "Zionism Equals Racism": The Campaign. MIDSTREAM 31, 5 (May 1985) 33-36.

A revised version of remarks made at the seminar held at the State Department, Dec. 1984. Traces the use of traditional antisemitic themes in anti-Zionist attacks (by the USSR, the UN, the Arabs, Marxist ideologists, and Western journalists), and describes accusations against Israel of "Nazi behavior" and "genocide" during the Lebanon War. Describes US efforts to fight anti-Zionism at the UN.

0858. Broner, E.M. The Road to Nairobi. MOMENT 9, 10 (Nov 1984) 35-39.

Adapted from Broner's keynote address to the International Gathering of Women's Organizations (Paris, July 1984) in preparation for the 1985 UN Conference on Women in Nairobi. On pp. 37-38 describes the formation of the group Feminists Against Anti-Semitism following the 1980 women's conference in Copenhagen where prejudice was expressed against Israel and against Jews.

0859. Cohen, Yoel; Reuveny, Jacob. The Lebanon War and Western News Media. INSTITUTE OF JEWISH AFFAIRS: RESEARCH REPORT 6/7 (July 1984) 26 pp.

Discusses international press coverage of the war in Lebanon (1982) and reasons for the extremely anti-Israel positions often taken, and summarizes various critiques and defenses of the press. Certain observers, such as Conor Cruise O'Brien, see Christian antisemitism as one cause of the anti-Israel position.

0860. COUNTERATTACK: REFUTING THE LIBEL AGAINST ZIONISM. New York: Jacob Goodman Institute for Middle East Research and Information, Zionist Organization of America, 1985. 13 pp.

Excerpts from presentations given during the study day, "Refuting the Zionism=Racism Equation" held at the residence of the President of Israel, Jerusalem, 11 November 1984. (See also no. 872.)

0861. Griver, Simon. Die Diffamierung des Zionismus - der neue Antisemitismus. DAS NEUE ISRAEL 38, 6 (Dec 1985) 16-17.

UN resolution 3379 (Nov. 1975) identifying Zionism with racism was a turning-point in Jewish history, representing a new form of antisemitism - de-legitimizing Israel and the Jewish people. The main purveyors of this new and dangerous form of antisemitism are the USSR, the Arab states, and neo-Nazi groups in the western world.

0862. Harap, Louis. "Zionist-Nazi Collaboration" Refuted: Lenni Brenner's Trickery Exposed. JEWISH CURRENTS 38, 5 (May 1984) 4-9, 28-30.

A refutation of Brenner's "Zionism in the Age of Dictators" (Westport, CT: L. Hill, 1983) which "tries to show that the Zionist movement was not at all interested in rescue of Jews from the Holocaust and even collaborated with the Nazis."

0863. Hasson, Ariel; Springett, Sabino. Sionismo=racismo, otra de las grandes falsedades. LA UNION 92 (Mar 1984) 18-25.

An interview with Peruvian painter Sabino Springett, in which he denounces the 1975 UN resolution.

0864. THE IMPACT OF ANTI-ZIONISM THROUGHOUT THE WORLD. New York: Jacob Goodman Institute for Middle East Research and Information, Zionist Organization of America, 1984. 23 pp. (Inauguration Addresses, 22 February 1984).

Contains addresses by various people against the "Zionism equals racism" claims: an attack on anti-Zionism by Meir Rosenne, Israeli ambassador to the US, a speech on Christian antisemitism by Jacqueline Wexler, president of the National Conference of Christians and Jews, and a warning against the spread of anti-Zionism by Morris Abram, vice-chairman of the Commission on Human Rights.

0865. Korey, William. Letter from the UN - Raising the Ante on Anti-Semitism. HADASSAH MAGAZINE 65, 9 (May 1984) 22-23, 38. A Portuguese translation appeared in CORRENTE WIZO (July-Sept 1984).

Describes expressions of antisemitism in speeches delivered at the UN in Nov./Dec. 1983 by the ambassadors from Libya, Iran and Syria. The crude and vulgar language was directed against "Jews" as well as against "Zionism" which is the usual butt of attacks.

0866. Levine, Audrey. Sisterhood is Heartbreaking. NEW OUTLOOK 28, 10/11 <250-251> (Oct/Nov 1985) 15-18.

An account of the author's experiences at the UN Conference on Women in Nairobi. Despite some fruitful contacts with Arab women, a "torrent of abuse prevailed," Israel was accused of genocide, and Zionism equated with racism. Sometimes, openly antisemitic remarks were voiced.

0867. Limiti, Giuliana. L'UNESCO e l'antisemitismo. LA RASSEGNA MENSILE DI ISRAEL 50, 5-8 (May-Aug 1984) 281-294.

Analyzes UNESCO official acts and statements and proves their anti-Israeli or antisemitic character.

0868. Liskofsky, Sidney. A DISMAL ANNIVERSARY: A DECADE OF THE UN'S "ZIONISM EQUALS RACISM" RESOLUTION, 1975-1985. New York: Jacob Blaustein Institute for the Advancement of Human Rights, American Jewish Committee, 4 November 1985. 14 pp. Unseen.

0869. Manor, Yohanan. L'antisionisme. REVUE FRANCAISE DE SCIENCE POLITIQUE 34, 2 (Apr 1984) 295-323. An extract appeared in REGARDS 124 (27 Sept-10 Oct 1984) 48-49 and a shortened English version in THE JERUSALEM QUARTERLY 35 (Spr 1985) 125-144.

Examines various explanations for antisemitism, and puts forward the view that the post-World War II period of freedom from antisemitic ideology is coming to an end and "a new anti-Jewish ideology is being established: anti-Zionism. This time its rationale will be political." Describes Arab and Soviet anti-Zionist propaganda and its success in legitimizing antisemitism.

0870. Moynihan, Daniel Patrick. LOYALTIES. New York: Harcourt Brace Jovanovich, 1984. Unseen.

Includes discussion of the 1975 UN resolution equating Zionism with racism, and the role of the USSR in passing that resolution.

0871. Moynihan, Daniel Patrick. Telling the Truth about the Lie. MOMENT 10, 3 (Mar 1985) 20-21.

The text of a speech delivered at the State Department in December 1984 (see no. 854). Gives an overview of works written about the UN resolution equating Zionism with racism since 1975, and of the study day convened in Jerusalem in November 1984 (see no. 860). Discusses also the Soviet anti-Zionist propaganda campaign.

0872. Moynihan, Daniel Patrick. "Z=R, plus 9." FORUM ON THE JEWISH PEOPLE, ZIONISM AND ISRAEL 54/55 (Spr 1985) 1-6.

Keynote address delivered at the study day refuting the Zionism=Racism equation, Jerusalem, 11 November 1984 (see no. 860). The UN resolution was the culmination of a virulent anti-Zionist propaganda campaign launched by the Soviet Union after the Six Day War, and which continues today. Discusses the ramifications of the resolution in international politics, where Zionism has been delegitimized, especially in the eyes of the Third World. Also mentions anti-Zionism propagated in Arab countries by Islamic fundamentalism.

0873. Rubin, Jeff. Zionism=Racism. B'NAI B'RITH INTERNATIONAL JEWISH MONTHLY 99, 6 (Feb 1985) 37-38, 48.

B'nai B'rith sponsored a seminar to explore the origin and effects of the "Zionism equals racism" UN resolution of 10 Nov. 1975.

0874. Schoemberg, Harris. En la ONU un Nazi habló sobre derechos humanos. HERENCIA JUDIA 32 (1985) 21-25.

The antisemitic declarations of a few members of the UN never seem to end. The complacent and indifferent attitudes of other members allow the diffusion of the antisemitic message.

0875. Stellman, Henri. ANTI-ZIONISM AND ANTI-SEMITISM (AND THE UNITED NATIONS). London: Britain/Israel Public Affairs Committee, 1985. 4 pp. (Focus, October 1985). Unseen.

0876. Stoehr, Martin. Ein Christ ueber Israel. JUDAICA 40, 1 (Mar 1984) 3-15.

Deals with present-day Christian criticism of and theological attitudes towards the State of Israel, some of which are tainted with antisemitic arguments.

0877. Strouse, Evelyn. End of a Long Decade. HADASSAH MAGAZINE 67, 2 (Oct 1985) 44-46.

The success of the American and Israeli delegations at the United Nations' Women's Conference in Nairobi, July 1985, in eliminating the "Zionism equals racism" equation from the final document of the conference was preceded by productive exchanges at the preliminary Non-Governmental Organizations Forum.

0878. Syrkin, Marie. Some Progress in Nairobi. MIDSTREAM 31, 8 (Oct 1985) 49-51.

Compared to the disastrous Copenhagen conference of 1980, the UN Conference for Women in Nairobi was a limited success for the Jewish representatives. Thanks to the US delegation, Zionism was deleted from the list of the world's ills, and the USSR acquiesced. Though Zionism was attacked with illogical and false accusations, some Palestinian-Israeli dialogue was possible.

0879. Tanembaum, Manuel. La ultima calumnia antijudía. LA UNION 112 (Nov 1985) 30-31.

A speech by one of the leaders of the WJC in Argentina condemning the Zionism=Racism UN resolution. Gives a short review of the history of contemporary antisemitism.

0880. Tarnero, Jacques. Israël, cet obscur objet du délire. JUDAISME ET DROITS DE L'HOMME, ed. Emmanuel Hirsch. Paris: Librairie des Libertés, 1984. Pp. 175-181.

Describes the contemporary world political situation and attacks on Israel, mainly caused by problems within the Third World and the growth of extreme right and neo-Nazi groups. Anti-Zionism is a universal and irrational madness which plays the part once taken by antisemitism in Europe.

0881. Tarnero, Jacques. Tiers mondisme antisioniste: Une figure de la redemption de la culpabilité occidentale à l'égard des Juifs. TRACES 9/10 (1984) 200-223.

Discusses anti-Zionism as an essential component of Third World ideology. The theme of Israel in the 1980s occupies in the Third World the place that the Jewish question had in Europe at the end of the 19th century.

0882. Wisse, Ruth R. Blaming Israel. COMMENTARY 77, 2 (Feb 1984) 29-36.

Examines recent manifestations of anti-Israel sentiment: media coverage of the Lebanon War, Arab anti-Zionist propaganda, Zionism=racism, Roald Dahl, Jacobo Timerman, the State University of New York Stony Brook campus affair.

0883. Wistrich, Robert S. ANTI-ZIONISM AS AN EXPRESSION OF ANTISEMITISM IN RECENT YEARS. Jerusalem: Hebrew University, Institute of Contemporary Jewry, Vidal Sassoon International Center for the Study of Antisemitism, Shazar Library, 1985. 44 pp. (Study Circle on World Jewry in the Home of the President of Israel, 10 December 1984). Appeared simultaneously in Hebrew.

Antisemitism and anti-Zionism are antithetical ideologies; however, they have become interrelated and Israel is the prime focus for modern-day antisemitism. There is a conscious effort on the part of various bodies - the USSR primarily, but also the UN, the Left, Islamic fundamentalists, and others - to delegitimize Jewish self-definition.

1945-1985: Australia and New Zealand

0884. Borg, Christian. WHO ARE THE JEWS? Bullsbrook, Western Australia: Veritas, 1984. ix, 278 pp.

In 1977, a leader of the New Zealand Nazi party, Durward Colin King-Ansell, was accused of "inciting racial disharmony." In the subsequent court case, it was established that the Jews are an ethnic group protected by the race relations laws. Provides a detailed account of the defense submissions claiming that the Jews are a religious group only, that the principle of free speech was being infringed and that "World Jewry" had influenced recent dictionary definitions of the word "ethnic."

0885. THE LEAGUE OF RIGHTS: AN EVALUATION OF AUSTRALIA'S FOREMOST ORGANISATION PROMOTING RACIAL AND RELIGIOUS HATRED. Melbourne: Executive Council of Australian Jewry, 1985. 9 pp.

This pamphlet was issued in order to inform the public of the true nature of the Australian League of Rights, an organization which poses as a respectable right-wing body. In fact, the League is an extremely radical racist and antisemitic body, founded in 1946 by supporters of the Social Credit movement of C.H. Douglas, who claimed he would solve the world economic crisis caused by a conspiracy of Jewish financiers. The League also supports Holocaust denial and anti-Zionist activities.

1945-1985: The Islamic World

0886. בארי, ידידיה. התקשורת המצרית מתרפקת על העבר הנאצי. בארץ ישראל 161 (יולי 1985) 16.

[Be'eri, Yedidya. The Egyptian Media Yearns for the Nazi Past. B'ERETZ ISRAEL 161 (July 1985) 16.]

Egyptian journalists, writing in May 1985 on the occasion of Reagan's visit to Bitburg, claimed that Jewish objections were meant only to stir up trouble between Western allies, and that the actuality of the Holocaust "has not been scientifically proven." The journalists expressed other "Nazi" accusations against the Jews.

0887. Foxman, Abraham H.; Jacobson, Kenneth. Egyptian Poison. ADL BULLETIN 42, 5 (May 1985) 3-5.

Some vicious antisemitic writings have recently been published in Egypt - in the daily newspapers, in books, and in magazine articles.

0888. Gruen, George E. Los 5,000 rehenes Judíos en Siria. LA UNION 91 (Feb 1984) 26-27. See also an article in the April 1984 issue (pp. 30-31).

The 5,000 Jews in Syria are hostages of the government. Forbidden to emigrate, they are exposed to acts of murder and brutality by government officials and private individuals. Several cases are described.

0889. Haim, Sylvia G. Islamic Anti-Zionism. JEWISH QUARTERLY 31, 2 <114> (1984) 48-51. An adaptation appeared in HUMANISTIC JUDAISM 13, 1 (Spr 1985) 47-51, entitled "Islamic Anti-Semitism."

Contends that European antisemites now parade their hatred in the guise of anti-Zionism. The Muslim world, particularly Islamic fundamentalism, has adopted the tools of old-style antisemitism, disseminating writings such as "The Protocols of the Elders of Zion" and the works of Henry Ford. Judaism is equated with Zionism, and hatred is vented against both.

0890. Israeli, Raphael. PEACE IS IN THE EYE OF THE BEHOLDER. Berlin (West): Mouton, 1985. xxii, 389 pp. (New Babylon: Studies in the Social Sciences, 46).

A study of Arab hostility towards Jews, Zionism and Israel as expressed in Arab media coverage of Israel-related affairs from 1975 to 1979. Analyzes most of the important newspapers, and also radio and television programs, in the Middle East and North Africa, with special emphasis on Egypt, Syria, Jordan and Lebanon. Includes numerous excerpts from the sources, and a chapter on antisemitic cartoons (pp. 283-357). Arab antisemitism stems from three sources: the Islamic religion, European antisemitism, and the Arab-Israeli conflict.

0891. Mayer, Thomas. The UN Resolution Equating Zionism with Racism: Genesis and Repercussions. INSTITUTE OF JEWISH AFFAIRS: RESEARCH REPORT 1 (Apr 1985) 11 pp.

After the October 1973 War, Arab politicians thought the time was ripe to spread the "Zionism is racism" proposition in the international arena. The UN resolution prompted a Western backlash. Arab attempts to further reduce Israel's recognition in the diplomatic arena have not succeeded, but a propaganda campaign in the West has had some impact.

0892. Nettler, Ronald L. Islam vs. Israel. COMMENTARY 78, 6 (Dec 1984) 26-30.

The first and most important Sunni Muslim fundamentalist organization was the Muslim Brothers, founded in 1928. Muslim fundamentalism is deeply antagonistic towards Israel, rejecting absolutely the legitimacy of Jewish statehood. This attitude is based on traditional Islamic conceptions of Jewish inferiority, and fear of a Jewish-Zionist conspiracy to undermine Islam and spread westernization.

0893. Sivan, Emmanuel. ISLAMIC FUNDAMENTALISM AND ANTISEMITISM. Jerusalem: Hebrew University, Institute of Contemporary Jewry, Vidal Sassoon International Center for the Study of Antisemitism; Shazar Library, 1985. 24 pp. (Study Circle on World Jewry in the Home of the President of Israel, 18 February 1985). Appeared simultaneously in Hebrew, and in Spanish in RUMBOS 12 (Spr 1985) 57-70.

Before 1967, Islamic fundamentalism, as embodied in the Muslim Brethren, sought to preserve the Muslim heritage against westernizing influences, and anti-Zionism was a marginal issue. After 1967, hot-headed young militants gave more prominence to anti-Zionist ideology. Since 1977/78 (due to Sadat's peace initiative, the Iranian revolution, and a younger leadership), and even more since the Lebanon War, anti-Zionism is presented as "the modern-day incarnation of the authentically Islamic hostility to the Jews." Jews are seen as the ever-present enemy who must be eliminated.

0894. Wigoder, Geoffrey. Antisemitismo en Egipto. LA UNION 106 (May 1985) 14.

The process of peace with Egypt is pragmatic in origin; it does not preclude antisemitic incidents and publications. Officially, the authorities differentiate between Jews and Zionists; in practice, the press expresses contempt toward Jews, Zionists, and Israelis alike.

1945-1985: Latin America

0895. Aronsfeld, C.C. Progress in Argentina: Old Prejudice and a New Law. JEWISH AFFAIRS 39, 12 (Dec 1984) 33, 35, 37.

Antisemitism still exists in Argentina, even after the demise of the military junta. Describes various antisemitic incidents and classical accusations against the Jews expressed by groups (particularly right-wing) and individuals (particularly Catholics), including anti-Zionist statements. A bill designed to outlaw discrimination was recently presented to Parliament.

0896. Bergstein, Nahum; Friedler, Egon; Jerozolimski, José. Anti-Zionism and Anti-Semitism in Latin America Today. ZIONIST IDEAS 8 (Spr 1984) 28-35.

Excerpts from a panel discussion which took place at a seminar on Zionist thought organized by the Circulo de Reflexión Judía (CCIU), Uruguay, March 1983.

0897. Comisión Nacional sobre la Desaparición de Personas. NUNCA MAS. Buenos Aires: Eudeba, 1985. 492 pp.

A collection of documents on the repressive activities of semi-official units in Argentina during the military regime. These units frequently displayed antisemitism - the Jews detained suffered more punishment and torture because of their Judaism. Provides many documents on the subject apart from those included in the chapter on antisemitism (pp. 67-75).

0898. DIARIO DEL JUICIO. Buenos Aires: Perfil, 1985-1986. 36 issues.

The protocols of the sessions (27 May 1985-28 Jan 1986) of the trial of the military junta which ruled Argentina between 1976 and 1983. On antisemitic attitudes towards Jews, see issues no. 1, 2, 11, 15, 21, 24, 27.

0899. Elkin, Judith Laikin. "We Knew but We Didn't Want to Know." JEWISH FRONTIER 52, 2 (Feb 1985) 7-11.

The Argentinian Jewish community is bitterly divided over the events that took place during the rule of terror from 1976 to 1983. Discusses whether that terror was antisemitic or not, and the impact of the repression on the Jewish community.

0900. Giraud, Michel. Crispation identitaire et antisémitisme en Martinique: Le cas d'"Antilla." TRACES 11 (1984) 129-151.

The Martinique weekly newspaper "Antilla" launched a violent antisemitic campaign under the guise of anti-Zionism in the wake of the Lebanon War. The writer and publishers were brought to court and fined.

0901. Hasson, Ariel; Amiel, Ricardo. Amiel: Somos tercos! Llegará el momento en que el pueblo diga si! al PPC. LA UNION 91 (Feb 1984) 18-25.

In a wide-ranging interview, Ricardo Amiel, a Peruvian political leader, expresses respect for the Jewish people and the State of Israel. He believes that antisemitism and anti-Zionism today result from envy of a people that is achieving its aspirations. He also believes that the PLO is encouraging neo-Nazi and antisemitic activity in Latin America.

0902. Herman, Donald L. Israel's Latin American Immigrants. AMERICAN JEWISH ARCHIVES 36, 1 (Apr 1984) 16-49.

Pp. 22-25 describe antisemitism in Latin America under the impact of social revolution - earlier in the 20th century in Mexico, Bolivia and Cuba, and more recently (1970s-80s) in Nicaragua, Guatemala and El Salvador. Pp. 25-29 discuss antisemitism in Argentina, and particularly the "Timerman controversy."

0903. Hirt-Manheimer, Aron; Meyer, Marshall. Argentina's Agony. REFORM JUDAISM 14, 1 (Fall 1985) 10-11.

An interview with Rabbi Marshall T. Meyer, who worked in Argentina between 1959 and 1984. Meyer states that over 1,000 Jews disappeared, but that only one or two were arrested solely because they were Jewish. The organized Jewish community failed to help because the leadership thought that good relations with the regime would reduce its antisemitism. (See also no. 914.)

0904. Kleiner, Alberto, comp. LOS POLITICOS ARGENTINOS Y EL ANTISEMITISMO. Buenos Aires: Libreros y Editores del Polígono, 1984. 3 vols. (ca. 90 pp.).

Proceedings of the national convention of DAIA, the organization of Argentinian Jewry, October 1983. Includes an opening speech by the chairman, Sion Cohen Imach, who discussed the recent outburst of antisemitism in Argentina, and speeches by several candidates in the presidential election, in which they condemned antisemitism. (See also no. 910.)

0905. Klich, Ignacio. Communal Policy under the Argentine Junta. THE JEWISH QUARTERLY 32, 2 <118> (1985) 13-19.

Criticizes the DAIA (Delegación de Asociaciones Israelitas Argentinas) for its failure to oppose antisemitic manifestations during the rule of the military junta, 1976-1983.

0906. Lerner, Nathan. A Continent in Turmoil: Jews in Latin America. SURVEY OF JEWISH AFFAIRS 1 <1982> (1984) 236-249.

A survey of Latin American Jewry during 1982. Mentions antisemitism as an endemic problem, especially in Argentina and occasionally in Brazil. Reactions to the Lebanon War are also covered.

0907. Levine, Robert. Anatomía de un antisemita brasileño y el conflicto arabe-israelí. RUMBOS 10 (Mar-June 1984) 127-139.

The Brazilian press's hostility towards Israel was intensified by the Lebanon War and by Brazil's economic dependence on the Arab countries. Paulo Francis, a reporter for the "Folha de São Paulo," uses a very aggressive tone in describing Israeli policy, and his coverage is also antisemitic.

0908. La ley antirracista y antidiscriminatoria en Argentina. SEMANA 761 (14 Nov 1984) 21.

An extract from the law recently presented to the Argentinian Congress in order to fight antisemitism.

0909. Newton, Ronald C. The United States, the German-Argentines, and the Myth of the Fourth Reich, 1943-1947. HISPANIC AMERICAN HISTORICAL REVIEW 64, 1 (Feb 1984) 81-103.

The US exerted pressure on Argentina to suppress the German-Argentines and to destroy their institutions and economic base, claiming that the Germans were planning to establish a Fourth Reich and were a threat for "Western Hemisphere security." The true motive for the US's action was its "interest in uprooting German economic competition in Argentina." The extent of German and Nazi involvement in Argentina is explored, with mention of Jews and antisemitism.

0910. PONENCIAS SOBRE EL ANTISEMITISMO EN ARGENTINA. Buenos Aires: Centro Max Nordau, 1984. 37 pp.

An offprint of two lectures delivered at the DAIA convention, October 1983 (not included in the volumes listed in no. 904): Mario Gorenstein: Antisemitismo -

antisionismo (3-19); Nehemias Resnizky: Factores globales que inciden en la problematica comunitaria (21-37).

0911. Rosenthal, Morton M. A Hopeful Era for Argentine Jewry. ADL BULLETIN 41, 1 (Jan 1984) 3-5.

Large numbers of Jews were attracted to President Alfonsin's Radical Civic Union Party and he moved quickly to bring prominent Jews to key positions in his government. This was in sharp contrast to the hundreds of antisemitic incidents during the election campaign period.

0912. Sarmiento, Sergio. Antisemitismo en México: Discriminación en el Congreso. LA UNION 92 (Mar 1984) 6.

Mexican federal deputy Miguel Olea Enríquez expressed anti-Jewish opinions in Congress. In view of Mexico's long tradition against discrimination, Olea Enríquez's views are an expression of personal prejudice and an attempt to cover up economic problems by attacking the Jews.

0913. Sobel, Henry I. América Latina: Realidades políticas, sociales y económicas actuales. RUMBOS 10 (Mar-June 1984) 119-126.

Surveys the Jewish communities in Latin America and focuses on antisemitism, especially in Argentina under the military regime. Examines the anti-Israel and anti-Zionist activities of Arab representatives in Brazil.

0914. Timerman, Uri; Meyer, Marshall. After the Junta's Fall: Jews and the New Argentina - Uri Timerman Interviews Marshall Meyer. JEWISH FRONTIER 51, 4 (Apr 1984) 10-12.

Meyer, an American-born Conservative Rabbi, discusses antisemitism during the reign of the Junta, and his activities on behalf of the Jews who disappeared. (See also no. 903.)

0915. URUGUAY 1984: EL ANTISEMITISMO EN LAS PLATAFORMAS DE LOS PARTIDOS POLITICOS Y OTROS DOCUMENTOS SOBRE PROPUESTAS PARTIDARIAS. Montevideo: Instituto de Estudios Latinoamericanos, 1984. 43 pp.

A collection of documents describing the transition from military rule to democratic government in Uruguay, in which antisemitic propaganda played a role. Examines the response of the Jewish community to antisemitic expressions in some of the parties' platforms.

0916. Weisbrot, Robert. Dateline Managua: Anti-Semitism or Anti-Climax? MOMENT 9, 9 (Oct 1984) 12-17.

Under the impact of revolutionary upheaval, the local Jewish community is rapidly disappearing. Claims that the Sandinista government is antisemitic frequently conflict with available evidence. Special measures were taken against Jewish businessmen because of their past dealings with the dictator Somoza; many Jews saw these measures as antisemitic. Government anti-Zionism may also slip into antisemitism. This article is followed by an exchange of views between two experts. Cynthia Arnson (pp. 18-22) describes the "Jewish connection" with the Nicaragua problem as largely a creation of the Reagan administration and the ADL. Morton Rosenthal (pp. 22-24) explains the substance of that connection. There may have been no "official policy" of persecution but there was Sandinista harassment of Jews as Jews.

1945-1985: The USA and Canada

0917. אלמן, ישראל. יהדות אמריקה בחברה פלוראליסטית. תל-אביב: ספרית פועלים, 1985. 422 עמ'.

[Ellman, Israel. AMERICAN JEWRY IN A PLURALISTIC SOCIETY. Tel Aviv: Sifriat Poalim, 1985. 422 pp.]

Discusses antisemitism in America on pp. 395-404. See the index for other references to antisemitism.

0918. גאלדקארן, יצחק. אפלייקענער פון געשיכטע. דרום אפריקע 37 (אפר-יוני 1985) 21-23.

[Goldkorn, Yitzchak. Deniers of History. DOREM AFRIKE 37 (Apr-June 1985) 21-23.]

Describes the trial of neo-Nazi Ernst Zundel in Toronto and calls for stronger measures against neo-Nazis and those who deny the Holocaust.

0919. דרוקער, ה. נאצי-גרופן אין אמעריקע און אין קאנאדע. אונזער צייט 9 <524> (סעפט 1985) 15-17.

[Druker, H. Nazi Groups in America and Canada. UNSER TSAIT 9 <524> (Sept 1985) 15-17.]

Describes neo-Nazi activities uncovered in the 1980s in the USA and Canada.

0920. יהודים ושחורים באספקלריית הבחירות בארצות-הברית. תפוצות ישראל 22, 3/4 (סתיו/חורף 1984).

[Jews and Blacks as They Are Reflected in American Politics. TEFUTSOT ISRAEL 22, 3/4 (Fall/Win 1984).]

The entire issue is devoted to this subject, consisting of articles translated from English, three of which are listed separately (nos. 946, 962, 982). Other articles dealing with antisemitism: Nat Hentoff: Unmasking Farrakhan (44-50) [THE VILLAGE VOICE, 29 May 1984]; A.C. Brownfield and J.A. Parker: In the Right with Two or Three (85-92) [The American Council for Judaism's ISSUES, Fall 1984]; Marvin Weitz: The Shattered Alliance (190-202) ["Patterns of Prejudice," May/June 1978]; Carl Gershman: Blacks and Jews (203-217) ["Midstream," Feb. 1976]; Sol Roth: Black Antisemitism: Diagnosis and Treatment (218-224) ["Judaism," Summmer 1981]; Nathan Perlmutter: Black-Jewish Relations: A Two-Way Street (225-229) ["Judaism," Summer 1981].

0921. Ages, Arnold. Canada's Trials and Investigations. B'NAI B'RITH INTERNATIONAL JEWISH MONTHLY 100, 3 (Nov 1985) 24-27, 36.

The trials of Ernst Zundel and James Keegstra, and the Conservative government's formation of the Deschesnes Commission to investigate the presence of war criminals in Canada, show that virulent antisemitism has managed to take root in Canada. Previous Liberal governments refused to take action on the war criminals issue because of pressure by Baltic ethnic groups. Many Canadian Jews felt that the media gave Zundel's allegations unnecessary publicity. However, the convictions of Zundel and Keegstra reassured them.

0922. Anti-Zionism, Anti-Semitism, Reaganism: Statement on a Harmful Document. JEWISH CURRENTS 38, 5 (May 1984) 17-19. The statement is signed: Paul Novick and Haim Suller for the "Morgn Freiheit," Itche Goldberg for "Yiddishe Kultur," Morris U. Schappes for "Jewish Currents."

A reaction to the text of a speech prepared by Victor Perlo of the US Communist Party for the International Anti-Zionist Conference in Havana, Cuba, November 1983. Perlo did not go to Havana, but the text of his speech was printed in the New York "Daily World" (5 Jan 1984) and the San Francisco "People's World" (7 Jan 1984). The statement declares that Perlo's speech is "replete with open and poorly-masked anti-Semitic overtones and implications," the effect of which will be to unite Jews in support of Reagan, and defeat the purpose of the Left.

0923. As Blacks See It. MOMENT 9, 9 (Oct 1984) 25-34.

In July 1984, "Moment" invited four leaders of Boston's Black community for an evening's discussion on Black-Jewish relations, and specifically on the Jewish reaction to Jesse Jackson as Blacks see it. The participants - Charles Stith, Ricardo Millet, Barbara Arnwine, Joseph Washington - felt that Jews give Jackson a bad press because he is critical of Israel, and that Israel is getting in the way of Black-Jewish understanding. Jews accuse Jackson of antisemitism over an issue that is strictly political policy. Jews must understand that Jesse Jackson represents the "cumulative aspiration of Black people," and that Farrakhan is just a "fringe thing." Blacks, though, must try to understand the centrality of Israel to the Jews.

0924. Auerbach, Jerold S. Fighting Anti-Semitism at Wellesley. SH'MA 15 <281> (16 Nov 1984) 1-3.

Accuses Wellesley College of continuing discrimination against Jews. A formal quota system restricting Jewish students to 8-10 percent of each class existed until the late 1940s. Bible study was required of every student until 1969; until then, no Jewish scholar was hired in the Religion Department because they were considered unqualified to teach the New Testament. Contends that antisemitism still exists on campus today. This view is refuted (on pp. 3-6) by Rabbi Richard J. Israel and Marshall I. Goldman.

0925. Barnes, Fred. Farrakhan Frenzy. NEW REPUBLIC 193, 18 (28 Oct 1985) 13-15.

Louis Farrakhan's antisemitic attacks have attracted media attention, built him up as a national figure, and widened the Jewish liberal-Black split. Moderate Black politicians have been the main sufferers. They fear losing their own base by denouncing him, and tend to be indifferent to his antisemitism. Reducing sensational press coverage of Farrakhan is the best policy.

0926. Barrett, Stanley R. Fascism in Canada. CONTEMPORARY CRISES 8, 4 (Oct 1984) 345-377.

A sociological study of the extreme Right in Canada from the 1930s until the present. Antisemitism is a central component of Canadian fascist ideology. Describes and analyzes leading organizations and individuals, based on archival material and personal interviews.

0927. Barrett, Stanley R. Racism, Ethics and the Subversive Nature of Anthropological Inquiry. PHILOSOPHY OF THE SOCIAL SCIENCES 14, 1 (Mar 1984) 1-25.

A discussion of the ethics of anthropological fieldwork which is often subversive to the host community studied. Attempts to solve the problem by shifting the focus of research from the victims and the powerless to the victimizers, such as racists. The study of several "white supremist" extreme right-wing groups in Canada revealed that antisemitism is the main ideological factor motivating them.

0928. Berman, Paul; Green, Philip. Jackson and the Left: The Other Side of the Rainbow. THE NATION 238, 13 (7 Apr 1984) 407-412.

Paul Berman (pp. 407-410) discusses the "rainbow coalition" of white liberals and Blacks and whether Jackson's antisemitic remarks have affected the white liberal, particularly Jewish, vote. Philip Green (pp. 410-412) defends Jackson, stating that he is a "true left-winger" and, as a political opportunist, is no worse than other politicians in high office.

0929. Berson, Cathy S.; Mark Silverberg. Reality of Hatred in the 1980s: A CJO Interview with Mark Silverberg. CANADIAN JEWISH OUTLOOK 23, 3 (Mar 1985) 5-6, 8.

Mark Silverberg, of the Canadian Jewish Congress, accounts for the rise in antisemitism in Canada. Traditional racist antisemites, such as the Aryan Nations Organization, have few members. They are dangerous terrorists but not a threat to the system, unlike the "credible ultra-right." Organizations like the Canadian League of Rights, with thousands of members including prominent people, disseminate anti-Zionism and Holocaust denial claims. The Zundel trial is a test case for the enforcement of a 1980 law against hate literature.

0930. Bevilacqua, Anthony J. Catholic-Jewish Relations in the USA. CHRISTIAN JEWISH RELATIONS 17, 3 (Sept 1984) 51-58.

A slightly shortened version of an address by the Bishop of Pittsburgh to the American Jewish Committee, June 1984. Reviews Catholic-Jewish relations since the "Nostra Aetate" declaration, emphasizing particularly the condemnation of antisemitism and the need for continued dialogue.

0931. Blitzer, Wolf. BETWEEN WASHINGTON AND JERUSALEM: A REPORTER'S NOTEBOOK. New York: Oxford University Press, 1985. xii, 259 pp.

An examination of the relationship between the USA and Israel in the 1970s-1980s by the Washington correspondent of the "Jerusalem Post." Pp. 151-153 describe antisemitic incidents during the 1982 Congressional campaign. Blacks and fundamentalist Christians are also mentioned as possible sources of antisemitism.

0932. Blumberg, Janice Rothschild. ONE VOICE: RABBI JACOB M. ROTHSCHILD AND THE TROUBLED SOUTH. Macon, GA: Mercer University Press, 1985. xi, 239 pp.

An account of the career of a Reform rabbi and civil rights activist in Atlanta, Georgia during the period of desegregation (1950s-1960s). In Oct. 1958 his synagogue was bombed during a wave of bombings by neo-Nazis of synagogues and Jewish community centers in the South. Describes the antisemitism aroused by Jewish support for integration and the Jewish communities' fears, although no general wave of antisemitism resulted. Black antisemitism is mentioned as well.

0933. Brickner, Balfour. Black-Jewish Dialogue? THE JEWISH SPECTATOR 50, 1 (Spr 1985) 23-27.

Discusses relations between Jews and Blacks in America in the past and today. Mentions American Black leaders, such as Jesse Jackson, who are anti-Israel and therefore seen as anti-Jewish, and explains the reasons for their attitudes.

0934. Byrski, Zbigniew. Pra-wybory Partii Demokratycznej w USA [The Democratic Party Primaries in the USA]. KULTURA 7/8 (July/Aug 1984) 82-86.

Discusses Jesse Jackson, and particularly his associate Louis Farrakhan, who wants to sow hatred of "White America" among Blacks. Much of his propaganda is antisemitic.

0935. Carmody, John. Judaism vis-à-vis Christianity: How to Make Changes. JOURNAL OF ECUMENICAL STUDIES 21, 3 (Sum 1984) 507-522.

Describes a project designed to discover how the images of Jews and Judaism in Christian religious educational materials in America can be improved. A questionnaire was sent to authors, publishers, directors of religious education, and classroom teachers, both Catholics and Protestants. The responses indicated that the negative stereotype still exists among students, the respondents were complacent about the present situation, and did not in general offer suggestions for improvement beyond what is already being done. The author presents his own recommendations on pp. 517-521.

0936. Carson, Claybourne. Blacks and Jews in the Civil Rights Movement. JEWS IN BLACK PERSPECTIVES: A DIALOGUE, ed. Joseph R. Washington. Rutherford, NJ: Fairleigh Dickinson University Press, 1984. Pp. 113-131.

A detailed analysis of developments within the civil rights movement during 1966/67, and the emergence of open Black antisemitism. Focuses on the SNCC (Student Non-Violent Coordinating Committee), a Black militant group supported by New York Jewish radical left circles. Black leaders found that socialist ideology did not attract the Black masses, and turned instead to nationalism and separatism. A virulent anti-Israel attack in the summer of 1967 served as a test of their break with the civil rights past and ties with whites. For the Jews it was a sign of growing Black antisemitism.

0937. Cattlemen's Gazette Promotes Anti-Semitism: One of Many Phoney Solutions to a Real Problem. THE HAMMER 6 (Spr 1984) 25-28.

Roderick (Rick) Elliott and his newspaper "The Primrose and Cattlemen's Gazette" have attempted to exploit the farm crisis by handing farmers solutions in the form of a combination of antisemitism and dubious legal remedies.

0938. Cohen, Kitty O. Black-Jewish Relations in 1984: A Survey of Black US Congressmen. PATTERNS OF PREJUDICE 19, 2 (Apr 1985) 3-18.

A summary of a report on interviews with 16 members of the Black Congressional Caucus of the 98th Congress, in which their attitudes to social and political issues affecting relations between the Black and Jewish communities were examined. Subjects discussed included: the image of the American Jewish community in Black eyes, the possibility that cooperation would reduce antisemitism, and Jewish opposition to Jesse Jackson. It was agreed that Black-Jewish relations had deteriorated in 1984, and unconscious antisemitism had surfaced.

0939. Copulos, Milton R. THE LAROUCHE NETWORK. Washington, DC: The Heritage Foundation, 1984. 10 pp. (The Heritage Foundation Institution Analysis, 28). Unseen.

0940. Culbertson, Philip. Seminarians, Judaism, and Christian Exclusivism. ENCOUNTER: CREATIVE THEOLOGICAL SCHOLARSHIP 43, 3 (Sum 1984) 213-220.

Examines attitudes toward Jews and Judaism of Episcopal seminarians in the USA who were asked to write an essay on the interpretation of John 14:6 for the purpose of interfaith dialogue between Christians and Jews. Concludes that the seminarians' knowledge regarding Jewish history and theology is inadequate, many old stereotypes are still adhered to, and some antisemitism was expressed as well - but more students are accepting of Judaism than are rejecting, and most are ashamed of the history of Christian persecution of the Jews.

0941. Davis, Harrison M. Mormon Attitudes toward Jews: A Theology of Blood and Race. HUMANISTIC JUDAISM 13, 1 (Spr 1985) 33-38.

Since 1978, Mormon Church officials have authorized a revision of Mormon scriptures, deleting various passages of a racially demeaning nature. Expresses hopes that the younger generation of Mormons in particular will denounce racism and antisemitism.

0942. Dawidowicz, Lucy. Politics, the Jews and the '84 Election. COMMENTARY 79, 2 (Feb 1985) 25-30.

A survey of Jewish involvement in politics from 19th century Europe to 20th century USA. Jews traditionally supported left-wing parties as a bulwark against antisemitism. Since the 1960s, antisemitism in the guise of anti-Zionism has been emanating from the Left much more than from right-wing Christian groups. In the 1984 elections, more than 60% of US Jews voted for the Democratic Party despite Jesse Jackson and Black antisemitism. Calls for Jews to rethink and change their political agenda.

0943. Donnelly, F.K. The Battle over Eckville: Prejudice in Canadian Provincial Politics. PATTERNS OF PREJUDICE 18, 1 (Jan 1984) 16-22.

Jim Keegstra, a secondary-school teacher in Eckville, Alberta, was dismissed by the school board in Dec. 1982 following complaints by parents regarding his teaching a blatantly antisemitic view of history. Keegstra is the mayor of Eckville, population about 870 (none of them Jews), and was also active in the Social Credit Party. Discusses Keegstra's views, reactions for and against him, the Social Credit Party, and political circles in Alberta.

0944. Downs, Donald Alexander. NAZIS IN SKOKIE: FREEDOM, COMMUNITY AND THE FIRST AMENDMENT. Notre Dame, IN: Notre Dame University Press, 1985. xii, 227 pp. (Notre Dame Studies in Law and Contemporary Issues, 1).

Based on interviews with representatives of all the groups involved in the dispute regarding the request of the National Socialist Party of America, led by Frank Collins, to march in Skokie in 1977 - the Holocaust survivors, the Nazi party, and the American Civil Liberties Union. Questions the decision of the court to permit the march. Opposes the protection of free speech as enshrined in the First Amendment when that speech is intended to assault or cause harm. Brings evidence for harm done to the survivors by permitting the march, and makes suggestions for legal reforms.

0945. Driedger, Leo; Clifton, Rodney A. Ethnic Stereotypes: Images of Ethnocentrism, Reciprocity or Dissimilarity? CANADIAN REVIEW OF SOCIOLOGY AND ANTHROPOLOGY 21, 3 (Aug 1984) 287-301.

Examines the concept of stereotypes as used by social scientists and the ethnocentric theory that ethnic groups rate themselves positively and other groups negatively. A study of Jewish, Ukrainian, French and German-origin high school students in Winnipeg shows that Jews were rated least favorably by the other three groups. Both Jews and non-Jews agreed that Jews are excitable, domineering, competitive, emotional, wealthy, etc., but the non-Jews included unfavorable traits such as dishonest and materialistic.

0946. Ellerin, Milton. Minister Louis Farrakhan, Leader of the Nation of Islam. BACKGROUNDER (Fall 1984). Unseen. A Hebrew trans. appeared in TEFUTSOT ISRAEL 22, 3/4 (Fall/Win 1984) 35-43.

0947. Fein, Leonard. Jesse Jackson and the Jews. MOMENT 9, 4 (Apr 1984) 13-14.

A survey of Jackson's views, Jewish reactions and Black-Jewish relations in 1984.

0948. Feingold, Henry L. Finding a Conceptual Framework for the Study of American Antisemitism. JEWISH SOCIAL STUDIES 47, 3/4 (Sum/Fall 1985) 313-326.

Describes the difficulties encountered by the historian studying antisemitism in a pluralistic society, where the prejudice is primarily latent rather than overt, where it is difficult to differentiate antisemitism from normal intergroup conflict in society and where the antisemitism is largely attitudinal and displays little ideological coherence.

0949. Gardner, Jigs. The Keegstra Affair. MIDSTREAM 31, 9 (Nov 1985) 7-9.

Surveys the implications of the trial of Jim Keegstra, who taught high school students for 14 years that the world was governed by a Jewish conspiracy and that the Holocaust was a hoax. The Social Credit Party suspended him, but many prominent members supported him. "What is so astounding and dismaying about the Keegstra affair is what one might call its lack of resonance: it is as if it occurred in an intellectual and imaginative void." In small-town Canada, Jews are viewed as alien and slightly sinister.

0950. Gibson, James L.; Bingham, Richard D. Skokie, Nazis, and the Elitist Theory of Democracy. WESTERN POLITICAL QUARTERLY 37, 1 (Mar 1984) 32-47.

Discusses the elitist theory of democracy - "elite support for democratic norms...[is] a necessary condition for the maintenance of civil liberties." The case in point is the Skokie-Nazi dispute of 1977/78, the elite being the American Civil Liberties Union which defended the Nazis' "rights of free speech and assembly."

0951. Glazer, Nathan. Jews and Blacks: What Happened to the Grand Alliance? JEWS IN BLACK PERSPECTIVES: A DIALOGUE, ed. Joseph R. Washington. Rutherford, NJ: Fairleigh Dickinson University Press, 1984. Pp. 105-112.

The Black-Jewish alliance, which fought successfully for anti-discriminatory laws in housing, education and employment in the 1940s and 1950s, was based on the principle of tests of abstract merit. In the 1960s it became clear that these tests helped few Blacks. "Affirmative action," or preference for Blacks, threatens Jewish interests and principles. The alliance can be revived, not on the basis of affirmative action, but on economic growth and progress for Blacks.

0952. Gold, Victor. Letter to Jesse, from Hymie's Son. NATIONAL REVIEW 36, 9 (18 May 1984) 28-29.

Gold, national correspondent for "Washingtonian" magazine, condemns Jesse Jackson as a bigot and racist; he relates a conversation he happened to overhear in 1969 on a flight to Washington when Jackson was sitting behind him and said to his companion "You just can't trust the Jews... I never have trusted those people."

0953. Goldstein, Clifford. Anti-Semitism. LIBERTY 79, 2 (Mar/Apr 1984) 14-16.

A survey of present-day expressions of antisemitism throughout the world and particularly in the United States.

0954. Hall, Gus. The Big Lie and the Jewish American Community. POLITICAL AFFAIRS 63, 8/9 (Aug/Sept 1984) 6-10.

A speech delivered at the 12th Annual Jewish Affairs Dinner, June 1984, by Gus Hall, General Secretary of the Communist Party (USA), in which he denounced American Jewry's accusation of antisemitism against the Soviet Union and other Communist countries and described Zionism as an ally of reactionary forces.

0955. Havelock, Ray. Funny, You Don't Look Canadian. REFORM JUDAISM 13, 3 (Spr 1985) 18-19, 31.

Discusses antisemitism in Canada, especially in Quebec and Alberta, and the antisemitic propaganda of James Keegstra.

0956. Hertzberg, Arthur. The Graying of American Jewry. SURVEY OF JEWISH AFFAIRS 1 <1982> (1984) 148-160.

1982 was a watershed for American Jews; their self-confidence and optimism were threatened as they had not been since the antisemitic 1930s. The 1982 Lebanon War led to polarization in the Jewish community and deep divisions over attitudes towards Israel. Nevertheless, despite their fears, antisemitism did not increase.

0957. Hux, Samuel. Affirmative Action, Anti-Semitism, and the Politics of Brave Triviality. MOMENT 9, 6 (June 1984) 59-62.

Argues that the Affirmative Action policy discriminates against whites. Supporters of the policy accuse the Jews of leading the opposition and express a contemptuous attitude towards Jewish suffering in the past and towards the Holocaust. One of the reasons for this accusation is antisemitism although those who are blaming the Jews deny it.

0958. It's Not Populism: America's New Populist Party - a Fraud by Racists and Anti-Semites. THE HAMMER 8 (Fall 1984) 19-29. Abridged version of a report by the Institute for Research and Education on Human Rights, published by the Anti-Klan Network, October 1984.

The new Populist Party offers a program of economic radicalism for dissatisfied young whites, and opposes racial equality. Extreme-right groups, including the Ku Klux Klan, are deeply involved in it and Willis Carto of the Liberty Lobby, with his newspaper "The Spotlight," is the driving force behind this incipient fascist party. The use of the Populist label is part of Carto's attempt to make antisemitism "respectable" in the USA and to expand his influence beyond fringe groups.

0959. Katchen, Alan S. The Station That Broadcast Hate. ADL BULLETIN 42, 2 (Feb 1985) 3-5.

Describes the reaction in Dodge City, Kansas to the radio broadcast "Victory with Jesus," by William P. Gale, in which people were incited to "kill Jews." Gale and James P. Wickstrom were leaders of the Posse Comitatus, a violent antisemitic organization. "Wickstrom and Gale told their listeners that behind the government and its policies stood a conspiracy of Jews."

0960. King, Dennis; Radosh, Ronald. The LaRouche Connection. THE NEW REPUBLIC 191, 21 (19 Nov 1984) 15-25.

Neo-Nazi political extremist Lyndon LaRouche and his followers have won access to a wide range of US administrative officials, and with it respectability. LaRouche's newspaper, "New Solidarity," has announced that Zionism is an evil cult, that a group of Jews controls organized crime, that the Holocaust was "mythical," and that B'nai B'rith "resurrects the tradition of the Jews who demanded the crucifixion of Jesus Christ."

0961. The Klan Tries to Enter a New Era: Forms Underground with Neo-Nazis, Uses Computer and Video Systems. THE HAMMER 9 (Spr 1985) 20-25.

Describes the connections between the Fifth Era, the new leadership of the Ku Klux Klan, who are more openly antisemitic and neo-Nazi than their predecessors, and the Aryan Nations group. The Aryan Nations established an underground army, known as The Order, which carried out several armed robberies, counterfeiting operations, and the murder of Alan Berg, a Jewish radio talk show host in Denver.

0962. Kristol, Irving. The Political Dilemma of American Jews. COMMENTARY 78, 1 (July 1984) 23-29. A Hebrew trans. appeared in TEFUTSOT ISRAEL 22, 3/4 (Fall/Win 1984) 13-19.

Discusses changes in the political landscape which are causing Jews anxiety: Black-Jewish relations, and particularly Jesse Jackson's anti-American, anti-Israel, and antisemitic stance; the Moral Majority and its pro-Israel stance; the UN's anti-Zionism. American Jewry wavers between a liberal internationalism which is more and more left-wing and anti-Israel and a desire for interventionist policies in relation to Soviet Jewry and to Israel. They must open their eyes to the "disengagement of the liberal coalition from Jewish interests."

0963. Lerman, Tony. Jewish Issues and the American Presidential Election, 1984. INSTITUTE OF JEWISH AFFAIRS: RESEARCH REPORT 12 (Oct 1984) 14 pp.

Republicans and Democrats are making fierce efforts to win the Jewish vote. "Each candidate is attempting to tar the other with the brush of the extreme wing of his party: Reagan is linked with the antisemitism inherent in Christian fundamentalism; Mondale is linked with the antisemitic statements of Jesse Jackson and some of his supporters."

0964. Lester, Julius. The Time Has Come. THE NEW REPUBLIC 193, 18 (28 Oct 1985) 11-12.

Louis Farrakhan's appearance at Madison Square Garden on 7 October 1985 demonstrated that he is America's preeminent Black leader. The crowd, while not members of his movement, responded enthusiastically to Farrakhan and to other speakers' antisemitic and anti-Zionist attacks. "The Jews are Farrakhan's scapegoat but all of America is his victim."

0965. Lester, Julius. You Can't Go Home Again: Critical Thoughts about Jesse Jackson. DISSENT 32, 1 (Jan 1985) 21-25.

Jackson's presidential candidacy aroused messianic hopes among the Blacks. However, his claim to moral leadership was tarnished by antisemitic remarks, his association with Louis Farrakhan, and reactionary racist nationalism. Jackson's real problem was his inability to obtain white support and address issues of general interest.

0966. Liebermann, Dov. Antisémitisme et néonazisme: La Constitution américaine protège le droit d'expression des antisémites les plus extrémistes. REGARDS 143 (July/Aug 1985) 10.

Describes neo-Nazi organizations in the US, mainly The Covenant, the Sword and the Arm of the Lord, and their activities.

0967. Lindsay, Robert. The Farrakhan Phenomenon. POLITICAL AFFAIRS 64, 12 (Dec 1985) 15-21.

An analysis of the success of Louis Farrakhan from a Communist viewpoint ties it to the new militant mood of "Afro-Americans" rebelling against Reagan's policies. "Farrakhan uses anti-Semitism to shield Reagan and the real class enemy" - the military-industrial complex - and endangers the Jewish-labor-Black alliance which alone can fight for true equality.

0968. Louis Farrakhan: An Update. ADL FACTS 30, 1 (Spr 1985) 14 pp.

Surveys Louis Farrakhan's antisemitic activities during 1984-1985. He stepped up the intensity of his antisemitic remarks and drew large audiences at public meetings and on college campuses. He also attracted much media attention which turned him into a "star." Describes support and criticism of Farrakhan in the Black community.

0969. Louis Farrakhan: In His Own Words. ADL SPECIAL REPORT (Oct 1985) 13 pp.

A selection of antisemitic remarks made by Farrakhan in the media and in speeches during 1984/85. Farrakhan's antisemitism has increased since 1984 and has not been clearly repudiated by leaders of the Black community. He claims that the Jewish lobby controls the media and the government, and that Jews and Israel are the enemies and exploiters of the Blacks.

0970. Lowe, David. Computerized Networks of Hate. ADL FACT FINDING REPORT (Jan 1985) 6 pp.

Describes two racist and antisemitic computer networks organized and operated by right-wing extremists, activists in the Aryan Nations and the Ku Klux Klan. The persons discussed are Louis Beam, George Dietz, Richard Butler, Glenn Miller.

0971. Lowe, David. Hatemongering by Computer. ADL BULLETIN 42, 6 (June 1985) 1, 12-13.

Use of computer technology marks a new trend for hate groups, one of which is the Idaho based Aryan Nations which disseminates racist and antisemitic propaganda.

0972. Lurie, Jesse Zel. "So Who Did You Vote for?" American Jews and the 1984 Presidential Elections. ISRAEL HORIZONS 33, 1/2 (Jan/Feb 1985) 7-9.

The explanation for Jewish support for the Democrats (64-66% of the vote) lies in the "gut issue" of antisemitism. A poll taken on election day showed that American Jews believe that antisemitism is widespread in the US, and that liberals and Democrats are perceived as being less antisemitic than Repubulicans and conservatives.

0973. Marable, Manning. Jackson and the Rise of the Rainbow Coalition. NEW LEFT REVIEW 149 (Jan/Feb 1985) 3-44.

An account of Jackson's campaign for the presidential nomination. See pp. 29-36 for Jackson's relations with the Jewish community. For much of Feb.-Mar. 1984, Jackson's campaign was bogged down with charges that he is an antisemite. Hundreds of liberal and left-wing activists, Jewish and non-Jewish, left the Rainbow Coalition.

0974. Mehler, Barry. The New Eugenics: Academic Racism in the US Today. ISRAEL HORIZONS 32, 1/2 (Jan/Feb 1984) 22-28.

In 1937, two eugenics activists established the Pioneer Fund, which is used today to fund the activities of academically respectable racists. Many of these individuals and organizations are linked to far-right groups. By distributing free copies to universities, the works of these researchers, often published by reputable publishing houses, are spread throughout the academic world.

0975. Mintz, Frank P. THE LIBERTY LOBBY AND THE AMERICAN RIGHT: RACE, CONSPIRACY AND CULTURE. Westport, CT: Greenwood Press, 1985. 251 pp. (Contributions in Political Science, 121).

A large portion of the study is devoted to the antisemitic and anti-Zionist position of the Lobby. Unseen.

0976. Mischel, Ellis. Anti-Semitism and Jewish Self-Hatred. REFORM JUDAISM 13, 2 (Win 1984/1985) 26.

The author, a practicing psychoanalyst in the US, has set up and worked with support groups to combat Jewish self-hatred. "The Jewish person who is the object of antisemitism often hates both persecutor and self."

0977. Morganthau, Tom et al. Jackson's Albatross: A Supporter's Remarks Make News - and Trouble. NEWSWEEK (23 Apr 1984) 31-32.

On antisemitic statements made by Louis Farrakhan (with a section containing quotes), and Jesse Jackson's evasive response to charges of antisemitism.

0978. Neusner, Jacob. ISRAEL IN AMERICA: A TOO-COMFORTABLE EXILE? Boston: Beacon Press, 1985. xi, 203 pp.

A collection of essays about the Jewish experience in the US, including the influence of antisemitism in Europe and in the US in shaping that experience (see the index). Part 3 (pp. 75-94), "Issues in Black, White and Jewish," consists of two chapters - on antisemitism in South Africa, and relations between Jews and Blacks in the US.

0979. "Populist" vs "Populist" - Viguerie and Carto Compete for Extreme-Right Following: An Analysis of Differing Programs. THE HAMMER 6 (Spr 1984) 14-21.

Analyzes the ideas of Richard Viguerie, the conservative publisher, and compares them with those of Willis Carto of the Liberty Lobby. Although both the New Right, as represented by Viguerie, and the Revolutionary Right of Carto present themselves as populists, Carto is also racist and antisemitic whereas Viguerie supports Israel.

0980. Puddington, Arch. Jesse Jackson, the Blacks and American Foreign Policy. COMMENTARY 77, 4 (Apr 1984) 19-27.

Discusses Jackson's Middle East policy, among other topics. Raises the possibility that his anti-Israel views are a cover for antisemitic sentiments.

0981. Purcell, J.Q.; Weisburd, Ellen. The Other Libel Suit. ADL BULLETIN 42, 5 (May 1985) 1, 11-13.

The ADL had charged that the writings of Lyndon H. LaRouche, Jr. included "crass antisemitism." When LaRouche sued for libel, a US District Court jury in Alexandria, VA ruled that LaRouche had neither been defamed by the ADL nor by NBC television.

0982. Rainbow's End: The Agony Imposed by Jackson's Campaign Deepens. THE NEW REPUBLIC 190, 17 (30 Apr 1984) 7-9. A Hebrew translation appeared in TEFUTSOT ISRAEL 22, 3/4 (Fall/Win 1984) 25-29.

On the racism and antisemitism expressed by Jesse Jackson and his supporter Louis Farrakhan and the damage they are causing to Democrats and liberals in the US.

0983. THE REVIEW OF ANTISEMITISM IN CANADA, 1984. Downsview, Ont.: B'nai B'rith Canada, League for Human Rights, 1984. 23, 23 pp. English and French.

Includes a preliminary comparative analysis for 1983 and 1984 from a research project on Canadian attitudes towards Jews, Italians and Poles. Unseen.

0984. Rosenfeld, Rita. It Can Happen Here. CANADIAN JEWISH OUTLOOK 23, 3 (Mar 1985) 4-5, 18.

Describing recent incidents of antisemitism in Canada, including the Keegstra and Zundel trials, compares Canada today with the situation during World War II when Jewish refugees were not welcome and Japanese Canadians were interned. The need for constant vigilance against antisemitism is emphasized.

0985. Ruby, Walter. Battle over Anti-Zionist Teachings. GENESIS 2 15, 4 (Feb/Mar 1984) 5.

On the "controversy over academic freedom and anti-Zionism at the Stony Brook campus of the State University of New York (SUNY)." The issue was a course entitled "The politics of race," taught by Ernest Dube, a Black

South African, who was teaching that Zionism is a form of racism.

0986. Schwartz, Alan. Louis Farrakhan. ADL FACTS 29, 1 (Spr 1984) 24 pp.

A survey of the activities of the antisemitic Black Muslim preacher. Discusses the history of the Black Muslim movement and the Nation of Islam faction, Farrakhan's involvement with Jesse Jackson, his antisemitic and anti-Zionist statements, and his financial and ideological ties with Libya and with Arab organizations.

0987. Seltzer, Arthur. "The Dube Affair." ADL BULLETIN 41, 8 (Oct 1984) 3-6.

A review of actions taken by the local ADL at the State University of New York (SUNY) at Stony Brook against Ernest Dube's misuse of academic freedom to teach that "Zionism is racism."

0988. Sher, Julian. The Propaganda of Hatred. CANADIAN FORUM 64 <744> (Dec 1984) 20-21.

Canada has become a major source of hate propaganda that finds its way to Europe and especially West Germany. The laws against such propaganda are weak, giving free rein to antisemitic and racist literature.

0989. Silberman, Charles. A CERTAIN PEOPLE: AMERICAN JEWS AND THEIR LIVES TODAY. New York: Summit Books, 1985. 458 pp.

Despite pockets of discrimination, almost every occupation and position in American society is open to American Jews, compared to the situation in the 1930s when widespread and virulent antisemitism caused Jews to hide their identity. Although many Jews fear this change because of increasing assimilation, evidence shows that it also offers opportunities for a cultural and religious revival. Black antisemitism is presented as the exception to this optimistic view.

0990. Silberman, Jeffery M. Anti-Semitism in the Suburbs. HUMANISTIC JUDAISM 13, 1 (Spr 1985) 14-15.

On antisemitism in lower Fairfield County, Connecticut.

0991. Silverberg, Mark. The Six Percent Solution: An Analysis of Hate Legislation in Canada. JOURNAL OF JEWISH COMMUNAL SERVICE 61, 1 (Fall 1984) 54-63.

A recent poll reveals that approximately 6% of the Canadian population are hard-core antisemites. These include adherents of the Identity Movement Churches (Aryan Nations, Ku Klux Klan), and others, who disseminate hate literature throughout the world, particularly Holocaust denial. Discusses the shortcomings of Canada's federal and provincial legal codes in dealing with the problems of racism and manifestations of antisemitism. Suggests procedures for reviewing existing laws.

0992. Simon, Merrill; Falwell, Jerry. JERRY FALWELL AND THE JEWS. Middle Village, NY: Jonathan David, 1984. xiv, 172 pp.

Written in the style of questions and answers, Falwell discusses his attitudes toward Jews, Judaism and Israel. See the index for references to antisemitism.

0993. Singer, David G. American Catholic Attitudes toward the Zionist Movement and the Jewish State as Reflected in the Pages of "America," "Commonweal," and "The Catholic World," 1945-1976. JOURNAL OF ECUMENICAL STUDIES 22, 4 (Fall 1985) 715-740.

Examines Catholic attitudes to Zionism and Israel in the light of centuries of Christian hostility toward the Jews, and the present-day interfaith dialogue following Vatican II. Discusses also the anti-Israel and anti-Zionist views of a relatively small group of traditional Catholic thinkers in America.

0994. Singer, David G. Has God Truly Abrogated the Mosaic Covenant? American Catholic Attitudes toward Judaism as Reflected in Catholic Thought, 1945-1977. JEWISH SOCIAL STUDIES 47, 3/4 (Sum/Fall 1985) 243-254.

There are two broad lines of thought - the traditional one, which holds that Jesus abrogated the Mosaic law and that Jews will some day convert to Christianity; and the revisionist one, which holds that Jesus was a devout Jew, and that contemporary Judaism can enrich Christianity. Traditionalists refused to acknowledge the connection between Christianity and antisemitism. Vatican Council

II opened a path to Catholic-Jewish dialogue. Various problems associated with this dialogue are discussed.

0995. Singer, David G. Hate, Ambivalence and Exaltation: American Christian Attitudes toward Jews and Judaism. HUMANISTIC JUDAISM 13, 1 (Spr 1985) 24-27.

A majority of American Catholic thinkers deny the relationship between Christian beliefs and modern antisemitism. But a small group of Catholic revisionist thinkers blame the Church for historical antisemitism and call for sweeping changes in Catholic teachings and doctrines regarding the Jews. In March 1967, the American bishops issued guidelines for dialogue between Catholics and Jews.

0996. Stone, Ellen et al. Blacks, Catholics, Protestants and Jews. PRESENT TENSE 11, 4 (Sum 1984) 4-20.

Comprises five papers - by Ellen Stone, Jim Castelli, Basil Patterson, A. James Rudin, Virginia Olsen Baron - dealing with relations between Blacks and Jews, and Christians and Jews, in the US. Antisemitism is mentioned throughout the discussions.

0997. The Struggle Is Not Over. CANADIAN JEWISH OUTLOOK 23, 4 (Apr 1985) 4, 16.

A statement by the United Jewish People's Order, National Resident Board. The struggle against antisemitism in Canada continues. While the trial of the neo-Nazi Ernst Zundel exposed his activities, it also gave him a platform. The official Canadian Jewish community leadership is accused of cooperation and close relations with the anti-Soviet Canadian Ukrainian community which harbors criminals guilty of collaboration with the Nazis. A judicial inquiry is to investigate the entry of Nazi war criminals into Canada.

0998. Suall, Irwin; Lowe, David; Gans, Gail L. The KKK and the Neo-Nazis: A 1984 Status Report. ADL SPECIAL REPORT (Nov 1984) 12 pp.

Field reports show an overall reduction in Klan membership and attendance at gatherings - about 6000-6500 participants in 1984. Frustrated activists are threatening to resort to terrorist activity. Gives a regional profile of the Ku Klux Klan in the South, East, West and Midwest, and explains the decline in popularity. Pp. 10-12 discuss neo-Nazi organizations which today consist of very small, isolated sects.

0999. Suall, Irwin; Lowe, David; Gans, Gail L. "Propaganda of the Deed": The Far Right's Desperate "Revolution." ADL SPECIAL REPORT (May 1985) 11 pp.

A description of the extreme right-wing, racist, and antisemitic group called The Order, many of whose leaders were arrested in 1985 for violent criminal offences and for planning a revolution against the US government (labeled ZOG "Zionist Occupation Government"). Also describes activities of like-minded groups, such as the Aryan Nations, Ku Klux Klan, Posse Comitatus, and the CSA (The Covenant, the Sword, and the Arm of the Lord).

1000. Sullivan, John L. et al. POLITICAL TOLERANCE IN CONTEXT: SUPPORT FOR UNPOPULAR MINORITIES IN ISRAEL, NEW ZEALAND AND THE UNITED STATES. Boulder, CO: Westview Press, 1985. xv, 264 pp.

Discusses the question of tolerance towards unpopular groups, including neo-Nazis, especially on pp. 23-26, "Nazis, Skokie and Civil Liberties in the United States."

1001. Syrkin, Marie. Jackson: Demolition Not Coalition. MIDSTREAM 30, 6 (June/July 1984) 28-30.

A critique of the Jesse Jackson phenomenon - his antisemitic remarks, his relationship with Louis Farrakhan, his support for the PLO - as a detriment to the Democratic Party.

1002. Taub, Muni. Zundel Trial Must Be Viewed as an Educational Process. CANADIAN JEWISH OUTLOOK 23, 4 (Apr 1985) 5-6.

The trial of Ernst Zundel was justified as part of a process of educating the public about the Holocaust. The legal system was successfully used to counter libels such as the "Zionist conspiracy."

1003. Zager, Muriel Kagan; Zagan, Victor. Are the Falwells Good for Israel? JEWISH SPECTATOR 49, 3 (Fall 1984) 31-32.

Israel has been able to count on political and financial support from evangelical and fundamentalist Christian groups, such as Jerry Falwell's Moral Majority. But this support may boomerang; when their theological expectations are not realized, Israel could become the cause of a new wave of antisemitism.

1004. Zwicker, Barry. The Media and Ernst Zundel. CANADIAN JEWISH OUTLOOK 23, 6 (June 1985) 13-14.

Criticizes media coverage of the Zundel trial. The trial is "the latest in a string of examples dating back to the 1930s showing that the mainstream media is generally soft on Nazism." The media failed to investigate Zundel's background or to identify him as a neo-Nazi, and frequently quoted his statements uncritically.

1945-1985: The USSR and Eastern Europe

1005. אורמן, יוסף. די נישט אויסגעוויינטע קינה. פאלק און ציון 60 (סעפט/אקט 1984) 13-14.

[Orman, Yosef. The Unfinished Lamentation. FOLK UN ZION 60 (Sept/Oct 1984) 13-14.]

Stalin's antisemitic campaign in the USSR after World War II, which culminated in the execution of Yiddish writers and cultural leaders, and the "Doctor's Plot" of 1953, was intended to prepare the way for the extermination of the Jews in the Soviet Union.

1006. אטינגר, שמואל. הרהורים על התרבות היהודית בברית-המועצות. יהודי ברית המועצות 2 <8> (דצ 1984) 13-18.

[Ettinger, Shmuel. Reflections on Jewish Culture in the Soviet Union. THE JEWS OF THE SOVIET UNION 2 <8> (Dec 1984) 13-18.]

Discusses, inter alia, the impact of antisemitic propaganda, including works written in the 19th century, on Soviet Jewry today - some try to assimilate and forget that they are Jews, while others study Jewish culture in order to understand why antisemitism is so widespread.

1007. גוטמן, ישראל. היהודים בפולין אחרי מלחמת-העולם השנייה. ירושלים: מרכז זלמן שזר, 1985. 166 עמ'. (האוניברסיטה העברית: סדרת מחקרים של המרכז לחקר תולדות יהודי פולין ותרבותם).

[Gutman, Yisrael. THE JEWS IN POLAND AFTER WORLD WAR II. Jerusalem: Zalman Shazar Center, 1985. 170 pp. (Hebrew University: Studies of the Center for Research on the History and Culture of Polish Jews).]

Includes descriptions of the murder of Jews and pogroms which took place after the War, especially the pogrom at Kielce, 4 July 1946 (pp. 34-41) where 47 Jews were killed and 50 wounded. Discusses Stalin's antisemitic campaign between 1948 and 1953 and its impact in Poland, where antisemitism was used as a tool by political factions until 1967/68, when the anti-Jewish and anti-Zionist campaign came to a head and most remaining Jews were "expelled" from Poland.

1008. גפן, אבא. אשנב למסך הברזל. תל-אביב: ספרית מעריב, 1985. 256 עמ'.

[Gefen, Abba. A WINDOW TO THE IRON CURTAIN. Tel Aviv: Sifriat Maariv, 1985. 256 pp.]

A description of the author's activities during his five years as Israel's Ambassador in Romania (1978-1982) - the only Communist country which did not sever diplomatic relations with Israel. See pp. 171-176 for antisemitism in Romania in the 1980s.

1009. לאקעטש, משה. צום אנדענק פון די אומגעקומענע יידישע שרייבער אין סאוועט-רוסלאנד. אונזער צייט 524 (סעפט 1985) 15-13.

[Loketch, Moshe. In Memory of the Yiddish Writers Who Were Murdered in the Soviet Union. UNSER TSAIT 524 (Sept 1985) 13-15.]

A brief summary of Stalin's negative attitude towards the Jewish intelligentsia in the 1930s and 1940s, which culminated in the murder of 24 Soviet-Jewish writers in the summer of 1952, and of Communist ideology which advocates assimilation (and eventual annihilation) of the Jewish people.

1010. פיגא, ישראל. דער גלח און דער פרעזידענט. אונזער צייט 516
(ינואר 1985) 17-22.

[Figa, Yisrael. The Priest and the President. UNSER TSAIT 516 (Jan 1985) 17-22.]

Jerzy Urban, journalist, Minister and Spokesman of the present-day Polish government, an assimilated Jew, anti-Zionist and anti-Church, was accused by the Catholics of incitement to murder the priest Jerzy Popieluszko in October 1984. Urban retaliated by accusing the Catholics of launching an antisemitic campaign against him, similar to their campaign in 1922 against Gabriel Narutowicz, the first president of Poland. Figa claims that Jaruzelski appointed Urban as spokesman so that the Jew could later be blamed for the crimes of the dictatorial regime.

1011. פינקוס, בנימין. הקיום הלאומי היהודי בברית המועצות: מספר
גישות-יסוד. יהודי ברית המועצות 2 <8> (דצ 1984) 37-79.

[Pinkus, Binyamin. The National Existence of the Soviet Jews. THE JEWS OF THE SOVIET UNION 2 <8> (Dec 1984) 37-79.]

A comprehensive study of Soviet Jewish and non-Jewish attitudes towards the "Jewish question" as expressed by political leaders, propagandists, scientists, writers, and dissidents. Antisemitism is also discussed, particularly official attempts to delegitimize the Jewish nation, the Jewish religion, and Zionism, and ideological antisemitism expressed by modern Slavophile nationalists.

1012. פרידגוט, תיאודור. היהודים בתקשורת הסובייטית לאחר עליית
צ׳רננקו: "לא ציונות ולא אנטישמיות." יהודי ברית-המועצות
2 <8> (דצ 1984) 27-36.

[Friedgut, Theodore. The Jews in the Soviet Media after Chernenko's Election: "Neither Zionism Nor Antisemitism." THE JEWS OF THE SOVIET UNION 2 <8> (Dec 1984) 27-36.]

Discusses the radicalization of antisemitic and anti-Zionist propaganda following the outbreak of the Lebanon War. Zionism was described as an international conspiracy out to destroy the Soviet Union, aided by the Jews who control the Western economies and politics. This radicalization abated after Andropov's death and was replaced by a policy guided by Brezhnev's dictum "neither Zionism nor antisemitism."

1013. ציגלמן, לודמילה. לב קורנייב. מבטא האנטישמיות הסובייטית
בשנות השבעים והשמונים. יהודי ברית המועצות 3 <9> (דצ
1985) 270-288.

[Tsigelman, Ludmilla. Lev Korneev, the Mouthpiece of Soviet Antisemitism in the 1970s and 1980s. THE JEWS OF THE SOVIET UNION 3 <9> (Dec 1985) 270-288.]

Traces the development of the Soviet ideological antisemitic propaganda campaign, based on anti-Zionism, from the 1970s to the present. It began with the publication of "Beware: Zionism" by Yuri Ivanov in 1969. Describes Ivanov's works, which expressed classic antisemitic accusations such as the world conspiracy theory, and other writings which were printed mostly in literary journals in the 1970s. The Soviet campaign continued with the UN resolution equating Zionism with racism, and went even further to equate Zionism with Nazism. Lev Korneyev began publishing works in 1977 expressing neo-Nazi accusations: Zionist-Nazi collaboration, Holocaust denial, Zionist falsification of history. Describes several of Korneyev's anti-Zionist and anti-Jewish writings.

1014. קולקר, יורי. מארטינוב: לוחם זכויות האדם ומגן על זכויות
היהודים בלנינגראד. יהודי ברית המועצות 2 <8> (דצ 1984)
94-98.

[Kolker, Yuri. Martynov: Champion of Human Rights and of the Rights of Jews in Leningrad. THE JEWS OF THE SOVIET UNION 2 <8> (Dec 1984) 94-98.]

Describes Martynov's fight against antisemitism in the USSR today. (See no. 1064.)

1015. שמואלי, אפרים. דיוקנה של מדינה: פולין בימינו (בעקבות
ביקור). בצרון 6 <23> (ספט 1984) 37-43.

[Shmueli, Ephraim. Portrait of a State: Poland Today. BITZARON 6 <23> (Sept 1984) 37-43.]

Poland has undergone considerable political, economic, and social changes since World War II, but antisemitism has persisted. Although there is now no Jewish community in Poland, antisemitism is evident in the official party line, expressed in anti-Israel and anti-Zionist policies.

Israel and the Zionists are blamed for all political misfortunes or governmental mishandling of internal issues.

1016. Alexeyeva, Ludmilla. SOVIET DISSENT: CONTEMPORARY MOVEMENTS FOR NATIONAL, RELIGIOUS AND HUMAN RIGHTS. Trans. by Carol Pearce and John Glad. Middletown, CT: Wesleyan University Press, 1985. xxii, 521 pp. + 32 pp. of plates. Originally published as ISTORIIA INAKOMYSLIIA V SSSR (Benson, VT: Khronika Press, 1984).

A study of the dissident movement in the USSR, by a Russian emigré writer, based mainly on "samizdat" (illegally published) material. Ch. 10 (pp. 175-198), "The Jewish Emigration Movement," describes the repression of Jews seeking to emigrate, antisemitism as a factor in the desire to emigrate, and the suppression of attempts to revive Jewish culture. Ch. 19 mentions antisemitism among Russian nationalist dissidents.

1017. Altshuler, Mordecai. The Jewish Anti-Fascist Committee in the USSR in Light of New Documentation. STUDIES IN CONTEMPORARY JEWRY 1 (1984) 253-291.

The Jewish Anti-Fascist Committee was established in 1942 as a tool to spread propaganda for the Soviet regime, particularly in the West. However, as the only representative Jewish body permitted to function, it also served as an address for the problems of Soviet Jewry, including complaints of antisemitism. The Committee was disbanded in 1948; most of its members were executed in 1952 by order of Stalin. Pp. 264-291 contain documents recently acquired from the archive of Solomon Mikhoels, including details of antisemitic incidents.

1018. Aronsfeld, C.C. Jews and Christians in Eastern Europe. JEWISH AFFAIRS 39, 6 (June 1984) 23-26.

Summarizes Christian-Jewish dialogue in recent years in Hungary, Poland, and East Germany.

1019. Aronsfeld, C.C. The Sources of Soviet Propaganda. JEWISH AFFAIRS 40, 5 (May 1985) 27-36.

Soviet propagandist Lev Aleksandrovich Korneyev has recently accused Jewish bankers of financing Hitler's accession to power, thereby enabling him to carry out the Final Solution. This libel originates from a booklet published in Amsterdam in 1933 by "Sidney Warburg," the non-existent son of Felix Warburg; the work was in fact a fabrication of J.G. Schoup, a Belgian journalist. A pro-Nazi Swiss writer, René Sonderegger, twice translated the booklet into German and identified the writer as "James Warburg." Felix Warburg exposed the fraud in 1949.

1020. Aronsfeld, C.C. Soviet Propaganda: Hitler and the Zionists. MIDSTREAM 31, 9 (Nov 1985) 13-16.

A slightly revised version of the preceding entry.

1021. Bákonyi, Péter; Kárdos, Gyoergy G. Egy eloeitélet háttere [The Background of a Prejudice]. FORRAS 5 (1984) 26-37.

A conversation with the Hungarian-Jewish writer Gyoergy G. Kárdos on neo-Nazism, the persistence of a Jewish stereotype, prejudice against Jews in Hungary today, and the influence of Israel on the level of antisemitism in Europe.

1022. Bell, David A. The Jews Left Behind. THE NEW REPUBLIC 192, 7 (18 Feb 1985) 12, 14.

Official antisemitism is threatening Soviet Jewry. The traditional response of US Jews and the US government to press the Soviets on the emigration issue is not enough; activists should fight for the right of Jews to live as Jews in the USSR.

1023. Bieńkowski, Wladyslaw. Polskiego dramatu ciąg dalszy [The Polish Drama: The Continuing Story]. KULTURA 5 <440> (May 1984) 3-42.

Discusses social conflict in Poland after the Second World War, including remarks on the antisemitic campaign in 1968 (pp. 15-16).

1024. Burt, Richard R. Soviet Crackdown on Jewish Cultural Activists. U.S. DEPARTMENT OF STATE BULLETIN 2097 (Apr 1985) 47-48.

Soviet authorities have been suppressing Hebrew teaching and other Jewish cultural activities through arrests, searches, beatings, and threats. An antisemitic campaign in the Soviet media, led by the "Anti-Zionist Committee of Soviet Society," is causing considerable concern.

1025. Eroes, Ferenc; Kovács, András; Lévai, Katalin. "Comment j'en suis arrivé à apprendre que j'étais juif." ACTES DE LA RECHERCHE EN SCIENCES SOCIALES 56 (Mar 1985) 63-68.

Excerpts from interviews with young Jews in Hungary today, relating to their Jewish identity. The children of Communist party workers wished either to camouflage or to ignore the issue, but it was forced on them by their environment which was more or less pervaded by antisemitism. Some reacted by experiencing traumas or by rejection of the truth. Notes the continued existence of popular antisemitism among the rural population.

1026. Eskenasy, Victor. A Note on Recent Romanian Historiography on the Jews. SOVIET JEWISH AFFAIRS 15, 3 (Nov 1985) 55-60.

The historiography of Romanian Jewry has always been characterized by polemics against the Jews and apologetics by Jewish writers. Virtually no new material has been published in the last 40 years, but a few pre-war publications by Romanian historians have recently been reissued. However, in these works, information on the Jews is often truncated, antisemitic interpretations are perpetuated, and critical introductions or notes are lacking.

1027. Ettinger, Shmuel. The "Jewish Question" in the USSR. SOVIET JEWISH AFFAIRS 15, 1 (Feb 1985) 11-16.

Article from the Proceedings of the Experts' Conference on Soviet Jewry, London, 4-6 Jan. 1983. There is much evidence that the so-called anti-Zionist attacks in the USSR are part of an antisemitic, anti-Jewish campaign. "The indiscriminate use of the 'anti-Zionist' argument, intertwined with anti-Jewish remarks and quotations, is intended to present a picture of the Jews as a totally negative element in society and in history generally."

1028. Ettinger, Shmuel. SOVIET ANTISEMITISM AFTER THE SIX DAY WAR. Jerusalem: Hebrew University, Institute of Contemporary Jewry, Vidal Sassoon International Center for the Study of Antisemitism, Shazar Library, 1985. 48 pp. (Study Circle on World Jewry in the Home of the President of Israel, 27 February 1984). Appeared simultaneously in Hebrew.

The main expression of antisemitism in the USSR today is anti-Zionism. Discusses similarities between anti-Zionism and classical Tsarist antisemitism. Today different groups within Soviet society use antisemitism as a tool for political advancement or to curry favor with one or more groups. Describes attempts of Soviet propaganda to delegitimize the Jew.

1029. Evans, Mike. LET MY PEOPLE GO! Nashville, TN: Nelson Resource Management, 1985. 83, [37] pp.

The author, a Christian evangelist and the head of MEM (Mike Evans Ministries), described as an "intercessionary arm to the Jewish people," discusses the problems of Soviet Jews refused exit visas, and the religious persecution of Jews and Christians in the USSR. Points out similarities between Soviet and Nazi antisemitism.

1030. Freedman, Theodore, ed. ANTI-SEMITISM IN THE SOVIET UNION: ITS ROOTS AND CONSEQUENCES. New York: Freedom Library Press of the Anti-Defamation League of B'nai B'rith, 1984. xii, 664 pp. A reprint of "Anti-Semitism in the Soviet Union," issues 1-3, Jerusalem, 1979-1983.

Contents: Pt. I: "Proceedings of the Seminar on Soviet Anti-Semitism, Jerusalem 1978": Yakov Yanai: Introduction (3-7); S. Ettinger: The Historical Roots of Anti-Semitism (8-16); R. Nudelman: Contemporary Soviet Anti-Semitism (17-36); G. Ilin: The Character of Soviet Anti-Semitism (37-40); Y. Tsigelman: Anti-Semitism in Soviet Publications <Belles Lettres and Feature Stories> (41-53); D. Tiktina (Shturman): The Reception of Anti-Semitic Propaganda in the USSR (54-62); A. Voronel: The Reasons for Anti-Semitism in the USSR (63-71); E. Sotnikova: The Jewish Problem in Samizdat and the Emigration Press (72-80); L. Dimerski-Tsigelman: The Attitude toward Jews in the USSR (81-102); S. Hirsh: State and Popular Anti-Semitism in Soviet Lithuania (103-104); M. Azbel: Aspects of Anti-Semitism and the Fight against It (105-109); Discussion (110-131). Pt. II: "Proceedings of the International Colloquium on Anti-Semitism in the Soviet Union, Paris 1979": André Lwoff: Introduction (139-140); Leon Dulzin: The Status of Jews in Soviet Society (141-143); Chimen Abramsky: The Soviet Attitude toward Jews (144-150); William Korey: The Soviet "Protocols of the Elders of Zion" (151-159); Stephen J. Roth: Anti-Zionism and Anti-Semitism in the USSR (160-166); Umberto Terracini: Israel as a factor in Soviet Anti-Semitism (167-171);

Shmuel Ettinger: Historical and Internal Political Factors in Soviet Anti-Semitism (172-178); Laurent Schwartz: Soviet Anti-Semitism and Jewish Scientists (179-185); Emanuel Litvinoff: The Slavophile Revival and Its Attitude to Jews (186-192); Sofia Tartakovsky: Anti-Semitism in Daily Life <A Personal Account> (193-196). Pt. III: "Jewish Samizdat on Anti-Semitism": G.A. Freiman: I Am a Jew, It Turns Out (200-265); Ruth Okuneva: Anti-Semitic Notions: Strange Analogies (266-381). Pt. IV: "Studies": S. Ettinger: Introduction (385-393); Yaacov Tsigelman: "The Universal Jewish Conspiracy" in Soviet Anti-Semitic Propaganda (394-421); R. Okuneva: Jews in the Soviet School Syllabus (422-448); Maya Kaganskaya: Intellectual Fascism in Soviet-Russian Establishment Culture (449-485); Judith Vogt: When Nazism Became Zionism: An Analysis of Political Cartoons (486-514). Pt. V: "Excerpts from Soviet Publications and Samizdat" [of antisemitic material published in 1948-1980] (515-628); N. Bibichkova: Anti-Semitic and Anti-Israeli Publications in the USSR, 1960 to 1981 (629-639).

1031. Friedgut, Theodore H. Soviet Anti-Zionism and Anti-Semitism: Another Cycle. SOVIET JEWISH AFFAIRS 14, 1 (Feb 1984) 3-22. Appeared also as RESEARCH PAPER no. 54 of the Hebrew University's Soviet and East European Research Centre (Jan 1984) 31 pp.

A renewed ban on Soviet-Jewish emigration, renewal of the Cold War, and the Israeli invasion of Lebanon provide the background for a new anti-Zionist campaign in the USSR. Analyzes some features of the current press campaign, which is using blatantly antisemitic propaganda, and possible reasons for the establishment of AKSO (Anti-Zionist Committee of the Soviet Public). The activities of Lev Korneyev, the most prominent anti-Zionist writer, are described.

1032. Gidwitz, Betsy. Contemporary Anti-Semitism in the USSR. RUSSIA 11 (1985) 19-25.

The revived campaign of antisemitism in the USSR has been concentrated in two areas - the media and higher education. A number of antisemitic themes, directed against "Zionists," are disseminated widely in the press. Statistics show a major decline in university admissions of Jews, the sign of a nationwide quota system. Reasons for the campaign are discussed.

1033. Gidwitz, Betsy. Less than Meets the Eye. MOMENT 9, 10 (Nov 1984) 40-45.

There has been a radical decline in Jewish emigration from the Soviet Union and an upsurge in both officially imposed and popular Soviet antisemitism. Although Yiddish culture appears to be flourishing, it is controlled by the authorities and is intended to defuse Western criticism of anti-Jewish practices, serving as "a smoke-screen for intensifying official antisemitism..."

1034. Gilbert, Martin. Andropov: O homem que fechou os portões soviéticos [Andropov: The Man Who Locked the Soviet Gates]. HERANCA JUDAICA 56 (Mar 1984) 41-44.

The 15 month reign of Yuri Andropov was a somber period for the Jews. Antisemitic and anti-Zionist articles and caricatures increased markedly in the press, emigration was reduced drastically, and the treatment of Prisoners of Zion became harsher.

1035. Gilbert, Martin. THE JEWS OF HOPE: THE PLIGHT OF SOVIET JEWRY TODAY. London: Macmillan, 1984. 237 pp.

The chapter entitled "Antisemitism" (pp. 110-122) describes Soviet antisemitic propaganda which flaunts accusations of a Zionist conspiracy to undermine the Soviet Union, of Zionist-Nazi collaboration during World War II, that the Jews are alien to the Soviet historic experience, and portrays Israel as a neo-Nazi state. Cites especially the works of Lev Korneyev.

1036. Gilison, Jerome M. Soviet-Jewish Emigration, 1971-1980: An Overview. SOVIET JEWRY IN THE DECISIVE DECADE, 1971-1980, ed. Robert O. Freedman. Durham, NC: Duke University Press, 1984. Pp. 3-16.

Pp. 11-12 discuss increased overt and covert antisemitism during the 1970s, and the "anti-Zionism campaign" which affected emigration.

1037. Giniewski, Paul. Au coeur de la guerre du Liban: De Moscou à Beyrouth. TRIBUNE JUIVE 804 (13-19 Jan 1984) 32-33.

Lists four causes for the anti-Israel media distortion in reporting on the 1982 Lebanon War: traditional Christian antisemitism, Soviet anti-Zionist and antisemitic propaganda, Arab disinformation fed to the media, Jewish self-hatred.

1038. Goodman, Jerry. The Jews in the Soviet Union: Emigration and Its Difficulties. SOVIET JEWRY IN THE DECISIVE DECADE, 1971-1980, ed. Robert O. Freedman. Durham, NC: Duke University Press, 1984. Pp. 17-28.

Pp. 26-28 deal with the vitriolic antisemitic propaganda campaign and the trials of Jews in the USSR.

1039. Heifetz, Mikhail. Anti-Semitism of the "Adherents of State Nationalism" (Based on Books Published in the Series Zh.Z.L. in the Late 1970s and Early 1980s). JEWS AND JEWISH TOPICS IN SOVIET AND EAST EUROPEAN PUBLICATIONS 1 (Sept 1985) 4-14. Appeared in Hebrew in THE JEWS OF THE SOVIET UNION 2 <8> (Dec 1984) 80-91.

The popular series "Zhizn Zamechatelnykh Lyudei" (Lives of Great Men), appearing since 1933, enjoys great authority in the USSR and was previously not antisemitic. In the late 1970s, expansionist Russian nationalists, especially the group known as State Nationalists, gained control of the editorial board, and antisemitism in the series increased. Negative historical figures are given dubious Jewish ancestry. In their polemic against the Solzhenitsyn wing of the "Russian party," the State Nationalists present 19th century Russia as dominated by foreign capitalists, especially Jews, until liberated by the Revolution.

1040. Hillel, Marc. LE MASSACRE DES SURVIVANTS EN POLOGNE APRES L'HOLOCAUSTE, 1945-1947. Paris: Plon, 1985. 352 pp. An extract appeared in L'ARCHE 344 (Nov 1985) 77-81.

An account of the pogroms against Jewish survivors in Poland in 1945-1947, particularly in Kielce, July 1946.

1041. Jews and Jewish Identity in the Soviet Union: A Statement. JEWISH CURRENTS 38, 11 (Dec 1984) 12-14.

At a meeting in New York on 9 August 1984 (under the auspices of "Morgn Freiheit," "Yiddishe Kultur" and "Jewish Currents") called to honor the memory of Yiddish writers and cultural leaders executed in the USSR in 1952, a joint statement was adopted. "We accuse the Soviet government of tolerating, encouraging and often itself conducting a broad multi-faceted antisemitic propaganda campaign which has lately been hiding behind the mask of 'a struggle against Zionism'."

1042. Jicinski, B. The Politburo's Longest Campaign. MIDSTREAM 30, 7 (Aug/Sept 1984) 7-8.

Surveys the anti-Zionist antisemitic campaign waged by the Soviet Union since 1967, and its latest development - the establishment in April 1983 of the Anti-Zionist Committee of the Soviet Public. Mentions the Soviet aim "to sever Soviet Jews from the Jewish people," the equation of Israelis with Nazis and of Zionism and Judaism with racism, and the accusation of Zionist-Nazi collaboration.

1043. Kagedan, Allan L. Soviet Anti-Jewish Publications, 1979-1984. POLITICAL COMMUNICATION AND PERSUASION 3, 2 (1985) 167-183.

Analyzes antisemitic themes appearing in recent Soviet anti-Jewish and anti-Zionist publications, showing that they are borrowed from earlier antisemitic writings, particularly from the "Protocols of the Elders of Zion" and "Mein Kampf." The themes discussed are: the Jews as warmongers, as manipulators of the economy, as controllers of the media, as conspiring with Freemasons, as themselves fomenting antisemitism in order to promote Jewish unity, and the Jewish State as an operational base for the above activities. A new theme being voiced is that of Zionist-Nazi collaboration during World War II.

1044. Kende, Péter. Zsidóság antiszemitizmus nélkuel? Antiszemitizmus zsidóság nélkuel? [Judaism without Antisemitism? Antisemitism without Judaism?]. VALOSAG 8 (1984) 69-88.

A survey of the history of antisemitism in Hungary since 1945, including the period of anti-Zionist trials. The State of Israel and the image of the "fighting Israeli" helped to moderate antisemitism after 1967. During the last ten years it has been on the increase, as evidenced by the fact that the Jewish question has become a taboo subject.

1045. Kopelew, Lew. Brief an Roy Medwedjew: Zur "Juedischen Frage in der UdSSR." TRIBUENE 89 (1984) 89-100. Translated from the Russian.

An open letter, written in 1971, in response to Medvedev's "The Near East Conflict and the Jewish Question in the USSR" [source not given - ed.]. Mentions the antisemitic policy of the Soviet regime from Stalin's time to the present.

1046. Korey, William. Brezhnev and Soviet Anti-Semitism. SOVIET JEWRY IN THE DECISIVE DECADE, 1971-1980, ed. Robert O. Freedman. Durham, NC: Duke University Press, 1984. Pp. 29-37.

Analyzes the antisemitic media campaign in 1979/80 as a reflection of the growth of a chauvinistic and xenophobic Russian nationalism which threatened Brezhnev, his followers, and the policy of détente. In Brezhnev's speech to the 26th Communist Party Congress (1981), he made a rare statement against antisemitism which signified acknowledgement of the phenomenon in the USSR and public repudiation, but his accompanying condemnation of Zionism made the first ineffectual. Antisemitism in the media is evident in the hate literature still being published.

1047. Korey, William. Charting Chernenko. REFORM JUDAISM 12, 4 (Sum 1984) 2-3.

Views the new Soviet leader, Konstantin Chernenko, as favorable to détente, which may lead him to allow more Jewish emigration. Chernenko has condemned antisemitism in the past, though criticizing Zionism at the same time. His rival for leadership, Grigory Romanov, is virulently antisemitic. Also summarizes Soviet policy on the Jews since Lenin's time.

1048. Korey, William. The Soviet Public Anti-Zionist Committee. MIDSTREAM 31, 7 (Aug/Sept 1985) 11-17.

An account of the development and activities of the Committee, founded in April 1983, whose members are prominent "establishment Jews" such as David Dragunsky and Yuri Kolesnikov. The main aims of the Committee are to stop internal and external demands for the emigration of Jews and to channel anti-Zionist propaganda. The success of the Committee in establishing the "Zionism equals Nazism" equation in the Soviet press is documented.

1049. Kovács, András. La question juive dans la Hongrie contemporaine. ACTES DE LA RECHERCHE EN SCIENCES SOCIALES 56 (Mar 1985) 45-57.

Surveys continuity and changes in regard to "the Jewish question" in Hungary since 1945. Describes the antisemitism expressed against Jewish members of the "communist elite" during the 1956 revolution. In general, since 1945, Jews have had to reject their Jewish identity in order to be accepted. Jews and non-Jews express very different attitudes toward questions of Hungarian nationalism and independence, and toward antisemitic elements in Hungary's past.

1050. Krajewski, Stanislaw. Finding It. MOMENT 9, 4 (Apr 1984) 19-26.

An interview with Krajewski, translated from the Polish, which appeared in the 24 April 1983 issue of "Tygodnik Powszechny," a Catholic weekly. Krajewski, a mathematician living in Warsaw, discusses his Jewish and Polish identities, and Polish antisemitism ("rather shallow and not very aggressive").

1051. Madrigal Nieto, Rodrigo. Discriminación y persecución de los judíos en la Unión Sovietica. LA UNION 97 (Aug 1984) 14-15.

The USSR does not observe the principles of the contract signed with UNESCO (1960) against discrimination in education. Jews are the only national minority without schools and are discriminated against in higher education and in employment opportunities. The only hope for Jews is emigration.

1052. Magil, A.B. The Soviet Jewish Paradox. JEWISH CURRENTS 38, 6 (June 1984) 7-9, 30.

The text of a speech delivered on 12 August 1983, at a memorial meeting for Soviet Yiddish writers, regarding conflicting Soviet post-war policies towards the Jews. "Since at least the early 1960s a rising tide of anti-Semitic filth has poured out of Soviet printing presses ...mislabeled anti-Zionism, but it is often so crude, so redolent of the ideological cesspools of fascism and czarism that only the most ignorant can be deceived." (See also no. 1056.)

1053. Meacham, S.M. JUDEN IN DER SOWJET-UNION. Trans. by Heinz-Juergen Heuhsen. Asslar [West Germany]: Schulte und Gerth, 1984. 63 pp. Originally published as "It Is Still Not Too Late" (Jerusalem: International Christian Embassy, 1983).

Deals with the persecution of Jews, especially "refuseniks," in the USSR from a Christian point of view. Argues that the persecutions and anti-Zionist propaganda are similar to Nazi antisemitic policy. Calls on Christians to act and raise their voices in protest, in contrast to the Holocaust period when Christians were passive.

1054. Nezer, Zvi. The Emigration of Soviet Jews. SOVIET JEWISH AFFAIRS 15, 1 (Feb 1985) 17-24.

From the proceedings of the Experts' Conference on Soviet Jewry, London, January 1983. Summarizes Soviet policy regarding Jewish emigration, from Stalin's time (the lowest point being 1948 to 1953 when only 18 exit permits were issued) through 1982. From 1968 to 1982, 262,300 Jews left the USSR, but 381,700 were still waiting for permits. Mentions antisemitism in published works and in the mass media, and harassment of "refuseniks."

1055. Rayski, Adam. NOS ILLUSIONS PERDUES. Paris: Balland, 1985. 322 pp.

Memoirs of a Polish Jewish journalist who spent the war years underground in Paris as head of the Jewish section of the French Communist Party. In 1949 he returned to Poland but became disillusioned with Communism, partly because of anti-Jewish measures in 1950-1953.

1056. Robeson, Paul; Magil, A.B. Readers' Forum on Soviet Jews. JEWISH CURRENTS 38, 11 (Dec 1984) 32-36.

An "amplification" of A.B. Magil's "The Soviet Jewish Paradox" (see no. 1052). Robeson argues that Magil did not give the fundamental reason for persistent Soviet antisemitism: the legacy left by Stalinism of repression of non-Russian nations and nationalities. Includes a reply by Magil.

1057. Sándor, Anna. A Note on Jewish Identity in Hungary. SOVIET JEWISH AFFAIRS 15, 2 (May 1985) 45-51.

Based on a series of interviews with 50 Hungarian Jews aged 25-38, during 1979-1980, examines the role of antisemitism in shaping Jewish identity in Hungary today.

1058. Sarfati, Georges Elia. LA NATION CAPTIVE: SUR LA QUESTION JUIVE EN URSS. Paris: Nouvelle Cité, 1985. 299 pp.

The first part of the book provides an account of the author's stay in Riga and his contacts with "refuseniks." The second part traces the history of the Jews in the USSR. Discusses the "Jewish question" under Stalin and afterwards, quoting from documents, speeches, etc. Analyzes a typical case of antisemitism in relation to the trial of Y.Y. Berenstein, and the anti-Jewish stereotypes used by the press in describing the case. Ch. 4C (pp. 250-260), "Publications soviétiques antijuives," describes anti-Zionist publications, including cartoons.

1059. Scharf, Rafael F. A Good Sign from Poland. CHRISTIAN JEWISH RELATIONS 17, 1 (Mar 1984) 47-49.

A report on the Feb./Mar. 1983 issue of the Polish journal "Znak," issued by Catholic circles in Cracow, which deals with the subjects: Polish-Jewish relations, antisemitism in Poland, and Catholicism and Judaism.

1060. Shafir, Michael. From Eminescu to Goga via Corneliu Vadim Tudor: A New Round of Antisemitism in Romanian Cultural Life. SOVIET JEWISH AFFAIRS 14, 3 (Nov 1984) 3-14.

Describes developments in Romania since 1983, especially the activity of the nationalist poet C.V. Tudor whose poems and articles are anti-Jewish tracts. The Romanian Jewish community, led by Chief Rabbi Moses Rosen, held a meeting to protest against Tudor's attacks. The resolution adopted was banned from publication in the Jewish community's periodical.

1061. Spier, Howard. Fulfilling a Restricted Role: The Soviet Anti-Zionist Committee in 1984. INSTITUTE OF JEWISH AFFAIRS: RESEARCH REPORT 16 (Dec 1984) 5 pp.

The most important of the Anti-Zionist Committee's activities in 1984 was the May 15 press conference where "witnesses" told of harsh conditions in Israel which had led them to return to the USSR. Other "witnesses" refuted allegations of antisemitism in the USSR, criticized the Interparliamentary Group in Defence of Human Rights for its "pro-Zionist" sympathies, and rebutted "Zionist slander" regarding the Soviet attitude to the Holocaust.

1062. Spier, Howard. Jewish Issues in the Soviet VE Day Propaganda Campaign. INSTITUTE OF JEWISH AFFAIRS: RESEARCH REPORT 3 (May 1985) 6 pp.

In 1984/85 the USSR mounted a major propaganda campaign emphasizing the Soviet role in the defeat of Hitler. In October 1984, the Anti-Zionist Committee held a press conference, alleging Zionist-Nazi collaboration during the War and claiming that the Red Army had saved the Jews from annihilation. Israeli policy in Lebanon was compared to Nazism. In April 1985, a second press conference held by the Committee showed a marked shift towards a positive presentation of Jewish involvement in World War II.

1063. Spier, Howard. Pravda Equates Zionism with Fascism. INSTITUTE OF JEWISH AFFAIRS: RESEARCH REPORT 2 (Mar 1984) 6 pp.

On 17 January 1984, "Pravda" published an article by Vladimir Bolshakov, "Fascism and Zionism: The Roots of Kinship," in which Zionism is equated with Nazi fascism. (An English translation appeared in "Soviet Jewish Affairs," February 1984.) Bolshakov insists that anti-Zionism is not antisemitism and that there is no antisemitism in the USSR, yet he uses antisemitic devices in his arguments. The importance of his article lies in the fact that it appeared in "Pravda," thus endowing the Zionism-fascism equation with an ideological authoritativeness. Also discusses the apparent decline of the Anti-Zionist Committee of the Soviet Public.

1064. Spier, Howard; Martynov, Ivan Fedorovich. Jews and Russian Culture. SOVIET JEWISH AFFAIRS 14, 2 (May 1984) 55-63.

Martynov, a non-Jewish historian and bibliographer living in Leningrad, has repeatedly applied to emigrate from the USSR. Together with his wife and other "refuseniks" Martynov tried to obtain the exclusion from the scholarly and journalistic communities of Lev Aleksandrovich Korneyev, the USSR's most prolific anti-Zionist and antisemitic writer and propagandist. Martynov's "open letter" to the Presidium of the USSR Academy of Sciences (Sept. 1983) is given in English translation.

1065. Suekoesd, Mihály. Koezlemények a zsidókérdesroel [Publications on the Jewish Question]. VALOSAG 8 (1984) 89-95.

A survey of Hungarian works published in 1984 on Jewish subjects and on antisemitism in Hungary. Contends that it is difficult to conduct reliable research as there is not sufficient data on Hungarian Jewry today. The Jewish question has always been the index of democracy in Hungarian society.

1066. Szczepański, Jan Józef. Prosze nie przysylać mi wiecej tych bredni [Please Don't Send Me Any More of This Rubbish]. TYGODNIK POWSZECHNY 9 (3 Mar 1985) 8.

Describes anonymous antisemitic texts which the writer received in the mail, accusing the Jews and their "world conspiracy" of causing all the ills in Poland. Such texts prove the existence of a nationalist, right-wing group in Poland today which cannot operate openly.

1067. Trials of Soviet Jewish "Refuseniks" and Activists, 1980-July 1985. INSTITUTE FOR JEWISH AFFAIRS: RESEARCH REPORT 5 (Sept 1985) 6 pp.

Harassment of Jewish "refuseniks" and cultural activists by the Soviet authorities was stepped up in the period from 1980 to July 1985, especially during 1984/85. Convictions have been obtained under article 190-1 of the Criminal Code - circulation of fabrications defaming the Soviet system. Activists have also been imprisoned for possession of drugs and a firearm, planted on them by the authorities.

1068. Tudor si dedesubturile [Tudor and the Undercurrents]. IZVOARE 14-16 (July 1985) 104-107.

A reaction to the leaflet written by Corneliu Vadim Tudor, the Romanian nationalist and antisemitic writer, which was distributed unofficially in Romania, in which he attacks Jews, Jewish Romanian writers, and Israel. Tudor belongs to a small Romanian cultural group with fascist and antisemitic views, which even though not representative still indicates an alarming trend.

1069. Vogt, Judith. Der Stuermers efterfoeljare [The Stuermer's Successor]. JUDISK KROENIKA, special nr. 2: "Judarna i Sovjet" (Apr 1984) 12-13.

On anti-Zionist caricatures in the Soviet press similar to Nazi caricatures of Jews, with six examples.

1070. Wieviorka, Michel. LES JUIFS, LA POLOGNE ET SOLIDARNOSC. Paris: Denoël, 1984. 210 pp.

Analyzes the Solidarity movement against the background of Polish history since World War II, and in relation to the "Jewish question." Antisemitism is not part of Solidarity's policy, although many anti-Jewish stereotypes persist in Polish society. Touches on the antisemitic campaign of 1968 and the Church's attitude towards the Jews. Denies the contention that antisemitism was a unifying factor for the Polish people in the 19th and 20th centuries; in fact, it was a divisive force.

1071. Wistrich, Robert S. The New War against the Jews. COMMENTARY 79, 5 (May 1985) 35-40.

Contrary to the general view, the recent attempt to link Nazism with Zionism is not due to the 1982 war in Lebanon but is the result of a long-prepared ideological offensive triggered off by the reparations agreement concluded between West Germany and Israel in 1952. "Using a crude anti-Semitic Marxism of a type fashionable among German Communists in the early 1930s, the new Soviet literature suggests that there was a class basis to the common language of Zionism and Nazism."

1945-1985: Western Europe

1072. אורון, יאיר. יחס הנוער היהודי המאורגן בצרפת לשואה ולאנטישמיות. יהדות זמננו 2 (1984) 209-235.

[Auron, Yair. The Attitude of Organized Jewish Youth in France to the Holocaust and Antisemitism. YAHADUT ZEMANENU 2 (1984) 209-235.]

Based on a study carried out in 1977-1979, including samples from Zionist and non-Zionist youth movements, and compared to attitudes of Israeli youth.

1073. זליגמן, חיים. על סכנת הניאו-נאציזם בגרמניה. מבפנים 46, 4 (נוב 1984) 591-596.

[Seligman, Haim. On the Danger of Neo-Nazism in Germany. MIBIFNIM 46, 4 (Nov 1984) 591-596.]

Surveys neo-Nazism in West Germany since World War II and makes the following points: neo-Nazis have connections with right-wing political parties; two-thirds of the adherents are young people, born after the war; they are motivated by varied factors and it is difficult to fight against their antisemitism; neo-Nazi books and periodicals are being published regularly.

1074. ישועה-ליית, עפרה. היהודי מברלין על כוונת הניאו-נאצים. הדאר 63, 21 (6 אפר 1984) 326-327.

[Yeshua-Leith, Ofra. The Jew from Berlin In the Sights of the Neo-Nazis. HADOAR 63, 21 (6 Apr 1984) 326-327.]

Describes the ongoing battle against neo-Nazism and Holocaust denial of Heinz Galinsky, head of West Berlin's Jewish community, who claims that the neo-Nazis in West Germany view him as their no. 1 enemy.

1075. ניואול, ונישיה. דם של גויים: כמה דוגמאות של פולקלור אנטישמי בימינו בבריטניה. מחקרי ירושלים בפולקלור יהודי 8 (מרס 1985) 78-88.

[Newall, Venetia. "Goy" Blood: Some Examples of Recent Antisemitic Folklore in Britain. JERUSALEM STUDIES IN JEWISH FOLKLORE 8 (Mar 1985) 78-88.] Trans. from English [source not given - ed.]

Surveys articles and caricatures in the press of the extreme Right and Left in Britain of the 1980s which accuse the Jews of a conspiracy to dominate the world through Zionism, controlling the media, and controlling the world of finance. Other accusations: promoting sexual promiscuity in order to destroy British society, spreading left-wing and liberal views, Zionist-Nazi collaboration, Israelis=Nazis, Holocaust denial.

1076. Ahlmark, Per. Anti-Semitism in Europe. ADL BULLETIN 41, 5 (May 1984) 3-5.

Discusses the rise of antisemitism disguised as anti-Zionism in Europe in the 1970s and 1980s.

1077. Alter, Hermann. Neonazi-Prozess in Frankfurt. FRANKFURTER JUEDISCHES GEMEINDEBLATT 17, 3 (June-Aug 1984) 11-12.

Describes the trial of a neo-Nazi member of the "Aktionsfront Nationaler Sozialisten/Nationale Aktivisten" taking place in Frankfurt. The main allegation against the accused is his denial of the Holocaust.

1078. Antisemitismus wieder salonfaehig. JUEDISCHER PRESSEDIENST 1/2 (1984) 35-36.

Describes an article published in PSYCHOLOGIE HEUTE 11, 2 (Feb 1984) 28-33, discussing the antisemitic views of two members of the West German "peace movement" - Peter Rubeau and Wolfgang Westermann - who claim that a small but influential group of American Zionist Jews, seeking revenge, power, and money, is pressuring the American government to destroy Germany by causing atomic war in Europe.

1079. Aronsfeld, C.C. The German Far Right Press and the 40th Anniversary of VE Day. INSTITUTE OF JEWISH AFFAIRS: RESEARCH REPORT 4 (May 1985) 8 pp.

The German Far Right press presented the 40th anniversary of Germany's defeat as a day of mourning for a national catastrophe. The press criticized those Germans who accept the Allies' reproaches for the crimes of their fathers. They claim that Germany's guilt is no greater than that of other nations which committed mass murder, and that these accusations of guilt are spread by the Jewish lobby in the USA and the leaders of the German Jewish community.

1080. Baker, David L. A.K. Chesterton, the Strasser Brothers and the Politics of the National Front. PATTERNS OF PREJUDICE 19, 3 (July 1985) 23-33.

The new leadership of the British National Front claims to have adopted the ideas of Gregor and Otto Strasser. However, the BNF's new "cultural fascism" owes much to the ideas of Arthur Kenneth Chesterton (1899-1973), influential exponent of cultural nationalism and antisemitism. In 1953, Chesterton founded an extreme right-wing pressure group, the League of Empire Loyalists, and during the 1950s-60s he wrote thousands of articles for his journal "Candour." His most influential work, also antisemitic, is "The New Unhappy Lords" (1965), now in its fourth edition.

1081. Barnes, I.R. Creeping Racism and Anti-Semitism. MIDSTREAM 30, 2 (Feb 1984) 12-14.

Discusses the New Right in France today, especially the group called GRECE.

1082. Batz, Georg. Staerkere Selbstdarstellung gegen Antisemitismus. DER LANDESVERBAND DER ISRAELITISCHEN KULTUSGEMEINDEN IN BAYERN 2 (1984) 9.

Although organized antisemitism exists only among small neo-Nazi groups, one finds widespread antisemitic prejudices and attitudes among the general population of West Germany, expressed in the form of anti-Zionism.

1083. Benamou, Georges-Marc. Propos diffamatoires et antisémites à "Apostrophes": Réactions des milliers de téléspectateurs. LA DROIT DE VIVRE 509 (Mar 1985) 19.

Describes reactions of protest against the appearance of Marc-Edouard Nabé on the television program "Apostrophes" on 15 Feb. 1985, in which he incited racial hatred while speaking about his book "Au régal des vermines."

1084. Benayoun, Chantal. Les Juifs et l'imaginaire politique: Lectures de quatre quotidiens français. TRACES 9/10 (1984) 224-235.

An analysis of the language used to describe Jews in four French newspapers ("Le Figaro-Aurore," "Libération," "L'Humanité" and "Le Matin") in October 1980, following the terrorist attack on the synagogue in the rue Copernic, Paris. Describes religious and economic terminology used to denigrate the Jews, the Jew viewed as victim and as guilty party, and the deliberate non-use of the term "antisemitism."

1085. Benima, Tamara. Knel tussen papierschaarste en polemiek: Joodse berichten in de niel-joodse pers [Caught between Paper-Scarcity and Polemic: News on Jews in the Non-Jewish Press]. LE-EZRAT HA-AM - HET VOLK TER HULPE: HET EERSTE JOODSE BLAD IN 1945 [To the Aid of the People: The First Jewish Newspaper in 1945], eds. T. Benima, F.J. Hoogewoud. Assen: Van Gorcum, 1985. Pp. xlii-li.

A survey of Jewish affairs appearing in the Dutch press in 1945, immediately after the liberation. The topic of antisemitism was much discussed. Certain trends in Dutch society, such as proposals to restrict Jewish influence, seemed to stem from Nazi propaganda. Sometimes, German Jews were treated as Germans, whom the Dutch hated.

1086. Benjamin, Jessica; Rabinbach, Anson. Germans, Leftists, Jews. NEW GERMAN CRITIQUE 31 (Win 1984) 183-193.

Discusses the debate touched off in West Germany by a special issue of "Aesthetik und Kommunikation" (June 1983), entitled "Germans, Leftists, Jews." Describes the contents of that issue, which reflect the anger of young left-wing activists at having to bear the responsiblity for the deeds of their fathers, and their resentment against the Jews. Their accusations against Jews "clearly enunciate left-wing antisemitism," particularly as expressed by one of the editors, Eberhard Knoedler-Bunte. Marion Kaplan, in her reaction to this article (Ibid. pp. 195-199), condemns the historical ignorance of Knoedler-Bunte and his mouthing of stereotypes against the Jews.

1087. Bensaïd, Norbert. La double connivence. LE GENRE HUMAIN 11 (Fall 1984/Win 1985) 251-275.

Discusses the prevalence of racism and antisemitism in France today and the tendency to understand or justify the attitudes of Jean-Marie Le Pen. Many claim that it is not wrong to despise other ethnic groups or act against them; it is wrong only to make a doctrine of racism. The existence of racial groups with a different essence than one's own is assumed to be natural, and Jews or Arabs are hated because of their nature rather than their characteristics. Concludes that one must recognize one's own "natural" prejudice against people who are different in order to overcome it.

1088. Benz, Wolfgang, ed. RECHTSEXTREMISMUS IN DER BUNDESREPUBLIK: VORAUSSETZUNGEN, ZUSAMMENHAENGE, WIRKUNGEN. Frankfurt a.M.: Fischer Verlag, 1984. 318 pp.

Contents: W. Benz: Die Opfer und die Taeter: Rechtsextremismus in der Bundesrepublik (11-44); Claus Heinrich Meyer: Die Veredelung Hitlers (45-67); Hermann Graml: Alte und neue Apologeten Hitlers (68-96); Stefan Klein: Von den Schwierigkeiten der Justiz im Umgang mit KZ-Schergen und Neonazis (97-114); Ulrich Chaussy: "Speerspitze der neuen Bewegung": Wie Jugendliche zu Neonazis werden - ein Bericht ueber die "Junge Front" (115-137); Id.: Eine Nazi-Operette wird ernst: Ueber die "Junge Front" und die VSBD ["Volkssozialistischen Bewegung Deutschlands"] (138-154); Hermann Weiss: Alte Kameraden von der Waffen-SS: Ist die HIAG rechtsextrem? (155-166); Gert Heidenreich: Die organisierte Verwirrung: Nationale und internationale Verbindungen (167-186); W. Benz: Judenvernichtung aus Notwehr? Vom langen Leben einer rechtsradikalen Legende (187-208); Peter Kritzer: Die Wut der Unbelehrten: Wie die "Deutsche Nationalzeitung" mit der Wahrheit umgeht (209-223); Barbara Distel: Diffamierung als Methode: Erfahrungen an der Gedenkstaette des ehemaligen Konzentrationslagers Dachau (224-237): Rudolf Mueller: Schule des Terrorismus: Die Wehrsportgruppe Hoffmann und andere militante Neonazis (238-254); Ino Arndt: Zur Chronologie des Rechtsradikalismus: Daten und Zahlen 1946-1983 (255-294).

1089. [Berg, Roger]. A travers les manuels scolaires: D'Auschwitz à l'Etat d'Israël. TRIBUNE JUIVE 839/840 (12-18 Oct 1984) 20-21.

Various antisemitic and anti-Zionist concepts have appeared in history textbooks and have been expressed by history teachers in France. To correct this situation, the PACEJ (Programme d'Action et de Coopération pour l'Education Juive) has encouraged the publication of a new textbook, "Les Juifs dans l'histoire, de 1933 à nos jours" (see no. 239).

1090. Bezymensky, Lev. Who Forged the "Hitler Diaries" and Who Benefits. NEW TIMES 13 (Mar 1984) 24-30.

A detailed account of the "Hitler diaries" affair. The forged diaries and the attempt to publish them in 1983 were the work of neo-Nazis in West Germany. The money paid by "Stern" magazine for the diaries was given to HIAG, the mutual aid society of the former Waffen-SS, "a rallying centre for war criminals," who are putting out books and pamphlets to "whitewash" the SS.

1091. Bierhoff, Hartwig. Der organisierte Rassenhass: Vor 50 Jahren in Kraft getreten - die Nuernberger Rassengesetze. TRIBUENE 96 (1985) 30-32.

West German social democrats held a meeting on 20 September 1985, on the 50th anniversary of the enactment of the Nuremberg Laws. The lecturers analyzed German racism in the past and present, contending that racism directed against Jews and others (Blacks, Turks, etc.) did not end with the fall of the Third Reich.

1092. Billig, Michael. Anti-Jewish Themes and the British Far Left. PATTERNS OF PREJUDICE 18, 1 (Jan 1984) 3-15; 18, 2 (Apr 1984) 28-34.

Examines antisemitism as expressed in the anti-Zionist positions of some sectors of the Far Left in Britain. Antisemitism is defined as opposition to Jews or Judaism per se, a desire for the elimination of the Jewish people, or criticism of Israel as a "Jewish" state. Discusses Marx's "On the Jewish Question" as the inspiration for the Left's ideological arguments against the Jews, and analyzes revolutionary Left publications in Britain today. Part II discusses the equation of Zionism with Nazism and the accusation of Zionist-Nazi collaboration.

1093. Brasz, Ineke. Bevrijdingsjaren jaren van bevrijding? [Years after the Liberation Also Years of Liberation?]. LE-EZRAT HA-AM - HET VOLK TER HULPE: HET EERSTE JOODSE BLAD IN 1945 [To the Aid of the People: The First Jewish Newspaper in 1945], eds. T. Benima, F.J. Hoogewoud. Assen: Van Gorcum, 1985. Pp. xvii-xli.

An introductory essay, dealing also with Dutch post-war antisemitism and with the controversy over Dutch Jewish war orphans in which anti-Jewish feeling was expressed. The Resistance and the Commission for War Foster Children demanded that custody of the children go to the foster-parents rather than to the Jewish community.

1094. British National Front Seeks White Working Class Backing: Strasserism a Continuing Legacy. THE HAMMER 8 (Fall 1984) 15-18, 29.

The new leadership of the National Front considers itself anti-capitalist and stresses its affinity to Otto and Gregor Strasser, identified by many scholars as Nazi socialist ideologists. Examines Gregor Strasser's thought and shows that antisemitism played a major role in his attack on big business and the bourgeoisie. The British National Front plans to continue this antisemitic and racist tradition.

1095. Brozik, Karl. "Fremd in der eigenen Stadt": Streitgespraech in der Alten Oper ueber das Verhalten juedischer Mitbuerger zu Frankfurt. FRANKFURTER JUEDISCHES GEMEINDEBLATT 17, 3 (June-Aug 1984) 13.

During a discussion held in May 1985 in Frankfurt, one of the speakers stated that latent antisemitism in everyday life is more dangerous than militant neo-Nazism. One example, typical of everyday life in West Germany, is the threatening letters sent to Jews in their work places.

1096. Bulawko, Henry. Le racisme à l'ordre du jour...: Racisme et pluralisme culturel. CAHIERS BERNARD LAZARE 106 (Jan 1984) 31-38.

Discusses reasons for the renewal of racism in France. After World War II, racism and antisemitism rarely found expression because of the revelation of the horrors perpetrated against the Jews by the Nazis. But in recent years racism and xenophobia have arisen once more.

1097. Calvert, Hildegund M. Jews in Nazi Germany: What West German Textbooks Say. INDIANA SOCIAL STUDIES QUARTERLY 37, 1 (Spr 1984) 43-53. Unseen.

1098. Campelli, Enzo; Cipollini, Roberta. CONTRA IL SEME DI ABRAMO: INDAGINE SULL'ANTISEMITISMO A ROMA. Milano: Franco Angeli, 1984. 324 pp. (Sociologia e ricerca sociale).

A sociological study of antisemitism, including a survey of antisemitism throughout the ages and proposals for research models on the subject of prejudice. Analyzes effects of the 1982 Lebanon War on antisemitic attitudes in Italy, based on questionnaires filled out by 678 inhabitants of Rome and on a study of the press. Includes statistical tables regarding the image of the Jew, stereotypes and degrees of intolerance in the Italian population.

1099. Camus, Jean-Yves. L'extrême gauche française et Israël: Les sous-entendus de l'antisionisme. TERRE RETROUVEE 950 (May/June 1984) 24-25.

A brief but detailed survey of the extreme Left in France and its fanatical anti-Zionism and antisemitism.

1100. Caputo, Giuseppe, ed. IL PREGIUDICIO ANTISEMITICO IN ITALIA: LA COSCIENZA DEMOCRATICA DI FRONTE AL RAZZISMO STRISCIANTE. Roma: Newton Compton, 1984. 242 pp.

Contents: Bernardino Cocchianella: L'antisemitismo nella cultura e nei comportamenti della Destra eversiva, 1968-1978: Una ricerca sull'area veneto-emiliana (13-38); Andrea Zanotti: Le radici cattoliche dell'antisemitismo (39-57); Alceste Santini: L'antisemitismo nella pubblicistica di Sinistra (58-68); Eugenio Melani: Sinistra marxista e antisemitismo (69-75); Emanuele Ascarelli; Mario Toscano: Manifestazioni antisemitiche ed evoluzione politica in Italia (76-103); Anna Isolina Di Nola: il caso di Trani (104-115); Lucia Mazzola: Antisemitismo e scuola dell'obbligo: L'insegnamento della religione attraverso i libri di testo (116-130); Loredana Gianluca: Antisemitismo e scuola dell'obbligo: L'insegnamento della storia attraverso i libri di testo (131-143); Giuseppe Caputo: Dalla libertà degli uguali alla libertà dei diversi (antisemitismo e teoria dei diritti di libertà) (147-162); Massimo Jasonni: Diritto delle minoranze e diritto delle formazioni sociali: La "minoranza ebraica" (163-175); Raffaele Botta: L'attuazione dei principi costituzionali e la condizione giuridica degli ebrei in Italia (176-230).

1101. Cass, Mike. The West German Law Makers. CANADIAN JEWISH OUTLOOK 23, 6 (June 1985) 4, 12.

Criticizes the West German Bundestag for its delays in passing a law against Holocaust denial. The law eventually passed describes Holocaust denial as an insult to survivors rather than as a criminal offence. Thus, the state cannot prosecute offenders; only the Jews can.

1102. Cohen, Brigitte-Fanny; Glucksmann, André. Pacifisme et antisémitisme: Un entretien avec André Glucksmann par Brigitte-Fanny Cohen. NOUVEAUX CAHIERS 76 (Spr 1984) 58-61.

An interview with Glucksmann about his book "La Force de Vertige" (Paris: Ed. Grasset, 1983), and especially his ideas regarding the Green Party in West Germany. Their 1983 "Second Nuremberg Trial" was directed mainly against the Allies and their actions during the War (from 1943). The Greens "forgot to mention" the gas chambers. Their "trial" blots out the memory of Auschwitz and is, perhaps unconsciously, antisemitic.

1103. Coren, Michael. When Underdog Bites Underdog. THE NEW STATESMAN 109, <2817> (Mar 1985) 16-17.

Surveys relations between Black and Jewish groups in Great Britain. Claims that antisemitic and anti-Zionist views voiced by the Blacks, as well as mutual physical violence, cause tension between the two groups.

1104. Cunz, Martin. Stehen wir vor einer Neuauflage des Antisemitismus, oder gelingt uns endlich eine fruchtbare Begegnung mit dem Judentum? DER FREUND ISRAELS 147, 3 (June 1984) 9-13.

A wave of antisemitism and anti-Zionism swept Switzerland after the Lebanon War. The Israelis were compared to the Nazis and Swiss Jews were threatened and insulted. These antisemitic feelings have deep roots in the souls of Christians, who should not accuse the Jews (Israel) of being immoral.

1105. Dudek, Peter. Kaum verhuellte NS-Ideologie. TRIBUENE 93 (1985) 22-26.

The racial agitation expressed by neo-Nazi youth newspapers in West Germany includes attacks against the Jews in the form of Holocaust denial.

1106. Dumont, Serge. Des "Le Pen" belges? REGARDS 145 (12-25 Sept 1985) 58-59.

Describes two small Belgian right-wing racist and antisemitic parties: Forces Nouvelles and Front National. The latter party, similar to Le Pen's Front National in France, is not dangerous at present.

1107. Dumont, Serge. Extrême droite: La percée européenne. REGARDS 149 (7-21 Nov 1985) 12-13.

The recent elections to the Belgian legislature show that the extreme right has made little progress. In Switzerland, a new extreme-right nationalist party, "Vigilance," scored considerable success in Geneva. In Britain, competing groups of "skinheads" close to the National Front have attacked immigrant and Jewish targets. In France, a recent book and newspaper articles have exposed the antisemitism of Jean-Marie Le Pen and his movement.

1108. Dumont, Serge. Voyage en "vraie France." REGARDS 118 (31 May-13 June 1984) 16-17.

A report on the yearly commemoration of Joan of Arc, which brings together various factions of the French Right in addition to German neo-Nazis and Italian neo-fascists. Jean-Marie Le Pen is lionized.

1109. Einhorn, Maurice. Wallon, écolo et raciste? REGARDS 129 (6-19 Dec 1984) 13.

A report on antisemitic caricatures which appeared in the Walloon journal "Coq d'Aousse" (no. 7, July/Aug 1984) published in the south of Belgium.

1110. Epstein, Simon. L'ANTISEMITISME FRANCAIS AUJOURD'HUI ET DEMAIN. Paris: Pierre Belfond, 1984. 255 pp.

Since the late 1970s, a wave of antisemitism is sweeping France, comparable to the period of the 1920s-1930s. Jewish communal authorities have adopted strategies similar to those of the earlier period - reliance on allies among the socialists, the communists, and the Church, and on the protection of the State and its laws - strategies not likely to succeed. Describes attempts of German Jews to organize a defense against Nazism, and the option of self-defense as advocated by the French organization LICA in the 1930s. French Jewry today denies the extent and importance of antisemitism, expressed by neo-Nazism and anti-Zionism; they have a false sense of security.

1111. Feichtlbauer, Hubert. Neonazismus im Alltag. DIE GEMEINDE 317 (8 May 1984) 7.

Deals with Austrian neo-Nazism in everyday life.

1112. Feldman, Lily Gardner. THE SPECIAL RELATIONSHIP BETWEEN WEST GERMANY AND ISRAEL. Boston: G. Allen and Unwin, 1984. xix, 330 pp.

See the index for references to antisemitism and anti-Zionism.

1113. The "Front National" in France: Nazi, Neo-Nazi and Anti-Semitic Connections. ADL EUROPEAN REPORT (Dec 1985) 6 pp.

Documents antisemitic and anti-Zionist statements in publications of the Front National party. It appears that the party will win 13% of the vote in the Spring 1986 elections [it actually won 10% - ed.] and enter the French Parliament, encouraging further antisemitism.

1114. Fubini, Guido. L'image du Juif dans l'opinion publique italienne en 1982. TRACES 9/10 (1984) 236-259.

Shows how the 1982 war in Lebanon profoundly affected the Jews of Italy. Discusses the self-image of the Jew, going back to the emancipation, Jewish culture and identity in Italy, the community organization and attitude towards the State of Israel. Analyzes the image of the Jew as seen by non-Jews in the period before and after 1982, and gives examples of antisemitism in Italy today.

1115. German Protestant Church Declarations. CHRISTIAN JEWISH RELATIONS 17, 3 (Sept 1984) 30-34.

In April 1950, the Synod of the Protestant Church in West Germany passed a resolution on the "guilt vis-à-vis Israel" and called on Christians to repudiate and resist all forms of antisemitism. In January 1960, following antisemitic outrages, the Provincial Synod of Berlin-Brandenburg reaffirmed the 1950 ruling, as did the Baden Provincial Synod of the German Evangelical Church in May 1984.

1116. Gleichmann, Gabi. Mot antisemitism och rasism i frankrike [Antisemitism and Racism in France]. JUDISK KROENIKA 53, 1 (Feb 1985) 6-7.

Describes the background and activities of the Ligue Internationale Contre la Racisme et l'Antisémitisme (LICRA).

1117. Griotteray, Alain. A propos des liens entre le socialisme et le fascisme. REVUE DES DEUX MONDES 2 (Feb 1984) 333-338.

Mentions antisemitism on the Right and Left (p. 337).

1118. Gruber-Ejnes, Pascale. Le "père fouettard" des antisémites. REGARDS 150 (21 Nov-4 Dec 1985) 33-35.

A survey of twenty years of activity by "Regards," the Belgian Jewish community newspaper, in combatting antisemitism on the Left and the Right, neo-Nazism, and anti-Zionism.

1119. Gutman, Nelly. The Rise of the National Front in France. INSTITUTE OF JEWISH AFFAIRS: RESEARCH REPORT 11 (Oct 1984) 8 pp.

Describes the development of Le Pen's Front National party and its program as outlined in his book "Les Français d'abord." Le Pen is overtly racist but argues that he is not antisemitic. "With overt racism no longer taboo, this may lead, in the long run, to the latent antisemitism in France being flaunted openly."

1120. Gutman, Nelly; Tarnero, Jacques. L'antisémitisme en France. SENS 36, 5/6 (1984) 221-226.

In France today, right-wing and left-wing antisemites propound common antisemitic positions and arguments. Israel has been "diabolized" and Zionism has become a metaphor for absolute evil. Faurisson's denial of the Holocaust attracted support from both the Right and the Left. Preconditions for this phenomenon are: historical amnesia, the ideological void, the taste for spectacle and novelty, and media manipulation.

1121. Harthoff, Bernhard. Ein skandaloeser Urteilsspruch. TRIBUENE 92 (1984) 14-15.

Deals with the rise of neo-Nazism in West Germany. Describes a children's game in which the play-figures (Jews) are put into the gas chamber. In addition to such games, there is a noticeable increase in neo-Nazi books and pamphlets.

1122. Hilsenrath, Edgar. Brief aus Berlin. CHESCHBON 7 (Fall 1984) 14-16.

Old-fashioned antisemitism is today replaced by a new sort. The left-wing sons and daughters of Nazis compare the deeds of their fathers to every brutal act occurring in the world, and claim that the Israelis are themselves Nazis because of their actions in Lebanon.

1123. Hoch, Marie-Thérèse. A Survey of Jewish-Christian Relations in France in Recent Years. JOURNAL OF ECUMENICAL STUDIES 22, 4 (Fall 1985) 869-875; 23, 1 (Win 1986) 185-192.

Christian attitudes toward Jews are defined by "indifference tinged with hostility based on ignorance." Summarizes the history of Christian hostility, and describes anti-Zionist and antisemitic terrorist acts in France of the 1980s, perpetrated by the PLO and by neo-Nazi groups. Discusses the new climate of reconciliation and dialogue between Christians and Jews, particularly the "Nostra Aetate" declaration and its consequences.

1124. Hoffman, Bruce. Right-Wing Terrorism in Europe. CONFLICT 5, 3 (1984) 185-210.

Examines recent right-wing terrorism in Italy, West Germany and France. "The distinction between 'right' and 'left' has become...controversial." In this regard, the phenomenon of "Nazi-Maoism" is described. Antisemitism is especially marked among German and French groups. Ties between the Hoffmann Military Sports Group and the PLO are discussed.

1125. Kaplan, Jacob. N'OUBLIE PAS. Paris: Editions Stock, 1984. 175 pp.

Addresses by the French Chief Rabbi Jacob Kaplan. See especially pp. 98-100 on the reappearance of antisemitism in post-war France, and pp. 159-160 for antisemitism disguised as anti-Zionism.

1126. Kuschel, Karl-Josef. Ecumenical Consensus on Judaism in Germany? A Theological Analysis of Recent Catholic and Protestant Statements on the Jewish Question. CHRISTIAN JEWISH RELATIONS 17, 2 (1984) 3-20. Appeared previously in the "Journal of Ecumenical Studies," Summer 1983.

Christian-Jewish dialogue has a two-fold direction: while it must be carried out between Christians and Jews, Christians should also be discussing among themselves an appropriate understanding of the Jews. Reviews inroads and points of conflict in the dialogue of the last forty years.

1127. Laemmermann, Godwin. Christliche Motivierung des modernen Antisemitismus? Religionssoziologische und -paedagogische Ueberlegungen zu einem sozialen Problem. ZEITSCHRIFT FUER EVANGELISCHE ETHIK 28, 1 (Jan-Mar 1984) 58-84. Unseen.

1128. Landau, Lazare. L'Eglise catholique de France et les Juifs. TRIBUNE JUIVE 816 (6-12 Apr 1984) 10-15.

Analyzes the importance of the "Declaration on the Jews" delivered by the Archbishop of Marseilles, Cardinal Etchegaray, at the Synod in Rome, October 1983 (see no. 773.)

1129. Leder, Danny. La crispation autrichienne: Les tentations néo-nazies du parti libertaire, membre de la coalition du gouvernement de Vienne. TRIBUNE JUIVE 810 (24 Feb-1 Mar 1984) 16-17.

Discusses neo-Nazism in Austria, particularly in the Freiheitliche Partei.

1130. Lemoine, Philippe. Informatique: Vers une race artificielle? LE GENRE HUMAIN 11 (Fall 1984/Win 1985) 29-51.

Deals with racial problems (including antisemitism) and human rights in relation to the development of information techniques in the modern world. Discusses identity cards in France, which included the racial origin of the card-bearer until this practice was forbidden in 1981, but it is still used for migrant workers.

1131. Levitte, Georges; Gutman, Nelly. A Maturing Community Faces Anti-Semitism: French Jewry in 1982. SURVEY OF JEWISH AFFAIRS 1 <1982> (1984) 210-226.

The 1982 Lebanon War resulted in a climate of media hostility towards Israel and towards Jews and their "ties to Israel." At the same time 15 serious acts of terrorism against Jews occurred in France. French Jews felt that the government and the media were responsible for giving antisemitism new legitimacy. The Communist Party was especially blamed, as well as the "Christian Left" group which combined pro-Palestinian sympathies with traditional Christian antisemitism. Nevertheless, opinion polls do not suggest a rise in antisemitism in the general population.

1132. Lucas, Noah. Jewish Students, the Jewish Community and the "Campus War" in Britain. PATTERNS OF PREJUDICE 19, 4 (Oct 1985) 27-34.

Recently there have been attempts to ban Jewish societies from university campuses in Britain on the grounds that they support Zionism which is identified as racism. Most students are either sympathetic or indifferent to Israel, and a minority of politically active students, led by Arabs, head the anti-Zionist attack. Jewish students and the Jewish community should not engage in a "propaganda war" with them; they should demand that academic institutions act to prevent racist measures.

1133. Magnus, Naama. NS-Wiederbetaetigung in Salzburg, und viele Seltsamkeiten. DIE GEMEINDE 317 (8 May 1984) 7-8.

A description of neo-Nazi activities in Salzburg, Austria, carried out by former members of the Austrian army and police. Hints that the local police would not charge the criminals.

1134. Magnus, Naama. Urteil im Neonaziprozess: 9 Schuldsprueche. DIE GEMEINDE 317 (8 May 1984) 8-9.

A description of the actions of and subsequent punishments handed down to nine Austrian neo-Nazis found guilty of Holocaust denial, racism, bomb-planting, etc.

1135. Malka, Victor. Grão-rabino Samuel Sirat: "Minha prioridade é a educacão" [Chief Rabbi Samuel Sirat: "My Priorities in Education"]. HERANCA JUDAICA 56 (Mar 1984) 73-76.

An interview with the Chief Rabbi of France, René-Samuel Sirat. Regarding antisemitism in France, he states that it is a continuing problem, and quotes statistics of antisemitic attacks in France between 1975 and 1980. He also discusses interreligious relations.

1136. Marcus, Jonathan. France: The Resurgence of the Far Right. THE WORLD TODAY 40, 12 (Dec 1984) 507-513.

Discusses the electoral rise of Jean-Marie Le Pen's Front National. Le Pen denies that he is racist and antisemitic.

1137. Markovits, Andrei S. Germans and Jews: The Continuation of an Uneasy Relationship. JEWISH FRONTIER 51, 4 (Apr 1984) 14-20.

Discusses West Germany's attitudes toward and relationship with Jews and with Israel since 1945, including over-simplified explanations regarding the Nazi period, reparations, vestiges of antisemitism, philo-Semitism toward Israel before 1967 and anti-Zionist views after 1967, and attitudes of the present-day Right and Left toward Israel.

1138. Marrus, Michael R. Are the French Antisemitic? THE JERUSALEM QUARTERLY 32 (Sum 1984) 81-97. A Spanish translation appeared in COLOQUIO 14 (1985) 31-52.

Challenges the view - based on terrorist attacks on Jews and the anti-Jewish bias of the press in 1982 - that France is undergoing a revival of antisemitism. Compares present-day attitudes to those in the 1930s (pp. 86-91). Concludes that anti-Jewish feeling has in fact diminished except for neo-Nazi activity. Prejudice and group tensions exist, but they are directed mostly against other groups.

1139. Mass, Heino. Israel und Libanon in den Schlagzeilen: Wissenschaftliche Auswertung der deutschen Presseberichterstattung. TRIBUENE 89 (1984) 76-80.

Results of research dealing with the attitude of the West German press towards the war in Lebanon, including the frequency of antisemitic and anti-Israel expressions.

1140. Matagrin, Gabriel. Bilan et perspectives d'avenir. SENS 37, 10/11 (Oct/Nov 1985) 333-340.

A survey of the influence of the "Nostra Aetate" declaration on Jewish-Christian relations in France. Although anti-Jewish stereotypes are widespread among French Catholics, interfaith dialogue has changed Catholics' view of Judaism, even if only for a minority.

1141. May, Michael. The Elections to the European Parliament, June 1984. INSTITUTE OF JEWISH AFFAIRS: RESEARCH REPORT 10 (Sept 1984) 15 pp.

Analyzes the results of the June 1984 elections in which Le Pen's National Front gained 11% of the vote. The extreme right-wing, neo-fascist faction in the European parliament consists of 16 members - from France, Italy, and Greece. The West German neo-nazi NPD party was roundly defeated. Issues of Jewish concern are discussed on pp. 10-13, including the resurgence of antisemitism in western Europe and in the USSR.

1142. Moltmann, Juergen. Theology in Germany Today. OBSERVATIONS ON THE "SPIRITUAL SITUATION OF THE AGE": CONTEMPORARY GERMAN PERSPECTIVES, ed. Juergen Habermas. Cambridge, MA: MIT Press, 1984. Pp. 181-204. Originally published as "Stichworte zur `geistige Situation der Zeit´" (Frankfurt: Suhrkamp Verlag, 1979).

A survey of the spiritual situation of the Churches and religious life in Germany today. Pp. 198-204 deal with effects of the Nazi period on the German Churches, the attempt to repudiate antisemitism and to rediscover the Old Testament, and the kinship of Christians and Jews.

1143. Mommsen, Hans. The Burden of the Past. OBSERVATIONS ON THE "SPIRITUAL SITUATION OF THE AGE": CONTEMPORARY GERMAN PERSPECTIVES, ed. Juergen Habermas. Cambridge, MA: MIT Press, 1984. Pp. 263-281. (See the above entry.)

Recent events in Germany have shown that "the burden of the Nazi past has not been lightened, that the historical consequences of the `Thousand Year Reich´ have not been resolved." Renewed interest in the Holocaust has revived questions regarding the responsibility of the older generation and the political consequences of Nazism. Neo-Nazism among youth is a facet of revolt against official authority and of refusal to deal seriously with historical burdens and social problems.

1144. Nittenberg, Joanna. "Auschwitz-Luege": Zum Tag des Holocaust. ILLUSTRIERTE NEUE WELT 5 (May 1985) 6.

Neo-Nazi groups in Austria are active mainly in the schools, where antisemitic material denying the Holocaust is distributed among students and teachers.

1145. Passauer, Paul. Schach den Geschichtsklitterern! Anmerkungen zur Strafbarkeit der "Auschwitz-Luege." TRIBUENE 95 (1985) 6-8.

Approves the initiative taken by some West German federal states to pass a law which will enable the courts to punish Holocaust denial.

1146. Plenel, Edwy; Rollat, Alain. The Revival of the Far Right in France. PATTERNS OF PREJUDICE 18, 2 (Apr 1984) 20-27.

Focuses on the Front National led by Jean-Marie Le Pen. Though he does not openly profess antisemitism, some of his associates do. The daily "Présent" expresses virulent antisemitism, denouncing the prominent role of Jews in French politics and culture.

1147. Prudence, Rose. "500,000 chomeurs, 400,000 juifs en trop." LES TEMPS MODERNES 455 (1984) 2330-2345.

Criticizes the Front National party in France, and Le Pen's politics of racism and antisemitism. Compares Le Pen to Hitler, and the atmosphere in today's France to that in Austria in the 1930s.

1148. Pudlowski, Gilles. LE DEVOIR DE FRANCAIS. Paris: Flammarion, 1984. 220 pp.

Reflects on questions of French and Jewish identity, inspired by the author's travels in provincial France. Declares himself obsessed by the question whether a Jew and a first-generation Frenchman can be "more French than the French," especially in view of events during the Holocaust. For antisemitism, see especially pp. 191-195.

1149. Regel, Marek. Bardzo niebezpieczne "zabawy" [Very Dangerous "Games"]. POLITYKA 23 <1466> (June 1985) 12.

Describes a neo-fascist organization in West Berlin and its activities. The organization (about 500 members) wishes to follow in the footsteps of the "Hitlerjugend" and has achieved some popularity among youth circles in Berlin. It also disseminates publications denying the Holocaust.

1150. Rollat, Alain. LES HOMMES DE L'EXTREME-DROITE: LE PEN, MARIE, ORTIZ ET LES AUTRES. Paris: Calmann-Lévy, 1985. 236 pp. (Questions d'actualité). Another edition was published by Calmann-Lévy in 1985 entitled LES HOMMES DE L'EXTREME-DROITE: LE PEN, JEAN-MARIE, ORTIZ ET LES AUTRES (252 pp.).

Discusses the activities of the extreme Right in France, particularly of Le Pen and the Front National. For racism and antisemitism see ch. 5 (pp. 109-141). Concludes that Le Pen's ideology is a direct political heritage from Pétain and Vichy.

1151. Rosenberg, David. Racism and Antisemitism in Contemporary Britain. THE JEWISH QUARTERLY 32, 1 <117> (1985) 23-27.

Organized attacks against ethnic minorities, including Jews, are increasing in Britain. Racism has been institutionalized through discriminatory immigration laws, and made legitimate ideologically by the New Right, influential in the Conservative party. Jewish communal leaders attribute antisemitic incidents to the "lunatic fringe" and prefer to trust in the protection of the State. The community should ally with other ethnic groups and take responsibility for its own defense.

1152. Samuels, Shimon. An Abiding Prejudice: The Tenacity of Anti-Semitism in Europe. THE VOICE OF AUSCHWITZ SURVIVORS IN ISRAEL 28 (Sept 1984) 8-16.

The author, European Director of the ADL, cites "a constant quantitative growth in anti-Semitic incidents matched by a qualitative increase in their level of violence." The attacks are coming from the extreme Right and Left, and PLO-sympathizers. Discusses reasons for this phenomenon, and a prognosis for its continuation.

1153. Schwinghammer, Georg. Politischer Eklat in Bremen. TRIBUENE 95 (1985) 92-101.

Christa Wilmes, author of a paper published by the Wissenschaftliche Institut fuer Schulpraxis, Bremen, claims that the State of Israel and Zionism share the character and policies of Nazi Germany. The fact that this antisemitic document appeared in Bremen, a city ruled by the Social Democrats, and not all local politicians objected, gives cause for concern.

1154. Short, Philip. The National Front in France: M. Le Pen Has Made Extremism Seem Respectable. THE LISTENER (28 June 1984) 5-6, 18.

Sketches the career of Jean-Marie Le Pen and discusses the impact of the Front National's achieving 11% of the vote for the European Parliament. Le Pen's political friends included "prominent neo-Nazis." His publishing company issued an album of Nazi songs, which led to a conviction for "seeking to excuse war crimes."

1155. Siegele-Wenschkewitz, Leonore. The Contribution of Church History to a Post-Holocaust Theology: Christian Anti-Judaism as the Root of Anti-Semitism. THE HOLOCAUST AS INTERRUPTION, eds. Elisabeth Schuessler Fiorenza and David Tracy. Edinburgh: T. and T. Clark, 1984. Pp. 60-64. Appeared in French in LE JUDAISME APRES AUSCHWITZ (Paris: Beauchesne, 1984, pp. 97-104).

In the immediate post-war period, the German Confessing Church saw itself as a victim of Nazism and a defender of the Jews. Since the 1960s, the Christian share in Nazi persecution and the centrality of anti-Judaism in Christian theology have been admitted. Nevertheless, the academic faculties of theology avoid the subject, as it would expose their collaboration with the Nazis in "de-Judaizing" Christianity.

1156. Skapinker, Michael. The Glory That Was Greek Jewry. B'NAI B'RITH INTERNATIONAL JEWISH MONTHLY 99, 4 (Dec 1984) 10-16, 34.

Greece's Jews were decimated by the Holocaust; now the Jewish community is distressed by recent antisemitism. The war in Lebanon sparked off a number of antisemitic and anti-Israel incidents.

1157. Slama, Jean-Luc. Racisme, antisémitisme, et fascisme. SENS 36, 5/6 (1984) 215-220.

Attacks current French hostility towards immigrants, seen as a movement towards fascism resulting, in part, from racist ideas and compared with pre-1945 French antisemitism (e.g. Drieu La Rochelle). The New Right (e.g. GRECE, Alain de Benoist) is opposed to the Jewish-Christian tradition as well.

1158. Stein, Richard A. Antisemitism in the Netherlands: Past and Present. PATTERNS OF PREJUDICE 19, 1 (Jan 1985) 17-24.

At times, in the past, the Netherlands was more favorable to the Jews than some other European countries, but antisemitism always existed as well, becoming activated under specific circumstances. "Today, one again observes antisemitic statements, publications and incidents," particularly manifested as anti-Zionism, expressed by journalists, clergymen, and politicians.

1159. Steinbach, Peter. "Revisionisten" melden sich zu Wort: Widerstaende bei der Aufarbeitung der Geschichte des Nationalsozialismus. TRIBUENE 96 (1985) 119-126.

Warns against "revisionist" historiography and Holocaust denial spread by extreme right-wing circles in West Germany today. Political criticism of this trend is not sufficient; it must be fought by the publication of serious historical research, based on sources.

1160. Struck, Hanna. Antisemitismus: Unausrottbares Vorurteil? TRIBUENE 96 (1985) 34-35.

Describes two meetings held during 1985, organized by Catholic and Evangelical academics in West Germany, on the subject "Antisemitism after 1945." Deals with neo-Nazi groups as well as with the New Left whose extreme anti-Zionist attitude, according to one lecturer, is now becoming more moderate.

1161. Tarnero, Jacques. Jacques Vergès ou le terrorisme judiciaire au service de la haine. TRIBUNE JUIVE 809 (17-23 Feb 1984) 18-19.

Jacques Vergès, the defense lawyer for Klaus Barbie, has previously defended left-wing terrorists but also has links with a neo-Nazi Swiss banker. He plans to turn Barbie's trial into a trial of the French regime, and claims that Western society, based on violence and massacres, has no right to accuse Barbie of war crimes. Israel, described as a fascist and racist state, is the focus of Vergès's hatred.

1162. Tarnero, Jacques. Qui n'est pas de gauche? VOUS AVEZ DIT FASCISMES?, ed. Antoine Spire. Paris: Editions Montalba, 1984. Pp. 153-190.

Discusses the anti-Israel, anti-Zionist Right in France and the fact that, for many, anti-Zionism is the same as antisemitism. Also mentions the Left-Right connection with Holocaust denial.

1163. TERRE RETROUVEE 949 (Apr 1984). "Dossier": Reuven Ben Moshé: Vous avez dit antisémitisme? Non, antisionisme! (20); Pierre-André Taguieff: Vus d'extrême-droite - Judaisme, Sionisme, Israël (21-23); Jacques Tarnero: L'Antisionisme "vertueux" de la gauche (24-25); Léon Poliakov: Trucage verbal, désinformation (25).

1164. TRIBUNE JUIVE 808 (10-16 Feb 1984). "Dossier extrême-droite": J. Grunewald: Editorial: Le Pen critère des nationalismes égoïstes (4-5); Edwin Eytan: Jean-Marie Le Pen - tel que je suis (6-7); Jean-Yves Camus: Le Front National, Israël et les Juifs (8-10); Reine Silbert: L'émergence de l'effet Le Pen (10); Emmanuel Haymann: Pas d'épouvantail pour les Juifs de Dreux (12-13); Henri Smolarski: Le Pen à l'assaut (14-15).

1165. Weinberg, Henry H. Facing the Left and the Right in France. MIDSTREAM 31, 3 (Mar 1985) 3-6.

Discusses dormant antisemitic feelings in France today, attacks from the Right (particularly from Le Pen and the Front National), and the hostility of the Left toward Zionism (particularly as expressed by the press in 1982). French Jewry must remain watchful.

1166. Weiss, Hilde. ANTISEMITISCHE VORURTEILE IN OESTERREICH: THEORETISCHE UND EMPIRISCHE ANALYSEN. Wien: Wilhelm Braumueller, 1984. vi, 155 pp. (Sociologica, I).

An empirical study of antisemitic attitudes in Austria of the 1970s. Constructs a theory based on sociological concepts to explain the origins of antisemitism, and compares it with traditional models.

1167. Zanger, Georg. Neonazismus an der Universitaet. ILLUSTRIERTE NEUE WELT 5 (May 1985) 7.

Unemployment in Austria and a tradition of antisemitism have increased the power of several neo-Nazi groups, some of which are now trying to penetrate the universities.

ANTISEMITISM IN LITERATURE AND IN THE ARTS

1168. גאלדקארן, יצחק. דער פראנצויזישער רענעסאנס און די יידן:
אלפרעד דע-וויניס אנטיסעמיטיזם. דרום אפריקע 36, 10
(יולי-סעפט 1984) 27-29; 36, 11 (אקט-דעצ 1984) 18-20.

[Goldkorn, Yitzchak. The French Renaissance and the Jews: Alfred de Vigny's Antisemitism. DOREM AFRIKE 36, 10 (July-Sept 1984) 27-29; 36,11 (Oct-Dec 1984) 18-20.]

Examines the personality of Count Alfred de Vigny (1797-1863), French Romantic poet, novelist, and playwright, and the antisemitic views expressed in his diary and literary works. Vigny's attacks against Jews were economic in nature, and were caused by jealousy of their wealth, and a belief in the privileges of nobility as opposed to socialism.

1169. גיטליס, ברוך. קולנוע ותעמולה: הסרט הנאצי האנטישמי.
גבעתיים: רביבים, 1984. 270 עמ'.

[Gitlis, Baruch. FILM AND PROPAGANDA: THE NAZI ANTI-SEMITIC FILM. Givatayim: Revivim, 1984. 270 pp.]

An analysis of anti-Jewish stereotypes and propaganda techniques used in the Nazi films "Jud Suess," "Der ewige Jude," "Die Rothschilds," and "Robert Webertram."

1170. וולקוב, שולמית. זחיחות-הדעת ושנאה עצמית: יהודים-גרמנים
בתחילת המאה ה-20. זמנים 14 (חורף 1984) 28-41.

[Volkov, Shulamit. Pride and Self-Hatred: German Jews at the Beginning of the 20th Century. ZMANIM 14 (Win 1984) 28-41.]

Expressions of Jewish self-hatred, particularly in literature (Rathenau, Weininger, Schnitzler, Kafka, Wassermann, Lessing), are analyzed historically, sociologically and psychologically.

1171. שטיין, אריה. דמות היהודי בחיי החברה בגרמניה ביצירות סופרים לא-יהודיים בהבט היסטורי, משנות האיחוד הלאומי עד תקופת וויימאר. דיסרטציה - אוניברסיטת תל-אביב, מאי 1985. 455, xx עמ׳ בשני כרכים.

[Stein, Arjeh. THE IMAGE OF THE JEW IN GERMAN SOCIETY ACCORDING TO WORKS OF GERMAN NON-JEWISH AUTHORS, DURING THE PERIOD OF NATIONAL UNIFICATION UNTIL THE WEIMAR ERA AS SEEN FROM A HISTORICAL ASPECT. Dissertation - Tel-Aviv University, May 1985. 455, xx pp. in 2 vols.]

A study of the negative stereotype of the Jew in German novels, drama, and poetry of the 19th and 20th centuries (up to 1933), reflecting the antisemitic views of German-speaking society (including the Austro-Hungarian Empire).

1172. Albertsen, Leif Ludwig. Der Jude in der deutschen Literatur, 1750-1850. ARCADIA 19, 1 (1984) 20-33.

As a result of the rise of romanticism and the idea of the Christian nation-state at the beginning of the 19th century, antisemitic trends appeared in German literature which were not present during the Enlightenment.

1173. Arbos, Cristina. Los cancioneros castellanos del siglo XV como fuente para la historia de los judíos españoles. JEWS AND CONVERSOS: STUDIES IN SOCIETY AND THE INQUISITION, ed. Yosef Kaplan. Jerusalem: World Union of Jewish Studies; Magnes Press, Hebrew University, 1985. Pp. 74-82.

The "cancioneros" (collections of songs) of 15th century Spain contain sharp criticisms against Jews, conversos, and courtiers of Jewish descent. The "cancioneros" were used as evidence in the trials of the Inquisition. The main motifs under attack were continued observance of Jewish rituals and the Jews' economic activities.

1174. Archer, John. The Structure of Anti-Semitism in the "Prioress's Tale." THE CHAUCER REVIEW 19, 1 (1984) 46-54.

Examines Chaucer's antisemitic views in terms of three categories: murder-sacrifice, economy, and law.

1175. Arneson, Richard J. Shakespeare and the Jewish Question. POLITICAL THEORY 13, 1 (Feb 1985) 85-111.

Analyzes Shakespeare's thinking about commerce in the "Merchant of Venice," partly in comparison to Marx's "On the Jewish Question." Suggests that Shakespeare used the conventional stereotype of the Jew to examine the morality of the free market, and holds that if the play reveals "Shylock to be morally a worse character than the Christians, then it is disquieting that no voice within the play challenges the Christian and anti-Semitic explanation of his badness."

1176. Ash, Timothy Garton. The Life of Death. NEW YORK REVIEW OF BOOKS 32, 20 (19 Dec 1985) 26-39.

Claude Lanzmann's film "Shoah" is compared to the German film "Heimat" directed by Edgar Reitz. While Reitz's position is amoral, showing pre-war and wartime Germany as Germans wish to remember it, Lanzmann is fiercely moral and obsessed with the historical truth of the Holocaust. However, on the issue of Polish collaboration with the Nazis, Lanzmann makes a vivid but confused statement. He emphasizes the primitive Christian antisemitism of the peasants, ignoring other aspects of Polish-Jewish relations which should be properly studied and debated in Poland.

1177. Bentley, James. OBERAMMERGAU AND THE PASSION PLAY: A GUIDE AND A HISTORY TO MARK THE 350TH ANNIVERSARY. Harmondsworth: Penguin Books, 1984. 89, [23] pp.

An illustrated historical and thematic examination of the Oberammergau Passion Play. Includes discussion of the various attempts, since the Holocaust, to eliminate antisemitism from the text.

1178. Bitton-Jackson, Livia E. De joodse vrouw in de christelijke literatuur [The Jewish Woman in Christian Literature]. NES AMMIM LEZINGEN: GESPREKKEN IN ISRAEL 10, 2 (1984) 22 pp.

Translation of a lecture given in English at Nes Ammim, 11 Jan. 1984. Discusses the image of the Jewish woman in Christian literature, both in works hostile to Jews (e.g.

"The Merchant of Venice," "The Jew of Malta") and sympathetic works (e.g. "Ivanhoe," "The Source"). Examines the deicide and Shylock myths as well as the blood libel.

1179. Black, Jeff. The Role of the Film in Nazi Propaganda. JEWISH AFFAIRS 40, 11 (Nov 1985) 33-36.

Describes how Josef Goebbels' Ministry of Propaganda used the portrayal of Jewish negative stereotypes in films to strengthen antisemitic feelings in the German population.

1180. Blot, Jean. L'Antisémitisme de Soljénitsine. L'ARCHE 344 (Nov 1985) 82-87.

Denies the accusation that Aleksandr Solzhenitsyn is an antisemite. The charge originates from rumors spread by the Soviet government to discredit the respected dissident. Nevertheless, Solzhenitsyn's Jewish characters are stereotypes, often favorable, but not viewed on their own terms. Examples from his new novel "November 16" are given; antisemitic sentiments in the book are explained by his mystical and religious conception of Russia, in which Jews have no part.

1181. Blum, Jakub [pseud.]; Rich, Vera. THE IMAGE OF THE JEW IN SOVIET LITERATURE: THE POST-STALIN PERIOD. New York: Ktav, 1985. 275 pp.

Consists of two parts - J. Blum, "Soviet Russian Literature" (pp. 1-97, trans. from the Russian ms.) and V. Rich, "Jewish Themes and Characters in Belorussian Texts" (pp. 99-271). In Blum's study, two sections are devoted to antisemitism: "The Depiction of Soviet Antisemitism in Works Concerning the Second World War" (pp. 50-53) and "Nazi Antisemitism in Soviet Literature" (pp. 53-55). Includes discussion of the Soviet anti-Zionist campaign of the 1960s-70s in literature.

1182. Boasson, Charles. Jewish Problems in Dutch Poetry. DUTCH JEWISH HISTORY: PROCEEDINGS OF THE SYMPOSIUM...NOV. 28-DEC. 3, 1982, TEL-AVIV-JERUSALEM, ed. Jozeph Michman. Jerusalem: Hebrew University, Institute for Research on Dutch Jewry, 1984. Pp. 363-378.

Describes Dutch poets who sympathized and identified with the Jews, from the 17th century until the aftermath of the Holocaust, mentioning only one who was antisemitic - Joost van den Vondel (1587-1679).

1183. Broński, M. Żydzi i Polacy dzisiaj [Jews and Poles Today]. KULTURA 3 (Mar 1984) 25-33.

Comments on the American TV serial "The Winds of War," based on the novel by Herman Wouk. The film suggests that Poles collaborated with the Germans in the extermination of the Jews. Rejects this view and calls for a boycott of influential personalities who use the media to spread the view that the Poles carried out Hitler's designs.

1184. Brophy, Hope. Charges of Anti-Semitism at Oberammergau. AMERICA 152 (23 Mar 1985) 234-235. Unseen.

1185. Brumberg, Abraham. What Poland Forgot. THE NEW REPUBLIC 193, 25 (16 Dec 1985) 46-48.

Regarding Claude Lanzmann's film "Shoah," the official Polish press has charged him with defaming the Polish people by accusing them of complicity in the Holocaust. Lanzmann is accused of diverting attention from French war-time collaboration and racism today, and of manipulation by "well-known anti-Polish Zionist circles." But critics of the film cannot deny the existence of antisemitism in pre-war Poland.

1186. Calle, Marie-France. Théâtre Cauchemar. L'ARCHE 345 (Dec 1985) 62-63.

Asks why the supporters of Rainer Werner Fassbinder's play "Garbage, the City and Death" insist on the performance of this mediocre and possibly antisemitic play. The "rich Jew" in the play is shown making a fortune out of the bad conscience of the Germans. Supporters of the play say their aim is to expose antisemitism in Frankfurt.

1187. Casillo, Robert. Plastic Demons: The Scapegoating Process in Ezra Pound. CRITICISM 26, 4 (Fall 1984) 355-382.

Shows "the integral and indispensable place of anti-Semitism" in Pound's thought and writings. Pound identified the Jews with usury, which he believed was the cause of confusion in the world, and from his hatred of usury he went on to scapegoat the Jews as the major cause of all the world's ills. Analyzes the language and symbols in the "Cantos" which indicate Pound's anti-Jewish views.

1188. Cernyak-Spatz, Susan E. GERMAN HOLOCAUST LITERATURE. New York: Peter Lang, 1985. 144 pp. (American University Studies, I: Germanic Languages and Literature, 29).

A study of works by German and German-Jewish writers up to 1979. Concludes that characterizations of the Nazi and of the Jewish victim have progressed from stereotypes of good and evil to the depiction of individuals with psychological motivations. This process indicates a willingness among young German writers to accept the responsibility of the whole nation for the Holocaust.

1189. Crane, John Kenny. THE ROOT OF ALL EVIL: THE THEMATIC UNITY OF WILLIAM STYRON'S FICTION. Columbia, SC: University of South Carolina Press, 1984. ix, 168 pp.

The works of William Styron reflect a central theme, best identified in his book dealing with the Holocaust "Sophie's Choice." He propounds a theory of individual development based on egoism, which leads one to attempt to remold men and events to one's will, losing moral scruples in the process. Antisemitism, Southern racism and anti-feminism can all be explained by this theory.

1190. Daalder, Joost. Senecan Influence on Shylock's "Hath Not a Jew Eyes?" Speech. ENGLISH STUDIES 65, 5 (Oct 1984) 405-408.

Concerned with the impact of Seneca on Shakespeare, the author believes that, far from being antisemitic, Shakespeare wished to reveal "what evil is caused by the way in which those who are in power treat the weak."

1191. Doneson, Judith E. THE HOLOCAUST IN AMERICAN FILM. Dissertation - Hebrew University of Jerusalem, January 1985. 324, 14 pp. With a Hebrew summary.

Ch. 1 (pp. 17-77) is entitled "Reflections of Anti-Semitism in Film, 1933-1947, and the Nazi Persecution of the Jews." The other three chapters deal with films made from the 1950s to the end of the 1970s, with mention of antisemitism interspersed throughout.

1192. Duggan, D. ASPECTS DE L'ANTISEMITISME DANS LE ROMAN ANGLAIS CONTEMPORAIN: GRAHAM GREENE, C.P. SNOW. Dissertation - Université de Paris XIII, January 1985. 434 pp. Unseen.

1193. Durham, Carolyn A. William Styron's "Sophie's Choice": The Structure of Oppression. TWENTIETH CENTURY LITERATURE 30, 4 (Win 1984) 448-464.

"Styron's novels - and the distinction is important - are not oppressive, but about oppression, not racist but about racism, not anti-Semitic but about anti-Semitism, and, I shall argue, not sexist although, in the instance of 'Sophie's Choice' especially, are persistently about sexism."

1194. Ehrlich, Evelyn. CINEMA OF PARADOX: FRENCH FILMMAKING UNDER THE GERMAN OCCUPATION. New York: Columbia University Press, 1985. 235 pp.

Ch. 4 (pp. 57-70), "The Film Industry and the Jews," deals with the Vichy and German attempt to remove Jewish influence from the French cinema, and with antisemitic propaganda supporting the myth of "Jewish control" of the cinema. One antisemitic film was made in France by French personnel - "Les Corrupteurs" (1942). Some French filmmakers helped Jewish colleagues to survive, but most shut their eyes to the Jews' exclusion from the industry.

1195. Erens, Patricia. THE JEW IN AMERICAN CINEMA. Bloomington, IN: Indiana University Press, 1984. xiii, 455 pp. (Jewish Literature and Culture).

For antisemitism see especially the sections: "Pogrom Films" (57-63); "Hitler's Rise and Hollywood's Response" (148-157); "Anti-Semitism and the War's Aftermath" (173-181); "The HUAC Investigations" (192-196).

1196. Feinberg, Anat. Jewish Fate in German Drama 1933-1945. LEO BAECK INSTITUTE YEAR BOOK 29 (1984) 57-71.

Several plays were written in German from 1933 to 1945 depicting the Jewish experience, past and contemporary. A survey of 14 of them, 12 of which were written in exile, is presented here. The plays portray a wide range of antisemitic statements, from echoes of the "medieval accusation of a Jewish plot to poison the Christian community or the violent rape of innocent Christian maids by

Jews, to anti-Jewish allegations in line with the stereotypes set up by the ideologists of the Nazi race theory."

1197. Field, Leslie. Thomas Wolfe's Attitudes toward Germany and Jews. JOURNAL OF MODERN LITERATURE 11, 1 (Mar 1984) 180-185.

Wolfe's fiction, letters, and notes reveal bigotry and prejudice. He had a strong affinity for Germans and Teutonic culture, but in his trips to Germany in 1935 and 1936 he was horrified by Nazi culture and sensed that "anti-Semitism and humanity were incompatible."

1198. Fox, Terry Curtis. The Hollywood Novel. FILM COMMENT 21, 2 (Mar/Apr 1985) 7-13.

A survey of novels about the film industry written since the 1920s. Pp. 10-12 discuss antisemitism in these works, especially in Budd Schulberg's "What Makes Sammy Run." Antisemitism played an important part in Hollywood - "economic power was kept by one hated group of American outsiders [Jews] while power over content was wielded by another [Catholics]." Their relationship was uneasy.

1199. Frankel, Anne. Images of the Jew. THE JEWISH QUARTERLY 32, 1 <117> (1985) 28-32.

The European films shown at the Jewish Film Festival in London in 1985 portray Diaspora Jews as threatened by Gentile society. Three films dealt with the Holocaust period - the experience of Jews in pre-war Germany and of refugees in 1947. "Fear not, Jacob," made in West Germany by Radu Gabrea, examines the roots of Christian antisemitism in a fable about a persecuted Jew in a Portuguese village.

1200. Friedman, R.M. Exorcising the Past: Jewish Figures in Contemporary Films. JOURNAL OF CONTEMPORARY HISTORY 19, 3 (July 1984) 511-527.

Analyzes films made from 1933 to 1982. Discusses the "retro" movement which arose in France in 1974, characterized by re-staging the past, obliterating history, utilizing stereotypes of Jews, treating concentration camps as erotic, and blurring Nazi and Jewish identities.

1201. Friedman, Saul S. THE OBERAMMERGAU PASSION PLAY: A LANCE AGAINST CIVILIZATION. Carbondale, IL: Southern Illinois University Press, 1984. xxvii, 270 pp.

Traces the origin of passion plays, and discounts the legend that the Oberammergau play was first performed in 1634 after the village was saved from a plague. Its true origin is in religious zealotry, antisemitism, and the profit motive. Concludes that the play falls short of aesthetic demands, creates harmful stereotypes of Jews, and perpetuates the charge of deicide. Describes changes in the play during the Nazi era, its revival after World War II for financial profit, and recent unsuccessful efforts to revise the text.

1202. Gelber, Mark H. Thomas Mann y el antisemitismo. COLOQUIO 13 (Spr 1984) 7-19. Trans. from the English ("Patterns of Prejudice" 17, 1983).

An examination of Thomas Mann's literary works and his personality reveals a complex attitude towards Jews. Literary antisemitism was common in his novels and short stories (e.g. "Betrachtungen," "Waelsungenblut," "Doktor Faustus") but he also denounced antisemitism and joined forces with Jewish organizations to fight Nazism.

1203. Gelber, Mark H. Wandlungen im Bild des "gebildeten Juden" in der deutschen Literatur. JAHRBUCH DES INSTITUTS FUER DEUTSCHE GESCHICHTE 13 (1984) 165-178.

Analyzes the positive and negative images of the "cultivated Jew" in German literature, from the 18th to 20th centuries. States that even liberal authors, like Thomas Mann and Gustav Freytag, were not free from antisemitic stereotypes and prejudices.

1204. Gelber, Mark H. What is Literary Antisemitism? JEWISH SOCIAL STUDIES 47, 1 (Win 1985) 1-20.

Defines literary antisemitism as "the potential or capacity of a text to encourage or positively evaluate antisemitic attitudes or behaviors." The history of early antisemitism shows the development of a myth about the Jewish people and religion as hostile to society. The emphasis on Jewish guilt for the death of Jesus was carried into Christian literature (e.g. the passion play) giving rise to a negative Jewish stereotype, later amplified by racial and cultural elements.

1205. Gibault, François. CELINE: DELIRES ET PERSECUTIONS (1932-1944). Paris: Mercure de France, 1985. 378 pp.

The second part of a three-volume biography of Louis-Ferdinand Céline. Pp. 147-172 deal with Céline's antisemitism as an important aspect of his racism, and discuss especially his pamphlet "Bagatelles pour un massacre." Pp. 100-103 refer to the origins of Céline's antisemitism. He hated Soviet communism and American capitalism, and viewed both as creations of the Jewish "clique."

1206. Ginzel, Guenther-Bernd et al. MIT HAENGEMAUL UND NASEN-SINKEN - ERZIEHUNG ZUR UNMENSCHLICHKEIT: MEDIENPAKET FUER GRUPPENLEITER UND LEHRER. Duesseldorf: DKV - Der Kleine Verlag, 1984. 174 pp. + 20 slides.

The text of an antisemitic book for children, with caricatures, published in 1934 by the Stuermer Press, accompanied by present-day explanations (pp. 26-67, text and explanation on opposite pages). Preceded by an introduction on the history of antisemitism from early Christianity until the Final Solution, and followed by source material, including documents and excerpts from books and from the press.

1207. Glickman, Nora. Viñas's "En la Semana Trágica": A Novelist's Focus on an Argentinian Pogrom. MODERN JEWISH STUDIES ANNUAL 5 (Fall 1984) 64-71.

David Viñas's novel is an account of the "tragic week" of 7-14 January 1919, in Buenos Aires. After violent clashes with the police during a strike, the Jews were accused of plotting to establish a Bolshevik regime in Argentina. The Church, which viewed the Jew as a diabolical agent of change, also incited the populace and a full-scale pogrom broke out. Viñas's main interest is in his protagonist, Camilo Pizarro, a representative of the fascist well-born youth of Argentina.

1208. Harap, Louis. Jews in American Drama 1900-1918. AMERICAN JEWISH ARCHIVES 36, 2 (Nov 1984) 136-152.

Analyzes the changing nature of the Jewish image in American drama during the Progressive Era. Concludes that "the pre-World War I period saw the removal of the Jewish stage stereotype from the dead center to a less prominent and less insidious role in the American theater."

1209. Hirschson, Niel. Shakespeare, Shylock and the Marrano Factor. MIDSTREAM 31, 9 (Nov 1985) 51-54.

Shakespeare's "Merchant of Venice" must be read in comparison with Christopher Marlowe's openly antisemitic "The Jew of Malta" and in the context of the social background of the play. It is an apology for the marranos who were then entering English society, appearing in the wake of the Lopez case in which a Portuguese convert was accused of poisoning the Queen. Antonio, the enigmatic "Merchant of Venice," is in fact an apostate, as was Shakespeare's own family. This explains his need to show, through Shylock, that Jews are not a menace to society.

1210. Hollstein, Dorothea. Dreimal Jud Suess: Zeugnisse "Schmaehlichster Barbarei." DER DEUTSCHUNTERRICHT 37, 3 (1985) 42-55.

A comparison between three artistic treatments of the figure of the Court Jew, Joseph Suess Oppenheimer - Wilhelm Hauff's short novel of 1827, Lion Feuchtwanger's novel of 1925, and the Nazi film of 1940. This comparison makes clear the process by which literary material was transformed into antisemitic propaganda.

1211. Horak, Jan-Christopher. ANTI-NAZI-FILME DER DEUTSCHSPRACHIGEN EMIGRATION VON HOLLYWOOD, 1939-1945. Muenster: MAkS-Publikationen, 1984. xxii, 473 pp. Dissertation - Muenster University. Unseen.

1212. Insdorf, Annette. L'Holocauste à l'écran. CINEMACTION 30 (1985) 190 pp.

The entire issue is devoted to the Holocaust in the cinema, and constitutes an updated French version of the author's "Indelible Shadows: Film and the Holocaust" (New York: Random House, 1983). Discusses reflections of Nazi antisemitism and attitudes towards persecuted Jews in the occupied countries as depicted in films. Pp. 49-52 analyze Ingmar Bergman's film "The Serpent's Egg" (1977) which depicts antisemitism in pre-Nazi Germany.

1213. Janz, Rolf-Peter. Professor Bernhardi - 'eine Art medizinischer Dreyfus'? Die Darstellung des Antisemitismus bei Arthur Schnitzler. ARTHUR SCHNITZLER UND SEINE ZEIT: Akten des Internationalen Symposiums, Bari 1981, ed. Giuseppe Farese. Bern: P. Lang, 1985. Pp. 108-118.

In Schnitzler's play "Professor Bernhardi" (1912), a Jewish physician prevents a priest's visit to a young girl, thereby forestalling her finding out about her impending death. The play criticizes trends in society, including antisemitism. Schnitzler saw no solution to the problem of antisemitism.

1214. Jaron, Norbert; Rudin, Baerbel. DAS OBERAMMERGAUER PASSIONSSPIEL: EINE CHRONIK IN BILDERN. Dortmund: Harenberg, 1984. 216 pp.

Describes developments and changes in the Oberammergau Passion Play (considered to be antisemitic), and its performances, from 1634 to 1984.

1215. Joffe, Josef. Postcard West Germany: Curtains. THE NEW REPUBLIC 193, 24 (9 Dec 1985) 9-10.

The attempt to produce Rainer Werner Fassbinder's play "Garbage, the City and Death" in Frankfurt was an example of the contemporary German desire to "overcome the past." Fassbinder's defenders claim that his aim was to attack the "urban system," but only antisemitism can explain the use of a Jew as the symbol of exploitation and destruction of society. Moreover, the postwar Jew is "existentially guilty" for reminding Germans of their past.

1216. Kissel, David L. Politics and Play Reform in Oberammergau: An Anthropologist's View. FACE TO FACE 12 (Win 1985) 10-15.

Attempts to reform the text of the Passion Play used since 1853 must be understood against the background of political and economic factional strife in the village, which is economically dependent on tourists attending the play. This strife began in 1961 over updating the text. In 1967, Munich church authorities directed the village to revise the text to exclude all antisemitism, but the revision was rejected. (See also no. 1231.)

1217. Knilli, Friedrich; Zielinski, Siegfried. Der Jude als Sittenverderber: Kleine Mediengeschichte des Joseph Suess Oppenheimer. TRIBUENE 89 (1984) 108-118.

A survey tracing various presentations of the court-Jew Oppenheimer from the 18th century to the present. Some of them, especially the Nazi film "Jud Suess," described him as corrupting virtuous German maidens by sexual temptation. This antisemitic stereotype exists even today.

1218. Krane, Edna. Literary Criticism and Theological Anti-Semitism. MIDSTREAM 30, 1 (Jan 1984) 47-50.

A defense of Shakespeare against critics who claim that his works reflect Christian medieval antisemitism. Contends that his works actually reflect a satirical view of Christian dogma.

1219. Krane, Edna. The Perfectly Innocent Victim. MIDSTREAM 30, 9 (Nov 1984) 50-52.

A discussion of Northrop Frye's book "The Anatomy of Criticism" (Princeton, NJ: Princeton University Press, 1973). Frye's theory of Christian literature supports the author's belief that many great writers generally considered antisemitic were in fact criticizing Christian society. Figures like Shylock and Fagin should be seen not as anti-Jewish portraits, but as ironic figures of "perfectly innocent victims" of society, like Jesus, persecuted because they were Jewish.

1220. Krane, Edna. Shylock - Symbol or Stereotype. MIDSTREAM 31, 5 (May 1985) 56-58.

Shakespeare's portrayal of Shylock is not a product of antisemitism but is deliberately ambiguous. "The Merchant of Venice" is viewed as a satire on St. Augustine's "City of God," on the Roman Catholic sacraments, and on the established Church.

1221. Landman, Nathan M. Orwell's "1984": The Jewish Dimension. THE JEWISH SPECTATOR 49, 2 (Sum 1984) 20-21.

Discusses George Orwell's views on antisemitism and on the Jewish role in history. The Jews are nay-sayers to every form of idolatry, including nationalism and totalitarianism. The price of their distinctiveness is antisemitism. The Jew is the victim of totalitarianism, as is the protagonist Goldstein in "1984."

1222. Lecco, Alberto. DON CHISCIOTTE EBREO OVVERO L'IDENTITA CONQUISTATA: SAGGI LETTERARI E CINEMATOGRAFICI SU EBRAISMO E ANTISEMITISMO 1961-1985. Roma: Carucci, 1985. 322 pp.

A collection of articles by Lecco - on literature, film and television - which appeared in the Italian press from 1961 to 1985, relating to problems of Judaism and antisemitism (e.g. L.-F. Céline; the films "Sophie's Choice," "Kapo," "Behind the Walls"; anti-Zionism and antisemitism in the media as a result of the 1982 Sabra and Shatila massacres, etc.). Includes an essay about Don Quixote.

1223. Lewis, Stephen. ART OUT OF AGONY: THE HOLOCAUST THEME IN LITERATURE, SCULPTURE AND FILM. Toronto: CBC Enterprises, 1984. 194 pp.

Based on programs aired on the CBC radio series "Stereo Morning," 30 May-3 June 1983. Includes interviews with Aharon Appelfeld, Jurek Becker, Yaffa Eliach, Annette Insdorf, George Segal, George Steiner, William Styron, Hans Juergen Syberberg, D.M. Thomas and Elie Wiesel. Some of them discuss antisemitism as well as the Holocaust.

1224. Manilla, Morton. Narcissism in Daniel Deronda. MIDSTREAM 30, 8 (Oct 1984) 44-47.

Presents the thesis that George Eliot's liberalism towards the Jews was motivated by a desire to expedite their conversion to Christianity.

1225. Mintz, Alan. HURBAN: RESPONSES TO CATASTROPHE IN HEBREW LITERATURE. New York: Columbia University Press, 1984. xiv, 283 pp.

Parts I-II (pp.15-154) discuss the pre-Holocaust period, including the Crusader martyrdoms and the pogroms of 1648, 1881/2 and 1905 - literary works written at the time of occurrence, and by modern Hebrew writers about these events. Part III (pp. 155-269) is devoted to the response to the Holocaust in modern Hebrew literature.

1226. Montaut, Annie. Médecine, théorie du "style" et antisémitisme chez Céline. LITTERATURE 58 (1985) 42-59.

Céline, a physician, believed that the "judaization" of medicine prevented him from becoming a medical pioneer. Adopting eugenics and Nazi racial biology, he hoped to bring salvation to mankind. Analyzes "Bagatelles pour un massacre" and its language to show the processes at work in Céline's antisemitism.

1227. Mork, Gordon R. The 1984 Oberammergau Passion Play in Historical Perspective. FACE TO FACE 12 (Win 1985) 15-21.

Analyzes the 1984 production of the Oberammergau play, based on the 1980 text which incorporated some revisions. However, of the 28 specific changes suggested by Leonard Swidler, only six were actually made. The villagers' demand to retain their tradition while freeing the play from the taint of antisemitism should be respected. (See also no. 1231.)

1228. Mueller, Heidy M. DIE JUDENDARSTELLUNG IN DER DEUTSCH-SPRACHIGEN ERZAEHLPROSA (1945-1981). Koenigstein/Ts.: Forum Academicum, 1984. 217 pp. (Hochschulschriften Literaturwissenschaft, 58). Based on the author's dissertation, 1983.

A study of Jewish characters in the literary works of fifty non-Jewish German-language writers shows the unconscious influence of their anti-Jewish cultural tradition, contrary to their conscious intentions to present Jews in a more realistic and positive light. The characters emerge as negative stereotypes.

1229. Navrozov, Lev. Solzhenitsyn's World History: "August 1914" as a New "Protocols of the Elders of Zion." MIDSTREAM 31, 6 (June/July 1985) 46-53.

Most of the first volume of the new Russian version of "August 1914" is devoted to the 1911 assassination of Peter Stolypin, depicted as the incarnation of pure Russian nationality and goodness; his assassin, portrayed as a Jew, depicts sickness, falsehood and evil. Although presented as historical fact, Solzhenitsyn's account is fictionalized and perpetuates the myth of a Jewish plot against Russia. US anti-communist bodies are helping to spread this book in the USSR.

1230. Newman, Mordecai. Naughty Nazis: A Review of [Mel Brooks's Film] "To Be or Not to Be." JEWISH FRONTIER 51, 3 (Mar 1984) 24-26.

Discusses "Brooks's preoccupation with comic anti-Semitism" and "his seeming compulsion to shape the sources of Jewish persecution in comic form."

1231. Oberammergau: Christian Folk Religion and Anti-Judaism. FACE TO FACE 12 (Win 1985) 35 pp.

The first part of this issue consists of papers (see nos. 250, 1216, 1227) given at a symposium on the Oberammergau Passion Play, held by the German Studies Association in Denver, October 1984. These are followed by a response to the papers by Saul S. Friedman (pp. 21-24), in which he calls for further revision of the play's text, and suggestions for revisions by Leonard Swidler and Gerard Sloyan (pp. 24-25).

1232. Oesterreicher, J.M. Oberammergau; Tampering with History. AMERICA 152 (11 May 1985) 384-385. Unseen.

1233. Ophuls, Marcel. Closely Watched Trains. AMERICAN FILM 11, 2 (Nov 1985) 18-22, 79.

Ophuls, the director of "Le Chagrin et la Pitié" on the fate of the Jews in war-time France, praises Claude Lanzmann's film "Shoah." He expresses impatience with debates as to whether the film is "anti-Polish," similar to the debates aroused by his own film. "Shoah" illuminates the psychology of ordinary "non-participating" witnesses as well as that of war criminals.

1234. Oudejans, Nico. DE JOOD IN DE MIDDELNEDERLANDSE LITERATUUR: EEN ONDERZOEK NAAR DE JOOD ALS TYPE IN DE LETTERKUNDE TOT 1600 [The Jew in Middle Dutch Literature: A Study of the Jew as a Type in the Literature until 1600]. Amsterdam: Universiteit van Amsterdam, 1984. 107, 45 pp. M.A. thesis.

Analyzes the figure of the Jew in medieval Dutch literature according to stereotypes delineated by Joshua Trachtenberg in "The Devil and the Jews" (New Haven: Yale University Press, 1943). Focuses on the "exempel" genre, a short, didactic, but entertaining story illustrating themes of faith and morality, dating mostly from the 13th century. The Jew is described as a hater of the Virgin

Mary, a murderer of Christ and of Christian children. But the themes of the devilish Jew, the magician, and the usurer are absent.

1235. Pally, Marcia; Bannert, Walter. "The Inheritors" - New Face of Nazism: An Interview with Walter Bannert. FILM COMMENT 21, 2 (Mar/Apr 1985) 76-79. Translated from the German.

The rise in antisemitic incidents in Europe in recent years, especially after the 1982 Lebanon war, caused the Austrian filmmaker Walter Bannert to make "The Inheritors," a film about a middle class teenager caught up in a neo-Nazi youth group. Bannert warns that in the current economic crisis, fascist activity may be the prelude to a resurgence of Nazism.

1236. Pleticha, Heinrich, ed. DAS BILD DES JUDEN IN DER VOLKS- UND JUGENDLITERATUR VOM 18. JAHRHUNDERT BIS 1945. Wuerzburg: Koenigshausen und Neumann Verlag, 1985. 240 pp.

A collection of articles stressing the historical and sociological background to the positive image of the Jew in the 18th century and the development of the negative stereotype in the 19th and 20th centuries. The contents: Ingrid Belke: Die soziale Lage der deutschen Juden im 18. und 19. Jhdt.(9-28); Leander Petzold: Der ewige Verlierer (29-60); Theodor Brueggemann: Das Bild des Juden in der Kinder- und Jugendliteratur von 1750-1850 (61-83); Hans Otto Horch: Admonitio Judaica: Juedische Debatten ueber Kinder- und Jugendliteratur im 19. und beginnenden 20. Jhdt. (85-102); Hans Lamm: Juedische Kinder- und Jugendliteratur in Deutschland vor und nach 1933: Antijuedische Kinderbuecher nach 1933 (103-106); Rainer Erb: Die Wahrnehmung der Physiognomie der Juden: Die Nase (107-126).

1237. Prawer, Siegbert. The Death of Sigismund Markus: The Jews of Danzig in the Fiction of Guenter Grass. DANZIG, BETWEEN EAST AND WEST: ASPECTS OF MODERN JEWISH HISTORY, ed. Isadore Twersky. Cambridge, MA: Harvard University Press, 1985. Pp. 93-108.

Analyzes the figure of Sigismund Markus, the sympathetic Jewish shopkeeper who commits suicide when his shop is destroyed on "Kristallnacht" in Grass's novel "The Tin Drum." Grass works both with and against anti-Jewish stereotypes; Markus's story is a parable of the failure of German Jews to assimilate, and the loss that Germany has sustained by rejecting and destroying them.

1238. Ragazzini, Giuseppe. EBREI E USURAI NELLA SOCIETA E NEL DRAMMA ELISABETTIANI: IL LINGUAGGIO MERCANTILE IN SHAKESPEARE E MARLOWE. Bologna: Ed. CLUEB (Cooperativa Libraria Universitaria Editrice), 1984. 247 pp.

The introductory chapter provides a history of the Jews in England from 1066 to 1290 and of crypto-Jews up to the end of the 17th century. Describes usury as viewed by thinkers, from Plato and Aristotle to the mercantilists. Analyzes the Jewish villain in pre-Shakespearean drama, and usury and the usurer in the poetry of Shakespeare and Dante. The figure of Barabbas in "The Jew of Malta" is a typical example of Elizabethan antisemitism, whereas Shylock is an archetypical example of the Jew.

1239. Rancour-Laferriere, Daniel. Solzhenitsyn and the Jews: A Psychoanalytical View. SOVIET JEWISH AFFAIRS 15, 3 (Nov 1985) 29-54.

Aleksandr Solzhenitsyn has been described both as an antisemite and as pro-Jewish. There is some psychological validity in both views although he is, properly speaking, neither. The emotional conflict of Solzhenitsyn's childhood, between his religious, anti-Bolshevik family and the ideology of the regime, represented by his fervently communist Jewish classmates, created a "Jewish shadow identity." Examples are given from his novels and writings which show sympathy or even identification with Jews, and the desire to repress this identification in a manner which may be seen as antisemitic.

1240. Rex, Richard. Chaucer and the Jews. MODERN LANGUAGE QUARTERLY 45, 2 (June 1984) 107-122.

Chaucer was a poet of humanity and compassion and it is wrong to charge him with antisemitism. Anti-Jewish statements made by characters in his works reflect contemporary attitudes, not necessarily his own. Quotes sources from 14th century England which show that various theologians and poets (e.g. William Langland) preached tolerance towards the Jews. Chaucer knew these people and probably held the same views.

1241. Roskies, David G. AGAINST THE APOCALYPSE: RESPONSES TO CATASTROPHE IN MODERN JEWISH CULTURE. Cambridge, MA: Harvard University Press, 1984. xii, 374 pp.

Examines the responses to the pogroms of the late 19th and early 20th centuries in Russia, and to the Holocaust, as depicted in literature (in Hebrew and Yiddish) and in art, by East European Jewish intellectuals. Pp. 196-310 deal with the Holocaust period.

1242. Ryan, J.S. Australian Novelists' Perceptions of German Jewry and National Socialism. AUSTRALIAN JOURNAL OF POLITICS AND HISTORY 31, 1 (1985) 138-146.

Examines the Nazi persecution of Jews and the Holocaust as depicted in the works of Geoff Taylor, Patrick White, and David Martin (pseudonym of Ludwig Detsinyi, of Hungarian-Jewish origin).

1243. Saalmann, Dieter. Holocaust Literature: José Emilio Pacheco's Novel "Morirás lejos." HISPANOFILA 83 (Jan 1985) 89-105.

The novel, published in Mexico in 1967 following a wave of antisemitic acts in Mexico City in 1966, focuses on the pursuit of a Nazi criminal doctor in Mexico City, but encompasses persecution of Jews throughout history - from the destruction of the Temple in 70 A.D., through the expulsion from Spain in 1492, to the Nazi deportation of the Jews of Salonica, and the Warsaw ghetto uprising. The novel's ideological concern is with racial persecution, religious intolerance, and civilization as opposed to barbarism.

1244. Sanders, Ivan. Sequels and Revisions: The Hungarian Jewish Experience in Recent Hungarian Literature. SOVIET JEWISH AFFAIRS 14, 1 (Feb 1984) 31-45.

A study of Hungarian literature dealing with Jewish themes, written by Jews and non-Jews in the 1970s and early 1980s. The themes include traditional Jewish life before the War, the Holocaust, and questions of assimilation and rejection. The Jewish self-image in most of the works is either ambivalent or negative. Mentions an essay on Hungarian antisemitism by G. Száraz, written in 1976 (see no. 261), which makes clear that antisemitism has been a ubiquitous feature of Hungarian Jewish history.

1245. Schamschula, Eleonore. Das Fleischpfand: Mot. J 1161.2 in Volkserzaehlung und Literatur. FABULA 25, 3/4 (1984) 277-295.

A comparative analysis of the "pound of flesh" motif, found in Shakespeare's "The Merchant of Venice" and in stories, plays, and ballads widespread in various countries and cultures. In the majority of cases examined, the Jew is depicted as a bloodsucking moneylender.

1246. Séebold, Eric. ESSAI DE SITUATION DES PAMPHLETS DE LOUIS-FERDINAND CELINE. Tusson, Charente: Ed. du Lérot, 1985. 143 pp.

An account of Céline's pamphlets (including antisemitic material) and their reception by different political circles then, and how they are viewed today. Discusses critics' explanations of Céline's antisemitism and racism and pleads for a new edition of the pamphlets (which have not been issued since the War) arguing that the public should know Céline's work in its entirety. Claims that since literature has little effect on life and history, their publication will cause no harm.

1247. Sharp, Nicholas A. Shakespeare's Shylock and Ours. MENORAH REVIEW 3 (Spr 1985) 3-5.

Approaches to "The Merchant of Venice" which portray Shylock as a heroic victim of bigotry are a modern imposition on the play. Shylock was "created by an anti-Semite, and he expresses and promotes a set of bigoted, ignorant and stupid prejudices against Jews." At the same time, he is one of the earliest and still the greatest portrayal of a Jew as a human being, the insight from which all arguments against antisemitism must proceed.

1248. Sicher, Efraim. BEYOND MARGINALITY: ANGLO-JEWISH LITERATURE AFTER THE HOLOCAUST. Albany, NY: State University of New York Press, 1985. xv, 235 pp. (SUNY Series on Modern Jewish Literature and Culture).

A study of the effects of antisemitism, the Holocaust, and the search for Jewish identity on Anglo-Jewish writers. Pre-World War II literature reflected the antisemitism of working-class Jewish districts, while many post-war writers describe the inability of middle-class Jews to integrate fully into English society.

1249. Simson, Otto von. Ecclesia und Synagoge am suedlichen Querhausportal des Strassburger Muensters. WENN DER MESSIAS KOMMT: DAS JUEDISCH-CHRISTLICHE VERHAELTNIS IM SPIEGEL MITTELALTERLICHER KUNST, eds. Lieselotte Koetzsche, Peter von der Osten-Sacken. Berlin (West): Institut Kirche und Judentum, 1984. Pp. 104-125.

Argues against the accepted thesis that the two famous statues of Church and Synagogue in the Cathedral of Strasbourg were designed with antisemitic intentions. Influenced by interpretations of the "Song of Songs," the Synagogue was viewed as the "sister-bride" who is destined to return to Christ, her spouse.

1250. Sobel, Ronald B. The Oberammergau Passion Play. ADL BULLETIN 41, 8 (Oct 1984) 7-9.

In May 1984, a delegation of the ADL's Intergroup Relations Committee viewed the Oberammergau Passion Play. They witnessed "the most blatant, glaring manifestations of medieval stereotypic anti-Semitism." Describes discussions with various persons and groups in an effort to change the text and production of the play.

1251. Socor, V. Antisemitism in Official Publications Recurs. RADIO FREE EUROPE RESEARCH, SITUATION REPORT: ROMANIA 9 (14 June 1984) 12-17.

Discusses the volume of poetry by Corneliu Vadim Tudor, "Saturnalia," published in Bucharest in 1983. The book contains two violently antisemitic poems, attacking Moses Rosen, the Chief Rabbi of Romania, and the Jewish people. There is every indication that its publication took place with the support of the highest authorities. The book created an international scandal and was withdrawn from bookstores. (See also nos. 1060, 1068.)

1252. Sonnenfeld, Albert. The Poetics of Anti-Semitism. ROMANTIC REVIEW 76, 1 (Jan 1985) 76-93.

The language of 19th century Romantic authors expresses antisemitic attitudes by devices such as the use of alien and exotic proper names for Jews or a peculiarly Jewish style of speech. Romantic works, such as Wagner's operas, the works of Dostoevsky, and those of French writers, are analyzed as parables of antisemitism - rejection of the modern world of commerce, represented by the Jew, and espousal of "a fairy-tale world of mysterious harmony" from which the Jew is excluded.

1253. Steiman, Lionel B. FRANZ WERFEL - THE FAITH OF AN EXILE: FROM PRAGUE TO BEVERLY HILLS. Waterloo, Ont.: Wilfrid Laurier University Press, 1985. xi, 244 pp.

A study of the thought of the Austrian Jewish writer, many of whose works reflect the deep ambivalence of the Jews' relationship with Western culture and Christianity. The Jewish characters in his books are often stereotypes, influenced by Werfel's education by antisemitic monks. Ch. 13 (pp. 165-188), "A Special Relationship," deals with Werfel's attitude to Judaism, and pp. 177-188 with his theory of antisemitism and Nazism. While believing in Christ, he viewed the rejection of Christ by the Jews, and antisemitism, as theologically necessary and refused to convert.

1254. Turowicz, Jerzy. "Shoah" w polskich oczach ["Shoah" in Polish Eyes]. TYGODNIK POWSZECHNY 45 <1898> (10 Nov 1985) 1, 3.

Argues against the thesis of Claude Lanzmann's film "Shoah" that extermination of the Jews on Polish territory was possible because of Polish antisemitism and indifference to the fate of the Jews. Points out differences between the condition of Jews in Poland and other countries, and describes Polish and Catholic antisemitism, concluding that these alone could never have resulted in the extermination of the Jews.

1255. Weinberg, David. Approaches to the Study of Film in the Third Reich: A Critical Appraisal. JOURNAL OF CONTEMPORARY HISTORY 19, 1 (Jan 1984) 105-126.

Mentions the aryanization of the film industry and the antisemitic film "Jud Suess" (pp.115-116).

APPENDIX I

CURRENT ANTISEMITIC PERIODICALS

ACTION
Sanctuary Press Ltd.
76A Rochester Row, London SW1
Ed.: Robert Row

ARYAN NATIONS
Teutonic Unity Publications
POB 362, Hayden Lake, ID 83835
Ed.: R.G. Butler

DIE BAUERNSCHAFT
Kritik Verlag
2341 Mohrkirch, West Germany
Ed.: Thies Christopherson

BEHIND THE NEWS
POB 1564, Krugersdorp 1740, South Africa
Ed.: Ivor Benson

BIBLE RESEARCHER: REVISIONIST HISTORY
Mardnadsvagen 289, S-183 34 Taby, Sweden
Ed.: Ditlieb Felderer

BRITAIN AWAKE
49A Park Street, Horsham, Sussex
Ed.: A. Ryan

BRITAIN FIRST
50 Pawsons Road, Croydon, Surrey CRO 2QF
Ed.: Richard Lawson

BRITISH NATIONALIST
POB 446, London SE23 2LS
Ed.: Ronald Rickard

BRITISH NEWS
316 Stanks Drive, Leeds 14
Ed.: Eddy Morrison

BULLDOG
50 Pawsons Rd., Croydon, Surrey CRO 2QF
Ed: Joe Pearce

CANDOUR
Candour Pub. Co.
Forest House, Liss Forest, Hampshire GU33 7DD

CARPATII: REVISTA DE CULTURA SI ACTIUNE ROMANEASCA IN EXIL
Calle Conde de Peñalver 82, 28006 Madrid
Ed.: Traian Popescu

THE CDL REPORT
POB 493, Baton Rouge, LA 70821

CEDADE: REVISTA NACIONALSOCIALISTA
Apartado de Correos, 14.207, 08080 Barcelona
Ed.: Joaquin Bochaca

CHRISTIAN VANGUARD
POB 426, Metairie, LA 700

COBRA INFORMATION
BP 1917, F-37019 Tours
Ed.: Olivier Devalez

COMBAT
POB 192, Manor Park, London E12
Ed.: Kevin Randall

COURRIER DU CONTINENT
Case Ville 2428, Lausanne
Ed.: G.A. Amaudruz

CURIERUL
POB 95, Santa Clara, CA
Ed.: Gabriel Balanescu

DAVID McCALDEN REVISIONIST NEWSLETTER
POB 3849, Manhattan Beach, CA 90266
Ed.: David McCalden

DEFENSE DE L'OCCIDENT
BP 184, 75228 Paris
Ed.: Maurice Bardeche

DEFIANCE
[No address], USA
Ed.: Karl Hand

DEUTSCHE WOCHEN-ZEITUNG
DVG-Deutsche Verlagsgesellschaft
Brueckenstr. 1, Postfach 270, 8200 Rosenheim, West Germany
Eds.: E. Kernmayr, W. Schuetz

DEUTSCHER ANZEIGER
DSZ Verlag
8000 Munich 60

LE DEVENIR EUROPEEN
1 Rue du Rhône, 44100 Nantes
Ed.: Goulven Pennaod

DON BELL REPORTS
POB 2223, Palm Beach, FL 33480

ECRITS DE PARIS
Centre d'Etudes des Questions Actuelles,
Société Parisienne d'Editions et de Publications
9 Passage des Marais, 75010 Paris
Ed.: Madeleine Malliavin

EIDGENOSS
CH-8401 Winterthur, Switzerland
Ed.: Max Wahl

ELEMENTS
SEPP-Société d'Editions et de Publicite Professionelles
5 Place du Colonel Fabien, 75491 Paris
Ed.: Michel Marmin

EUROPA LIBRE
Ap. Cor. 9043, Valencia
Ed.: José Miguel García Brull

THE EUROPEAN
NSAP (Watford)
BCH Box 2047, London WC1N 3XX

EUROPEAN HUMAN RIGHTS (EHR)
Marknadsvagen 289, S-183 34 Taby, Sweden
Ed.: Dietlieb Felderer

FACT FINDER
95A Chester Road East, Deeside, Clwyd, Wales

FIII DACIEI: REVISTA DE OPINIE SI ACTIUNE ROMANEASCA
Boian News Service
POB 713, 300 E. 91 St., New York, NY 10028
Ed.: George F.A. Boian

LE FLAMBEAU EUROPEEN
[No address], France
Ed.: Louis Jeancharles

FROM THE MOUNTAIN
POB 331, Cohoctah, MI 48816
Ed.: Robert E. Miles

DER GAULEITER
[No address], Arkansas

GOLDEN DAWN
Skonfor 11, Koridallos, Piraeus, Greece
Ed.: Giannis Poriotis

GOTHIC RIPPLES
Thorgarth, Greenhow Hill, Harrogate, N. Yorks. H93 5JQ
Ed.: J. Pearce, N. Griffin et al.

HALT
Volksbewegung
Prinz-Eugen Str. 74/2, 1040 Wien
Ed.: Gerd Honsik

HOLOCAUST NEWS
Centre for Historical Review
POB 40, London E15

INSTAURATION
Howard Allen Enterprises, Inc.
POB 76, Cape Canaveral, FL 32920
Ed.: Wilmot Robertson

JOURNAL OF HISTORICAL REVIEW (includes IHR NEWSLETTER)
Institute of Historical Review
POB 1306, Torrance, CA 90505

JUVENTUDE EUROPEIA
Apartado 131, 4801 Guimaraes, Portugal

KANSALLIS - KDP (National Democratic Party)
POB 41, 005111, Helsinki 51
Ed.: Pekka Siitoin

THE KLANSMAN
POB 700, Denham Springs, LA 70726
Ed.: Bill Wilkinson

KOMMENTARE ZUM ZEITGESCHEHEN
Webgasse 11, 1060 Wien

LEAGUE REVIEW
League of St. George
9/11 Kensington High St., London
Ed.: J. Sibley

LECTURES ET TRADITION
Diffusion de la Pensee Francaise
Chire-en-Montreuil, 86190 Vouille, France
Ed.: Jean Auguy

LECTURES FRANCAISES: REVUE DE LA POLITIQUE FRANCAISE
Same as preceding entry

LEGAL EAGLE
Patriots Tax Committee [and] Layman Education Guild at Law
9600 Cedar Lake Rd., Pinckney, MI 48169

LA LEGITIMITE
BP 462-08, 75366 Paris 08

LETTRE DE LYNX-CLUB
Synd. Nat. de la Presse Ind.
26 Rue Volambert, 95100 Argenteuil, France
Ed.: Henry-Robert Petit

LETTRES POLITIQUES
BP 16, 75767 Paris 16
Ed.: J. Ploncard d'Assac

LIBERTATEA
47-15 44th St., Apt. 1R, Woodside, NY 11377
Ed.: Nicolae Niţă

LIBERTY BELL
Liberty Bell Publications
Reedy, WV 25270
Ed.: George P. Dietz

MERCURY
POB 73523, Houston, TX
Ed.: La Vonne Dodea Furr

MERIDIANE (Formerly MINCINOSUL)
88-10 Whitney Ave., Elmhurst, NY 11373
Ed.: Rodica Andrei

MILITANT: REVUE NATIONALISTE POPULAIRE D'ACTION EUROPEENNE
44 Quai Jemmapes, BP 104, 75010 Paris
Ed.: M. Bousquet

MONITOR
Centre for Historical Review
POB 228, Manor Park, London E12

NASJONALISTEN
National Party
POB 104, Skoeyen, Oslo 2

NATION EUROPA: MONATSSCHRIFT IM DIENST DER EUROPAEISCHEN ERNEUERUNG
Nation Europa Verlag
Bahnhofstr. 25, Postfach 670, Coburg, West Germany

NATIONAL FRONT NEWS
N.F.N. Press
50 Pawsons Rd., Croydon, Surrey CRO 2QF
Ed.: Martin Wingfield

NATIONAL VANGUARD: TOWARD A NEW CONSCIOUSNESS, A NEW ORDER, A NEW EUROPE
National Alliance
Box 3535, Washington, DC 20007
Ed.: William L. Pierce

NATIONALISM TODAY: THE RADICAL VOICE OF BRITISH NATIONALISM
N.T. Press
50 Pawsons Road, Croydon, Surrey CRO 2QF
Ed.: Joe Pearce

NEA DYNAMIS
Tach Thyris 3819, Athens

NEUE ANTHROPOLOGIE
[No address], West Germany
Ed.: J. Rieger

THE NEW ORDER
NSDAP-AO
POB 6414, Lincoln, NE 68506
Ed.: Gerhard Lauck

NORDISK KAMP
Solhsulet
POB 162, 15201 Strangnas, Sweden

THE NORTHLANDER
The Northern League
POB 1796, Amsterdam

NOTRE EUROPE
BP 76, 75462 Paris 10
Ed.: Jean-Claude Domino

NS BULLETIN: OFFICIAL NEWSLETTER OF THE NEW ORDER
[No address], Arlington, VA

NSIWP & NSPUK (National Socialist Irish Workers' Party & National Socialist Party UK)
69 Eugene St., Dublin 8

NS NATIONALER
Clifford Herrington
POB 388, Bartlesville, OK 74005
Ed.: R.L. Halle

NSV REPORT
National Socialist Vanguard
POB 328, The Dalles, OR 97058

PORUNCA VREMII: REVISTA DE PRESTIGIUL SI DREPTURILE NEAMULIU NOSTRU
Boian News Service
POB 713, 300 E. 91 St., New York, NY 10028
Ed.: George F.A. Boian

RACE AND NATION (Formerly NATIONAL SOCIALIST MOBILIZER, NS KAMPFRUF)
World Service
POB 12444, San Diego, CA 92112
Ed.: Russell Veh

RAUTARISTI
POB 41, 00511 Helsinki 51

REVISION
Centro de Estudios Historicos Revisionistas Español
Apartado de Correos 603, 03080 Alicante, Spain

REVUE L'HOMME LIBRE: FILS DE LA TERRE
Cercle d'Etudes Psychologiques
BP 205, 42005 St. Etienne, France
Ed.: Marcel Renoulet

RIVAROL
9 Passage des Marais, 75010 Paris
Ed.: Camille-Marie Galic

ROMANIAN NEWS & WORLD REPORT
Boian News Service
POB 713, 300 E. 91 St., New York, NY 10028
Ed.: George F.A. Boian

SAMISDAT NEWS
206 Carlton St., Toronto

THE SCORPION
Heritage Books
BCM 5766, London WC1N 3XX
Ed.: Michael Walker

SIEG
Leiblachstr. 9, A-6912 Hoerbranz, West Germany
Ed.: Walter Ochensberger

SIEGE
POB 17, Chillicothe, OH 45601
Ed.: James Mason

SOCIAL JUSTICE
American Workers' Party - National Socialist Movement
POB 41503, Cincinnati, OH 45241

SONS OF LIBERTY BOOK LIST
POB 214, Metairie, LA 70004

SOUTHERN NATIONAL NEWSLETTER
Southern National Party
POB 18214, Memphis, TN 38118
Ed.: Benjamin L. Hooks

SPEARHEAD
Seacroft, 52 Westbourne Villas, Hove, Sussex
Ed.: John Tyndall

THE SPOTLIGHT (Formerly LIBERTY LOWDOWN, NATIONAL SPOTLIGHT, LIBERTY LETTER)
Cordite Fidelity Inc.
300 Independence Ave. S.E., Washington, DC 20003
Ed.: Vincent J. Ryan

DER STOSSTRUPP
Postfach 98, 1096 Wien
Ed.: Martin Nirschl

SUSSEX FRONT
National Front
POB 80, Worthing, Sussex BN14 8EG
Ed.: Martin Wingfield

SWORD OF CHRIST (Spotlight)
Box 88, Good News Ministries, London, ARK 72847
Ed.: Ralph P. Forbes

TABOE
Pub.: A. DeGrauwe, Destelbergen
P. Hendrickx, Wandelweg 21, B-2241 Zoersel, Belgium
Ed.: Peter Hendrickx

TALON/EURO-AMERICAN QUARTERLY
POB 2-1776, Milwaukee, WI 53221

TARA SI EXILUL: CURIER INFORMATIV AL MISCARII LEGIONARE
Pl. República Dominicana, 1-3D, 28016 Madrid
Ed.: Gheorghe Costea

TEMPLE BIBLICAL NEW [sic]
Lowell Davis Enterprises
Box 4341, Waco, TX 76705

TEUTONIC UNITY
A.E., POB 11116, Station E, Buffalo, NY 14211
Ed.: Manfred Roeder

THE TORCH
White Peoples Committee
POB 88, Bass, ARK 72612
Ed.: Thom Arthur Robb

TRIBUNA NOASTRA: ZIAR CANADIAN [sic] IN LIMBA ROMANA
The National Association of Americans of Romanian Descent
in the United States
POB 713, New York, NY 10028
Ed.: Stefan Penes

UNABHAENGIGE NACHRICHTEN
Postfach 40 0215, 4630 Bochum 4, West Germany

VANGUARDA
Apartado 162, 2700 Amadora, Portugal
Ed.: Luis Henriques

VATRA: FOAIE ROMANEASCA DE OPINIE SI INFORMATIE
Muenchhofstr. 12, Freiburg, West Germany

VOICE
Box 11116, Buffalo, NY 14211
Ed.: Karl B. Heinrich

WAPA
POB 65, Fallbrook, CA 92028

THE WHITE CAROLINIAN
Route 1, Box 386, Angier, NC 27501

WHITE POWER: THE REVOLUTIONARY VOICE OF NATIONAL SOCIALISM
NS Publications, The National Socialist White People's Party
and The New Order
POB 5505, Arlington, VA 22205 (or 2507 North Franklin Rd.,
Arlington, VA 22201)
Ed.: Martin Kerr

YOUNG NATIONALIST
16 Vale Lodge, Perry Vale, London SE23 2LG
Ed.: R. Edmonds

YVELINES SOLIDARISTES
BP 59, 78001 Versailles

APPENDIX II

BIBLIOGRAPHIES ON ANTISEMITISM AND THE HOLOCAUST PUBLISHED PRIOR TO 1984

1877

Steinschneider, Moritz. POLEMISCHE UND APOLOGETISCHE LITERATUR IN ARABISCHER SPRACHE, ZWISCHEN MUSLIMEN, CHRISTEN UND JUDEN, NEBST ANHAENGEN VERWANDTEN INHALTS, MIT BENUTZUNG HANDSCHRIFTLICHER QUELLEN. Leipzig: F.A. Brockhaus. xii, 456 pp. 182 items in Arabic and Latin. Annotated. Includes appendixes: Christian polemical works (pp. 218-243) and Jewish polemics against Islam (pp. 244-388).

1885

Jacobs, Joseph. THE JEWISH QUESTION, 1875-1884: BIBLIOGRAPHICAL HAND-LIST. London: Truebner & Co. xi, 96 pp. 571 items. Books, pamphlets, articles, speeches, reports of meetings and societies, published in Europe and America.

1893

Westphal, P. ILLUSTRIERTER FUEHRER DURCH DIE ANTISEMITISCHE LITTERATUR. Nossen i.S.: Verlag von P. Westphal, Spezialbuchhandlung fuer antisemitische Litteratur. 112 pp. Antisemitic books in German. Partially annotated.

1905

Desachy, Paul. BIBLIOGRAPHIE DE L'AFFAIRE DREYFUS. Paris: Edouard Cornély et Cie. vii, 71 pp. 728 items. Books and articles in European languages.

1906

Hayn, Hugo. UEBERSICHT DER (MEIST IN DEUTSCHLAND ERSCHIENENEN) LITTERATUR UEBER DIE ANGEBLICH VON JUDEN VERUEBTEN RITUALMORDE UND HOSTIENFREVEL. Jena: H.W. Schmidt's Verlagsbuchhandlung (G. Tauscher). 30 pp. 121 items, partly annotated. Mostly German books, with some in Latin and French.

1926

LITERATUR-WEGWEISER FUER DEN K.C.: EINE UEBERSICHT UEBER DIE FUER DEN K.C.ER WICHTIGSTE LITERATUR. Hrsg. von der Schriftleitung der K.C.-Blaetter. Berlin: Der Kartell-Convent der Verbindungen deutscher Studenten juedischen Glaubens. 20 pp. German books. See antisemitic works on pp. 12-18: "Judengegnerschaft."

1930

נאדעל, ב.; עליאוויטש, י. ליטערעטור וועגן דער נאציאנאלער פראגע, אנטיסעמיטיזם און יידישער ערד-איינארדנונג אין ראטנפארבאנד: ביבליאגראפישער אנווייזער פאר פראפאגאנדיסטן, געזערד-אקטיוויסטן און געזערד-קרייזלעך. כארקאוו: אוקרגעזערד. 56 עמ׳.

[Nadel, B.; Eliovitch, I. LITERATURA PRO NATSIONAL'NE PITANNYA BOROT'BU Z ANTISEMITIZMOM TA PRO ZEMEL'NE VLASHTUVANNYA EVREISKOI BIDNOTI: BIBLIOGRAFICHNII POKAZNIK DLYA PROPAGANDISTIV OZET-AKTIVISTIV TA OZET-OSEREDKIV. Kharkov: Vidannya ukrozetu. 56 pp.] Books and articles, in Yiddish and Russian. Pp. 13-16: "Antisemitism."

1938

Eichstaedt, Volkmar. BIBLIOGRAPHIE ZUR GESCHICHTE DER JUDENFRAGE. BD.1: 1750-1848. Hamburg: Hanseatische Verlagsanstalt. x, 267 pp. 3016 items. A Nazi bibliography of books and articles on Judaism (mostly German, some French) published in the 18th-20th centuries. Includes antisemitic works and works about antisemitism.

1941

Baron, Salo Wittmayer. BIBLIOGRAPHY OF JEWISH SOCIAL STUDIES, 1938-39. New York: Conference on Jewish Relations. 291 pp. Reprinted from JEWISH SOCIAL STUDIES 2, 3/4 (1940). 4231 items. Books and articles. Multilingual. Pp. 509-520: "Antisemitism."

Menzel, Joachim. SCHRIFTTUM ZUR JUDENFRAGE: EINE AUSWAHL. Muenchen: Zentralverlag der NSDAP. 32 pp. (Schriftenreihe zur weltanschaulichen Schulungsarbeit, Heft 4). "Hrsg. vom Amt Schrifttumspflege der NSDAP." An annotated list of antisemitic German books, mostly published during the Third Reich.

1945

Weinreich, Max. DESIDERATA OF NAZI LITERATURE ON THE JEWS: HELP PROCURE THESE BOOK FOR SCIENTIFIC RESEARCH. New York: YIVO. 40 pp. 422 books and 84 periodicals. German only.

1951

Neumann, Inge S.; Rosenbaum, Robert A. EUROPEAN WAR CRIMES TRIALS: A BIBLIOGRAPHY. New York: Carnegie Endowment for International Peace. 113 pp. 746 items. Books and articles published between 1941-1950, in the US and Western Europe.

1953

Friedman, Philip. THE BIBLIOGRAPHY OF THE WARSAW GHETTO (ON THE TENTH ANNIVERSARY OF THE UPRISING IN THE WARSAW GHETTO). New York: Jewish Book Council of America. 8 pp. Reprinted from JEWISH BOOK ANNUAL 11 (1952/3). Multilingual. Annotated.

1957

Chojnacki, Wladyslaw; Pospieszalski, Karol Marian; Serwański, Edward. MATERIALY DO BIBLIOGRAFII OKUPACJI HITLEROWSKIEJ W POLSCE, 1939-1945. Warszawa: Panstwowe Wydawnictwo Naukowe. 64 pp. (Polska Akademia Nauk. Instytut Historii). Books and articles in Polish. See the index for material on the extermination of the Jews.

1958

Geyer, Arthúr. A MAGYARORSZAGI FASIZMUS ZSIDOUELDOEZESENEK BIBLIOGRAFIAJA, 1945-1958. Budapest: Magyar Izraeliták Országos Képviselete. 167 pp. Pp. 7-44 contain an annotated list of 240 books (in Hungarian) on the Holocaust period in Hungary. Pp. 47-148 list archival material.

Wolff, Ilse R. GERMAN JEWRY: ITS HISTORY, LIFE AND CULTURE. London: Vallentine, Mitchell, for the Wiener Library. 279 pp. (Wiener Library Catalogue Series, 3). 3434 items. Books and articles in European languages. Pp. 205-236: "Antisemitism." See continuation in 1978.

1960

נשמית, שרה. השואה והמרד: חומר ביבליוגרפי. הוכן על-ידי "בית לוחמי הגיטאות" והוגש ע"י שרה נשמית. תל-אביב: מזכירות הקיבוץ המאוחד, ועדת החנוך, המדור לבתי ספר. 35 עמ'.

[Nishmit, Sara. THE HOLOCAUST AND RESISTANCE: BIBLIOGRAPHIC MATERIAL. Prepared by the Ghetto Fighters House. Tel-Aviv: Hakibbutz Hameuchad, Education Committee, Section for Schools. 35 pp.] Books in Hebrew and European languages. Annotated.

פרידמן, פיליפ. ביבליוגרפיה של הספרים העבריים על השואה ועל הגבורה. ירושלים: יד ושם; ניו-יורק: ייווא. 433, x עמ'. (מפעלים משותפים, סדרה ביבליוגראפית, ב).

[Friedman, Philip. BIBLIOGRAPHY OF BOOKS IN HEBREW ON THE JEWISH CATASTROPHE AND HEROISM IN EUROPE. Jerusalem: Yad Vashem; New York: YIVO. 433, x pp. (Joint Projects, Bibliographical Series, 2).] 1246 items. Annotated.

Hochmuth, Ursel. WAECHST GRAS DARUEBER? 400 LITERATURHINWEISE ZUM THEMA "UNBEWAELTIGTE VERGANGENHEIT." Jugenheim a.d.B.: Weltkreis Verlags GmbH. 59 pp. Also appeared in the series DAS WERDENDE ZEITALTER 7 (July 1960). 400 German books on the Holocaust period. For persecution of the Jews see the subject index.

Robinson, Jacob; Friedman, Philip. GUIDE TO JEWISH HISTORY UNDER NAZI IMPACT. New York: YIVO; Jerusalem: Yad Vashem. xxxi, 425 pp. (Joint Documentary Projects, Bibliographical Series, 1). 3634 items. Multilingual. Includes books, articles and archival material. Reprinted in 1973. A first draft appeared in 1958, entitled: GUIDE TO RESEARCH IN JEWISH HISTORY, 1933-1945.

Wolff, Ilse R. PERSECUTION AND RESISTANCE UNDER THE NAZIS. 2nd rev. ed. London: Vallentine, Mitchell, for the Wiener Library. 208 pp. (Wiener Library Catalogue Series, 1). 1943 items. Books and articles in European languages. The 1st ed., entitled PERSECUTION, TERROR AND RESISTANCE IN NAZI GERMANY, appeared in 1949 (74 pp.) and was reissued, with a supplement, in 1953.

1962

גאר, יוסף; פרידמן, פיליפ. ביבליאגראפיע פון יידישע ביכער וועגן חורבן און גבורה. ניו-יארק: ייווא; ירושלים: יד ושם. xxxi, 330 עמ׳. (בשותפותדיקע דאקומענטאציע-פראיעקטן, ביבליאגראפישע סעריע, 3).

[Gar, Joseph; Friedman, Philip. BIBLIOGRAPHY OF YIDDISH BOOKS ON THE CATASTROPHE AND HEROISM. New York: YIVO; Jerusalem: Yad Vashem. xxxi, 330 pp. (Joint Documentary Projects, Bibliographical Series, 3).] 1771 items. See the continuation in 1970.

Braham, Randolph L. THE HUNGARIAN JEWISH CATASTROPHE: A SELECTED AND ANNOTATED BIBLIOGRAPHY. New York: YIVO; Jerusalem: Yad Vashem. xxv, 86 pp. (Joint Documentary Projects, Bibliographical Series, 4). 752 items. Multilingual.

1963

Goodman, Philip. THE WARSAW GHETTO UPRISING: A RESOURCE FOR PROGRAMMING. New York: National Jewish Welfare Board. 33 pp. English books and audio-visual material. Annotated.

Mark, Bernard. MECZENSTWO I WALKA ZYDOW W LATACH OKUPACJI: PORADNIK BIBLIOGRAFICZNY. Warszawa: Bibliotek Narodowa, Instytut Bibliograficzny. 44 pp. 114 books and articles in Polish. Annotated.

Wolff, Ilse R.; Kehr, Helen. AFTER HITLER: GERMANY 1945-1963. London: Vallentine, Mitchell, for the Wiener Library. x, 261 pp. (Wiener Library Catalogue Series, 4). 2694 items. Books and articles in European languages. Pp. 229-231: "Antisemitism."

1964

Devoto, Andrea. BIBLIOGRAFIA DELL'OPPRESSIONE NAZISTA, FINO AL 1962. Firenze: Leo S. Olschki. ix, 149 pp. 1503 items. Books and articles in European languages. See continuation in 1983.

LA FRANCE DE L'AFFAIRE DREYFUS A NOS JOURS. Paris: Bibliothèque du Centre de Documentation Juive Contemporaine. xii, 264 pp. (Catalogue no. 1). Books, mostly French but including other languages as well, and mainly dealing with antisemitism and the Holocaust period.

Wolff, Ilse R. FROM WEIMAR TO HITLER: GERMANY 1918-1933. 2nd rev. ed. London: Vallentine, Mitchell, for the Wiener Library. x, 269 pp. (Wiener Library Catalogue Series, 2). 2990 items. Books and articles in European languages. Pp. 180-199: "Antisemitism." The 1st ed. appeared in 1951.

1966

פיקאז׳, מנדל. השואה והגבורה באספקלריה של העיתונות העברית: ביבליוגרפיה. כר׳ 1-4. ירושלים: יד ושם; ניו-יורק: ייווא. ל, 368, viii; 371-896; 899-1345; 244 עמ׳. (מפעלי תיעוד משותפים, סידרה ביבליוגראפית, ה-ח).

[Piekarz, Mendel. THE JEWISH HOLOCAUST AND HEROISM THROUGH THE EYES OF THE HEBREW PRESS: A BIBLIOGRAPHY. Vol. 1-4. Jerusalem: Yad Vashem; New York: YIVO. [30], 368, viii; 371-896; 899-1345; 244 pp. (Joint Documentary Projects, Bibliographical Series, 5-8).] 23188 items. Lists material from September 1939 until 1960 (daily and weekly periodicals until the end of 1950). See continuation in 1978.

1966-1969

גאר, יוסף. ביבליאגראפיע פון ארטיקלען וועגן חורבן און גבורה אין יידישער פעריאדיקע. באנד I-II. ניו-יארק: ייווא; ירושלים: יד ושם. xxiv, 306; x, 338 עמ׳. (בשותפותדיקע דאקומענטאציע-פראיעקטן, ביבליאגראפישע סעריע, 9-10).

[Gar, Joseph. BIBLIOGRAPHY OF ARTICLES ON THE CATASTROPHE AND HEROISM IN YIDDISH PERIODICALS. Vol. I-II. New York: YIVO; Jerusalem: Yad Vashem. xxiv, 306; x, 338 pp. (Joint Documentary Projects, Bibliographical Series, 9-10).] 3597; 5717 items. Covers periodicals from 1939 to 1950.

1966-1978

Lowenthal, E.G. In the Shadow of Doom: Post-War Publications on Jewish Communal History in Germany. LEO BAECK INSTITUTE YEAR BOOK 11 (1966) 306-335; 15 (1970) 223-242; 23 (1978) 283-308. German works covering medieval times through the Holocaust.

1968

LA FRANCE, LE TROISIEME REICH, ISRAEL. Paris: Bibliothèque du Centre de Documentation Juive Contemporaine. xi, 252 pp. (Catalogue no. 2). Books, mostly French but including other languages as well. For antisemitism, see the index and table of contents. Continues the previous catalogue (see 1964).

TEN YEARS OF YAD VASHEM PUBLICATIONS, 1957-1967. Jerusalem: Yad Vashem. 20 pp. Books and periodicals in English, Hebrew, and Yiddish.

1969

Neut, E.M. van der. HET LOT DER JODEN IN NEDERLAND TIJDENS DE TWEEDE WERELDOORLOG: BIBLIOGRAFIE. Amsterdam: [The Author]. 51 pp. 175 items. Books and articles, mostly Dutch.

1969-1974

ילינק, ישעיהו. שואת יהודי סלובאקיה בראי המחקר והספרות. ילקוט מורשת יא (נוב 1969) 161-157; טו (אוקט 1972) 184-175; יח (נוב 1974) 194-185.

[Jelinek, Yeshayahu. The Holocaust of the Jews of Slovakia in Research and Literature. YALKUT MORESHET 11 (Nov 1969) 157-161; 15 (Oct 1972) 175-184; 18 (Nov 1974) 185-194.] 87, 148, 126 items respectively. Books and articles. Multilingual.

1970

באס, דוד. ביבליאגראפיע פון יידישע ביכער וועגן חורבן און גבורה. ניו-יארק: ייווא; ירושלים: יד ושם. 54 עמ׳. (בשותפותדיקע דאקומענטאציע-פראיעקטן, ביבליאגראפישע סעריע, 11).

[Bass, David. BIBLIOGRAPHY OF YIDDISH BOOKS ON THE CATASTROPHE AND HEROISM. New York: YIVO; Jerusalem: Yad Vashem. 54 pp. (Joint Documentary Projects, Bibliographical Series, 11).] 456 items. Continues the previous bibliography (see 1962).

על השואה והגבורה: רשימה ביבליוגרפית. ירושלים: העיריה, המחלקה לחינוך, הספריה העירונית ע"ש פרופ׳ י. קלוזנר. 32 עמ׳.

[ON THE HOLOCAUST AND HEROISM: A BIBLIOGRAPHICAL LIST. Jerusalem: Municipality, Department of Education, Municipal Library. 32 pp.] Hebrew books.

Garsse, Yvan van. A BIBLIOGRAPHY OF GENOCIDE, CRIMES AGAINST HUMANITY AND WAR CRIMES. Vol. 1. Sint Niklaas: Studiecentrum voor Kriminologie en Gerechtelijke Geneeskunde. 1750 items. A mimeographed list of books and articles. Multilingual. See the index for antisemitism.

Lispschutz, Léon. UNE BIBLIOTHEQUE DREYFUSIENNE: ESSAI DE BIBLIOGRAPHIE THEMATIQUE ET ANALYTIQUE DE L'AFFAIRE DREYFUS. Paris: Société Littéraire des Amis d'Emile Zola et Editions Fasquelle. 103 pp. 551 items. Books and articles in European languages. Annotated.

1971

Kehr, Helen. PREJUDICE - RACIST, RELIGIOUS, NATIONALIST. London: Vallentine, Mitchell for the Institute of Contemporary History. viii, 385 pp. (Wiener Library Catalogue Series, 5). 4511 items. Books and articles in European languages.

Kisch, Guido. The Jews in Medieval Germany: A Bibliography of Publications on Their Legal and Social Status, 1949-1969. REVUE DES ETUDES JUIVES 130, 2-4 (Apr-Dec 1971) 271-294. Pp. 292-294: "Jewish Persecutions."

Wood, James E. A Selected and Annotated Bibliography on Jewish-Christian Relations. JOURNAL OF CHURCH AND STATE 13, 2 (Spr 1971) 317-340 and JEWISH-CHRISTIAN RELATIONS IN TODAY'S WORLD, ed. J.E. Wood. Waco, TX: Baylor University Press. Pp. 139-162. Books in English.

1972

ארדיטי, בנימין. הספרות האנטישמית בבולגריה: רשימה ביבליאוגרפית. חולון: ב. ארדיטי. 79 עמ'.

[Arditti, Benyamin. ANTISEMITICHESKATA LITERATURA V BULGARIA. Holon: B. Arditti. 79 pp.] 226 items. Books and journals in Bulgarian, with Hebrew translations and annotations.

THE STUDY OF JUDAISM: BIBLIOGRAPHICAL ESSAYS. [Vol. 1]. New York: ADL. 229 pp. Vol. 2 appeared in 1976 (see below). See the essays: Frank Talmage: Judaism on Christianity: Christianity on Judaism (81-112); Henry Friedlander: The Holocaust: Anti-Semitism and the Jewish Catastrophe (207-229).

1972/73

Friedlander, Henry. ON THE HOLOCAUST: A CRITIQUE OF THE TREATMENT OF THE HOLOCAUST IN HISTORY BOOKS ACCOMPANIED BY AN ANNOTATED BIBLIOGRAPHY. New York: ADL. Unseen.

1973

Ball-Kaduri, Kurt Jakob. Bibliographie des in Israel erschienenen Schrifttums zur Geschichte der Juden in Deutschland waehrend der Jahre 1933 bis 1945. JAHRBUCH FUER DIE GESCHICHTE MITTEL- UND OSTDEUTSCHLANDS 22 (1973) 242-246. Books, articles, and dissertations published in Israel - in German, English, and Hebrew.

Bass, David. Bibliographical List of Memorial Books Published in the Years 1943-1972. YAD VASHEM STUDIES 9 (1973) 273-321. 342 items. Multilingual. Listed simultaneously in the Hebrew edition, pp. 223-265. See addenda by Z. Baker, 1979/80.

Robinson, Jacob. THE HOLOCAUST AND AFTER: SOURCES AND LITERATURE IN ENGLISH. Jerusalem: Israel Universities Press. 334 pp. At h. of t.p.: Jerusalem: Yad Vashem; New York: YIVO. (Joint Documentary Projects, Bibliographical Series, 12). 6637 items. Books and articles. Partly annotated.

1974

פייקאז׳, מנדל. השואה וספיחיה בספרים העבריים שיצאו לאור בשנים
1933-1972: ביבליוגראפיה. כר׳ 1-2. ירושלים: יד ושם. 495,
vii; 499-920, vii עמ׳. (סידרה ביבליוגראפית משותפת, יג-יד).

[Piekarz, Mendel. THE HOLOCAUST AND ITS AFTERMATH: HEBREW BOOKS PUBLISHED IN THE YEARS 1933-1972. Vol. 1-2. Jerusalem: Yad Vashem. 495, vii; 499-920, vii pp. (Joint Documentary Projects, Bibliographical Series, 13-14).] 4006 items.

Wahlen, Verena. Select Bibliography on Judenraete under Nazi Rule. YAD VASHEM STUDIES 10 (1974) 277-294. 215 items. Books and articles. Multilingual. Listed simultaneously in the Hebrew edition, pp. 209-225.

1975

אייבשיץ, יהושע. מורשת הקהילות היהודיות באירופה שנחרבו: תערוכת
השואה והגבורה שנערכה בספריה הציבורית בקרית-אתא בימים כ"ז בניסן
-כ"ז סיון תשל"ה. קטלוג וילקוט ביבליוגרפי. קרית-אתא: העיריה,
המחלקה לחינוך ולתרבות, הספריה הציבורית. 39 עמ׳.

[Eibeschuetz, Yehoshua. THE LEGACY OF THE EUROPEAN JEWISH COMMUNITIES WHICH WERE DESTROYED: AN EXHIBITION OF THE HOLOCAUST AND HEROISM, NISSAN-27 SIVAN 5735. A CATALOGUE AND BIBLIOGRAPHY. Kiryat Ata: Municipality, Department of Education and Culture. 39 pp. A list of books, mostly Hebrew.

EUROPEAN JEWISH COMMUNITIES, 1933-1945: HISTORIES, MEMOIRS, DIARIES, MEMORIAL BOOKS. WITH SUPPLEMENT: BOOKS ON CONCENTRATION-CAMPS. Los Angeles: University of California Library, Jewish Studies Collection. 65 pp. UCLA Library holdings. Multilingual.

Farkas, Sara. Lest We Forget: Books on the Holocaust. SCHOOL LIBRARY JOURNAL (May 1975) 37-38. Unseen.

Roskies, Diane K. TEACHING THE HOLOCAUST TO CHILDREN: A REVIEW AND BIBLIOGRAPHY. New York: Ktav. 65 pp. Pp. 54-65 contain a list of books, articles, and periodicals in English and Yiddish.

Singerman, Robert. THE JEWS IN SPAIN AND PORTUGAL: A BIBLIOGRAPHY. New York: Garland. 364 pp. Over 5000 items. Books and articles. Multilingual.

1976

Eppler, Elizabeth E. INTERNATIONAL BIBLIOGRAPHY OF JEWISH AFFAIRS 1966-1967: A SELECTED ANNOTATED LIST OF BOOKS AND ARTICLES PUBLISHED OUTSIDE ISRAEL. London: André Deutsch, for the Institute of Jewish Affairs. ix, 401 pp. Pp. 154-159, 347-353: "Antisemitism." See also 1983.

THE STUDY OF JUDAISM. VOL. 2: BIBLIOGRAPHICAL ESSAYS IN MEDIEVAL JEWISH STUDIES. New York: ADL. viii, 392 pp. Vol. 1 appeared in 1972 (see above). See the essays: Ivan G. Marcus: The Jews in Western Europe: Fourth to Sixteenth Century (17-105); Kenneth F. Stow: The Church and the Jews: From St. Paul to Paul IV (107-165); Mark R. Cohen: The Jews under Islam: From the Rise of Islam to Sabbatai Zevi (167-229).

YAD VASHEM PUBLICATIONS. Jerusalem: Yad Vashem. ix, 15 pp. Mostly Hebrew, but includes English and Yiddish works. Annotated.

1977

Cargas, Harry James. THE HOLOCAUST: AN ANNOTATED BIBLIOGRAPHY. Haverford, PA: Catholic Library Association. 86 pp. Books and articles in English.

Stachura, Peter D. THE WEIMAR ERA AND HITLER, 1918-1933: A CRITICAL BIBLIOGRAPHY. Santa Barbara, CA: Clio Press. 275 pp. Unseen.

1978

פייקאז׳, מנדל. השואה וספיחיה באספקלריית כתבי-עת עבריים:
ביבליוגראפיה. ירושלים: יד ושם. 493 עמ׳.

[Piekarz, Mendel. THE HOLOCAUST AND ITS AFTERMATH AS SEEN THROUGH HEBREW PERIODICALS: A BIBLIOGRAPHY. Jerusalem: Yad Vashem. 493 pp.] 7109 items. A continuation of the previous bibliography (see 1966) up to and including 1975.

Busi, Frederick. A Bibliographical Overview of the Dreyfus Affair. JEWISH SOCIAL STUDIES 40, 1 (Win 1978) 25-40. Books in English and French.

Henrix, Hans Hermann. In der Entdeckung von Zeitgenossenschaft: Ein Literaturbericht zum christlich-juedischen Gespraech der letzten Jahre. UNA SANCTA: ZEITSCHRIFT FUER OEKUMENISCHE BEGEGNUNG 33, 3 (1978) 245-260. A bibliographical essay on 30 German books and articles.

Kehr, Helen. GERMAN JEWRY, PART II: 1959-1972. Additions and Amendments to Catalogue no. 3. London: Institute of Contemporary History. 363 pp. (Wiener Library Catalogue Series, 6). Items 3435-6818. See Part I in 1958.

ON THE HOLOCAUST: BIBLIOGRAPHIES. Philadelphia: National Institute on the Holocaust. Various pagings. Bibliographies for courses on the Holocaust from various colleges and universities in the US.

1979/80

Baker, Zachary M. Bibliography of Eastern European Memorial Books: Updated and Revised. TOLEDOT 3, 2/3 (Fall 1979/Win 1980) 7-42. 449 items. Comprises David Bass's bibliography (see 1973) with additions and revisions. Addenda to Baker's list, by David Einsiedler, appeared in ROOTS-KEY 6, 2 (Sum 1985) [3 pp.].

Mensch, Terry G. Psychohistory of the Third Reich: A Library Pathfinder and Topical Bibliography of English Language Publications. JOURNAL OF PSYCHOHISTORY 7, 3 (Win 1979/80) 331-354. 338 items. Books and articles. Pp. 334-335: "Anti-Semitism."

1980

Gurewitsch, Bonnie. BIBLIOGRAPHY. Brooklyn, NY: Center for Holocaust Studies. 26 pp. English books on the Holocaust.

Hirshberg, Jeffrey. The Holocaust in Literature, 1978-79: A Bibliography. SHOAH 2, 1 (Spr 1980) 25-30. 100 items, in English. Annotated. Includes literature, memoirs, biographies, and essays.

Joseph, Sharon. THE HOLOCAUST: AN ANNOTATED BIBLIOGRAPHY. Montreal: National Holocaust Remembrance Committee, Canadian Jewish Congress, [1980?]. 34 pp. English books and audio-visual material.

1980/81

Eckardt, A. Roy. Recent Literature on Christian-Jewish Relations. JEWISH BOOK ANNUAL 38 (1980) 47-61 and JOURNAL OF THE AMERICAN ACADEMY OF RELIGION 49, 1 (Mar 1981) 99-111. A survey of English and German books and articles.

1981

איבשיץ, יהושע. שואה וגבורה: ילקוט ביבליוגרפי, מתוך ספרים, כתבי-עת, עתונים ופרסומים הנמצאים ברשות הספריה בקרית-אתא. קרית-אתא: העיריה, המחלקה לחינוך ולתרבות. 93 עמ'.

[Eibeschuetz, Yehoshua. HOLOCAUST AND HEROISM: A BIBLIOGRAPHICAL LIST FROM BOOKS, JOURNALS, NEWSPAPERS AND PUBLICATIONS FOUND IN THE KIRYAT ATA LIBRARY. Kiryat Ata: Municipality, Department of Education and Culture. 93 pp.] Hebrew only.

Drew, Margaret; Strom, Margot Stern; Parsons, William. Facing History and Ourselves: The Nucleus of a Bibliography for Students and Teachers. MORAL EDUCATION FORUM 6, 2 (Sum 1981) 49-58. 48 items. English books, fiction and non-fiction, on the Holocaust. Annotated. "Excerpted from the FHAO Curriculum Guide."

THE HOLOCAUST - HITLER AND NAZI GENOCIDE: PERSECUTION AND RESISTANCE. London: Hammersmith Books, [1981?]. 22 pp. (Catalogue no. 67). 1092 items. Multilingual.

1982

Bensimon, Doris. BIBLIOGRAPHIE: LES JUIFS EN FRANCE DURANT LA DEUXIEME GUERRE MONDIALE. Clichy: Centre de Documentation et de Recherche, Etudes Hébraïques et Juives, Modernes et Contemporaines - INALCO, Paris III. v, 19 pp. Books in French. Annotated.

Eitinger, Leo. PSYCHOLOGICAL AND MEDICAL EFFECTS OF CONCENTRATION CAMPS: RESEARCH BIBLIOGRAPHY. Haifa: University of Haifa, Ray D. Wolfe Centre for Study of Psychological Stress, [1982?]. 122 pp. 808 items. Books and articles. Multilingual.

Freidenreich, Fradle. Materials for Teaching the Holocaust. THE PEDAGOGIC REPORTER 33, 2 (Mar 1982) 26-29. An annotated list of English fiction and non-fiction, for children and adults. Adapted from the JEWISH CURRICULUM AND RESOURCE GUIDE FOR THE ARMED FORCES (1981).

Kehr, Helen; Langmaid, Janet. THE NAZI ERA, 1919-1945: A SELECT BIBLIOGRAPHY OF PUBLISHED WORKS FROM THE EARLY ROOTS TO 1980. London: Mansell. xvi, 621 pp. 6523 items. Books and some articles, in European languages (mostly English and German), published since 1919.

Laska, Vera. NAZISM, RESISTANCE & HOLOCAUST IN W.W.II: A BIBLIOGRAPHY. Weston, MA: [The Author]. 50 pp. Over 1300 items, in European languages.

Muffs, Judith Herschlag. THE HOLOCAUST IN BOOKS AND FILMS: A SELECTED ANNOTATED LIST. Revised and expanded. New York: ADL, Center for Studies on the Holocaust. 67 pp. Over 400 items, in English. The previous edition appeared in 1978 and was prepared by Roselle Chartock, Ruth Routtenberg Seldin, and Henry Friedlander.

Singerman, Robert. ANTISEMITIC PROPAGANDA: AN ANNOTATED BIBLIOGRAPHY AND RESEARCH GUIDE. New York: Garland. xxxvii, 448 pp. 1915 items. The bibliography (1437 items) includes English books, pamphlets, and articles published from 1871 to 1981. The research guide (items 1438-1915) includes English books and articles about antisemitism.

1983

כהנא, ליבי; טננבאום, רות. ארבעים שנה למרד גיטו ורשה: מבחר ספרי זכרונות, עיון ותיעוד. תערוכה, ירושלים, סיון תשמ"ג. ירושלים: בית הספרים הלאומי והאוניברסיטאי. 23 עמ׳.

[Kahane, Libby; Tenenbaum, Ruth. FORTY YEARS SINCE THE WARSAW GHETTO UPRISING: A SELECTION OF MEMOIRS, RESEARCH AND DOCUMENTATION. Jerusalem: Jewish National and University Library. 23 pp.] Catalogue of an exhibition. Books. Multilingual.

Devoto, Andrea. L'OPPRESSONE NAZISTA: CONSIDERAZIONI E BIBLIOGRAFIA, 1963-1981. Pref. di Giovanni Spadolini. Firenze: Leo S. Olschki. xv, 207 pp. 1701 items. Books and articles in European languages. Continues the previous listing (see 1964).

Eppler, Elizabeth E. INTERNATIONAL BIBLIOGRAPHY OF JEWISH AFFAIRS 1976-1977: A SELECTIVELY ANNOTATED LIST OF BOOKS AND ARTICLES PUBLISHED IN THE DIASPORA. Boulder, CO: Westview Press, for the Institute of Jewish Affairs. xiii, 402 pp. Pp. 164-171, 341-347: "Antisemitism." See also 1976.

In addition, the following are ongoing bibliographies in the field of Judaica which regularly list material on antisemitism and the Holocaust:

ARTICLES OF INTEREST IN CURRENT PERIODICALS. New York: American Jewish Committee, Blaustein Library, 1950- Mainly English. Annotated.

BIBLIOGRAPHY OF NEW ACQUISITIONS. Tel-Aviv: Wiener Library, Tel-Aviv University, 1982- Multilingual.

INDEX OF ARTICLES ON JEWISH STUDIES. Jerusalem: Jewish National and University Library, 1969- Multilingual. Covers material from 1966 on.

INDEX TO HEBREW PERIODICALS. Jerusalem: Center for Public Libraries in Israel, for the University of Haifa, 1978- Hebrew only. Covers material from 1977 on.

INDEX TO JEWISH PERIODICALS. Cleveland Heights, OH, 1964- English only. Covers material from 1963 on.

KIRYAT SEFER: CURRENT BIBLIOGRAPHY OF ISRAEL PUBLICATIONS AND JUDAICA-HEBRAICA ABROAD. Jerusalem: Jewish National and University Library, 1924- Multilingual. Annotated in Hebrew.

POST-WAR PUBLICATIONS ON GERMAN JEWRY: A SELECTED BIBLIOGRAPHY OF BOOKS AND ARTICLES. London: Leo Baeck Institute, 1956- Multilingual. Appears annually in the LBI YEAR BOOK.

RECENT ADDITIONS TO THE LIBRARY. New York: American Jewish Committee, Blaustein Library, 1940- Books, mainly English. Annotated.

AUTHOR INDEX

SUBJECT INDEX